The Covenantal Structure of Christian Economics

WRITTEN BY GARY NORTH

Marx's Religion of Revolution
An Introduction to Christian Economics
Unconditional Surrender
Successful Investing in an Age of Envy
Government By Emergency
The Last Train Out
Backward, Christian Soldiers?
75 Bible Questions Your Instructors Pray You Won't Ask
Coined Freedom
12 Deadly Negatrends
Conspiracy
Unholy Spirits
Honest Money
Fighting Chance (with Arthur Robinson)
Dominion and Common Grace
Inherit the Earth
The Pirate Economy
Liberating Planet Earth
Healer of the Nations
Is the World Running Down?
Puritan Economic Experiments
When Justice Is Aborted
Political Polytheism
The Hoax of Higher Criticism
Victim's Rights
The Judeo-Christian Tradition
Millennialism and Social Theory
Westminster's Confession
Christian Reconstruction (with Gary DeMar)
The Coase Theorem
Salvation Through Inflation
Rapture Fever
Tithing and the Church
Crossed Fingers
The War on Mel Gibson
The Five Pillars of Biblical Success
The Covenantal Tithe
Gertrude Coogan's Bluff
Mises on Money
Conspiracy in Philadelphia
God's Covenants
Stay of Execution
Christian Economics in One Lesson
The Covenantal Structure of Christian Economics
Christian Economics for Students
Christian Economics for Teachers
Christian Economics for Activists
Christian Economics for Scholars
Protectionism and Poverty
The Five Pillars of Biblical Leadership
The Biblical Structure of History

An Economic Commentary on the Bible (31 vols.)

EDITED BY GARY NORTH

Foundations of Christian Scholarship
Tactics of Christian Resistance
The Theology of Christian Resistance
Theonomy: An Informed Response
The Journal of Christian Reconstruction (1974–1981)

The Covenantal Structure of Christian Economics

A Primer on Economics from a Biblical Worldview

Gary North

AXEHEAD
PRESS

To view a copy of the original work as it appeared when this Axehead Press
edition was produced, visit AxeheadPress.com/tcsoce-original.

For a description of changes to this work, visit AxeheadPress.com/tcsoce-changelog.

First published by Axehead Press in 2024
Version 2.0

Submit typos and corrections to typos@axeheadpress.com.

Published by
Axehead Press
Moulton, Alabama

The NASB's convention of setting New Testament quotations of Old Testament material
in all capitals has been changed to normal sentence case for readability purposes. For the same
purpose, first lines of poetry have been lowercased when quoted when appropriate.

Paperback ISBN: 978-1-956329-11-7
Library of Congress Control Number: 2022951376

This book is dedicated to

PAX NORTH & BISHOP NORTH

Cousins

Contents

PART I

The Economic Structure of the Dominion Covenant

PART II

The Economic Structure of the Individual Covenant

PART III

The Economic Structure of the Family Covenant

PART IV

The Economic Structure of the Church Covenant

PART V

The Economic Structure of the Civil Covenant

Foreword

(to be read)

A. The Lord's Prayer

I am going to give you the opening words of what is known as the Lord's prayer. Can you complete this prayer? "Our Father, who art in heaven. . . ."

This prayer is in the language of the King James Bible, which was published in 1611. Most English-speaking Protestants who were born prior to 1960 grew up listening to the language of this version of the Bible. Even today, over half of all the Bibles purchased in the United States are King James Bibles. This is after half a century of the publication of dozens of new translations of the Bible. The translation in second place, the New International Version, accounts for under 20% of sales. All the others are marginal.[1] People say they cannot easily understand the King James. They say the language is difficult. But, when push comes to shove, they recite the Lord's prayer and the twenty-third psalm in the King James translation. They probably would have trouble reciting any other version.

Can you recite the prayer?

There are two versions. One is in Matthew. One is in Luke. Most people who have memorized it have memorized Matthew's version.

> Our Father which art in heaven, Hallowed be thy name. Thy kingdom come, Thy will be done in earth, as it is in heaven. Give us this day our

1. Sarah Eekhoff Zylstra, "The Most Popular and Fastest Growing Bible Translation Isn't What You Think It Is," *Christianity Today*, March 13, 2014, christianitytoday.com/news/2014/march/most-popular-and-fastest-growing-bible-translation-niv-kjv.html.

> daily bread. And forgive us our debts, as we forgive our debtors. And lead us not into temptation, but deliver us from evil: For thine is the kingdom, and the power, and the glory, for ever. Amen. (Matt. 6:9b–13)

You probably got it wrong. Most people say, "who art in heaven." It is "which." Most people say "done on earth," It is "done in earth."

Luke's version is shorter.

> Our Father which art in heaven, Hallowed be thy name. Thy kingdom come. Thy will be done, as in heaven, so in earth. Give us day by day our daily bread. And forgive us our sins; for we also forgive every one that is indebted to us. And lead us not into temptation; but deliver us from evil. (Luke 11:2b–4)

For the purposes of this Foreword, Luke's version is clearer: "as in heaven, so in earth."

How much thought have you given to this phrase? Probably not much. That is why I am beginning here.

Exactly what is to be done "as in heaven, so in earth"? The text in both versions of the prayer are the same: "thy will." What about God's will? Is it different in heaven from what it is on earth? No. Then what is source of the difference on earth? *People's willingness and ability to do God's will.* God's will is the same in both realms. People's responses are different on earth from what they are in heaven. Why? Sin. There is no sin in heaven.

Jesus assigned this prayer. The prayer specifically calls for a world in which His will is done on earth, just as it is in heaven. How much clearer could this be?

How much thought have you given to this? How much thought have you given to the implications of this in history—in your history and in everyone's history? Let me venture a guess: not much.

Let me press the issue. Do you think Jesus has given His people a prayer that He does not expect God to answer? I hope not. Do you think Jesus has given His people a prayer that He does not expect His people to pray? I hope not. Do you think Jesus' people have prayed this prayer for almost two millennia? I hope so. So, if they have prayed it, has He answered it? He has not answered it perfectly, for there is still sin. But has He answered it progressively?

Let me cite another part of the prayer: "Give us this day our daily bread." Do you have daily bread? Yes. Do you have a little too much bread? You may have a few Cheetos, too. Chips and dip. Pizza. Dessert. Second helpings. Could you stand to lose a few pounds?

Do you worry about where your next meal is coming from? No. But there are people in the world who do worry about this. Most of them live in non-Christian societies.

God has answered this prayer over the last two centuries to a degree that He never did before in recorded history. How much gratitude has He received? If you read a textbook on economic history, I guarantee you that the author does not attribute this historical development to God's answer to this prayer. This prayer first began to be answered on a permanent basis in the British Isles and English-speaking North America: the early phase of the Industrial Revolution. This began around 1800 (sometime between 1780 and 1820). The last famine in the West was in Ireland in the 1840s, which was not an industrial nation. So, this part of the Lord's prayer has been answered in the West, beginning in Protestantism's most entrepreneurial nations.[2] It has spread around the world.

The economic historians' explanations for this development are numerous, but none of them holds up under cross-examination.[3] They all have this in common: they give all of the credit to autonomous man and his institutions. We have been warned about this explanation for mankind's success. "Otherwise, you may say in your heart, 'My power and the strength of my hand made me this wealth.' But you are to remember the LORD your God, for it is He who is giving you power to make wealth, in order to confirm His covenant which He swore to your fathers, as it is this day" (Deut. 8:17–18).[4]

Let us return to my original questions. Do you think God has given His people a prayer that He does not intend to answer? Do you think God has given His people a prayer that He does not expect His people to

---

2. This began in Holland in the late sixteenth century, but it was not sustained after 1650. Economic growth slowed.

3. Deirdre N. McCloskey, *Bourgeois Dignity: Why Economics Can't Explain the Modern World* (Chicago: University of Chicago Press, 2010).

4. Gary North, *Inheritance & Dominion: An Economic Commentary on Deuteronomy* (Moulton, Alabama: Axehead Press, [1999, 2012] 2026), chaps. 21, 22.

pray? Do you think God's people have prayed this prayer for almost two millennia? So, if they have prayed it, has He answered it progressively?

Specifically, when you pray this prayer, do you expect God to answer it progressively? Do you believe that if our grandchildren continue to pray this prayer, that they will see more evidence that God is answering it? If not, why not? In other words, do you believe that things will become less sinful over time if Christians pray this prayer consistently, and also in faith? Remember James' words: "But if any of you lacks wisdom, let him ask of God, who gives to all generously and without reproach, and it will be given to him. But he must ask in faith without any doubting, for the one who doubts is like the surf of the sea, driven and tossed by the wind. For that person ought not to expect that he will receive anything from the Lord, being a double-minded man, unstable in all his ways" (James 1:5–8). If your answer is "no, things will get more sinful over time," then why do you think Christ told us to pray the Lord's prayer? Why do you think that things will get progressively worse rather than progressively better? Why do you think God will answer this prayer as follows? "Thy will not be done, in earth as it is in heaven."

Let me get to the famous bottom line. *Is your eschatology consistent with the Lord's prayer?*

B. Economics and Confession

Modern economists are mostly atheists or functional atheists. They do not think that economic theory is in any way related to Christianity. They do not think the Bible provides insights into the way the world works economically, or is supposed to work economically. They believe that economic theory is autonomous.[5] They do not think that it rests on morality, theology, or any other academic discipline.[6] They think that economic laws—what they may prefer to call predictable patterns of behavior—are autonomous: self-reinforcing in all seasons.

I think economic theory, as with all other social sciences, is depen-

5. Gary North, *Christian Economics for Students* (Moulton, Alabama: Axehead Press, [2017] 2025), ch. 7.

6. A growing number of economists, called behavioral economists, believe that economics and psychology are intimately related. Most economists reject this assumption.

dent on God's revelation in the Bible. So, I do not begin with Adam Smith in my quest to understand economics. I also do not begin with the Spanish Scholastic economists of the sixteenth century, who rested their case for economics and politics on Aristotle's defense of natural law. I do not begin with the assumption of man's autonomy. I begin with the Bible's revelation of God, man, and historical causation. In this, I am different from other economists, including Christians who are academic economists.

In this book, I bring together into a coherent form—I hope—a set of conclusions that I have reached, which are based on a series of studies that I have labored on for over half a century. I offer these conclusions in terms of an assumption: *God's five-point biblical covenant model is the appropriate model for all social theory, including economic theory.* More than this: I argue that all systems of social theory rest implicitly on this five-point structure, although not necessarily in the biblical order. Social theorists must deal with the issues of all five points if they are to offer consistent analysis. Social theorists are not self-conscious about this, but they cannot successfully escape the five points.

Here is the structure: sovereignty, authority, law, sanctions, and inheritance. Put politically: sovereignty, representation, law, voting, and succession. Put economically: ownership, stewardship, law, feedback, and economic growth. Put theologically: God, man, law, sanctions, and eschatology. Every social system has a theory of each of these categories, as well as a theory of their interaction. Here is the version for modern economics.

1. Sovereignty: man (either individual or collective)
2. Authority: reason
3. Law: evolutionary
4. Sanctions: profit/loss or bureaucratic
5. Inheritance: economic growth

In this book, I set forth a description of how biblical economic theory manifests the covenant's five-point structure. I also set forth the content and logic of these five categories in the five covenants of the Bible: the dominion covenant, the individual covenant, the family covenant, the church covenant, and the civil covenant. *These are oath-bound covenants.* There is no covenant apart from a specific oath before God, either explicit or implicit. He holds every covenant member responsible in time and eternity for adhering to His standards of each covenant. Men substitute other standards. They suffer the consequences: negative sanctions.

C. Inheritance and Disinheritance

This is the first book that has presented economic theory in terms of the five-point covenant model and its five covenants.[7] The logic of the presentation will be unfamiliar to economists. It presents a new paradigm.

The number-one shift in the paradigm is with respect to sovereignty: God, not man. The second shift deals with authority: the Bible, not man's unaided reason. The third shift deals with law: revelational, not autonomous. The fourth shift deals with sanctions: imposed (exogenous), not merely autonomous (endogenous). Finally, inheritance: the wealth of the sinner is laid up for the just (Prov. 13:22b).[8]

The manifestation of this shift can be seen in my starting point. I begin with ownership, not scarcity. *Ownership is central because the universe is theocentric.* God created the heaven and the earth. Man did not. Man is the son of God, not the son of the Big Bang. The crucial question for every person is therefore this: "Am I an adopted child or a disinherited child?" Society will inevitably reflect the dominance of one of these two families: adopted or disinherited.

Economics, more than any other social science, is a science of inheritance. This book presents the biblical case for the economics of inheritance. But this presentation is necessarily also a theory of the economics of disinheritance.

D. The Kingdom of Man and the Kingdom of Satan

I use the two terms interchangeably. Here is why. When Adam and Eve decided to act in terms of the words of the serpent, who represented

7. My 1987 book, *Inherit the Earth*, did not consider all five covenants.

8. Gary North, *Wisdom & Dominion: An Economic Commentary on Proverbs* (Moulton, Alabama: Axehead Press, [2012] 2029), ch. 41.

Satan as a trustee, they switched their covenantal allegiance from God to Satan. They moved from grace to wrath. But there is a theological issue here that is rarely discussed. Man is higher in the creation's hierarchy than Satan and his fallen angels. Paul wrote of covenant-keepers: "Or do you not know that the saints will judge the world? If the world is judged by you, are you not competent to form the smallest law courts? Do you not know that we will judge angels? How much more matters of this life?" (I Cor. 6:2–3). *This is a judicial hierarchy.* Man is superior to the angels, not in terms of power, but in terms of authority. Think of a petite female judge in a courtroom. She is facing a hulk of a man who has just been convicted by a jury of first-degree murder. She has the responsibility of declaring the penalty: either life in prison or execution. Who is in charge? The judge or the murderer?

Adam could not forfeit this office in the name of mankind. It is a God-given office. There is no escape by covenant-keepers from this office either in history or eternity. So, while it looks as though the kingdom of Satan is the only rival kingdom to God's kingdom, this is an illusion. It is an illusion that is inherently Satanic. It imputes far more credit to Satan's authority in the creation's hierarchy than Satan deserves. He likes this, of course, but I doubt that he is fooled. However, it is conceivable, in an old American phrase, that he believes his own press releases. Self-deception is a common affliction among humans. Maybe it also bedevils devils.

Covenant-breaking men only rarely self-consciously worship Satan. Satanism has always been a tiny cult. Men have instead worshiped physical idols: creations of their hands. "Their idols are silver and gold, The work of human hands. They have mouths, but they cannot speak; They have eyes, but they cannot see; They have ears, but they cannot hear; They have noses, but they cannot smell; They have hands, but they cannot feel; They have feet, but they cannot walk; They cannot make a sound with their throat. Those who make them will become like them, Everyone who trusts in them" (Ps. 115:4–8). In modern times, millions of formally educated people have worshiped intellectual idols: creations of their minds.[9] They impute to some elusive god what they

9. Herbert Schlossberg, *Idols for Destruction: Christian Faith and Its Confrontation with American Society* (Nashville, Tennessee: Thomas Nelson, 1983).

like best about themselves. Others worship mammon: the alluring god of the religion of "more for me in history." These are ways for fallen man to worship himself. He is a faithful servant in the kingdom of man.

Preface

A. Background to This Book

I began thinking about the question of Christian economics in the spring of 1960. I was in the second semester of my freshman year in college. I have been thinking about this ever since.

I recognized in 1959 that the approach in the four-page tabloid, *Christian Economics*, was not Christian. It came out every two weeks. It was funded by the richest Calvinist in history, J. Howard Pew of Sun Oil. It was edited by a Quaker who, as far as I could see, was not a Trinitarian. He was an evolutionist. The featured authors were usually agnostics. It began publication in 1950. It was mailed free of charge to every minister in the United States.[1] It was the most widely circulated free market publication in the world, although it is forgotten today. The conservative magazine, *National Review*, began publishing in 1955. *The Freeman* began in 1956. Until then, *Christian Economics* had an operational monopoly on free enterprise journalism.

I began reading *The Freeman* and *Christian Economics* in 1958. I kept seeing the same authors in both publications. In the summer of 1959, I became a Christian. I immediately recognized that *Christian Economics* was not Christian theologically. Its economic content was not different from *The Freeman*, which had no theological pretensions. By 1960, I wanted to know what connection there was, or wasn't, between the economics of these two publications and the Bible. I bought Ludwig von Mises' *Human Action* and F. A. Hayek's *The Constitution of Liberty*

1. Ronald Lora and William Henry Longton (eds.), *The Conservative Press in Twentieth-Century America* (Westport, Connecticut: Greenwood Press, 1999), 164–167.

in June of 1960. I wrote down this date in the inside front covers.

By early 1960, I became aware of the fact that there had never been a book defending an explicitly biblical economic theory, as distinguished from Roman Catholic scholasticism, which rested on Aristotle. There was no awareness among free market economists that such a thing could exist. I was on my own, intellectually speaking. A major part of my motivation for spending half a century on developing Christian economics is this: to keep some young scholar in the future from being equally alone. Today, Christians college students have at least some Christian academic sources to use to get them through their systematically secular higher educations. These materials are not generally very good, either intellectually or conceptually, but at least there are places to begin reading. Students need not feel as alone as I did in the fall of 1959.

As an undergraduate from fall 1959 to spring 1963, I continued to read Austrian School economists, but only sporadically. I was busy earning my degree in history. My immersion in Austrian School economics came in the three months that I worked for the William Volker Fund (Center for American Studies) in the summer of 1963. I was paid to read, which I did. I read Murray Rothbard's *Man, Economy, and State* (1962), *America's Great Depression* (1963), and *The Panic of 1819* (1962). I finally finished Mises' *Human Action*. I read Mises' *Socialism* (1922) and *The Theory of Money and Credit* (1912).

I attended Westminster Theological Seminary in Philadelphia for one academic year, 1963–1964. There, my thinking became Reformed, though not yet Presbyterian. I abandoned my hyperdispensationalism as a result of a course I audited on the book of Romans. It was taught by John Murray. His exposition of Romans 11[2] converted me to postmillennialism. I also audited his course on sanctification. There, he introduced me to the three-part concept of sanctification: definitive, progressive, and final.[3] While I did not at that time perceive that this tripartite structure also applies to covenantal collectives, it later re-shaped my thinking about economics.

I began writing for *The Freeman* in graduate school. My first article

2. John Murray, *The Epistle to the Romans* (Grand Rapids, Michigan: Eerdmans, 1965), vol. II, 46ff.

3. John Murray, *Collected Works of John Murray* (Edinburgh: Banner of Truth, 1982), vol. II, chaps. 21–25.

was in February 1967.[4] I continued to write for *The Freeman* for the next 26 years.

My book, *Marx's Religion of Revolution*, appeared in 1968.[5] I used biblical social theory and Austrian School economics to refute Marx's system. *An Introduction to Christian Economics* appeared in 1973.[6] It was a compilation of articles. In February of 1973, I began to write my economic commentary on the Bible for the *Chalcedon Report*. I finished writing in late January, 2012, two weeks before my August 1977 vow expired. I had committed ten hours a week, 50 weeks a year, to that project, to end on my 70th birthday. (On that day, my son got married. I had begun fulfilling my vow in the month he was born.) I also had to raise the funds to publish the books through my Institute for Christian Economics, which I launched in 1975. I did not take a salary or book royalties. I shut it down in December 2001 because I saw that I could publish everything I wrote for free on the Internet. My fund-raising days ended after 25 years. That work had taken me at least 20 hours a week, 50 weeks a year, from 1976 to 2001, in addition to the time I devoted to researching and writing the commentaries. In short, the commentary project cost me around 38,000 hours, 1973–2012. That was my "homework." In 2017 and 2018, I am bringing this work to completion.

B. The Biblical Covenant

The most important influence in my thinking after I began writing my economic commentary was Ray Sutton's development of the five-point covenant model. An early variant appeared in Meredith Kline's 1963 commentary on Deuteronomy, *Treaty of the Great King*. He in turn got the idea for this from George Mendenhall, who wrote about it in 1954.[7]

4. Gary North, "Domestic Inflation versus International Solvency" *The Freeman* (Feb 1967).

5. Gary North, *Marx's Religion of Revolution: Regeneration Through Chaos* (Moulton, Alabama: Axehead Press, [1968, 1989] 2023).

6. Gary North, *An Introduction to Christian Economics* (Moulton, Alabama: Axehead Press, [1973] 2025).

7. George Mendenhall, "Covenant Forms in Israelite Tradition," *Biblical Archaeologist*, vol. 17 (1954), 50–76. Mendenhall, *Law and Covenant in Israel and the Ancient Near East* (Pittsburgh: The Presbyterian Board of Colportage of Western Pennsylvania, 1955). For a detailed analysis of his thesis, see René Lopez, "Israelite Covenants in the Light of Ancient

Sutton's book was far more developed than Kline's. I helped him edit the manuscript in 1986 and 1987. It went through several major revisions before my Institute for Christian Economics published it in 1987: *That You May Prosper: Dominion By Covenant.* Sutton presented the covenant model in this form:

1. God (transcendent yet immanent)
2. Hierarchy
3. Ethics
4. Sanctions
5. Continuity

A reader recommended this re-structuring:

1. Transcendence/presence
2. Hierarchy
3. Ethics
4. Oath
5. Succession

The acronym is THEOS, the Greek word for God.

In my 1980 book, *Unconditional Surrender: God's Program for Victory*, I instinctively adopted the first three: God, man, and law. In the third edition, published in 1988, I added time. In the 2011 edition, I completed it by adding sanctions. I hope that this is the final edition. Here are the five inescapable components of covenant theology.

1. God
2. Man
3. Law
4. Sanctions
5. Time

This structure is visible in the structure of the Pentateuch.

1. Genesis (origins)
2. Exodus (authority)[8]

Near Eastern Covenants, Part 1," *CTS Journal*, vol. 9 (2003); part 2 in ibid., vol. 10 (2004).

8. The book is divided into five sections: (1) sovereign God (1–17); (2) judicial appeals courts (18); (3) laws (21–23:13); (4), oath (23–24); (5) inheritance (25–40). The Ten

3. Leviticus (law)[9]
4. Numbers (sanctions)
5. Deuteronomy (inheritance)[10]

I put all this into one short (for me) book: *God's Covenants* (2014).[11] I also discussed the five covenants in history: dominion, individual, family, church, and state.

This laid the foundation for my identification of the five inescapable factors in all social theory.

1. Sovereignty
2. Authority
3. Law
4. Sanctions
5. Succession

It took me all those years to come up with my outlines for Christian economics. Only after I finished the commentaries did I formulate my theory. It comes in two parts, judicial and economic. Here are the judicial principles of Christian economics.

I begin with God. Here are the theocentric judicial principles of economics in 15 words.

JUDICIAL (THEOCENTRIC)
1. God owns everything.
2. God delegates ownership.
3. God prohibits theft.
4. God evaluates performance.
5. God mandates growth.

I cover this in Chapter 1.

Commandments are two sets of five points each: priestly, kingly.

9. The book is divided into five sections: (1) five sacrifices (1–7); (2) priestly, hierarchical cleansing of God's house and man's house, including the land—a means of deliverance (8–16); (3) laws of separation (17–22); (4) covenant-renewal festivals and covenant-breaking acts (23–24); (5) inheritance (25–27). The five sacrifices are structured in terms of the covenant.

10. The book is divided into five sections: (1) transcendence (1:1–5); (2) hierarchy (1:6–4:49); (3) ethics (5–26); (4) sanctions (27–30); and (5) continuity (31–34).

11. Gary North, *God's Covenants: Understanding His Eternal Purposes & Decrees* (Moulton, Alabama: Axehead Press, [2006, 2014] 2023).

God designates men as His trustees. As trustees, they are authorized to act in God's name as judicial representatives. Here are the rules of trusteeship in 15 words.

JUDICIAL (REPRESENTATIVE)

1. Owners are trustees.
2. Trustees possess authority.
3. Trusts are binding.
4. Trustees are accountable.
5. Trustees designate successors.

There are also economic aspects of delegated ownership. God requires men to act as stewards. These are responsibilities of property management. Men must act on God's behalf. They must put His interests above their own. The laws governing men's stewardship are structurally the same as God's laws of ownership, but suitable for creatures. Here are the rules of stewardship in 15 words.

STEWARDSHIP LAWS

1. Purpose precedes planning.
2. Priorities structure planning.
3. Ownership involves exclusion.
4. Owners evaluate performance.
5. Owners designate heirs.

I cover these in Chapter 2.

Trusteeship has two aspects: judicial and economic. The judicial aspect is a matter of guardianship. The economic aspect is stewardship. This distinction goes back to God's designation of Adam as His trustee over the creation. The garden was Adam's testing place. God told Adam to dress the garden and keep it (Gen. 2:15). Stewardship was economic. Guardianship was legal. Stewardship involved *increasing the value of the property*. This is the meaning of "dress." Guardianship involved *defending God's property from unlawful invasion*. This is the meaning of "keep." Other translations translate "keep" as "work." Stewardship is trusteeship *on behalf of*. Guardianship is trusteeship *in the name of*. Both responsibilities are aspects of ownership: God's original ownership and man's delegated ownership.

Ownership is an inescapable concept. It is never a question of hierarchical ownership vs. no hierarchical ownership. It is always a question of who is the supreme owner. This structure of ownership leads to laws of economics. These laws are not autonomous. They are the results of God's covenantal ownership. These laws govern the structure of production. Here are these laws in 15 words.

ECONOMIC LAWS

1. Owners adopt purposes.
2. Prices provide information.
3. People prefer more.
4. Scarcity imposes costs.
5. Growth reduces scarcity.

I cover this in Chapter 3.

Here, in 60 words, are the foundations of Christian economics. I came up with a preliminary version of this formulation in early 2015: the first edition. This was before I wrote the first two volumes of my proposed four-volume set, *Christian Economics*. I completed the manuscript of volume 1, *Christian Economics for Students*, on June 2, 2017. I completed the manuscript of volume 2, *Christian Economics for Teachers*, in mid-September 2017. I completed the outline for volume 3, the activist's edition, in August. These forced me to re-structure some of the 45 points that I originally posted in 2015. The main difference is my consideration of purpose in this edition. I had ignored this in 2015.

I still plan to write a scholar's edition, along the lines of *Human Action*, but much broader in scope. Mises considered only what he called *catallactics*: market exchange. Economics is far broader than market exchange. The free market operates in terms of exchange: substitution and free pricing. Ask yourself: "Can a man sell his wife?" Put differently: "Does a husband own his wife?" The answer to both questions is "no." Therefore, the family is not governed by the laws of the free market, either the judicial laws or the economic laws.

C. Fundamental Law

The dominion covenant defines mankind.

> Then God said, "Let Us make mankind in Our image, according to Our likeness; and let them rule over the fish of the sea and over the birds of the sky and over the livestock and over all the earth, and over every crawling thing that crawls on the earth." So God created man in His own image, in the image of God He created him; male and female He created them. God blessed them; and God said to them, "Be fruitful and multiply, and fill the earth, and subdue it; and rule over the fish of the sea and over the birds of the sky and over every living thing that moves on the earth." (Gen. 1:26–28)[12]

Therefore, all social thought must begin here. By "must," I mean a moral imperative. I also mean an epistemological imperative. But few Christians begin here. No humanists begin here.

Implicitly, all social thought does begin here. But social theorists are not self-conscious about this. They implicitly assume concepts of sovereignty, authority, law, sanctions, and time, but only rarely do they spell out in detail what their definitions of these categories are, and never in terms of the five consecutive points of the biblical covenant. But every system of social theory has all five points. It takes effort to discover this structure. Any Christian who comes to any rival system of social theory owes it to his readers to identify these five points, and then analyze the system by means of, and in terms of, the biblical structure and content of these categories. But this is never done. Neither Christians nor their rivals are self-conscious about the biblical covenant model. Christian readers are not provided with the most important tool of analysis: the biblical covenant model.

I am using this book as an example of how Christian social theory should be conducted, both from the point of view of laying the foundations of a specific area of social theory and as a model of analysis. If I had understood this in 1960, I would have saved a great deal of time. I hope to save other Christian social thinkers a great deal of time.

When we begin with the covenant, we begin with fundamental law:

12. Gary North, *Sovereignty & Dominion: An Economic Commentary on Genesis* (Moulton, Alabama: Axehead Press, [1982, 2012] 2022).

biblical law. This is where all social theory should begin. There are specific aspects of how biblical law applies to any social institution. But before these can be adequately developed, the Christian should understand the overall structure of fundamental law. This is the integrating framework.

Fundamental law preceded social law, both temporally and structurally. We must start with God's judicial sovereignty. God, as the Creator, laid down the law. He enforces the law. The Creator is the final Judge. He judges in terms of His law.

This means that law cannot be neutral with respect to God. This is why all neutrality is a myth. The quest for universal laws that stand apart from the doctrine of creation and final judgment is futile. Every alleged neutral system of law always imports highly unneutral assumptions into the procedure. Sometimes this is self-conscious. Usually, it isn't.

In the field of economic theory, the most widely used back-door operation is found in economic advice. Economists offer conclusions about what economic theory reveals is the most efficient solution. But this concept of efficiency is always deeply biased. Why? Because modern economics officially rests on the assumption of methodological individualism. This principle is violated by every policy recommendation. Why? Because, according to modern economic theory, it is impossible to compare individual subjective utilities. In the language of economist Lionel Robbins, a disciple of Ludwig von Mises, it is scientifically impossible to make interpersonal comparisons of subjective utility.[13] I return to this theme often in this book. Every policy recommendation breaks this law. There is no way to measure social utility.

In their quest for neutrality, meaning value-free economic theory, economists seek a starting point that does not invoke a theory of original ownership. The most popular approach to evading the issue of original ownership is to begin with scarcity. Adam Smith began this tradition. He began *The Wealth of Nations* (1776) with a discussion of scarcity. In doing so, he weakened the case for the free market. Socialists were able to proclaim socialism as a morally superior economic system because it does not start with the acceptability of any initial distribution of wealth.

13. Lionel Robbins, *An Essay on the Nature and Significance of Economic Science* (New York: Macmillan, 1932, ch. VI.

Not until Ludwig von Mises in 1920 refuted the idea that socialism can be used to organize economic life rationally did the socialists lose the advantage of occupying what they said was the high moral ground. But the economics profession, other than followers of Mises, simply ignored his argument, or dismissed it as irrelevant, until the end of the Soviet Union on December 25, 1991.

I do not begin with the division of labor. I begin with ownership. There is original ownership and delegated ownership. God possesses original ownership. Mankind possesses delegated ownership. Therefore, in my version of Christian economics, this judicial fact is central: ownership. An implication of this fact—the division of labor—is secondary.

This means that fundamental law undergirds economic theory. We must start with sovereignty, which is a judicial concept. We start with God's sovereignty. His creation of the universe out of nothing is a manifestation of His sovereignty. The dominion covenant (Gen. 1:26–28) is an aspect of the laws of creation.

Conclusion

In this book, I present the structure of economic thought. This structure is covenantal, whether Christian or non-Christian. The five-point covenant is an inescapable concept. It is never a question of covenant vs. no covenant. It is a question of which covenant.

What you will read here is like nothing else you have ever read. This is the first time that the biblical covenant model has been applied to an academic discipline. This is a work of reconstruction. It is to serve as a model for reconstructions in the other social sciences and humanities. I am laying the foundations for a re-thinking of economic theory and therefore of economic action.

I have known for half a century that this reconstruction would have a limited market. The economists do not care about theology, and the theologians do not care about economic theory. I went ahead with this project anyway. I am not responsible for the response of the market. I believe in supply-side economics. Supply does not always create its own demand, even when it is offered for free, as the widespread resistance to Christ's gospel of redemption indicates. But without supply, customers will not be aware of what is available. Entrepreneurs must decide for them. Then the customers decide whether the entrepreneurs were correct.

The movie scene that drove this into my consciousness was in *Chariots of Fire* (1981). The sprinter Harold Abrahams has just been defeated by Eric Liddell in the 100-meter dash. (This never actually happened.) Abrahams is despondent. His girl friend tries to console him. (With a girlfriend that good looking, I would have been easily consoled.) He says: "If I can't win, I won't run." She replies: "If you don't run, you can't win."

I plan to continue to run.

Introduction

Introduction

This book seeks to provide answers to two questions, which are treated as one question: "What do economists know, and how can they know it?" It is therefore a book on the epistemology of economic reasoning. This is not a popular topic. It never has been.

Let us begin at the beginning. What is economics? This seems like a simple question. It *is* a simple question. It does not have a simple answer.

James Buchanan won the Nobel Prize in economic science in 1986. Over two decades earlier, he had asked this question: "What is economics?" Here was his answer, or at least his affirmation of Jacob Viner's answer. "Economics is what economists do." Then what do economists do? To answer this, Buchanan cited Viner's associate at the University of Chicago, Frank H. Knight. "Economists do economics."[1] I was amused by this circular explanation when I read it as a first-year student at Westminster Theological Seminary in Philadelphia in early 1964. I was probably the only seminary student in the United States who subscribed to the *Southern Economic Journal*.

The earliest definition was Xenophon's. About four centuries before the birth of Christ, he defined "economics" as "household management."[2] This definition prevailed for the next two millennia. This is from the *Online Etymological Dictionary*.

1. James Buchanan, "What Should Economists Do?" *Southern Economic Journal* (Jan. 1964). Reprinted in Buchanan, *What Should Economists Do?* (Indianapolis, Indiana: Liberty Fund, 1979), 18.

2. Xenophon, *The Economist*.

> 1530s, "household management," from L. oeconomia, from Gk. oikonomia "household management, thrift," from oikonomos "manager, steward," from oikos "house" (cognate with L. vicus "district," vicinus "near;" O.E. wic "dwelling, village;" see villa) + nomos "managing," from nemein "manage" (see numismatics). The sense of "wealth and resources of a country" (short for political economy) is from 1650s.[3]

Xenophon's original meaning is correct. Economics has to do with stewardship. The owner manages property. But for whom does he manage it? *On whose behalf*? This is the central question of Christian economics, as well as Christian everything else: "On whose behalf?" *Who is the original owner*? The correct answer is this: the God of the Bible. The shift of meaning of economics, and therefore stewardship, which took place in the 1650s, marked the advent of modern economic theory.[4] This launched a series of debates over the crucial issue: "On whose behalf?" These debates are still going on. They will continue to go on.

This raises second issue: hierarchy. *To whom do I report*? Is there a representative in between me and the owner? Do I deal directly with the owner? Is there a higher court of appeal above me? In sixteenth- and seventeenth-century political theory, there was a doctrine popular with English kings, the divine right of kings. It meant this: no higher court of appeal on earth. Unless there is a divine right of *me*, there has to be some institution above me. In terms of Christian social theory, there are more than one. This is because the concept of the divine right of anything in the creation is not biblically valid for anything except the Word of God: the resurrected Jesus and the Bible. There are always multiple institutional authorities in history. Each of these lawful authorities has its limited sphere of legitimate authority.

This raises a third issue: law. *What are the terms of stewardship*? There is no stewardship apart from legal obligations of the steward. There is no responsibility apart from contracts and custom. The steward owes something to somebody. There are multiple somebodies—an inescapable implication of multiple authorities.

This raises a fourth issue: sanctions. When the focus of economics

3. See etymonline.com/word/economy (accessed October 5, 2022).

4. William Letwin, *The Origins of Scientific Economics: English Economic Thought 1660–1776* (Cambridge, Massachusetts: M.I.T. Press, 1963).

shifted from the household to the nation-state, this mandated a new set of questions. They center on this issue: *What are economic success indicators*? The steward must have success indicators. Without these, he does not know if he is on the right track. The appropriate success indicators in a household are different from success indicators in a nation-state. The success indicators of a nation-state are different from success indicators in a free market. Success indicators are hypothetical if there are no sanctions. The success indicators must have a system feedback: motivation to honor the success indicators.

Finally, there is the issue of inheritance or legal succession. *How is legal responsibility transferred through time*? Men are mortal. They die. They are replaced.

So, there are five fundamental economic issues, all of which are inescapably related: (1) Who is the owner? (2) Who is the steward? (3) What are the terms of this stewardship? (4) Which success indicators must stewards use? (5) What are the means of succession? These are the issues of sovereignty, authority, law, sanctions, and time. They are inescapable in all social theory. They apply in unique ways in economics, and therefore also in economic theory.

These issues are covenantal. They are therefore legal. This means that economics in practice rests on a legal order. But it goes much deeper that this. Economic law is a development of the legal order, which in turn is derived from a moral order, which in turn is derived from a covenantal order. Conclusion: economic practice is never neutral. Therefore, economic theory cannot be neutral. Economic practice cannot be value-free. Therefore, economic theory cannot be value-free. *Any attempt at value-neutrality is misleading*. The values will be imported from some other realm. They will be sneaked in through an epistemological back door.

A. Five Covenants, Five Points

My work in economic theory ever since 1986 has been a series of explorations of the five points of the biblical covenant—God, man, law, sanctions, and time—as applied to the five oath-bound covenants: dominion, individual, family, church, and state. This systematic research and publication program began with the publication of Ray R. Sutton's book, *That You May Prosper: Dominion By Covenant.* I helped him edit it. My Institution for Christian Economics published it.[5] I self-consciously used this paradigm to write 29 of the 31 volumes of my comprehensive study, *An Economic Commentary on the Bible.*

The first edition of this book was the first book to consolidate my findings. That was in 2015. This book is not a treatise on the way that economies and economic institutions work. I cover these issues in my multi-volume series, *Christian Economics.* It is rather a treatise on the theoretical foundations that undergird the actual economy. It is also not a work on epistemology: "What can we know, and how can we know it?" I may eventually write such a book. I have explored the epistemology of post-1870 economic theory in previous writings.[6] The central issue in this volume is this: *the imputation of economic value.* First, whose imputations count most? Second, how do individual imputations produce reliable information for accountable decision-makers who act on behalf of covenantal organizations?

B. The Economists' Crucial Mistake

All varieties of textbook-based economic theory rest on a conceptual mistake. It is the is the mistake of not recognizing the inherently narrow scope of economic theory. Textbook-based theories of economic causation rarely apply outside of the institution of the market: an institutional arrangement for legally exchangeable goods and services. Applications of economic theory beyond this limited institutional sphere are derived from patterns of behavior that apply to this sphere. Economists assume that these same patterns of behavior also prevail in other spheres,

5. Ray R. Sutton, *That You May Prosper: Dominion By Covenant*, 2nd ed. (Tyler, Texas: Institute for Christian Economics, [1987] 1992).

6. Gary North, "Economics: From Reason to Intuition," in North (ed.) *Foundations of Christian Scholarship: Essays in the Van Til Perspective* (Vallecito, California: Ross House, 1976), reprinted below as the Appendix; North, *Sovereignty & Dominion: An Economic Commentary on Genesis* (Moulton, Alabama: Axehead Press, [1982, 2012] 2022), ch. 5; North, *Authority & Dominion: An Economic Commentary on Exodus*, vol. 5 (Moulton, Alabama: Axehead Press, [1985, 2012] 2025), Appendix H.

such as family, church, and state. They expect this transfer of market-based patterns of behavior to different legal and cultural domains to provide explanatory power. These explanations of behavior rarely work well.

Let me give what should be an obvious example. There is no market-based system for buying and selling wives. There used to be. There is a book about this, but it was not written by an economist: *Wives for Sale*.[7] It is not a well-known book. The practice of auctioning off wives in the public square went on for two centuries in Great Britain, ending only in the early 1900s. It was not a legal market, but laws against it were not always enforced. It would be legitimate to apply economic theory to this market retroactively: subjective value theory, marginal benefit and marginal cost theory, and so forth. But these analytical tools throw little light on the concept of pricing in marriage relationships in general. There is no price-based theory of exchange in marriage. There is no legal open entry and competitive bidding for services rendered.

Economics in its original sense of *household management* is at odds with textbook economics. What passes for economics today is an implicit denial of economics as defined from about 400 BC to AD 1650. Students are not told this. The authors ignore it because it has been ignored for over 350 years. But no theory of Christian economics should ignore it. This is because all institutions are judicially related to one or more of the three covenantal institutions: family, church, and state. All institutions are part of the general dominion covenant (Gen. 1:26–28). "Then God said, 'Let Us make mankind in Our image, according to Our likeness; and let them rule over the fish of the sea and over the birds of the sky and over the livestock and over all the earth, and over every crawling thing that crawls on the earth.' So God created man in His own image, in the image of God He created him; male and female He created them. God blessed them; and God said to them, 'Be fruitful and multiply, and fill the earth, and subdue it; and rule over the fish of the sea and over the birds of the sky and over every living thing that moves on the earth.' "[8] All covenants are governed by the dominion covenant.

---

7. Samuel Menefee, *Wives for Sale: An Ethnographic Study of British Popular Divorce* (London: Palgrave Macmillan, 1981). See also "Wife selling (English custom)." *Wikipedia*, Wikimedia Foundation, October 5, 2020.

8. Gary North, *Sovereignty & Dominion: An Economic Commentary on Genesis* (Moulton, Alabama: Axehead Press, [1982, 2012] 2022), chaps. 3, 4.

Therefore, modern economics rests on deception. It rests on a self-imposed limitation: a refusal to develop a comprehensive theory of resource allocation. Economists claim that their theory is comprehensive. It is not. It is narrowly bounded. It offers no guidance, meaning no theoretical model, for understanding the issues of ownership and stewardship outside of market transactions.

C. Mises on Praxeology and Catallactics

Early in the first chapter of *Human Action* (1949), Ludwig von Mises discussed what he called *praxeology*, the general science of human action and choice. He coined the term. It has not been used outside the narrow circles of his disciples. He believed that praxeology is a true science. But he faced a problem. He did not specify what it is, precisely, or how it works outside of the narrow confines of voluntary market transactions. He wrote: "The modern theory of value widens the scientific horizon and enlarges the field of economic studies. Out of the political economy of the classical school emerges the general theory of human action, *praxeology*. The economic or catallactic problems are embedded in a more general science, and can no longer be severed from this connection. No treatment of economic problems proper can avoid starting from acts of choice; economics becomes a part, although the hitherto best elaborated part, of a more universal science, praxeology."[9]

What did he mean by "catallactic"? He meant the free market social order: the realm of exchange. He described this in detail in Chapter XIV. "The subject matter of catallactics is all market phenomena with all their roots, ramifications, and consequences."[10] More specifically, "Catallactics is the analysis of those actions which are conducted on the basis of monetary calculation. Market exchange and monetary calculation are inseparably linked together. A market in which there is direct exchange only is merely an imaginary construction. On the other hand, money and monetary calculation are conditioned by the existence of the market."[11]

9. Ludwig von Mises, *Human Action: A Treatise on Economics* (New Haven, Connecticut: Yale University Press, 1949), Introduction, sect. 2.

10. Ibid., ch. XIV, sect. 1.

11. Idem.

Catallactics is a subset of praxeology. "The scope of praxeology, the general theory of human action, can be precisely defined and circumscribed. The specifically economic problems, the problems of economic action in the narrower sense, can only by and large be disengaged from the comprehensive body of praxeological theory."[12] Mises presented his theory of praxeology in terms of individual ranking of values. Men make decisions at the margin, pursuing their highest value. They exchange conditions over time.

But there was a problem. *He never elucidated this theory of praxeology outside of catallactics.* In his most famous and most important contribution to economics, his theory of the irrationality of socialist economic planning, he stated that socialist economic planning is economically irrational. Central planners cannot plan rationally apart from prices generated on a free market. "Thus, in the socialist commonwealth, every economic change becomes an undertaking whose success can be neither appraised in advance nor later retrospectively determined. There is only groping in the dark. Socialism is the abolition of rational economy."[13] Socialism is irrational because there are no monetary prices that correspond with supply and demand. There is no market. There is no private ownership. "Calculation *in natura*, in an economy without exchange, can embrace consumption goods only; it completely fails when it comes to dealing with goods of a higher order [capital goods—G. N.]. And as soon as one gives up the conception of a freely established monetary price for goods of a higher order, rational production becomes completely impossible. Every step that takes us away from private ownership of the means of production and from the use of money also takes us away from rational economics."[14]

We could also say, "irrational is as irrational does." The planners are blind. They are not economically rational. But then what can we say about the nature of this irrationality? How can we specify its irrational characteristics in a scientific way? We can make lists of gluts and shortages, but we can explain these only by way of the logic of market exchange and monetary prices. *Without the market, there is no way to*

12. Idem.

13. Ludwig von Mises, *Economic Calculation in the Socialist Commonwealth* (Auburn, Alabama: Mises Institute, [1920] 1990), 23.

14. Ibid., 17.

analyze the nature of socialism's irrationality. There are no theories of irrational behavior that apply in a consistent, predictable way. There is no theory of socialist economics. Yet socialists do act. They just do not act rationally. So, praxeology has nothing to say about socialism, other than this: it is irrational. This places socialist economics outside the realm of rational economic analysis. He wrote:

> Without economic calculation there can be no economy. Hence, in a socialist state wherein the pursuit of economic calculation is impossible, there can be—in our sense of the term—no economy whatsoever. In trivial and secondary matters rational conduct might still be possible, but in general it would be impossible to speak of rational production any more. There would be no means of determining what was rational, and hence it is obvious that production could never be directed by economic considerations. What this means is clear enough, apart from its effects on the supply of commodities. Rational conduct would be divorced from the very ground which is its proper domain. Would there, in fact, be any such thing as rational conduct at all, or, indeed, such a thing as rationality and logic in thought itself?[15]

This leads to an inescapable conclusion of his epistemology. *There is no science of human action inside a purely socialistic commonwealth.* There are no axioms, no corollaries. There is no way to analyze the specific hierarchy of errors. There is no way to explain action in such a commonwealth. There are no profits or losses. There is only chaos. There is no science of chaos.

Then what of the family? The church? The state? Are there subdivisions in the science of human action? Are these subdivisions capable of being analyzed in the way that market transactions are? In a world without profit and loss revealed by means of monetary prices and double-entry bookkeeping, how can the science of human action be applied? These are not trick questions. They are the heart of economic science.

What Mises identified as catallactics has been the domain of economists ever since the seventeenth century. Here is where most of the advances have been made by economists. They have made only sporadic advances regarding those institutions outside of the market exchange process. These advances consist of insights into market-oriented decision-

15. Ibid., 18.

making within non-market institutions. Think of public choice theory. It applies a handful of market-deduced insights regarding the pursuit of individual self-interest, but inside the domain of civil government. The public choice economist searches for concealed non-monetary exchanges that would otherwise have taken place through market exchanges, except that they would have been illegal. Problem: *there is no broad theory of human action inside the confines of civil government, family government, and church government.* So, economics as the study of household management does not exist. The household is not an institution based on monetary exchange, competitive bidding, and product substitution. In this sense, it is like the socialist commonwealth. *By the standards of praxeolgy, these non-market institutions are irrational.*

I argue that they are not irrational. They are stewardship institutions. There will be a day of final accounting. There is ongoing accounting, which conveys accurate information regarding the final day of accounting.

D. Epistemology

Epistemology asks two questions, which are usually treated as one: "What can we know, and how can we know it?"

This question is almost never asked by economists. Historians have written extensively on epistemology. It has a different name: historiography. As an undergraduate history major in 1963, I had to take a course in historiography. I later collected dozens of books on this. I own almost no books on economic epistemology. That is because there are so few. I have never heard of a graduate level economics course on epistemology. I have not heard of one on methodology, which is close to epistemology. There are books on this, but they do not go into such issues as philosophical realism (inherent) vs. philosophical nominalism (imputed), which is at the heart of any theory of value. *The crucial issue of economic theory is the relationship between value and price.* Economic value is subjective, we are told, but prices are objective. How are these related? Economists cannot say, so they rarely discuss this systematically. Their silence does not mean that they do not operate constantly on the assumption that they have provided an answer. They assume that the problem has been solved, somewhere, by someone. It hasn't.

For all the seeming precision of mathematical equations (theory) and statistical correlations (history), economists have yet to show how, in theory, these equations in any way relate to the statistical correlations. The old statement, "correlation is not causation," is relevant here. This is the ancient problem of *theory*, which is in theory constant, and *history*, which is always changing. It is the debate of the pre-Socratic philosophers, Parmenides (theory) and Heraclitus (history). The debate has yet to be reconciled. Economists are always in the middle of it, yet they seem oblivious to its existence, let alone their immersion in it. One aspect of epistemology which is occasionally mentioned is the logic of deductive reasoning—axioms and corollaries—vs. inductive reasoning: facts-based, facts-derived theory.[16] Most economists pretend to be adherents of inductive reasoning. They aren't. They are notoriously governed by their theories of how the world just *has* to work.

The school of economic opinion known as behavioral economics, which appeared in the 1970s, relies heavily on rigorous psychological experiments to explain economic behavior. The experimenters find, again and again, that people do not act in terms of the theories of mainstream economics. The problem is, no behavioral economist has published a comprehensive theory that integrates the school's findings. So, most economists prefer to ignore behavioral economics, despite the fact that two of the founders have won Nobel Prizes: Daniel Kahneman (2002) and Richard Thayer (2017). Marketers do not dare ignore this field. I speak from experience as a marketer. Some of the discoveries of behavioral economists had been known and applied by marketers long before the 1970s, but conventional economists paid no attention. Most older mainstream economists dismiss behavioral economics as a fad.

The heart of the economists' philosophical problem is this. They argue that economic value is subjective. It is imputed by acting individuals. This was the great insight of Austrian economist Carl Menger in 1871. The problem is, once you accept this theory of subjectivism, you

16. I discussed this dualism in 1976: "Economics: From Reason to Intuition." in Gary North (ed.), *Foundations of Christian Scholarship: Essays in the Van Til Perspective* (Vallecito, California: Ross House, 1976), ch. 3. I have reprinted this in the Appendix.

must abandon the use of economic aggregates. You must also abandon accepting or offering all policy recommendations. Why? Because the imputations of value by individuals are said to be autonomous. *There is no common scale of economic value.* If there were, it would have to be objective. It would have to be measurable. No such value scale exists outside of the mind of an autonomous economic actor. *This fact undermines virtually all of modern economics.* It converts applied economics into a cacophony of competing subjective valuations. It undermines all claims that economics is a science. This has been known ever since 1938, when two economists debated it publicly: Roy Harrod, Keynes' colleague and disciple, and Lionel Robbins, Mises' disciple. I shall return to this theme repeatedly in this book. I have been hammering on this ever since 1982 in my book, *The Dominion Covenant: Genesis*, the first edition of the first volume in my 31-volume economic commentary on the Bible.

E. Mises on Epistemology

This book is my answer to an assertion by Mises. Mises wrote: "Theology and the metaphysics of history may discuss the ends of society and the designs which God wants to realize with regard to society in the same way in which they discuss the purpose of all other parts of the created universe. For science, which is inseparable from reason, a tool manifestly unfit for the treatment of such problems, it would be hopeless to embark upon speculations concerning these matters."[17] I disagree with his view of science. His view is the common view in this, the era of Immanuel Kant. Kant's assertion of a permanent epistemological separation of the theological-metaphysical realm—assuming that it even exists—from the realm of science is systematic on the part of modern scientists. University textbooks in every academic discipline reflect this separation. Economics was the first social science to adopt the assumption of theological and ethical neutrality.[18]

Mises extended his critique to include the idea of God's providence.

17. Mises, *Human Action*, ch. VIII, sect. 1.
18. Letwin, *Origins of Scientific Economics*.

In defending the idea of autonomous individuals in an autonomous social order, he wrote that "it is not necessary to have recourse to a doctrine, certainly offensive to a truly religious mind, according to which the original creation was so defective that reiterated superhuman intervention is needed to prevent its failure."[19] I reject his suggestion that the distant and aloof god of an alleged form of deism, which in fact has never had any adherents, is somehow the creedal affirmation of "the truly religious mind." I also reject his affirmation that either man or society is autonomous.

In this book, I present an explicitly Trinitarian approach to economic theory. I wrote a preliminary consideration of the structure of Christian economics in *Inherit the Earth: Biblical Blueprints for Economics* in 1987.[20] That book was shorter than this one. It did not deal systematically with all five oath-bound covenants: dominion, individual, family, church, and state. As in the case of this book, *Inherit the Earth* was structured in terms of the five points of the biblical covenant. In 2017, I wrote a follow-up book, *Christian Economics for Students*.[21] It is also structured in terms of the five points.

There have been a handful of economists who have argued in favor of one or another economic system in terms of its alleged conformity to Christianity. None of them has gone to the Bible as the starting point for his reasoning. None of them has been epistemologically self-conscious, challenging the presuppositions of modern economic theory in terms of biblical revelation. Most important, none of them has based his claims on 31 volumes of verse-by-verse expositions of biblical texts that deal with economics or issues intrinsic to economic reasoning. I have.

If we date the origin of modern economic theory with the School of Salamanca in the sixteenth century,[22] then economic theory orig-

---

19. Mises, *Human Action*, ch. 8, sect. 2.

20. Gary North, *Inherit the Earth: Biblical Blueprints for Economics* (Ft. Worth, Texas: Dominion Press, 1987).

21. Gary North, *Christian Economics for Students* (Moulton, Alabama: Axehead Press, [2017] 2025).

22. Murray N. Rothbard, "Late Medieval Origins of Free Market Economic Thought," *The Journal of Christian Reconstruction*, II (Summer 1975); Rothbard, "New Light on the Prehistory of the Austrian School," in Edwin G. Dolan (ed.), *The Foundations of Modern Austrian Economics* (Kansas City: Sheed & Ward, 1976), 52–74; Alejandro A. Chafuen, *Christians for Freedom: Late-Scholastic Economics* (San Francisco: Ignatius, 1986).

inally rested on natural law theory, not the Bible. Next, if we date its origin with the mercantilists of the late-seventeenth century, then modern economic theory rests on the assumption of the autonomy of the mind and the power of mathematical reasoning. English mercantilism was self-consciously opposed to any appeal to religion or morality. The founders were in reaction against the English Civil War between Puritans and the King's forces (1642–1649). They were also reacting against the Thirty Years' War in what is today Germany between Protestants and Catholics (1618–1648). These men had lost faith in the ability of men to come to any agreed-upon conclusions regarding either religion or morality. They tried to create a morally neutral science of economics on the basis of man's universal and autonomous logic.[23]

If we date economic theory with David Hume's mid-eighteenth century essays on trade, in which Hume reacted against the mercantilists' defense of government-controlled trade, we see that his methodology was equally committed to man's autonomous mind. The same is true of Adam Smith's *Wealth of Nations* (1776). The moralism and deism of his *Theory of Moral Sentiments* (1759) were completely absent from his later book. It was the second book, not *The Theory of Moral Sentiments*, which launched modern economics.

Smith began *Wealth of Nations* with a discussion of the division of labor. This was a conceptual blunder with negative consequences. It was a strategic blunder with even worse consequences. There is nothing unique about the division of labor under the free market compared with socialism. What is unique under capitalism is private property. Smith had begun the first lecture of the first series in his *Lectures on Jurisprudence* (1760) with an affirmation of private property. But this document was not published until 1978.[24]

The opening salvo against Smith's defense of capitalism came from William Godwin in 1793: *Enquiry Concerning Political Justice*.[25] He attacked the idea of private property. The connected questions of property and ownership became the supreme intellectual issues in economics over the next two centuries. In the twentieth century, they became

23. Letwin, *Origins of Scientific Economics*.

24. Tom Bethell, *The Noblest Triumph: Property and Prosperity Through the Ages* (New York: St. Martin's, 1998), 97.

25. Ibid., 103.

the supreme political issues: capitalism, fascism, socialism, and Marxian communism. Yet Smith devoted very little space to a discussion of private property in *Wealth of Nations*. This weakened the work of his successors. It also opened the door for socialist critics to offer rival views of economic cause and effect.

F. Trinitarian Economics

It is the great benefit of the Austrian School economists that they do begin with individual motivation and decision-making, namely, human action. This is why the Austrian School's approach to economics is more closely aligned with Christian economics than any other rival system of economics. More than any other interpretive school of economics, the Austrian School begins with subjectivism, meaning subjective value theory, and extends it to every aspect of the market process. There are limits epistemologically to this approach, but these limits are not nearly so debilitating conceptually as the assumption of corporate or aggregate economics. In other words, *microeconomics is the heart of economic theory, not macroeconomics*. In saying this, however, I am saying it in terms of the biblical covenantal structure of economics, which begins with God and not man. I am saying this as someone who believes that man is made in the image of God, a creature who thinks God's thoughts after Him, and who is totally responsible to God for his thoughts, motivations, and actions.

1. *The Image of a Trinitarian God*

Man is made in the image of God. This is true individually, and it is also true corporately. Christian economics teaches that God is both one and three. Mankind is therefore both individual and corporate. So, when we speak of economics, we must speak of microeconomics, which rests on the assumption of individual responsibility and legal authority, and also macroeconomics, which rests on the assumption of corporate responsibility and legal authority. We say that God is both one and many. We should say that there is an *equal ultimacy* of the one and the many. This is what theologians sometimes call the doctrine of the *ontological* Trinity. It deals with the essence of God's being.

Nevertheless, theologians also speak of a hierarchy of authority within the being of God. There is a Father, a Son, and a Holy Ghost. This is sometimes called the doctrine of the *economic* Trinity. This has nothing to do with prices and exchange. It has to do with the original Greek meaning of *eco*, namely, family or household (*oikos*). Economics is the law (*nomos*) of the household. Within the Trinity itself, there is a hierarchy. There is a system of authority. There is therefore the possibility of an inter-Trinitarian covenant or series of covenants. This is not much discussed by theologians, but it underlies all covenant theology. When God said "Let us make man in our own image," this was not hyperbole. This was not a "plural of majesty," as unitarians call it. This was a corporate decision.

If there is equal ultimacy of the one and the many in the Trinity, why isn't there an equal ultimacy of the one and the many in the methodology of economics? Why isn't macroeconomics equally ultimate to microeconomics? The Christian economist should reply that they are equally ultimate covenantally, meaning judicially. The law of God and the historical sanctions of God are equally ultimate, according to the Mosaic law. That is to say, judicially they are ultimate. They apply to individuals and institutions. But economics both in theory and practice is more about individual motivation than judicial structure. With respect to motivation, because of the nature of eternal sanctions on individuals, methodological individualism has greater motivational power, and therefore greater methodological power, than holism or collectivism. This is why Jesus constantly referred in His parables to individual motivation. Several of them were what I call pocketbook parables. They had to do with money.

2. *Judicial Representation*

Here is a preliminary conclusion: economic science rests more heavily on methodological individualism than political science does. Here is one application of this insight. There are methodological limits to that school of economic thought known as public choice theory. Public choice theory rests on this assumption: people who act in their capacity as agents of the civil government are not motivated differently from people who are agents of a small business which they own or which their family owns. They are equally governed by self-interest, says the public choice economist. They are, indeed. This is a fundamental implication of the doctrine of the final judgment. But this does not mean that civil office holders are as motivated by financial gain as an entrepreneur is. The covenantal structure of the civil government is different from the covenantal structure of a profit-seeking business. The rules are different. The sanctions are different.

The state is far more about judicial affairs than economic affairs. It is more about the exercise of power than about the accumulation of wealth. It therefore displays the characteristics of corporate action, which is individual action on behalf of a hierarchical agency. In the case of the civil covenant, personal motivation is strongly corporate. Again, this has to do with power more than money, and *power is corporate*. So, while we should not ignore personal motivation of state officials when we analyze the exercise of unitary civil authority, we should not elevate it over corporate motivation. When a person exercises corporate authority, he is not supposed to "look out for number one" (himself). Rather, he is to look out for the group. This is obvious in the case of the family covenant. It also applies to the civil covenant and the church covenant.

This sense of *covenantal obligation* in history is inherently strong in every office-holder. Why? Because God judges—evaluates and imposes sanctions—those people who serve as judges. He judges them in terms of a higher ethical standard than He judges individuals who do not possess judicial/covenantal authority. There is one passage in the Bible above all others that teaches this: Leviticus 4.[26] The fundamental principle of ethical responsibility is this: *with greater knowledge comes greater personal responsibility* (Luke 12:47–48).[27] This applies to judges—in family, church, and state—more than to other positions of institutional authority. Why? Because men in a covenantal office represent God in His office as the supreme Judge: the sanctions-bringer. This is why men are warned throughout the Bible not to use false weights and measures. In civil government, these are metaphors for false judgment. Judges

---

26. Gary North, *Boundaries & Dominion: An Economic Commentary on Leviticus* (Moulton, Alabama: Axehead Press, [1994, 2012] 2026), ch. 4.

27. Gary North, *Treasure & Dominion: An Economic Commentary on Luke* (Moulton, Alabama: Axehead Press, [2012] 2031), ch. 28.

must judge impartially (Lev. 19:15).[28] They must not seek bribes. They must uphold God's law. They know this. It is part of the work of the law written in their hearts (Rom. 2:14–15).[29]

I want to make crystal clear what I am saying here. Christian economics is fundamentally judicial. It is therefore fundamentally moral. It is not value-free. So, I begin my analysis with judicial categories:

1. God owns everything.
2. God delegates ownership.
3. God prohibits theft.
4. God evaluates performance.
5. God mandates growth.

Economic categories are applications of these judicial categories. This is why I begin with God's sovereignty. This is a *legal category,* not an autonomous economic category.

G. The Bible Provides Blueprints

In books and articles written by Protestant evangelical academic scholars, we read this phrase: "The Bible is not a blueprint on. . . ." The author will then list his academic discipline: economics, sociology, psychology, or whatever.

What does this phrase mean? It has objective meaning. It also has subjective meaning. Its objective meaning is this: "The Bible does not provide supernaturally authoritative principles that govern the theoretical foundations of an academic discipline, nor does it in any way govern the discipline's applications in practice." Its subjective meaning is this.

> I received an advanced economic degree from a university that is accredited by humanists. It was officially secular. Supernatural revelation was excluded as an authoritative source of propositional truth. I have not deviated from the outlook of that training. So, when I examine my academic discipline, I do not let supernatural revelation affect my

28. North, *Boundaries & Dominion,* ch. 14.

29. Gary North, *Cooperation & Dominion: An Economic Commentary on Romans* (Moulton, Alabama: Axehead Press, [2012] 2031), ch. 3.

> presuppositions. Therefore, I say with authority that the Bible is not a textbook on [fill in the field], because if it were a textbook, I would then be exposed as someone who sold his spiritual birthright for a mess of academic pottage. I do not want to consider this possibility, so I say with all of the authority that I possess because of my training, the Bible is not a textbook on [fill in the field].

I have seen this in book after book: "The Bible is not a textbook on economics." My favorite example is the 1984 book, *Wealth and Poverty: Four Christian Views of Economics.*[30] I was one of the four contributors. The others were defenders of rival approaches: Keynesianism's mixed economy, state central planning, and small-community agriculture with property held in common. Each of the other three authors insisted that the Bible is not a textbook in economics. That was because the Bible explicitly establishes a private property system that denies the legitimacy of each of the other three positions. I, in contrast, cited dozens of passages that explicitly affirm the legitimacy of private property.

I have written 31 volumes of economic commentaries on the Bible that demonstrate the truth of this position: "The Bible offers a blueprint for economics."

Conclusion

This book begins with the issue of ownership. It does so because the concept of ownership is an aspect of the doctrine of creation. Every academic discipline should begin where the Bible does: the doctrine of origins. Every academic discipline rests on a specific concept of origins. Because scholars like to pretend that their disciplines are ethically neutral, they find it convenient to avoid straightforward discussions of origins. This controversial and complex issue points back to theology, or at least to cosmology. Scholars regard both issues as peripheral in the construction of the social sciences. So, they build their systems in terms a set of assumptions about origins, but only rarely are these assumptions admitted publicly and used explicitly to develop the overall discipline.

30. Robert Clouse (ed.), *Wealth and Poverty: Four Christian Views of Economics* (Downers Grove, Illinois: InterVarsity Press, 1984).

But there is no escape from the concept of origins and its implications. These implications are smuggled into each academic discipline through the back door.

It is time to get the doctrine of origins front and center.

PART I

The Economic Structure of the Dominion Covenant

Introduction to Part I

In every field of thought, we are required by God to begin with two premises: (1) God is absolutely sovereign; (2) nothing in the creation is autonomous. These are implications of the biblical doctrine of creation. God created the universe out of nothing. The universe is totally dependent on the providence of God. God is in no way dependent on the universe.

The economy is not autonomous. *Economic theory must therefore not begin with any concept of man or society as autonomous.* This declaration is the heart, mind, and soul of this book and my theory of Christian economics.

The economy is under the authority of God. This authority is manifested covenantally. Covenants are established by men under God. Men bind themselves legally by an oath that involves penalties for disobedience. These are called *self-maledictory* oaths. They implicitly call down God's negative sanctions on the oath-takers for any future disobedience. There are five of these covenantal oaths in history: dominion, individual, familistic, ecclesiastical, and civil. Each of these covenants has stipulations governing the economic process. Conclusion: the economy is not autonomous.

The economy is under the authority of God. This authority is manifested covenantally. Covenants are established by men under God. Men bind themselves legally by an oath of allegiance that involves penalties for disobedience. These are called *self-maledictory* oaths. They implicitly call down God's negative sanctions on the oath-takers for any future disobedience. There are five of these covenantal oaths in history: dominion, individual, familistic, ecclesiastical, and civil. Each of these covenants has stipulations governing the economic process.

Economics is the study of production and consumption in a world governed by scarcity. Scarcity is defined as follows: "At zero price, there is greater demand than supply." When this is the case, scarce resources are allocated by price. The question is: What kind of price? Money? Power? Good looks?

The dominion covenant is the overall covenant for all mankind. It was established by God in the name of mankind before the first man was created. The confirming oath was made by God as a judicial representative of all mankind. God said what mankind must do. Man did not confirm this oath. It was an implicit oath. It is like citizenship. No formal oath is taken by native-born citizens, but it is implied. A citizen is allowed to vote at some age. But it takes no public oath of allegiance to obtain a voting card.[1]

The economy is primarily the outgrowth of the family, though to a lesser extent, individuals. This is because property is owned mostly by families. Both church and state are supported by revenues generated by families and individuals, including the modern judicial individual, the limited liability corporation. Thus, *economics is governed primarily by laws governing the family and individuals.*

The fundamental issue of economics is God's original ownership. The subordinate issues are man's stewardship, private property, scarcity, and economic growth. The great debate among humanistic economists is this: *Who owns what?* Competing schools of economic thought generally divide into two factions: defenders of private property and defenders of state property. This is a debate over *judicial sovereignty*, although the debaters rarely admit this. Most of them seem unaware of this fact.

Christian economics has its version of these same two factions, but Christian economists have usually come down heavily on the side of private property. I have written 31 volumes of Bible commentaries to demonstrate why this conclusion is warranted biblically.

The fundamental question for economic theory is almost never debated by economists, even by Christians who are economists: *To whom has God* ***delegated trusteeship*** *in history?*

Thus, in Chapter 1, I begin with God's ownership. God has a lawful

1. In the United States, a public oath is required of all foreign-born candidates for citizenship. They swear the oath immediately prior to being granted citizenship.

claim on everything, including all men. He has delegated ownership mainly to families and individuals, but also to civil governments and churches, which have lawful claims as God-ordained agencies. We must go to the Bible in our search for legal principles of jurisdiction over property. This, economists have not done in the past in a systematic fashion. They have turned to supposedly common ethical principles of supposedly autonomous law. I do not.

Chapter 1

The Judicial Sovereignty of God

I am the Lord, *and there is no one else;*
There is no God except Me.
I will arm you, though you have not known Me,
So that people may know from the rising to the setting of the sun
That there is no one besides Me.
I am the Lord, *and there is no one else,*
The One forming light and creating darkness,
Causing well-being and creating disaster;
I am the Lord *who does all these things.*

Isaiah 45:5–7

Analysis

Point one of the biblical covenant is the transcendence of God, yet also His presence with the creation.[1] As the Creator, God is absolutely sovereign over the creation. He is not part of it. He is also not removed from it.

When we begin our discussion of Christian economics, we must begin with this conceptual outline, which has to do with the judicial aspects of the covenant:

1. Transcendence/presence is point one of the biblical covenant. Ray R. Sutton, *That You May Prosper: Dominion By Covenant*, 2nd ed. (Tyler, Texas: Institute for Christian Economics, [1987] 1992), ch. 1.

1. God owns everything.
2. God delegates ownership.
3. God prohibits theft.
4. God evaluates performance.
5. God mandates growth.

These are judicial categories. They are what God demands, based on His office as the Creator and therefore the Owner. These categories have to do with original ownership. All economic thought implicitly reflects this judicial structure. Every system of economic theory deals with each of these five categories. They are inescapable concepts.

Point one is the legal issue of sovereignty. What is sovereignty? It is *autonomous power*. It answers to no one. There is no court of appeal higher than the court of the sovereign. Being absolutely sovereign because of its absolute autonomy, the court therefore also possesses *authority*. This court is legitimate. Those under its jurisdiction have a moral requirement to obey. Obedience is to be a manifestation of self-government under law.

Sovereignty is the ability to impose one's will both by force (power) and legitimate authority, which deserves obedience on moral grounds. Sovereignty establishes that which the subordinates owe the sovereign. Sovereignty can compel the payment of whatever is owed, whenever that which is owed is not paid. In the deepest sense, *sovereignty is personal*.

Sovereignty identifies the answer to this question: "Who's in charge here?" This is point one of the biblical covenant: the God who is transcendent and also present.

The sovereign is not required to explain his reasons for doing anything. He explains himself only by His grace: a gift unmerited by the recipient. The Book of Job is the premier book in the Bible on sovereignty. Job demanded an explanation from God (chapters 3–37). He was not entitled to one, yet he was given one. What was it? "I'm God, and you're not" (chapters 38–41).[2]

All human thought necessarily begins with an underlying presupposition regarding sovereignty. This is stated explicitly or else is implicitly presumed: either the sovereignty of God or the sovereignty of some

2. Gary North, *Predictability & Dominion: An Economic Commentary on Job* (Moulton, Alabama: Axehead Press, [2012] 2029), ch. 6.

aspect of the creation. In the modern world, the most widely believed alternative to the sovereignty of God is the sovereignty of man, either individual or collective.

Humanistic economic theory is Darwinist. Darwinian humanism officially begins with an assumption: the original sovereignty of an unplanned, evolving, impersonal universe. Yet the word "sovereignty" is carefully avoided. Instead, the doctrine of sovereignty is smuggled into the humanists' worldview by means of the same issue by which the doctrine of sovereignty is openly proclaimed in Christianity: the account of origins.

1. *Bait and Switch*

This is the first step in what police describe as a bait-and-switch operation. A bait-and-switch operation is a sales strategy by which a seller persuades shoppers to buy that which they had no intention of buying when they walked into the store. The seller's advertising campaign promises to sell a desirable item at a very low price. Once the customer walks into the store, the salesman tells him that the store is out of stock of the sought-after item. He then uses his sales skills to sell the customer a more expensive product. This tactic is illegal in most local jurisdictions in the United States. It is classified as a fraud. Why? Because it steals time from customers.

The bait in the modern concept of cosmic origins is the desire of covenant-breaking man to eliminate the God of the Bible from this world. Covenant-breaking man seeks cosmic autonomy. *Man's cosmic autonomy is the central theme in a vast advertising campaign, which is promoted by the modern educational system.* The world is said to have begun with the autonomous and totally impersonal Big Bang, rather than with God's creation of the universe out of nothing. The concept of something coming out of nothing in no way repels the modern cosmologist. After all, the infinitely dense and infinitely tiny substance that originally expanded within a tiny fraction of a second, which took place about 13.7 billion years ago, became the universe. It came out of nothing, or so most modern evolutionary cosmologists believe.[3]

3. A few cosmologists believe in an oscillating universe, with the universe always existing: expanding and contracting forever. "New Theory Provides Alternative to Big Bang,"

The modern cosmologist systematically rejects any suggestion that a sovereign being created the universe with a purpose in mind. Even the suggestion that the autonomous universe had its own autonomous purpose is rejected. This idea was Darwin's original target for destruction. It is today called "intelligent design." It is anathema to orthodox Darwinists, just as it was for Darwin. So, *it is the concept of* ***original purpose****, not the concept of* ***something from nothing****, which repels the modern cosmologist.* The cosmic expansion of the uncreated, unexplained, impersonal, and autonomous substance that comprised the source of everything that came later is said to be all there ever was and all there will ever be. This is the bait: a world without a sovereign God who has created heaven, hell (Luke 16), and the lake of fire (Rev. 20:14–15).

The universe is said to be very big. The universe is also said to be very old. The bigness of the universe is used to affirm its oldness.[4] The earth is a mere speck in this very big, very old universe. This *speck theory* is also an aspect of the bait. It is bait because it reduces man's immediate environment to *cosmic insignificance*. In doing this, the cosmologists are attempting to push the Creator God out of the universe by means of the universe's age and size. Man is thereby reduced to cosmic insignificance.

This step is crucial because the first chapter of Genesis affirms that man is the image of God (Gen. 1:26). The second chapter describes a hierarchy in which the sovereign Agent places a representative man under a law, and then announces the sanction of death for violating this law. Such a view of man's origins rests on a doctrine of God's sovereignty, which stems from His omnipotence in creating the universe and His omniscience in evaluating it, day by day, on His own authority: "It is good." *God is both original Creator and final Judge.* He is final Judge because He is the original Creator. So, to escape his legitimate fear of final judgment, humanist man is required to accept mankind's cosmic insignificance. But only briefly.

At some point in time—approximately 3.5 billion years ago, according to the latest widely accepted theory (sure to be revised)—life on

Science Daily, April 30, 2002, sciencedaily.com/releases/2002/04/020429080540.htm. This is hardly a new theory. It goes back thousands of years. The mathematics is new.

4. The prevailing theory linking time with size is the red-shift phenomenon.

earth evolved out of a lifeless environment. Life, like the universe, was originally uncreated, purposeless, and autonomous. The appearance of life, like the Big Bang, was a discontinuous event: the second discontinuous event.

This is bait. Then comes the switch. Over time, life evolved until the third cosmic discontinuity took place: the evolution of man. Man is said to be unlike anything that preceded him. Man is purposeful. He plans in terms of His purposes. He shapes the present in terms of a vision of the future. *With man, purpose entered what had been a purposeless environment.* This makes man fundamentally different from the rest of his environment, and possibly unique in the entire universe. Man arose out of purposelessness, but he now imposes change on his environment in terms of his purposes. Purpose is therefore original with mankind. ***Original purpose** is seen by humanists as the central factor in defining **sovereignty**.* In this regard, they agree with Christians. The debate is over who the original sovereign is: God or man.

2. *Origins and Sovereignty*

So, what begins with an affirmation of cosmic purposelessness, which is an assertion of the absence of cosmic sovereignty, soon becomes an affirmation of the unique sovereignty of man, at least on our little speck of the universe.[5] This is *sovereignty by default.*

Every post-Darwin academic discipline begins with this version of man's origins. The doctrine of cosmic origins shapes everything that follows. *The doctrine of cosmic origins conveys the doctrine of sovereignty.* This is why the Bible begins, "In the beginning God created the heavens and the earth" (Gen. 1:1). These words convey a specific doctrine of sovereignty: God, not the universe or any aspect of it, is sovereign.[6]

In all academic versions of economic thought, the sovereignty of man is the operating presupposition. Economists rarely discuss economics in terms of a seemingly political or even philosophical idea, which "sovereignty" surely is. The main exception was free market economist

5. Gary North, *Sovereignty & Dominion: An Economic Commentary on Genesis* (Moulton, Alabama: Axehead Press, [1982, 2012] 2022), Appendix A: "From Cosmic Purposelessness to Humanistic Sovereignty."

6. Ibid., ch. 1.

William H. Hutt. In 1935, he coined the term *consumer sovereignty.*[7] In free market circles, this phrase has caught on to a limited extent.

The question of sovereignty is inescapable. It can be concealed, but it cannot be avoided. The great debate between socialists and capitalists has been over the nature of the sovereign entity which should—an ethical issue—allocate economic resources, including labor: either the hypothetically impersonal free market or the politically personal civil government.

By raising the question of origins, I am moving the debate back to the fundamental issue: the sovereignty of autonomous God vs. the sovereignty of self-professed autonomous man.

I have already listed the five judicial categories. I will now extend my discussion.

A. God Owns Everything

Point one: God's sovereignty. God created the universe: an act of sovereignty. He therefore owns it. He is responsible for it. I argue that God has a purpose for the creation. He is responsible to Himself for seeing to it that this purpose is fulfilled in history and eternity. He is not responsible to man. Man is responsible to God. God does not answer to man (Job 38–41). Man answers to God. "But I tell you that for every careless word that people speak, they will give an account of it on the day of judgment" (Matt. 12:36).

If Christian economics is to be distinguished from humanistic economics, Christian economists must begin with the doctrine of creation. This is true of every science, including all of the social sciences. To begin anywhere else is to begin with man as autonomous. This is where all modern humanistic sciences begin. Christians must make a self-conscious break from the epistemology of humanism. They should do so by beginning where the Bible begins: "In the beginning God created the heavens and the earth" (Gen. 1:1).[8] Christian economists must also

7. W. H. Hutt, "The Nature of Aggressive Selling," *Economica* (August 1935); cf. Hutt, "The Concept of Consumers' Sovereignty," *Economic Journal* (March 1940).

8. Gary North, *Sovereignty & Dominion: An Economic Commentary on Genesis* (Moulton, Alabama: Axehead Press, [1982, 2012] 2022), ch. 1.

acknowledge that the specific action of creation was accomplished by the Second Person of the Trinity, later incarnated as Jesus Christ. Paul wrote of Christ as the Creator.

> ...giving thanks to the Father, who has qualified us to share in the inheritance of the saints in light. For He rescued us from the domain of darkness, and transferred us to the kingdom of His beloved Son, in whom we have redemption, the forgiveness of sins. He is the image of the invisible God, the firstborn of all creation: for by Him all things were created, both in the heavens and on earth, visible and invisible, whether thrones, or dominions, or rulers, or authorities—all things have been created through Him and for Him. He is before all things, and in Him all things hold together. (Col. 1:12–17)

This leads us to the distinguishing feature of Christianity, separating it from all other religions: the doctrine of the Trinity.

1. *The Trinity*

Here is where Christian economics departs from Jewish economics, which does not exist as a separate academic discipline, and Islamic economics, which does. "Then God said, 'Let Us make mankind in Our image, according to Our likeness; and let them rule over the fish of the sea and over the birds of the sky and over the livestock and over all the earth, and over every crawling thing that crawls on the earth'" (Gen. 1:26). The words are clear: "Our image."[9] With the advent of Jesus Christ, the second person of the Trinity, God the Son, Christianity was able to extend the implications of the Old Testament. This extension includes insights into the nature of the sovereignty of God.

God is both one and many. He is three persons in one being: Father, Son, and Holy Spirit. This means that there is an underlying cosmic foundation for all issues that reflect both the unity and plurality of man. Man is made in God's image. Mankind therefore reflects both the unity and plurality of the Godhead.

God has a purpose for the creation. He also has a plan to attain this purpose. First, God's purpose preceded the creation. Paul wrote:

9. Both Judaism and Islam speak of this plural language as a supposed "plural of majesty." In other words, they have no theologically consistent answer for it. Christianity does.

> Blessed be the God and Father of our Lord Jesus Christ, who has blessed us with every spiritual blessing in the heavenly places in Christ, just as He chose us in Him before the foundation of the world, that we would be holy and blameless before Him. In love He predestined us to adoption as sons and daughters through Jesus Christ to Himself, according to the good pleasure of His will, to the praise of the glory of His grace, with which He favored us in the Beloved. In Him we have redemption through His blood, the forgiveness of our wrongdoings, according to the riches of His grace which He lavished on us. In all wisdom and insight He made known to us the mystery of His will, according to His good pleasure which He set forth in Him, regarding His plan of the fullness of the times, to bring all things together in Christ, things in the heavens and things on the earth. (Eph. 1:3–10)

This leads to a conclusion: *the concept of God's purpose must be front and center in Christian economic theory*.

Second, God makes plans, as we see in His declaration of intent to create mankind. This planning operation was a joint process. There was cooperation and discussion. The creation of man is explicitly revealed by the text to have been preceded by a joint declaration: "Let us." The same is true of God's decision to destroy men's cooperation in building the tower of Babel. "Come, let Us go down and there confuse their language, so that they will not understand one another's speech" (Gen. 11:7).[10] This indicates that there was a reconciliation of plans before man's creation and before Babel's destruction took place. This concept of *plan reconciliation* is extremely important in developing an explicitly Christian economic theory.

God's purpose and His plan are conceptually distinct categories. They were pre-creation. They existed outside of time. There is no meaning to chronological sequence when applied to the world before the creation. But, for man, purposes and planning are sequential. This leads to a biblical principle: *purpose precedes planning*.[11]

---

10. North, *Sovereignty & Dominion*, ch. 19.

11. Gary North, *Christian Economics for Teachers* (Moulton, Alabama: Axehead Press, [2017], 2026), ch. 3.

2. *Creation and Providence*

God is the owner of the universe because of two things: His original creation of the universe and His providential administration of it subsequently. The completion of the creation on day six, coupled with God's declaration of its goodness, jointly constitute the starting point of any discussion of economics. "And God saw all that He had made, and behold, it was very good. And there was evening and there was morning, the sixth day" (Gen. 1:31).[12] This verse establishes God as a uniquely *transcendent* God: separate from and dominant over the creation. It also identifies God as the source of all imputations of value. The doctrine of *God as sovereign Imputer* is crucial for any discussion of economic value, as we shall see.

God used dust to create Adam. "Then the LORD God formed the man of dust from the ground, and breathed into his nostrils the breath of life; and the man became a living person" (Gen. 2:7). God did not speak man into existence, unlike His creation of the cosmos on days one through five. He also intervened directly to create Eve out of Adam's body (Gen. 2:21–22). Put explicitly, *God used existing resources to complete the creation.* He adopted a system of ends and means. He then progressively limited Himself to what was available in the creation. He added His own breath to the earth to create Adam. Next, he used Adam's body, which was alive, to create Eve, but without adding His breath. This leads to a conclusion: *God has progressively restricted His intervention into history by restricting Himself to using previously created means.* He intervenes in history more and more indirectly. A good example is the entrance of the Israelites into Canaan. The miracle of the providentially and miraculously supplied manna ceased forever (Josh. 5:12).[13] *God substitutes previously created means for miracles.* This does not reduce the degree of providence. It does lure covenant-breakers into denying providence (Rom. 1:18–22).[14]

Providence refers to God's active sustaining of the universe through time. *God's providence is the basis of all continuity.* The continuity of

12. North, *Sovereignty & Dominion*, ch. 5.

13. Gary North, *Disobedience & Defeat: An Economic Commentary on the Historical Books* (Moulton, Alabama: Axehead Press, [2012] 2029), ch. 2.

14. Gary North, *Cooperation & Dominion: An Economic Commentary on Romans* (Moulton, Alabama: Axehead Press, [2012] 2031), ch. 2.

the universe is not autonomous in any aspect. Christians affirm that God is present with His universe through time. He is not part of it, but He is present with it.[15]

With respect to God's providential administration of the world, Job 38–41 is a relevant passage. God answers Job's question—"Why me, Lord?"—with a long list of things He has seen and done. "Where were you when I laid the foundation of the earth? Tell Me, if you have understanding" (Job 38:4).[16] But no passage more forcefully declares God's sovereignty over the creation than Isaiah 45. The entire chapter constitutes an affirmation of the sovereignty of God, but these verses especially. "'It is I who made the earth, and created mankind upon it. I stretched out the heavens with My hands, And I ordained all their lights. I have stirred him in righteousness, And I will make all his ways smooth. He will build My city and let My exiles go free, Without any payment or reward,' says the LORD of armies" (Isa. 45:12–13).

The twin doctrines of creation and providence are the conceptual foundations of this declaration: "For every animal of the forest is Mine, The cattle on a thousand hills" (Ps. 50:10).[17]

The twin doctrines of creation and providence establish a fundamental distinction between God as Creator and any aspect of the creation. God is in no way dependent on the creation. The creation is in every way dependent on God. God is autonomous, establishing His law for Himself and the creation. The creation is not autonomous in any way.

3. *Neither Pantheism nor Deism*

God is not part of His creation. The creation is not an extension of God's being. It is fundamentally different from God. God created it out of nothing. He did not cut off a piece of Himself to form it. So, man does not contain a spark of divinity. In no sense is man divine. The creation is not infused with God's being. *All forms of pantheism are wrong.* God is in no way immersed in His creation. The Bible's doctrine of God's creation of the universe out of nothing mandates this conclusion.

---

15. Transcendence/presence is point one of the biblical covenant. Sutton, *That You May Prosper*, ch. 1.

16. North, *Predictability & Dominion*, ch. 6.

17. Gary North, *Confidence & Dominion: An Economic Commentary on the Psalms* (Moulton, Alabama: Axehead Press, [2012] 2029), ch. 10.

Similarly, the doctrine of God's providence militates against any version of deism. God establishes law for the creation. He also sustains it, moment by moment. Paul wrote of Christ, "He is before all things, and in Him all things hold together" (Col. 1:17). The deistic view of the universe, namely, that God created the world and then departed from it, leaving it to operate in terms of autonomous law, is incorrect. *All forms of deism are wrong.*

Conclusion: God is both transcendent to His creation and present with it. This assertion distinguishes Christianity from deism, which makes transcendence a function of distance. Deism's god is so different from the creation that it has no contact with it: *separation*. Deism's god is an outside god who ignores the universe. This is a hands-off god. Pantheism's god is so much like the creation that it cannot judge the creation or autonomously shape it: *immanence*. Pantheism's god is an inside god who cannot autonomously redeem the universe. This is a hands-in god. The Bible denies both positions. The Bible's God is a hands-on God.

B. God Delegates Ownership

Point two: hierarchy. Ownership is a manifestation of the Trinity. The God of the Bible established ownership of the cosmos as a unified team. The equal ultimacy of the three persons of the Trinity with respect to the being of God is affirmed by Christianity. This equal ultimacy is referred to by theologians as the doctrine of the *ontological Trinity*. But there is more to the doctrine of the Trinity than equal ultimacy of the three persons. There is also hierarchy. The three persons of the Trinity have different functions in relation to the creation. Theologians refer to this as the *economic Trinity*.

The New Testament does not speak of the Second Person of the Trinity as separate from Jesus Christ, who incarnates the Second Person. It does speak of the Holy Spirit as a separate person of the Godhead. The Son is spoken of only with respect to Jesus.

Jesus made it clear that He perfectly represents God the Father. "Jesus said to him, 'Have I been with you for so long a time, and yet you have not come to know Me, Philip? The one who has seen Me has seen the Father; how can you say, "Show us the Father"?'" (John 14:9).

Jesus also made it clear that His work was done in the name of the Father. He was therefore the Father's trustee.

> And He said to them, "Why is it that you were looking for Me? Did you not know that I had to be in My Father's house?" (Luke 2:49)

> "For not even the Father judges anyone, but He has given all judgment to the Son, so that all will honor the Son just as they honor the Father. The one who does not honor the Son does not honor the Father who sent Him." (John 5:22–23)

> "I can do nothing on My own. As I hear, I judge; and My judgment is righteous, because I do not seek My own will but the will of Him who sent Me." (John 5:30)

> "But the testimony I have is greater than the testimony of John; for the works which the Father has given Me to accomplish—the very works that I do—testify about Me, that the Father has sent Me. And the Father who sent Me, He has testified about Me. You have neither heard His voice at any time, nor seen His form." (John 5:36–37)

God the Father has delegated tasks to Jesus Christ. Together, they have delegated tasks to the Holy Spirit. "I will ask the Father, and He will give you another Helper, so that He may be with you forever; the Helper is the Spirit of truth, whom the world cannot receive, because it does not see Him or know Him; but you know Him because He remains with you and will be in you. I will not leave you as orphans; I am coming to you" (John 14:16–18). This is the issue of the delegation of authority. The persons of the Trinity perform different tasks. God the Father is supreme in terms of *functional hierarchy*. He gives the orders. The perfection of Jesus Christ in history was based on His perfect fulfillment of these orders.

Jesus's primary task was judicial: to fulfill God's law. "Your light must shine before people in such a way that they may see your good works, and glorify your Father who is in heaven. Do not presume that I came to abolish the Law or the Prophets; I did not come to abolish, but to fulfill" (Matt. 5:16–17). So, there is a hierarchy of work: from God the Father to the Son, and from the Son to His followers.

Jesus is the designated steward. This is fitting, for He was the Creator under God the Father. "For by Him all things were created, both in the heavens and on earth, visible and invisible, whether thrones, or dominions, or rulers, or authorities—all things have been created through Him and for Him. He is before all things, and in Him all things hold together" (Col. 1:16–17). He is therefore also the redeemer of the church. He acts as a steward for God over the church. "He is also the head of the body, the church; and He is the beginning, the firstborn from the dead, so that He Himself will come to have first place in everything. For it was the Father's good pleasure for all the fullness to dwell in Him, and through Him to reconcile all things to Himself, whether things on earth or things in heaven, having made peace through the blood of His cross" (Col. 1:18–20).

In Christ, we have the model of the faithful steward. God the Father has trusted Him to fulfill His tasks on behalf of the Father. Jesus claimed to have done this faithfully. This was confirmed publicly by God the Father in His announcement that He was well pleased with the Son's performance (Matt. 3:16–17; 12:18; 17:5).

C. God Prohibits Theft

Point three: ethics. This is manifested by biblical law. *The essence of law is boundaries.* Men are not to violate these boundaries. The legal boundary around the forbidden tree is the archetype of private property. First, God announced, "This tree is mine!" Second, Adam and Eve stole from God by eating from this tree. Third, after man's Fall, God placed the boundary of the angel with the flaming sword around the garden, to keep men away from the tree of life (Gen. 3:24).

In the third commandment, which corresponds to the third point of the biblical covenant, God placed a judicial boundary around His name. "You shall not take the name of the LORD your God in vain, for the LORD will not leave him unpunished who takes His name in vain" (Ex. 20:7).[18] This is the basis of the doctrine of holiness, which refers to God's

18. I did not see this in the 1986 edition of *The Sinai Strategy*, which I wrote before Ray Sutton wrote *That You May Prosper* (1987). I make the point clear in the 2012

special dealing with men and things. He *sets them apart*, which is the meaning of holiness in the Bible. It is also the basis of the biblical concept of *sacred space*. Sacred space was originally manifested by the forbidden tree. After God's judgment, it was manifested by the garden itself. Holiness was the meaning of the Levitical priesthood, which guarded the temple (Num. 3), which was holy space. The holy of holies, in which the Ark of the Covenant resided, was sacred space; so, only the high priest could enter it, and only once a year (Heb. 9:7). The interior of Ark of the Covenant was sacred space; to look inside brought death (I Sam. 6:19).

In the New Covenant, the church is sacred. It is called "the Israel of God" (Gal. 6:16) and the bride of Christ (Rev. 21:2). This indicates the existence of *lawful boundaries*—moral and legal—which must not be broken.

Time also is bounded. In creation week, God worked each day to begin and complete a project. He added something to the creation each day (Gen. 1). Then the work week was completed on day six.

There is a time for everything, Ecclesiastes teaches (Eccles. 3:1–8).[19] There will be an end to time. "For the Lord Himself will descend from heaven with a shout, with the voice of the archangel and with the trumpet of God, and the dead in Christ will rise first. Then we who are alive, who remain, will be caught up together with them in the clouds to meet the Lord in the air, and so we will always be with the Lord. Therefore, comfort one another with these words. Now as to the periods and times, brothers and sisters, you have no need of anything to be written to you. For you yourselves know full well that the day of the Lord is coming just like a thief in the night" (I Thess. 4:16–5:2). When will this day arrive? Jesus said: "But about that day and hour no one knows, not even the angels of heaven, nor the Son, but the Father alone" (Matt. 24:36). Not only is time bounded by God, God alone knows where this boundary is.

There was a beginning (Gen. 1:1). There will be an end: "and swore by Him who lives forever and ever, who created heaven and the things in it, and the earth and the things in it, and the sea and the things in it, that there will no longer be a delay" (Rev. 10:6). The concept of *linear time* is basic to biblical religion. This concept is the application of the

edition: *Authority & Dominion: An Economic Commentary on Exodus*, vol. 2, *Part II: Decalogue & Dominion* (Moulton, Alabama: Axehead Press, [1986, 2012] 2025), ch. 3.

19. Gary North, *Autonomy & Stagnation: An Economic Commentary on Ecclesiastes* (Moulton, Alabama: Axehead Press, [2012] 2030), ch. 7.

biblical principle of boundaries to the concept of time. Time belongs to God as surely as any other aspect of the creation belongs to Him. Time is scarce. More than any other scarce resource, there is greater demand for time than there is supply. Jesus in the parable of the barn-builder—capital accumulator—identified the essence of foolishness: "But God said to him, 'You fool! This very night your soul is demanded of you; and as for all that you have prepared, who will own it now?'" (Luke 12:20).[20]

The boundary between heaven and hell is unbreachable. Jesus in His parable of the rich man in hell and the poor man in heaven made this clear. "But Abraham said, 'Child, remember that during your life you received your good things, and likewise Lazarus bad things; but now he is being comforted here, and you are in agony. And besides all this, between us and you a great chasm has been set, so that those who want to go over from here to you will not be able, nor will any people cross over from there to us'" (Luke 16:25–26).[21]

D. God Evaluates Performance

Point four: sanctions. Sanctions are the outcome of God's judgment. A covenant is based on law (point three). Each law in the covenant must be applied to history. God does this day by day, as we learn from the account of the creation week in Genesis 1. God kept saying: "it is good." God is the cosmic Evaluator. With respect to economic value, He imputes value, based on His hierarchy of values. He enforces His own standards in history and at the end of time.

The doctrine of imputation is not much discussed, yet it is central in any concept of economics. Imputation is the way that modern economists explain economic value.

1. *Evaluation*

In Genesis 1, God pronounces judgment on His work at the end of five out of six days (not day two). He pronounces His day's work as

20. Gary North, *Treasure & Dominion: An Economic Commentary on Luke* (Moulton, Alabama: Axehead Press, [2012] 2031), ch. 25.

21. Ibid., ch. 40.

being good. God assesses the work of His creative word, day by day. He compares His work with some sort of standard. Here is the origin of all evaluation: the application of a fixed standard to the realm of creation. Theologians call this activity *casuistry*: the application of moral standards to human action.

God has a moral standard: *perfection*. "Therefore you shall be perfect, as your heavenly Father is perfect" (Matt. 5:48). God pronounces judgment at special times[22] and at the end of time. "Then I saw a great white throne and Him who sat upon it, from whose presence earth and heaven fled, and no place was found for them. And I saw the dead, the great and the small, standing before the throne, and books were opened; and another book was opened, which is the book of life; and the dead were judged from the things which were written in the books, according to their deeds. And the sea gave up the dead who were in it, and Death and Hades gave up the dead who were in them; and they were judged, each one of them according to their deeds" (Rev. 20:11–13).

God evaluates everything all the time. This is what the covenant-breaker denies. "He says to himself, 'God has forgotten; He has hidden His face; He will never see it'" (Ps. 10:11). The Psalmist warns evil men not to believe this. "They kill the widow and the stranger And murder the orphans. They have said, 'The LORD does not see, Nor does the God of Jacob perceive.' Pay attention, you stupid ones among the people; And when will you understand, foolish ones? He who planted the ear, does He not hear? Or He who formed the eye, does He not see?" (Ps. 94:6–9).

Imputation is associated with work, from Genesis 1 until Revelation 22. There is a standard; there is work in terms of this standard; there is evaluation; there is a declaration; and there is the imposition of sanctions. The Bible is *theocentric*: God's standard, God's work, God's evaluation, God's declaration, and God's sanctions. The temptation in the garden of Eden had to do with a rival standard, rival work, and God's negative evaluation and negative sanctions. The Bible teaches that some of the things which God does sovereignly, man should do subordinately.[23] Adam and Eve refused to accept this.

---

22. God's voice pronounced His pleasure with Jesus (Matt. 3:16–17; 12:18; 17:5).

23. This has to do with the communicable attributes of God. Some attributes are non-communicable: omniscience, omnipotence, and omnipresence.

God is omniscient. He sees all things. God is also omnipotent. What He has decreed, He will bring to pass. At the end of time, He will render judgment.

2. Decree

The meaning of decree is "to establish the future." God decrees the future. Then He brings it to pass. Probably the clearest statement of this is Isaiah 45.

> For this is what the LORD says, He who created the heavens (He is the God who formed the earth and made it, He established it and did not create it as a waste place, but formed it to be inhabited):
>
> "I am the LORD, and there is no one else.
> I have not spoken in secret,
> In some dark land; I did not say to the offspring of Jacob,
> 'Seek Me in a wasteland';
> I, the LORD, speak righteousness,
> Declaring things that are right.
> Gather yourselves and come;
> Come together, you survivors of the nations!
> They have no knowledge,
> Who carry around their wooden idol
> And pray to a god who cannot save.
> Declare and present your case;
> Indeed, let them consult together.
> Who has announced this long ago?
> Who has long since declared it?
> Is it not I, the LORD?
> And there is no other God besides Me,
> A righteous God and a Savior;
> There is none except Me.
> Turn to Me and be saved, all the ends of the earth;
> For I am God, and there is no other.
> I have sworn by Myself;
> The word has gone out from My mouth in righteousness
> And will not turn back,
> That to Me every knee will bow, every tongue will swear allegiance.
> (Isa. 45:18–23)

Isaiah extended this declaration with respect to His spoken word. "For as the rain and the snow come down from heaven, and do not return there without watering the earth and making it produce and sprout, and providing seed to the sower and bread to the eater; so will My word be which goes out of My mouth; it will not return to Me empty, without accomplishing what I desire, and without succeeding in the purpose for which I sent it" (Isa. 55:10–11).

E. God Mandates Growth

Point five: succession. There is sequence in history. This is based on God's sovereign decree (Isa. 45). What does His decree refer to? His kingdom, both in history and eternity. Again, citing Isaiah, "For a Child will be born to us, a Son will be given to us; And the government will rest on His shoulders; And His name will be called Wonderful Counselor, Mighty God, Eternal Father, Prince of Peace. There will be no end to the increase of His government or of peace On the throne of David and over his kingdom, To establish it and to uphold it with justice and righteousness From then on and forevermore. The zeal of the LORD of armies will accomplish this" (Isa. 9:6–7). Who is this child? Jesus Christ. He will be the heir of God in history, this passage asserts. Jesus announced the fulfillment of this prophecy after His resurrection. "And Jesus came up and spoke to them, saying, 'All authority in heaven and on earth has been given to Me. "Go, therefore, and make disciples of all the nations, baptizing them in the name of the Father and the Son and the Holy Spirit, teaching them to follow all that I commanded you; and behold, I am with you always, to the end of the age'" (Matt. 28:18–20).[24]

This is known as the Great Commission. It applies to the whole world.[25] His kingdom will expand. This means that *God will receive a positive rate of return in history on His investment*. His kingdom expands in history at the expense of Satan's kingdom. Whatever God wins, Satan loses. Economists call such a win-lose relationship a *zero-sum* arrange-

24. Gary North, *Priorities & Dominion: An Economic Commentary on Matthew* (Moulton, Alabama: Axehead Press, [2012] 2030), ch. 48.

25. Kenneth L. Gentry, *The Greatness of the Great Commission: The Christian Enterprise in a Fallen World*, 2nd ed. (Tyler, Texas: Institute for Christian Economics, [1990] 1992).

ment: nothing is added; whatever is won by one person is lost by the other.

Paul taught that Christ's bodily resurrection in history is proof of God's program of kingdom extension.

> But the fact is, Christ has been raised from the dead, the first fruits of those who are asleep. For since by a man death came, by a man also came the resurrection of the dead. For as in Adam all die, so also in Christ all will be made alive. But each in his own order: Christ the first fruits, after that those who are Christ's at His coming, then comes the end, when He hands over the kingdom to our God and Father, when He has abolished all rule and all authority and power. For He must reign until He has put all His enemies under His feet. The last enemy that will be abolished is death. For He has put all things in subjection under His feet. But when He says, "All things are put in subjection," it is clear that this excludes the Father who put all things in subjection to Him. When all things are subjected to Him, then the Son Himself will also be subjected to the One who subjected all things to Him, so that God may be all in all. (I Cor. 15:20–28)[26]

This is the fulfillment of Psalm 110:1: "The LORD says to my Lord: 'Sit at My right hand until I make Your enemies a footstool for Your feet.'" It is an aspect of *inheritance*: from God the Father to God the Son, and then, at the end, from God the Son to God the Father. "Then comes the end, when he delivers the kingdom to God the Father after destroying every rule and every authority and power" (I Cor. 15:24).

Conclusion

Christian economic theory begins with the idea of creation out of nothing by a Trinitarian God. The doctrine of the Trinity affirms the plurality of the Godhead, the equal ultimacy of the persons, and the hierarchy of functions among them. Who God is, what He has done in history, and what He has revealed about Himself in the Bible jointly determine the correct structure of economic theory. Any system of economic theory that does not begin with the idea of creation out of nothing by a

26. Gary North, *Judgment & Dominion: An Economic Commentary on I Corinthians* (Moulton, Alabama: Axehead Press, [2012] 2031), ch. 17.

Trinitarian God is not Christian. At best, it is baptized humanism.

The fundamental error of modern economics is shared by economists of many different traditions, methodologies, and conclusions. The fundamental error is this presupposition, which is regarded as an axiom: *the autonomy of man.* This axiom has five negative corollaries:

1. A sovereign God does not have a legal claim on everything in history.
2. Man does not answer in history to such a creator God.
3. A sovereign God does not determine the limits of the environment, especially mankind.
4. God does not bring sanctions in history.
5. The kingdom of man is the only kingdom in history.

To the extent that modern economists think consistently with these five presuppositions, economic theory is incorrect.

What I am saying is simple: *Christian economics is the* ***only*** *consistent form of economics.* I am not arguing that Christian economic theory is one system among many. I am arguing that all systems of economic theory that are not explicitly Christian are imitations of the truth, as surely as all rival religions to Christianity are imitations of the truth.[27] The reason why free market humanistic economists reject Christian economics is not because they reject all of its conclusions. They do not reject all or even most of its conclusions. They reject it because they reject Christianity's claim of being the only true religion and therefore supremely authoritative in every area of life, including economics.

Rival systems of economic theory lead to inescapable contradictions logically. They lead to erroneous conclusions about the nature of economic cause and effect. Only insofar as economists think inconsistently with these five presuppositions do they make accurate assessments of economic cause and effect.

Therefore, to the extent that humanistic economists are consistent, they are wrong. To the extent that they are accurate, they are inconsistent with their presuppositions, whether implicit or explicit.

27. Here, I am imitating Cornelius Van Til in his apologetic methodology. He did not argue that Christianity is the most likely option among many religious systems. He argued that it alone is true.

Chapter 2

The Economic Authority of Man

Then God said, "Let Us make mankind in Our image, according to Our likeness; and let them rule over the fish of the sea and over the birds of the sky and over the livestock and over all the earth, and over every crawling thing that crawls on the earth." So God created man in His own image, in the image of God He created him; male and female He created them.

Genesis 1:26–28

Analysis

Point two of the biblical covenant is hierarchy/authority.[1] Point two also has to do with God's covenant with man. We can see this with respect to the Book of Exodus. It is the second book in the Pentateuch. It is also supremely the book of the covenant. Speaking of Moses, Exodus declares: "Then he took the Book of the Covenant and read it as the people listened; and they said, 'All that the Lord has spoken we will do, and we will be obedient'" (Ex. 24:7). Exodus deals with the rival claims of two self-professed gods: the God of Israel and the Pharaoh.[2]

Authority is another word for *delegated sovereignty*. With respect to

1. Ray R. Sutton, *That You May Prosper: Dominion By Covenant*, 2nd ed. (Tyler, Texas: Institute for Christian Economics, [1987] 1992), ch. 2.

2. Gary North, *Authority & Dominion: An Economic Commentary on Exodus*, vol. 1, *Part I: Representation & Dominion* (Moulton, Alabama: Axehead Press, [1985, 2012] 2025), ch. 1.

economics, authority is a *judicial category*. This is because it is subordinate to God's original sovereignty. Here is the judicial structure:

1. God owns everything.
2. God delegates ownership.
3. God prohibits theft.
4. God evaluates performance.
5. God mandates growth.

This means that authority is a matter of representation. This representation is at bottom judicial. For judicial representation, I use the phrase "in the name of." As we shall see, there are also economic aspects of this representation. For economic representation, I use the phrase "on behalf of." Ownership is legally a matter of hierarchical representation: *trusteeship*. This is a stewardship function. As we shall see, there are also economic aspects of this representation. This also is a hierarchical stewardship function: *sharecropping*. It also is economically representative outward to the public at large: the *auctioneer* function. I deal with all three in this book.

When God delegates ownership to men, He requires them to act in His name. These are the laws of *judicial trusteeship*. This can also be described as guardianship.

1. Owners are trustees.
2. Trustees possess authority.
3. Trusts are binding.
4. Trustees are accountable.
5. Trustees designate successors.

The trustees are also economic stewards. They are required by God to act on His behalf. These are the laws of *economic stewardship*.

1. Purpose precedes planning.
2. Priorities structure planning.
3. Ownership involves exclusion.
4. Owners evaluate performance.
5. Owners designate heirs.

The science of economics reflects the continuing rivalry between two gods and two covenantal administrations. As is the case with all other modern academic disciplines, economic science rests on a presupposition: *the sovereignty of man*. Economists rarely state this explicitly, but they do so implicitly. They begin with man: either individual man or man as a social being. This tradition of beginning with man as sovereign goes back to Aristotle. As I explained in Chapter 1, this presupposition is incorrect.

In contrast, a consistently Christian economic theory must begin with a self-conscious and formal affirmation of the absolute sovereignty of God. This God is a Trinity. Any attempt to develop Christian economic theory by beginning with man, either individual or corporate, is a compromise with humanistic economic theory.

But if God is absolutely sovereign, then in what way is man empowered by God to exercise dominion? Answer: through God's delegated power and delegated authority. *Mankind necessarily acts in the name of God*. Individuals and societies can and do rebel against this obligation, but this obligation always defines man. There is no escape. "Then God said, 'Let Us make mankind in Our image, according to Our likeness; and let them rule over the fish of the sea and over the birds of the sky and over the livestock and over all the earth, and over every crawling thing that crawls on the earth'" (Gen. 1:26).[3] This original decree defines man in relation to God and the creation.

Covenant-breaking men seek to substitute a would-be god as the sovereign agent, usually mankind. With the exception of Muslims, when covenant-breaking men acknowledge the existence of any supernatural god, it is a partially sovereign god who either serves man or at least cooperates with man as a fellow creature. God and man affirm: "We're in this together." The God of the Bible never affirms this, except to Himself as a Trinity. With respect to the creation, God does not cooperate with man. Rather, He decrees. This fact, Job initially affirmed: "He said, 'Naked I came from my mother's womb, and naked I shall return there. The LORD gave and the LORD has taken away. Blessed be the name of the LORD'" (Job 1:21). Job then refused to confirm his confession. His constant questioning of God testified to a very different view of God. It is unwise to imitate Job in this regard.

---

3. Gary North, *Sovereignty & Dominion: An Economic Commentary on Genesis* (Moulton, Alabama: Axehead Press, [1982, 2012] 2022), ch. 3.

With respect to economics, as distinguished from judicial representation, I begin with economic representation: stewardship rather than guardianship. This means acting on behalf of God.

I begin with the creation week. Point one reflects God. God spoke the world into existence. Men cannot do this. Men are required to imitate God as creatures made in God's image. So, using the creation week as a model, I came up with five characteristics that reflect God's creativity.

A. Purpose Precedes Planning

Point one: God's sovereignty. In economics, point one is connected to God's creation. He is the sovereign Owner because he was the Creator. But this raises a problem. Man is not a creator in the way that God is. Man did not speak the creation into existence. So, we must look to God's creation as the archetype of man's creativity.

Human action is purposeful action. Ludwig von Mises developed a comprehensive deductive economic system based on this simple concept.[4] Mises used this approach to exclude God from any consideration in economic reasoning or historical events. He argued that God, being perfect and therefore content, cannot act. Perfection is antithetical to action.[5] Yet God does act, and He is perfect. We must therefore go beyond Mises' humanism. There is purpose in the universe because God created it purposefully and sustains it providentially.

The question is this: Whose purposes are authoritative? The biblical answer: God's. Therefore, men are to subordinate their purposes to God's purposes. God's purposes provide the standards of purpose, both individual and corporate. These standards are *ethical*. But they are also *eschatological*: the last things. They are therefore *historical*: getting

---

4. Ludwig von Mises, *Human Action: A Treatise on Economics* (New Haven, Connecticut: Yale University Press, 1949), ch. I, sect. 1.

5. Ibid., ch. II, sect. 11. Elsewhere, he wrote: "Perfect satisfaction and its concomitant, the absence of any stimulus to change and action, belong properly to the concept of a perfect being. This, however, is beyond the power of the human mind to conceive. A perfect being would not act." Ludwig von Mises, *Epistemological Problems in Economics*, 3rd ed. (Auburn, Alabama: Mises Institute, [1960] 2003), 25.

from now until then. This is *progressive sanctification*, both individual[6] and corporate. Here, I focus on history.

1. *Sequential Action*

In days two through five, God spoke sections of the universe into existence. On day one, He created the heavens and the earth out of nothing, meaning *into* nothing. Thereafter, each act of creation took place within an environment that had been re-shaped daily through sequence. We must always declare that the days of creation were sequential. Deny this, and you deny the biblical doctrine of creation.[7] Day by day, that which had been created served as the context for that which was created next. The creation's sequence was based on the causal principle of *necessary but not sufficient*. What preceded each day's creation was necessary, but it was not sufficient to produce that day's creation or the next day's creation. Something had to be added from outside the cosmos. In this sense, the biblical doctrine of creation is at odds with the doctrine of cosmic evolution, whose causal principle is *necessary and sufficient*. In Darwinism, nothing emerges explicitly today that was not available implicitly yesterday. The cosmos is all there is.

The week of creation was purposeful because the universe is not autonomous. This idea is the great affront of the biblical doctrine of creation to the Darwinist. He insists that the cosmos was not originally purposeful precisely because it was autonomous. In the Darwinian worldview, purpose arrived in the universe only with advanced forms of life. Life arose out of purposeless change. As far as Darwinists know, man alone has long-run purposes, which can be achieved only by complex planning. For the Darwinist, purpose was a great cosmic disconti-

---

6. John Murray, "Progressive Sanctification," *Collected Works of John Murray* (Edinburgh: Banner of Truth, 1982), II, ch. 23.

7. This is the great theological and conceptual error of the so-called framework hypothesis, which was Meredith G. Kline's attempt to get away from the plain teaching of Genesis 1. His colleague at Westminster Seminary, Edward J. Young, wrote the essays that were compiled as *Studies in Genesis 1* (Nutley, New Jersey: Presbyterian & Reformed, 1964) to reaffirm the fixed sequence of the days of creation. Some evolution-accepting Christians think Kline's thesis will make Genesis 1 more acceptable to evolutionary scientists. So far, it has only kept Christians with an interest in science from pressing the claims of the Bible on those scientists who reject the Bible and the God of the Bible.

nuity in an autonomous universe. For the Christian, the creation of the universe was a great discontinuity, which was completely separate from the autonomous Creator. Purpose is eternal. The universe is not. The universe is now without end, but it had a beginning not so long ago. *Purpose is therefore more fundamental than the universe.* Purpose precedes action because it preceded the creation.

Purpose preceded the curse of the world by God (Gen. 3:17–19). Scarcity existed before the fall because man is finite.[8] He is not omnipotent. Time constrains him. He cannot do everything he wants to do immediately. He acts sequentially. In this sense, he imitates God's days of creation. His lack of omniscience constrains him. He learns sequentially. His lack of resources constrains him. He accumulates resources sequentially. Ever since the fall, the world has resisted him.

As the image of God, man is purposeful. As the image of God, who acted sequentially in the creation week, man acts sequentially. He intervenes into the processes of his environment in order to create something that does not yet exist. Man is subordinately creative under God in ways that animals are not.

Higher animals display purposeful behavior. This is how we define "higher." The closer to man that an animal is in the chain of covenantal authority, the more it displays purposeful behavior. Purposeful behavior is a series of sequential actions in which learning takes place, thereby changing the actor's future sequence of actions in what seems to be a similar environment. The main change in the environment is the animal's mastery of new information regarding causation. It learns to manipulate its environment in order to achieve its goals. It learns new connections between ends and means. It remembers them.

God is transcendent, yet in achieving His ends on creation days two through six, He used means that were available in the creation. On day six, He used the earth to create Adam's body, breathing His spirit into it. He used Adam's rib to create Eve. This was an aspect of His role as a cosmic planner. "Let Us make mankind in Our image, according to Our likeness" (Gen. 1:26a).[9] This plan preceded its implementation. Its implementation was through created means.

---

8. North, *Sovereignty & Dominion*, ch. 12.

9. Ibid., ch. 3.

2. *One/Many*

Like the Trinity, man is both one and many. There are individuals. There are corporate entities. Responsibility is therefore both individual and corporate. So, *purpose is both individual and corporate.* Men act in an environment, and this environment is in part social. Man is a social being. An individual selects his purposes and a specific concept of causation in terms of what he has learned from his membership in multiple groups. *The concept of the autonomous individual is as incorrect as the concept of the autonomous group.* Christian epistemology must affirm both unity and diversity. Any discussion of economic causation must begin with both the acting individual and the acting group. It must begin with a discussion of the formation of individual plans as being, from the beginning, the product of previous plans that were themselves reconciled plans.

In discussing human action, we must begin with God as Trinity, as revealed in Genesis. We must not begin with Robinson Crusoe or any other solitary decision-maker. A true Crusoe is an heir of all of the implemented plans that influenced his thinking. He is responsible before God for a kingdom-enhancing formulation of new plans and their implementation. He is not autonomous. *He is an heir of capital supplied by God.* The most valuable form of capital is accurate knowledge, coupled with the wisdom and courage to implement it.[10]

B. Priorities Structure Planning

Point two: hierarchy. An inescapable aspect of production is the acknowledgment of hierarchy. Someone must be in charge. Someone must reward and punish. Production began with God. It has been financed by God: capital. The economic mark of man's subordination to God is the tithe. Abraham tithed to the priest, Melchizedek. "For this Melchizedek, king of Salem, priest of the Most High God, who

10. Carl Menger wrote: "Nothing is more certain than that the degree of economic progress of mankind will still, in future epochs, be commensurate with the degree of progress of human knowledge." Menger, *Principles of Economics* (Auburn, Alabama: Mises Institute, [1871] 2007), 74.

met Abraham as he was returning from the slaughter of the kings and blessed him, to whom also Abraham apportioned a tenth of all the spoils, was first of all, by the translation of his name, king of righteousness, and then also king of Salem, which is king of peace" (Heb. 7:1–2). Christ the high priest is modeled after Melchizedek (Heb. 5:6). Covenant-keeping people owe a tithe on their increase as a sign of their covenantal subordination.[11] This is the bare minimum. "Woe to you, scribes and Pharisees, hypocrites! For you tithe mint and dill and cumin, and have neglected the weightier provisions of the Law: justice and mercy and faithfulness; but these are the things you should have done without neglecting the others" (Matt. 23:23).[12] All of the tithe is owed to the member's local institutional church.[13]

1. *Representation*

Representation is trusteeship. This can be legal trusteeship: guardianship. It can be economic trusteeship: stewardship.

In his office as a legal guardian, an owner holds an asset as a legal guardian. He holds it in the name of God. His is hierarchical representation. He also holds it in the name of those under his authority. This usually refers to his family, but in some cases, it may be in the name of beneficiaries of a trust.

In his office as an economic steward, he acts on behalf of God (upward), those under his authority (downward), those outside the family who may buy from him in the future (outward), and his own goals (inward). Consider outward service. I call this the auctioneer function. He uses his assets to satisfy the expected future demand of those customers who will offer the highest monetary bids. But he may decide to act in a charitable way. He sells for less than the highest bids. In selling to these lower-bidding buyers, the owner forfeits the use of whatever extra money the highest bidders had bid. He cannot deliberately sell for less at zero cost to himself. He suffers a reduction of money income.

Economically, the market principle of *monetary high bid wins* is

---

11. Gary North, *The Covenantal Tithe: The Providential Plan for Fruitful Stewardship* (Moulton, Alabama: Axehead Press, [2011] 2026).

12. North, *Priorities & Dominion*, ch. 46. Cf. North, *Covenantal Tithe*, ch. 9.

13. Gary North, *Tithing and the Church* (Moulton, Alabama: Axehead Press, [1994] 2032).

a way for high bidders to gain cooperation from specific sellers. This forces the owner to consider *horizontal* representation. His customers are neither over him judicially nor under him judicially. They are his judicial equals. By bidding, they compete against each other to establish the highest bid. Turning down the highest bid costs the seller money.

2. *Pietism and Humanism*

There is a supreme purpose for covenant-keeping individuals: "But seek first His kingdom and His righteousness, and all these things will be provided to you" (Matt. 6:33).[14] Jesus said this to a multitude of people who were listening to Him teach: the sermon on the mount. He was comparing various earthly attainments. "Do not worry then, saying, 'What are we to eat?' or 'What are we to drink?' or 'What are we to wear for clothing?' For the Gentiles eagerly seek all these things; for your heavenly Father knows that you need all these things" (Matt. 6:31–32).[15] He was not comparing salvation from hell with the extension of God's kingdom.

Hundreds of millions of Christians assume that God's kingdom is less important than people's salvation from eternal negative sanctions. They think that people's avoidance of hell is more important to God than the extension of His kingdom. They assume that the gospel—the good news of Jesus Christ—is primarily the good news of individual deliverance from hell rather than the extension of God's kingdom in history. *This is operational humanism.* It puts men first. The Bible's doctrine of the sovereignty of God teaches otherwise. *God's kingdom, not man's salvation, is primary.* Ours is a theocentric universe, not an anthropocentric universe.

When discussing the ontological Trinity, we should speak of *the equal ultimacy of the one and the many.* We should do the same with respect to individual redemption in history and social redemption in history. To redeem is to buy back. Jesus' redemption is comprehensive. It applies to everything that is under Satan's squatter kingdom.[16] Redemption in Christ should be manifest in history, not just eternity.

---

14. Ibid., ch. 15.

15. Idem.

16. Gary North, *Is the World Running Down? Crisis in the Christian Worldview* (Moulton, Alabama: Axehead Press, [1988] 2029), Appendix C: "Comprehensive Redemption."

There is therefore a hierarchy of ends. Paul wrote: "Grace to you and peace from God our Father and the Lord Jesus Christ. Blessed be the God and Father of our Lord Jesus Christ, who has blessed us with every spiritual blessing in the heavenly places in Christ" (Eph. 1:2–3). Redemption is the means by which God the Father extends the kingdom of Jesus Christ in history. "No one can come to Me unless the Father who sent Me draws him; and I will raise him up on the last day" (John 6:44). But this is a mutual relationship. "Jesus said to him, 'I am the way, and the truth, and the life; no one comes to the Father except through Me'" (John 14:6). This is a process of *kingdom replacement*: God's kingdom reduces the jurisdiction of man's kingdom. It is therefore a process of *kingdom subordination*. This is not believed by most people or even most Christians. They place other goals higher than the goal of corporate redemption. So, their value scales reflect a different system of priorities from God's.

3. *Ranking: Ordinal vs. Cardinal*

Individuals are responsible for their ranking of goals, whether lifetime goals or goals in the next five minutes. They rank them *ordinally*: first, second, third, etc. They do the same with their various values. Each person has a scale of values at any point in time. There is no system of value-ranking that provides a measure of *exactly how much more* a person values one goal over another—what is called *cardinal* ranking. No one can do more than rank them ordinally.[17] Any suggestion that an individual or a committee can compare numerical measurements of human preference is an implicit affirmation the omniscience of man. *There is no cardinal measure of subjective value*, not even for the individual who evaluates his choices in terms of a scale of values.

Men have ends. They also have access to means. They select means in terms of their hierarchy of ends. Men are constrained by time and by limited resources.

17. Ludwig von Mises, *Human Action: A Treatise on Economics* (New Haven, Connecticut: Yale University Press, 1949), ch. IV, sect. 4.

C. Ownership Involves Exclusion

Point three: ethics. This is manifested in law. Here is the judicial issue of ownership: the legal authorization to use, lose, sell, rent, donate, or destroy a specific scarce resource, meaning a resource for which there is greater demand than supply at zero price. Biblically, ownership is *the right to include and exclude.* God possessed the legal right to grant to Adam access to the garden. He also had the right to forbid access to a specific asset.

1. *Name*

The third commandment refers to God's name, which men are not to use in vain (Ex. 20:7).[18] Applying this principle to an individual, his reputation must be protected by law, as surely his money is. Shakespeare understood this application of God's law.

> Good name in man and woman, dear my lord,
> Is the immediate jewel of their souls:
> Who steals my purse steals trash; 'tis something, nothing;
> 'Twas mine, 'tis his, and has been slave to thousands:
> But he that filches from me my good name
> Robs me of that which not enriches him
> And makes me poor indeed.[19]

Property is an extension of a person's name, by which he secures ownership. He signs legally binding contracts. He establishes bank accounts. There can be legal claims by him and against him. These legal claims establish personal responsibility on his part for the administration of his assets. This connection between name, assets, and responsibility is fundamental. It establishes a legal claim on the civil government: protection of private property.

This use of a name applies also to corporate institutions: families, churches, businesses, and other entities that are legally responsible for the administration of assets. Ownership is therefore corporate as well as individual: one and many.

---

18. Gary North, *Authority & Dominion, Part II: Decalogue & Dominion* ([1986, 2012] 2022), ch. 23.

19. *Othello*, III:3.

If I own something, I possess the legal authority to disown it. I can give it away. I can sell it. This broad right of disownership is the legal basis of contract. *There is no marketable ownership apart from the right of disownership.* Therefore, the concept of collective ownership through politics makes no sense. If I cannot sell my share of a collective good, I do not have an ownership claim.

2. *Rights*

Property rights belong to individuals or organizations. These are human rights: specified bundles of legal immunities and protections. *Property rights authorize exclusion.* They place legal boundaries around specific physical assets or relationships. They announce: "This is mine. Do not trespass." The archetype of this arrangement is the forbidden tree in the garden. *God symbolically announced His sovereignty over mankind by placing a legal boundary around the tree.* He later did the same by placing an angel with a flaming sword at the entry point into the garden.

An analogous boundary of exclusion is the basis of the marriage vow between husband and wife. Another is the boundary of exclusion around the sacraments of baptism and the Lord's Supper. These rights are defended by covenantal governments: church or state or both.

Theft is an owner-unauthorized transfer of assets from someone or some agency which has legal title. Owners make decisions concerning the use of assets. They have been entrusted with ownership by God through society. Again, God's goal is dominion. Man is acting as His agent. *Ownership establishes an enforceable hierarchy of responsibility.* Men will give a final account of their use of all assets entrusted to them. This was Jesus explicit teaching in His parable of the talents (Matt. 25:14–30).[20]

Anyone who interferes with this hierarchy of responsibility is acting as if he were God. He is asserting his sovereignty over the allocation of assets that God has sanctioned. Various Mosaic laws apply this principle to specific situations. The Mosaic laws prohibiting men from moving a landmark were part of the law against theft (Deut. 19:14;[21] 27:17[22]).

20. North, *Priorities & Dominion*, ch. 47.

21. Gary North, *Inheritance & Dominion: An Economic Commentary on Deuteronomy* (Moulton, Alabama: Axehead Press, [1999, 2012] 2028), ch. 43.

22. Ibid., ch. 67.

So were the laws governing weights and measures (Lev. 19:36;[23] Deut. 25:13[24]). The various Mosaic laws governing weights and measures, and the law's equation of weights and measures with the administration of civil justice, point to the importance of standards. The violation of these standards constitutes a violation of property rights. People make decisions in terms of standards. To violate them unilaterally is a form of theft.

3. *Contracts*

A contract is analogous to a covenant. A covenant is a legal bond under God. It lawfully invokes God's name. It is established by an oath or representative oath-sign. It is a vow taken before God and is enforceable by God. If it is an institutional covenant—family, church, or state—it is legally enforceable by one or more of these governments.

A contract is also legally enforceable by civil government, although a contract does not lawfully include a self-maledictory oath before God. It specifies the terms of exchange, either in the present or the future. A contract enables people to make increasingly accurate forecasts regarding other people's future performance. By lowering the costs of forecasting accurately, a contract encourages greater cooperation, which means greater specialization, which means greater expected output from whatever resources are invested in a production process.

D. Owners Evaluate Performance

Point four: sanctions. Sanctions are the result of exercising judgment: *the application of unchanging law to changing circumstances*. The doctrine of imputation in theology refers to God's judicial assessment of a person's guilt or innocence, or an institution's guilt or innocence. God evaluates all actions in terms of His standards, and He then makes a declaration. He does this as a Trinity: both one and many. God also imputes meaning to all events in terms of His comprehensive standards.

As God's agents, men impute both meaning and value to things and

---

23. Gary North, *Boundaries & Dominion: An Economic Commentary on Leviticus* (Moulton, Alabama: Axehead Press, [1994, 2012] 2026), ch. 19.

24. North, *Inheritance & Dominion*, ch. 64.

events. They pass judgment. They are responsible as individuals and as participants in organizations. They are one and many, as creatures made in God's image. Like God, they also use standards as guides.

Imputation is subjective. Each person assesses economic value in terms of the options that he believes are available to him. He decides what to do with his assets in the broadest sense. He chooses one path of action based on this assessment. Yet this imputation must be future-oriented. Every action moves us into the future. We evaluate expected outcomes in advance.

Imputation is also a retroactive procedure. God evaluated His work at the end of five of the six days: "It is good." Men are to assess the success of past efforts in terms of their assessment of God's final judgment. They are to think God's future thoughts after Him. So, they must forecast the future in order to evaluate the past. The future—final judgment—may be very distant. The past may be immediate. *Imputation is a form of rendering judgment.* The model is a courtroom. The jury or judge renders judgment after all of the testimony has officially been presented.

1. *Subjective/Marginal Value*

Each person is responsible before God for adopting and implementing his personal hierarchy of values and therefore also the *hierarchy of goals* that he adopts in pursuit of his values. So, ranking values and goals is a subjective procedure. A person must adopt a hierarchy of priorities. This is based on a hierarchy of values.

He must select an immediate goal. He has to do something. Life is a series of decisions. Decisions are based on priorities. People must do *this* rather than *that*. To attain any goal, we must pay a price: give up something. We live in a world of cursed scarcity (Gen. 3:17–18).[25] To obtain some of *that*, I must give up some of *this*. Life is marked by a constant series of exchanges.[26]

As we gain more of one scarce resource, we find that we want less of it, compared to how much we want another item. When we are thirsty,

---

25. Gary North, *Sovereignty & Dominion: An Economic Commentary on Genesis* (Moulton, Alabama: Axehead Press, [1982, 2012] 2022), ch. 12.

26. Mises, *Human Action*, ch. IV, sect. 4.

the first drink of water is satisfying. But as we drink more, we reach satiation. This is not merely a biological response. It is a universal response to the increased consumption or accumulation of any type of asset. Each additional unit provides less satisfaction than the one before. At the margin of our scale of values, satisfaction per additional unit falls in relation to the immediately preceding unit. Economists call this *marginal value theory*. It is based on individual subjective imputation. "I prefer this to that."

2. *Objective Value*

God imputes value: "It is good." He does this subjectively, based on His own personal scale of values. Yet we must affirm that this subjective evaluation is simultaneously objective. Why? Because God is sovereign. Something is good or bad *objectively* because God says so *publicly*, if only to Himself as Trinity. So, economic value is both subjective and objective. Methodological covenantalism affirms both objective value and subjective value, based on God's autonomous imputation of value to specific events or resources.

To say that economic value is *autonomously objective* is to adopt the humanistic Greek concept of *realism*. This is an extension and application of Greek humanism. Realism is represented by the classical Greek idea of the Idea: an independently existing, unchanging metaphysical realm that serves as the model (one) for the constantly changing realm of historical and physical facts (many). This includes the idea of the good. This is the tyranny of "the one," i.e., that which does not change, the thing by which change must be evaluated. Because it is autonomous, it is authoritative. It possesses final authority, for it represents or incarnates the unchanging standard of value. This concept leads to political tyranny. There must be a supreme interpreter of the objective good if this good is to secure its manifestation in history. This interpreter must possess a lawful monopoly, for it alone perceives what is good and declares this publicly and authoritatively. Yet this collective "it" is in fact a compilation of the many—a committee—except in the case of a monarch or dictator. Whatever this agency of declaration is, there is no appeal beyond it. It possesses what in sixteenth-century Europe was called *divine right*: no superior court of appeal.

On the other hand, to say that there is no objective value is to adopt the concept of *nominalism*. This is represented by the outlook of medievalist William of Occam and his many modern disciples: the assertion that *mankind names reality*, and *reality is whatever men declare*. But each man may assess the realm of facts differently from his neighbor. There are multiple standards. There are multiple imputers. This is the error of "the many." It leads to *epistemological fragmentation*.

Politically, nominalism can easily lead to the warlord society: *might makes right*. The equally authoritative autonomous value scales and priorities of autonomous individuals come into conflict whenever individuals come into conflict. There is no final declaration of the good because there is no original/final good beyond the imputations and assessments of individuals. *Economic value has no objective existence for the nominalist.* Some power-seekers conclude that there is no peaceful way to reconcile autonomous priorities. James wrote: "What is the source of quarrels and conflicts among you? Is the source not your pleasures that wage war in your body's parts? You lust and do not have, so you commit murder. And you are envious and cannot obtain, so you fight and quarrel. You do not have because you do not ask" (James 4:1–2). They seek to impose their exclusively subjective values on others by force. They seek the authority to hand out badges and guns to their representative trustees.

Economic theory ever since the 1870s has been officially subjectivist and marginalist, but in practice almost all economists defend their ability as scientists to recommend specific economic policies to politicians.[27] This leads to a rarely acknowledged clandestine importation of objective value theory back into economics. This importation is mandatory for social policy. In order for an economist to declare, in the name of economic science, that one policy is superior—preferable—to another, he must move from nominalism (subjectivism) to realism (objectivism), from the open-ended many to the statistically limited one. He must conclude that someone's value judgment does not count. Then he proposes a program in which the enforcing authority implements his assessment. There will be losers.

---

27. The only exception who comes to mind is Israel Kirzner. He has always avoided published considerations of good or bad effects of specific policies. He takes seriously the highly subjective theory of exclusively subjective economic theory.

3. *Interpersonal Comparisons of Subjective Utility*

A person can assess the economic value to him of obtaining an additional unit of a scarce resource. He can assess its value ordinally, although not cardinally. He can *rank* its value to him; he cannot *measure* its value to him.

If this inability to measure economic value is true for an individual who assesses his own scale of values, how much more true is it for an individual who is trying to assess someone else's scale of values compared to his own, or two people's scale of values compared to each other, or a million people's value scales?

You are not responsible for my scale of values, and I am not responsible for yours. You are not inside my head, and I am not inside yours. If you tell me, "I love my wife more than you love yours," all we can do to evaluate who loves his wife more is to see how we treat our wives in public. But this tells us nothing certain about the intensity of our respective love. A man could be very polite to his wife yet utterly cold to her emotionally. There is no objective measure of love. Neither is there an objective measure of satisfaction.

This applies to human beings' assessments. It does not apply to God. Jesus' assessment of the degree of sacrifice by the rich men and the poor widow indicates that God can assess subjective value and subjective cost. "Now He looked up and saw the wealthy putting their gifts into the temple treasury. And He saw a poor widow putting in two lepta coins. And He said, 'Truly I say to you, this poor widow put in more than all of them; for they all contributed to the offering from their surplus; but she, from her poverty, put in all that she had to live on'" (Luke 21:1–4).[28] Nevertheless, *what God can do perfectly, men can do provisionally*. We can say with a great degree of confidence that the value of an additional amount of income for a rich man is worth less to him than the same increase for a poor man. We just cannot say exactly how much more. We have no available objective measure.

If this ability did not exist, then lawful representatives in governments—ecclesiastical, familial, and civil—could not make any valid policy judgments: *this* policy rather than *that* policy. Yet God holds

---

28. North, *Treasure & Dominion*, ch. 50.

them responsible for making policy judgments. So, He has given men the ability to make rough estimations of other people's subjective utilities. Leaders can legitimately act on this assumption: "It is better to be rich and healthy than it is to be poor and sick." Most people accept this assessment. A corporate policy that can be shown to tend toward poverty and sickness should therefore be avoided.

Modern subjectivist economics officially denies that it is possible to make scientifically valid interpersonal comparisons of subjective utility.[29] Yet, when pushed to the inescapable conclusion, namely, that this would deny the scientific relevance of all public (state) policy, all but philosophical anarchists abandon the position. They secretly import objective value theory back into their economic theories.[30] Even zero-state libertarians usually succumb. Most of them speak of monetary inflation as the cause of price inflation, but price inflation implies an index number, and all index numbers are based on the interpersonal comparisons of subjective utilities.

In Christian economics, economic value is both subjective and objective because God's imputation is both subjective and objective. Christian economists need not sneak in objective economic value theory through the back door. They should open the front door and invite objective economic value theory to take up permanent residence—just not exclusive residence.

E. Owners Designate Heirs

Point five: succession. In economics, this is inheritance. Because men are mortal, they must find ways to preserve their legacy through time. Owners pass down (hierarchy) assets to their heirs. Legal authority over these assets is thereby transferred. The capital or wealth which they transfer as owners to their heirs will then be used by others, possibly in terms of the testamentary document written by the testator, but more likely according to the will of the heirs.

---

29. Lionel Robbins, *An Essay on the Nature and Significance of Economic Science* (London: Macmillan, 1932), ch. VI.

30. North, *Sovereignty & Dominion*, ch. 5.

The heirs can either be individuals or legal agents acting on behalf of a corporate body. Their responsibility may be individual or shared as administrators of the corporate entity. Inheritance is therefore both one and many. So is responsibility.

Because stewardship is necessarily covenantal, inheritance is covenantal. It should therefore conform to the requirement of the covenant: *confession supercedes name.* More precisely, stewards should confess Christ's name over the family's name. This means that the heirs should be co-members of the covenant. They should make the same confession and take the same oaths in each of the four covenantal administrations: personal, familial, ecclesiastical, and civil.

There can be cases of *common-grace confession* where inheritance is legitimate. There may be an organization that is doing something productive that no confessionally consistent organization is doing. This might have to do with medical research. In such cases, inheritance is legitimate on the basis of the absence of any confessional heir.

The primary goal of inheritance in the biblical worldview is the extension of the kingdom of God in history. People are mortal. This means that individuals cannot maintain ownership after they die. This brings up the issue of inheritance. Inheritance laws governed the Mosaic economy. Among these was the law of the jubilee: the return of rural land to the families of the conquest generation under Joshua (Lev. 25).[31] The basic law of inheritance was this: "A good person leaves an inheritance to his grandchildren, And the wealth of a sinner is stored up for the righteous" (Prov. 13:22).[32] This has not changed.

Jesus taught that covenant-keepers can transfer wealth to the world beyond the grave. "Do not store up for yourselves treasures on earth, where moth and rust destroy, and where thieves break in and steal. But store up for yourselves treasures in heaven, where neither moth nor rust destroys, and where thieves do not break in or steal; for where your trea-

---

31. This law was annulled at the time of the captivity. After the nation's return to Israel, the law was not reimposed, as Ezekiel had prophesied (Ezek. 47:21–22). Gary North, *Restoration & Dominion: An Economic Commentary on the Prophets* (Moulton, Alabama: Axehead Press, [2012] 2030), ch. 22.

32. Gary North, *Wisdom & Dominion: An Economic Commentary on Proverbs* (Moulton, Alabama: Axehead Press, [2012] 2029), ch. 41.

sure is, there your heart will be also" (Matt. 6:19–21).[33] They do this by transferring wealth to the needy in history. This enables them to lay up treasure in heaven. In medieval times, men on their deathbeds would transfer ownership of land to an agency of the church, such as a monastery. They did this as a way of laying up treasure in heaven. They sacrificed their heirs' inheritance, not their own. They used the property for as long as they could, and then they disinherited their children. They believed that this would fulfil Jesus' requirement for a successful transfer of wealth to heaven. They sought to take their wealth with them. They designated heirs outside their families. This permanently transferred ownership to an institution that would maintain control indefinitely. This ended when civil governments confiscated these landholdings. Henry VIII began the practice in the late 1530s by confiscating monastic lands. He sold them to raise money. The French Revolution imitated him in 1789. In this case, the state kept the land and printed money, with the land supposedly held in reserve to back the currency. This led to hyperinflation, since monetary inflation raised the price of the land, which in turn authorised the state to print more money.[34]

Conclusion

Economics operates in terms of a cosmic hierarchy: God over man over nature. Economic theory must reflect this or else drift into error. We see this most clearly in the concept of stewardship. Christian economics makes man a trustee of God. This means that God possesses sovereignty. Man possesses authority, which could also be called delegated sovereignty or subordinate sovereignty. God delegates to individuals and corporate entities responsibility for administering His property in His name and for His kingdom's benefit.

There is a conflict between rival kingdoms over title to the world's assets. This is the conflict between the kingdom of God and the kingdom of man. Economic science has been marked by a self-conscious commit-

33. North, *Priorities & Dominion*, ch. 38.

34. Andrew Dickson White, *Fiat Money Inflation in France* (New York: Appleton-Century, [1896] 1933).

ment to the kingdom of man. Historically, the debate over economics has been between those defending the kingdom of individual men vs. the kingdom of collective man. This is the division between the many and the one, between methodological individualism and methodological holism. What has not previously been self-consciously presented by Christian economists is a case for methodological covenantalism.

Methodological covenantalism in its Trinitarian form has a concept of stewardship that rests on the five pillars of the covenant: the sovereignty of God, the authority of man, the right to private property, predictable economic sanctions, and the triumph of God's kingdom in history. With respect to the ultimate stewardship—Christ's stewardship of the world for His Father—Paul was clear. Incorporating the imagery of Psalm 110, the "footstool psalm," he wrote of the resurrection:

> But each in his own order: Christ the first fruits, after that those who are Christ's at His coming, then comes the end, when He hands over the kingdom to our God and Father, when He has abolished all rule and all authority and power. For He must reign until He has put all His enemies under His feet. The last enemy that will be abolished is death. For He has put all things in subjection under His feet. But when He says, "All things are put in subjection," it is clear that this excludes the Father who put all things in subjection to Him. When all things are subjected to Him, then the Son Himself will also be subjected to the One who subjected all things to Him, so that God may be all in all. (I Cor. 15:23–28)[35]

Stewardship is economic. The rules are these:

1. Purpose precedes planning.
2. Priorities structure planning.
3. Ownership involves exclusion.
4. Owners evaluate performance.
5. Owners designate heirs.

35. Gary North, *Judgment & Dominion: An Economic Commentary on I Corinthians* (Moulton, Alabama: Axehead Press, [2012] 2031), ch. 16.

Chapter 3

The Economic Laws Governing Man

The Lord *God commanded the man, saying, "From any tree of the garden you may freely eat; but from the tree of the knowledge of good and evil you shall not eat, for on the day that you eat from it you will certainly die."*

Genesis 2:16–17

Analysis

Point three of the biblical covenant is ethics.[1] This is associated with law. God's laws are based on God's ethics. Without law, there is no covenant.

God's dominion covenant began with this law: "You may surely eat of every tree of the garden, but of the tree of the knowledge of good and evil you shall not eat, for in the day that you eat of it you shall surely die." This made it clear: *the most fundamental of all laws is the law against theft*. Man could not break covenant with God by any other act. This should warn mankind: be alert to the temptation to steal. Men should resist it.

In the commandment designated by non-Lutheran Protestants as the third commandment, we read: "You shall not take the name of the Lord your God in vain, for the Lord will not leave him unpunished

1. Ray R. Sutton, *That You May Prosper: Dominion By Covenant*, 2nd ed. (Tyler, Texas: Institute for Christian Economics, [1987] 1992), ch. 3.

who takes His name in vain" (Ex. 20:7).[2] This is found in the first section of the Decalogue: commandments one through five. In the third commandment in the second section of five, we read: "You shall not steal" (Ex. 20:15).[3] God placed boundaries around His name. He also placed boundaries around property. His name is His property. He protects it. This is why the state must protect it. Here is the judicial covenant. I covered this in Chapter 1.

1. God owns everything.
2. God delegates ownership.
3. God prohibits theft.
4. God evaluates performance.
5. God mandates growth.

In Chapter 2, I covered the economic laws of stewardship.

1. Purpose precedes planning.
2. Priorities structure planning.
3. Ownership involves exclusion.
4. Owners evaluate performance.
5. Owners designate heirs.

What about economic laws of property management? Are they also governed by the five points of the covenant? They are. Economic laws are inherent in every social order. Every society must deal with the economic issues raised by the social covenants. Every textbook on economics, if it is complete, deals with these issues. They are inescapable concepts. They are dealt with differently in different economic systems, but they are all dealt with, both in terms of theory and practice.

1. Owners adopt purposes.
2. Prices provide information.
3. People prefer more.
4. Scarcity imposes costs.
5. Growth reduces scarcity.

---

2. Gary North, *Authority & Dominion: An Economic Commentary on Exodus*, vol. 2, *Part II: Decalogue & Dominion* (Moulton, Alabama: Axehead Press, [1986, 2012] 2025), ch. 23.

3. Ibid., ch. 8.

A. Owners Adopt Purposes

Point one: God's sovereignty. Here, I repeat what I wrote in the previous chapter. In economics, point one is connected to God's creation. He is the sovereign Owner because he was the Creator. But this raises a problem. Man is not a creator in the way that God is. Man did not speak the creation into existence. So, we must look to God's creation as the archetype of man's creativity.

We look to what preceded the creation as the source of guidance to understand man's creativity. God had a purpose for the creation. He had a plan. He had a decree. These were not sequential chronologically. There was not yet time. But, logically, purpose preceded planning. How should this affect our understand of economics?

The supreme Christian purpose is this: "But seek first His kingdom and His righteousness, and all these things will be provided to you" (Matt. 6:33).[4] Men are to seek God's kingdom in their lives. "Ask, and it will be given to you; seek, and you will find; knock, and it will be opened to you. For everyone who asks receives, and the one who seeks finds, and to the one who knocks it will be opened" (Matt. 7:7–8).[5] This is a required procedure. Before someone can develop a plan of action, he needs purpose. There is no escape from the fundamental principle: *purpose precedes planning*. This is true in every area of life, not just economics.

God holds owners responsible for the administration of the property that He has entrusted to them. They cannot escape this responsibility without transferring ownership of the property to someone else. This transfer must be lawful. In an economic exchange, they become responsible for whatever they received in the trade.

God had a purpose for His creation. It is summarized in the dominion covenant.

> Then God said, "Let Us make mankind in Our image, according to Our likeness; and let them rule over the fish of the sea and over the birds of the sky and over the livestock and over all the earth, and over

4. Gary North, *Priorities & Dominion: An Economic Commentary on Matthew* (Moulton, Alabama: Axehead Press, [2012] 2030), ch. 15.

5. Ibid., ch. 16.

> every crawling thing that crawls on the earth." So God created man in His own image, in the image of God He created him; male and female He created them. God blessed them; and God said to them, "Be fruitful and multiply, and fill the earth, and subdue it; and rule over the fish of the sea and over the birds of the sky and over every living thing that moves on the earth." (Gen. 1:26–28)[6]

There is no escape from this covenant by either individuals or institutions. God spoke these words judicially in the name of humanity. This covenant defines both mankind and nature. Man did not exist at the time God established this covenant by an oath. It was a mutual oath within the Godhead: "Let Us." It was spoken representatively. Man was not yet on the scene. God had purposes for mankind before He implemented His plan.

B. Prices Provide Information

Point two: hierarchy. Men exercise dominion over nature and over other men in terms of their purposes. Plans begin with purpose. This is true all kinds of plans. Economic theory rests on this fact: *we have limited resources, including time*. We cannot achieve all of our goals at the same time. We must therefore establish a list of priorities: first, second, third, etc. We then compare this list with how much money we own. We will have to pay for whatever it is that we want. This is the factor of scarcity. Economists define scarcity as follows: "At zero price, there is greater demand than supply."

In our quest to come up with a plan of action, we find that we face an array of monetary prices. There are other people who wish to achieve their purposes. They also possess money or assets that they can exchange for money. They are constantly bidding for resources, just as we are. The free market is a gigantic auction. Its ruling principle is this: *monetary high bid wins*. I go into this in detail in Parts I and II of my book, *Christian Economics for Teachers* (2017).[7] Prices provide crucial

---

6. Gary North, *Sovereignty & Dominion: An Economic Commentary on Genesis* (Moulton, Alabama: Axehead Press, [1982, 2012] 2022), chaps. 3, 4.

7. Gary North, *Christian Economics for Teachers* (Moulton, Alabama: Axehead Press, [2017] 2026).

information. They tell us what we will have to pay in order to purchase scarce resources.

There is constant feedback between our list of priorities and the prices we must pay to achieve our goals. It is possible that the price of something we want to purchase will rise or fall so much that our priorities change. Our goals and our monetary resources are in constant flux. Jesus understood this. Jesus warned His listeners: "For which one of you, when he wants to build a tower, does not first sit down and calculate the cost, to see if he has enough to complete it? Otherwise, when he has laid a foundation and is not able to finish, all who are watching it will begin to ridicule him, saying, 'This person began to build, and was not able to finish!' Or what king, when he sets out to meet another king in battle, will not first sit down and consider whether he is strong enough with ten thousand men to face the one coming against him with twenty thousand? Otherwise, while the other is still far away, he sends a delegation and requests terms of peace" (Luke 14:28–32).[8] This is a biblical principle: *count the cost*. Prices enable us to count the costs more accurately. They are objective indicators of the costs of achieving our goals. These costs are subjective. They are based on our priorities. But the objectivity of prices is crucial in helping us make objective decisions.

In 1920, Ludwig von Mises wrote the most important work in his long career, which stretched from 1906 to 1966. It was an article critical of socialism. He argued that socialism is inherently irrational because socialist planners have no prices to use to plan production. They can copy prices from the free market, but this is no solution to the planners' problems of allocating scarce resources. The prices in the market are products of supply and demand. Real people are bidding to gain ownership of real goods. The socialists are planning for the future. They do not have indicators regarding the products that consumers are willing to pay for. The consumers do not have access to open markets.

Even more important, Mises argued, is the absence of markets for capital goods. Socialist planners do not know what capital costs. They cannot assess present production costs. They have no way to assess future demand by consumers. They have no way of knowing what to

8. Gary North, *Treasure & Dominion: An Economic Commentary on Luke* (Moulton, Alabama: Axehead Press, [2012] 2031), ch. 35.

produce in order to meet future demand by consumers. His long article was titled, "Economic Calculation in the Socialist Commonwealth."[9] It became the center of an academic debate that went on in the 1920s and 1930s. F. A. Hayek edited a book of essays on this in 1935: *Collectivist Economic Planning.*[10] A handful of socialist economists announced in the late 1930s that they had won the argument. Keynesian and mainstream neoclassical economists accepted their word for it by the end of the 1940s. Mises and his article were then forgotten. Mises was rarely mentioned in graduate programs in economics. Then, without warning, the economy of the Soviet Union collapsed, 1988 to 1991. A famous socialist economist, Robert Heilbroner, admitted in a September 10, 1990 article in *The New Yorker* that Mises had been correct all along. Heilbroner was a multimillionaire from book royalties. He had written the most popular college textbook on the history of economic thought, *The Worldly Philosophers*. He never mentioned Mises in his book. He announced in 1990: "Mises was right." On December 25, 1991, the Soviet Union literally went out of business.

In his most influential article, Mises' disciple F. A. Hayek argued in 1945 that knowledge is decentralized. Individuals own it. No socialist planning committee can ever have sufficient knowledge to match the knowledge that is made available constantly by the free market's system of pricing. Prices enable individual decision-makers to plan rationally. People with local, specialized, accurate knowledge can profit from their information in the capital markets. They can buy low and sell high because they possess better knowledge. This in the entrepreneurial function. This was an extension of Mises' argument 25 years earlier.[11]

C. People Prefer More

Point three: ethics. This is connected to law. We search for laws of economics. These laws let us understand economic cause and effect. Here

9. Ludwig von Mises, *Economic Calculation in the Socialist Commonwealth* (Auburn, Alabama: Mises Institute, [1920] 1990).

10. *Collectivist Economic Planning* (Routledge & Kegan Paul Ltd., 1935).

11. F. A. Hayek, "The Use of Knowledge in Society" (1945), reprinted in Hayek, *Individualism and Economic Order* (Chicago: University of Chicago Press, 1948), ch. 4.

is one of the most powerful of all economic laws: people prefer more. But this is not quite correct. It should read as follows: "People prefer more at the same price." This is a fundamental law of economics. If this were not true, there could be no science of economics.

There are two ways of describing this phenomenon. First, people want more at the same price. Second, people want the same amount at a lower price. The common way of phrasing this is less price: people want more for less. This leads to confusion. Which does a person want most? He cannot get both at the margin, which is where we make purchasing decisions.

The most famous case in the Bible of this phenomenon is Abraham's bargaining with God over the number of righteous people in Sodom. God announced that He was going to destroy Sodom. That was where Abraham's nephew Lot and his family lived. Abraham wanted a better deal. He argued on behalf of the righteous people in the city.

> Then the men turned away from there and went toward Sodom, while Abraham was still standing before the LORD. Abraham approached and said, "Will You indeed sweep away the righteous with the wicked? Suppose there are fifty righteous people within the city; will You indeed sweep it away and not spare the place for the sake of the fifty righteous who are in it? Far be it from You to do such a thing, to kill the righteous with the wicked, so that the righteous and the wicked are treated alike. Far be it from You! Shall not the Judge of all the earth deal justly?" So the LORD said, "If I find in Sodom fifty righteous within the city, then I will spare the entire place on their account." (Gen. 18:23–26)

But this was only his first offer. Abraham wanted an even better price. What about 45 righteous people? God agreed. What about 40? God agreed. Then 20. Then 10. Abraham wanted a steep discount. God could afford to offer this. He knew there were not ten righteous people in the city. There were only Lot, his wife, and their two daughters... and the women were not all that righteous.

The fact that people want more is related closely to the silent presumption of most people, namely, that they can obtain more benefits in life without a corresponding increase in personal responsibility. *They assume a permanently fixed price with respect to personal responsibility.* They assume, in short, that there really is such a thing as a free lunch in life. Christianity teaches that there is: salvation by grace through faith. Christianity teaches that there will be greater responsibilities, but nothing remotely sufficient to repay God for His grace. All payments are token payments. Apart from grace, all people are running up a huge debt to God.

People seek greater wealth. To obtain this, they must offer productive services to buyers unless they are the recipients of either charity or a state subsidy. This is a motivation for people to serve others. There are two mental approaches to this quest. One is to obtain more wealth for the purpose of consumption. This is the humanist view of economics. It goes back to Adam Smith's *Wealth of Nations*. "Consumption is the sole end and purpose of all production; and the interest of the producer ought to be attended to only so far as it may be necessary for promoting that of the consumer. The maxim is so perfectly self-evident that it would be absurd to attempt to prove it. But in the mercantile system the interest of the consumer is almost constantly sacrificed to that of the producer; and it seems to consider production, and not consumption, as the ultimate end and object of all industry and commerce."[12] The other approach is to seek out greater responsibility. This means seeking out more ways to serve others. But to continue this quest, there must be profits. No one can serve others if he goes bankrupt. The results are the same in both cases: more income through greater satisfaction of consumer demand. The first approach is mammon's: "More for me in history." The second is Christ's. Jesus taught: "No man can serve two masters: for either he will hate the one, and love the other; or else he will hold to the one, and despise the other. Ye cannot serve God and mammon" (Matt. 6:24, KJV).[13]

A lower price could also lead to greater capital accumulation. This could then be put to use for the kingdom of God. So, there is a legitimate reason to seek a discount.

---

12. Adam Smith, *An Inquiry into the Nature and Causes of the Wealth of Nations* (1776), Bk. IV:8:49.

13. North, *Priorities & Dominion*, ch. 14.

D. Scarcity Imposes Costs

Point four: sanctions. There are two kinds: positive and negative. In economics, these are called profit and loss. They are men's means of reducing the effects of scarcity.

There was scarcity prior to the fall. Adam had to work: name the animals (Gen. 2:19–20). Then they both had to dress the garden and defend it from any invader: a thief. They failed to defend it. So, there were costs of production in the garden. But these costs of production increased outside the garden due to God's curse of Adam and the ground (Gen. 3:17–19).[14]

Because scarcity imposes costs of production, people are pressured economically to cooperate with each other. There are economic benefits that flow from the division of labor. These benefits reduce scarcity. "Two are better than one because they have a good return for their labor; for if either of them falls, the one will lift up his companion. But woe to the one who falls when there is not another to lift him up! Furthermore, if two lie down together they keep warm, but how can one be warm alone? And if one can overpower him who is alone, two can resist him. A cord of three strands is not quickly torn apart" (Eccles. 4:9–12).[15]

Through trade, people can specialize in their production. They can concentrate on what they do best. Their output increases as a direct result of specialization. So does their income. The curses that God has imposed on man and nature therefore have an element of grace. Because people do not want to lose the benefits of voluntary trade, they want to avoid the economically separating effects of warfare, theft, violence, and fraud. Such actions reduce other people's willingness to cooperate. This would reduce most individuals' wealth. In other words, war, theft, violence, and fraud would increase the cost of production. Here is a fundamental economic law of pricing: "When costs rise, the quantity demanded falls." In this case, rising costs are imposed on evil behavior. Therefore, less is demanded.

Cursed scarcity is therefore a means of grace, both common grace (life-giving) grace and special (soul-saving) grace. It pressures people to

14. North, *Sovereignty & Dominion*, ch. 12.

15. Gary North, *Autonomy & Stagnation: An Economic Commentary on Ecclesiastes* (Moulton, Alabama: Axehead Press, [2012] 2030), ch. 14.

cooperate economically: common grace. It reminds people of the final judgment: special grace. It reminds people that God's covenant is still in force: positive and negative sanctions. This is both common grace and special grace. There is both common curse and special curse.

All forms of scarcity are incentives for men to work harder, longer, and smarter. People want more. To obtain more, they must increase their productivity. To increase their productivity, they must gain access to capital: tools of production. *The economic incentives that scarcity provides are engines of increased production.* Here is God's mandate: increased productivity. Increased productivity is the biblical way of subduing the earth, which remains the goal of the dominion covenant. This covenant is still binding on mankind.

E. Growth Reduces Scarcity

Point five: succession. In economics, this means inheritance. God mandates a positive rate of return on his capital. This is the message of the parable of the stewards (Matt. 25:14–30).[16] To achieve this, men must increase the economic value of their output. When output increases, men gain greater wealth. This can be used to increase consumption. It can be used to provide charity. It can be used for capital formation, which in turn leads to greater output when wisely allocated.

When I say that growth reduces scarcity, I mean objective scarcity. Objective scarcity is measured in terms of calories per day, clothing that protects against the environment, living conditions, and the number of goods and services. The economic value of these assets is assessed subjectively. If increased wealth leads to what behavioral economists call a *hedonic ratchet*—better known as the rat race or "keeping up with the Joneses"—then increased output can lead to greater scarcity, with scarcity defined as the subjective gap between assets owned and wealth hoped for. The gap may appear subjectively to increase. In such a case, there is no escape from the psychological burden of scarcity.

If scarcity is seen as the gap between the output of capital in the past and capital today, there has been a reduction of scarcity. Increased out-

16. North, *Priorities & Dominion*, ch. 47.

put because of better tools is real. Society is closer to the fulfillment of the dominion covenant. This means that society is closer to the day of judgment. This is an objective point of reference for God.

God mandates capital accumulation. This is not so that His people can live more leisurely lifestyles. It is so that they can become more productive. They are required by God to use their increased wealth to extend the kingdom of God in history. "But seek first His kingdom and His righteousness, and all these things will be provided to you" (Matt. 6:33). When "all these things" arrive, the covenant-keeper is to reinvest a portion of this increase. This is the message of the parable of the talents. The successful stewards are given authority over greater wealth.

The kingdom of God is not extended exclusively by non-profit organizations. The free market is based on service to consumers. This was the great insight of Adam Smith. Before Smith, economists had seen the growth of business and the growth of charity as mutually exclusive. They saw the two sides as being in competition for the public's money. After Smith, it became clear that increased output, increased employment, and increased knowledge are all potentially beneficial to the expansion of the kingdom of God. "Give a man a fish, and you feed him for a meal. Teach him how to fish, and you feed him for a lifetime." My version: "Give a man a handout, and he will stick his hand out again. Give him a marketable skill, and he will not have to stick his hand out again." *Profit as a success indicator can be harnessed for the kingdom of God.* It is a matter of the rich man's confession of faith, not his net worth, that matters. This was implied in Solomon's proverb: "A good person leaves an inheritance to his grandchildren, And the wealth of a sinner is stored up for the righteous" (Prov. 13:22).[17] This is an aspect of inheritance, the fifth point of the biblical covenant. So is economic growth.

If rich men always tithed to their local churches, this would extend the kingdom of God. Which pastors would prefer to have no rich men in their congregations? The idea that they might prefer this is absurd. The problem is rich men's refusal to tithe, not the fact that they are economically successful.

Jesus preached that the poor would always be with the disciples. "For

17. Gary North, *Wisdom & Dominion: An Economic Commentary on Proverbs* (Moulton, Alabama: Axehead Press, [2012] 2029), ch. 41.

you always have the poor with you, and whenever you want, you can do good to them; but you do not always have Me" (Mark 14:7).[18] He was speaking prior to His ascension. Did He set forth poverty as a standard to be adopted by the masses? No. Today, there is a serious possibility that starvation-producing poverty will no longer exist in 2050, except in war-torn poor nations. Is this not an answer to the Lord's prayer? "Give us this day our daily bread" (Matt. 6:11).[19] Why should Christians not rejoice at this prospect? Should they want non-Christians to starve? If so, why do they send money to charitable foreign missions to help a token handful of poor people? Wouldn't it be far better to wipe poverty from off the face of the earth?

Conclusion

There are common themes in free market economic theory: ends (purposes) and means, the price system as a way to gain access to better information, the desire to gain wealth, the close relationship between scarcity and costs, and economic growth as a way to reduce scarcity. Are they the most fundamental themes in economics? There are others. The idea of property rights is crucial. This idea is implicit in the concept of a price system. There can be no prices apart from exchange. There can be no exchange apart from private property. There can therefore be no rational monetary prices under socialism. This makes socialist economies impossible. That was Mises' point in his 1920 essay on economic calculation. So, we are back to private property: ownership (point one).

The idea of scarcity (point four) and the ideal of economic growth (point five) are the two most agreed-upon economic concepts in humanistic economics. What about point three: the desire for more? This is another fundamental theme in all schools of economic opinion. There is no such thing as a system of economic theory built on the idea of a universal desire to own less. There are books that proclaim this: "Small is beautiful." Or this: "Less is more." They offer no economic theory. They offer no analytical system of predictable causes and effects.

18. Gary North, *Trust & Dominion: An Economic Commentary on Mark* (Moulton, Alabama: Axehead Press, [2012] 2031), ch. 20.

19. North, *Priorities & Dominion*, ch. 12:B.

Chapter 4

The Economic Constraints on Man

Then to Adam He said, "Because you have listened to the voice of your wife, and have eaten from the tree about which I commanded you, saying, 'You shall not eat from it';

Cursed is the ground because of you;
With hard labor you shall eat from it
All the days of your life.
Both thorns and thistles it shall grow for you;
Yet you shall eat the plants of the field;
By the sweat of your face
You shall eat bread,
Until you return to the ground,
Because from it you were taken;
For you are dust,
And to dust you shall return."

Genesis 3:17–19

Analysis

Point four of the biblical covenant is sanctions: positive and negative.[1] There are two aspects of the constraints on man. The first constraint is

1. Ray R. Sutton, *That You May Prosper: Dominion By Covenant*, 2nd ed. (Tyler, Texas: Institute for Christian Economics, [1987] 1992), ch. 4.

man's finitude. He is a creature. The second constraint is God's curses on mankind and the ground in response to man's sin. Any attempt by man to escape completely from the limits of his creaturehood is a sin. The serpent tempted Eve in this regard: to be as God (Gen. 3:5). Second, God's curses imposed even greater constraints on man (Gen. 3:17–19).[2]

I begin with the constraints imposed by finitude. These are covenantal: five points. First, the fundamental pre-Fall economic constraint on man was that he is a creature. This is point one of the biblical covenant: God's transcendence, yet his universal presence with the creation. This is an incommunicable attribute of God. In contrast, man is finite. This finitude is inherent in man's being. Not being God, man cannot create something out of nothing. He cannot speak anything into existence out of nothing. He does not possess any of these incommunicable attributes of God: omniscience, omnipotence, and omnipresence. Neither one man nor mankind can evolve into divinity. "What is man that You think of him, And a son of man that You are concerned about him?" (Ps. 8:4).[3] "Woe to the one who quarrels with his Maker—A piece of pottery among the other earthenware pottery pieces! Will the clay say to the potter, 'What are you doing?' Or the thing you are making say, 'He has no hands'?" (Isa. 45:9). So, any attempt by man to attain these incommunicable attributes is a form of covenant-breaking.

The second pre-Fall constraint on man was his position as a steward in the hierarchy of creation. He oversaw the earth on behalf of God. He could not escape this economic hierarchy. It pointed to his position as a creature. To attempt to deny this hierarchy is a sin. Speaking of the king of Babylon (Isa. 14:4), Isaiah wrote: "How you have fallen from heaven, You star of the morning, son of the dawn! You have been cut down to the earth, You who defeated the nations! But you said in your heart, 'I will ascend to heaven; I will raise my throne above the stars of God, And I will sit on the mount of assembly In the recesses of the north. I will ascend above the heights of the clouds; I will make myself like the Most High.' Nevertheless you will be brought down to Sheol, To the recesses of the pit" (Isa. 14:12–15).

---

2. Gary North, *Sovereignty & Dominion: An Economic Commentary on Genesis* (Moulton, Alabama: Axehead Press, [1982, 2012] 2022), ch. 12.

3. Gary North, *Confidence & Dominion: An Economic Commentary on the Psalms* (Moulton, Alabama: Axehead Press, [2012] 2029), ch. 3.

The third pre-fall constraint on man is the finitude of creation. Creation is bounded. "After this I saw four angels standing at the four corners of the earth, holding back the four winds of the earth so that no wind would blow on the earth, or on the sea, or on any tree" (Rev. 7:1). This applies also to men's institutions. "And He will lift up a flag for the nations And assemble the banished ones of Israel, And will gather the dispersed of Judah From the four corners of the earth" (Isa. 11:12).

The fourth pre-fall constraint on man is scarcity. He cannot attain all of his goals by speaking them into existence. He cannot get everything he wants when he wants it at zero price. This limitation preceded the fall. It was original in the creation.

The fifth pre-fall constraint is the linearity of time. Man is bounded by linear time. While a man can do more than one thing at a time, he cannot do all things simultaneously. He must do things in a sequence. This creates the dual problems of planning and resource allocation. Each person has to schedule his actions. There is a necessary sequence in all life. This includes production. God made Adam name the animals of the garden before He gave him a wife (Gen. 2:19–22).[4]

These constraints constitute the general economic issue of scarcity. Scarcity is defined as follows: "At zero price, there is greater demand than supply." This fact produces prices. People bid competitively for scarce resources.

Then there are the limits imposed by God's curses in response to mankind's sin. Here are the major curses.

A. Blindness

Point one: God's sovereignty. Blindness is the negative sanction on man's ability to determine purpose. God is transcendent. He is the Creator. Adam and Eve rejected this doctrine. They decided that they possessed both the ability and the authority to judge between the word of God and the word of the serpent. God therefore brought them under judgment. The serpent's temptation was this: by eating from the tree, they would become as God, knowing good and evil. Their rebellion

4. Ibid., ch. 10.

produced the opposite effect. They lost the ability to make clear judgments about right and wrong, meaning life and death. From that day on, they needed guidance from God. That would be an act of grace on His part. Moses warned the generation of the conquest:

> "See, I have placed before you today life and happiness, and death and adversity, in that I am commanding you today to love the LORD your God, to walk in His ways and to keep His commandments, His statutes, and His judgments, so that you may live and become numerous, and that the LORD your God may bless you in the land where you are entering to take possession of it. But if your heart turns away and you will not obey, but allow yourself to be led astray and you worship other gods and serve them, I declare to you today that you will certainly perish. You will not prolong your days in the land where you are crossing the Jordan to enter and take possession of it. I call heaven and earth to witness against you today, that I have placed before you life and death, the blessing and the curse. So choose life in order that you may live, you and your descendants, by loving the LORD your God, by obeying His voice, and by holding close to Him; for this is your life and the length of your days, so that you may live in the land which the LORD swore to your fathers, to Abraham, Isaac, and Jacob, to give them." (Deut. 30:15–20)[5]

Choose life, Moses said. Adam and Eve had chosen death. They did this as judicial representatives of all mankind. This is the doctrine of original sin. Apart from God's grace, both special (soul-saving) and common (life-giving), all men are blind. Jesus described this affliction as blindness: "Leave them alone; they are blind guides of blind people. And if a person who is blind guides another who is blind, both will fall into a pit" (Matt. 15:14). Men can no longer clearly discern the truth.

Because of common grace, people have broad purposes in life. They are future-oriented. They also have goals, which are narrower purposes that are subservient to their broader purposes. These purposes and goals lead them to make plans for the future. Their goals can be long term or short term. These goals guide people in making plans. *Purpose precedes planning*. But when men's goals are opposed to God's purposes for them, they are led astray. They fall into a ditch, spiritually speak-

5. Gary North, *Inheritance & Dominion: An Economic Commentary on Deuteronomy* (Moulton, Alabama: Axehead Press, [1999, 2012] 2028), ch. 73.

ing. They sacrifice a part of the present for the sake of the future, but this future is self-destructive. They may possess great intelligence. What they lack is either the ability or interest in conforming their standards to God's standards. Cornelius Van Til, the Christian philosopher, put it this way. "If a circular saw is crooked, it does not matter how well you sharpen it. It will not cut straight." This is fallen man's problem from birth. Paul wrote: "But a natural person does not accept the things of the Spirit of God, for they are foolishness to him; and he cannot understand them, because they are spiritually discerned" (I Cor. 2:14). It requires God's grace to straighten the saw.

Blindness causes men to choose the wrong priorities. These priorities are foundational to the task of economic planning. People must allocate scarce resources to achieve their goals. They faced scarcity before the fall. They face cursed scarcity today. They cannot attain all of their goals at the same time. So, they must set priorities. In English, there is a word: "prioritize." They must choose which goals they want to attain. They must select a sequence of action: priorities. Then they must put together a plan of action (point two of the covenant). This process begins with an overall purpose. The Psalmist put it this way, speaking of evil-doers.

> They mock and wickedly speak of oppression; they speak from on high. They have set their mouth against the heavens, and their tongue parades through the earth. Therefore his people return here, and abundant waters are drunk by them. They say, "How does God know? And is there knowledge with the Most High?" Behold, these are the wicked; and always at ease, they have increased in wealth. Surely in vain I have kept my heart pure and washed my hands in innocence; for I have been stricken all day long, and punished every morning. If I had said, "I will speak this way," behold, I would have betrayed the generation of Your children. When I thought of understanding this, it was troublesome in my sight until I entered the sanctuary of God; then I perceived their end. You indeed put them on slippery ground; You dropped them into ruin. (Ps. 73:8–18)[6]

They are blind to the outcome of their plans. But their blindness extends beyond their faulty plans. They have chosen ends that lead to

6. Gary North, *Confidence & Dominion*, ch. 17.

destruction. Their plans may be consistent with their purposes. Their main problem is not the details of their plans. Their worldview has led them to adopt destructive purposes. This is a curse imposed by God. Paul wrote:

> What shall we say then? There is no injustice with God, is there? Far from it! For He says to Moses, "I will have mercy on whomever I have mercy, and I will show compassion to whomever I show compassion." So then, it does not depend on the person who wants it nor the one who runs, but on God who has mercy. For the Scripture says to Pharaoh, "For this very reason I raised you up, in order to demonstrate My power in you, and that My name might be proclaimed throughout the earth." So then He has mercy on whom He desires, and He hardens whom He desires. You will say to me then, "Why does He still find fault? For who has resisted His will?" On the contrary, who are you, you foolish person, who answers back to God? The thing molded will not say to the molder, "Why did you make me like this," will it? Or does the potter not have a right over the clay, to make from the same lump one object for honorable use, and another for common use? What if God, although willing to demonstrate His wrath and to make His power known, endured with great patience objects of wrath prepared for destruction? (Rom. 9:14–22)

The disciples asked Jesus why He spoke in parables. His answer was clear, but it is not what Christians want to hear, so they close their ears.

> And the disciples came up and said to Him, "Why do You speak to them in parables?" And Jesus answered them, "To you it has been granted to know the mysteries of the kingdom of heaven, but to them it has not been granted. For whoever has, to him more shall be given, and he will have an abundance; but whoever does not have, even what he has shall be taken away from him. Therefore I speak to them in parables; because while seeing they do not see, and while hearing they do not hear, nor do they understand. "And in their case the prophecy of Isaiah is being fulfilled, which says,
>
> > 'You shall keep on listening, but shall not understand;
> > And you shall keep on looking, but shall not perceive;
> > For the heart of this people has become dull,
> > With their ears they scarcely hear,
> > And they have closed their eyes,

> Otherwise they might see with their eyes,
> Hear with their ears,
> Understand with their heart, and return,
> And I would heal them.'
>
> But blessed are your eyes, because they see; and your ears, because they hear." (Matt. 13:10–16)[7]

This is why it takes God's grace to restore vision. It is not restored by working harder. It cannot be restored by a 12-step plan for self-improvement. Only after God's free grace is bestowed on someone can his purposes begin to correspond to God's purposes for him. The overall purpose is clear: "But seek first His kingdom and His righteousness, and all these things will be provided to you" (Matt. 6:33).[8] The restoration of spiritual sight comes from outside men's ends-means system of planning. In short, *purpose precedes planning*.

B. Rebellion

Point two: hierarchy. Hierarchy is associated with judicial representation. Man represents God to nature. This is the meaning of the dominion covenant. Man was to obey God. He rebelled. In response, God has increased nature's resistance to man's dominion. God implicitly announced to Adam: "You rebelled against me as my covenantal agent. Nature will henceforth rebel against you." This rebellion has made man's work more expensive.

1. *Nature Rebels*

The curse on Adam was not his finitude. He was finite before the fall. The curse was that nature would henceforth increase his costs of dominion. "Then to Adam He said, 'Because you have listened to the voice of your wife, and have eaten from the tree about which I commanded you, saying, "You shall not eat from it"; Cursed is the ground

7. Gary North, *Priorities & Dominion: An Economic Commentary on Matthew* (Moulton, Alabama: Axehead Press, [2012] 2030), ch. 27.

8. Ibid., ch. 15.

because of you; With hard labor you shall eat from it All the days of your life. Both thorns and thistles it shall grow for you; Yet you shall eat the plants of the field; By the sweat of your face You shall eat bread, Until you return to the ground, Because from it you were taken; For you are dust, And to dust you shall return'" (Gen. 3:17–19).[9]

The ground was under Adam's authority. It has now been made to suffer, along with Adam's heirs. God imposed the curse to bring sorrow to mankind, but it also has brought sorrow to the creation. Paul wrote: "For the eagerly awaiting creation waits for the revealing of the sons and daughters of God. For the creation was subjected to futility, not willingly, but because of Him who subjected it, in hope that the creation itself also will be set free from its slavery to corruption into the freedom of the glory of the children of God. For we know that the whole creation groans and suffers the pains of childbirth together until now" (Rom. 8:19–22).[10]

So, the hierarchy under man participates in the curse of man. This is an important aspect of hierarchy. There is a covenantal link between man and the creation. The creation shares in God's sanctions, both positive and negative.

Man is cursed by way of the creation. "Both thorns and thistles it shall grow for you; Yet you shall eat the plants of the field" (Gen. 3:18). They battle for their place in a bounded environment. Their costs rise.

2. *Work*

Man's work is hampered because of sin. God reminds men in their labor that there are consequences for rebellion. Man cannot escape the dominion covenant (Gen. 1:26–28).[11] He must work. He is compelled by inner drives as dominion man to extend his dominion. But the environment resists. This includes other men. "What is the source of quarrels and conflicts among you? Is the source not your pleasures that wage war in your body's parts?" (James 4:1).[12]

---

9. Gary North, *Sovereignty & Dominion: An Economic Commentary on Genesis* (Moulton, Alabama: Axehead Press, [1982, 2012] 2022), ch. 12.

10. Gary North, *Cooperation & Dominion: An Economic Commentary on Romans* (Moulton, Alabama: Axehead Press, [2012] 2031), ch. 5.

11. North, *Sovereignty & Dominion*, chaps. 3, 4.

12. Gary North, *Ethics & Dominion: An Economic Commentary on the Epistles* (Moulton, Alabama: Axehead Press, [2012] 2032), ch. 36.

The curse of scarcity has an element of grace in it. Men are now murderous. If they were left unrestrained by external resistance, they would pursue evil with greater intensity. But nature does not allow this. Men must battle against thorns and thistles. This leaves them less time and fewer resources to battle against each other. *Cursed scarcity is a blessing in disguise.* To overcome it, men must cooperate in joint ventures and voluntary exchange.

Labor was not initially cursed. Adam labored in the garden, naming the animals. His labor after the fall became difficult. "By the sweat of your face You shall eat bread, Until you return to the ground, Because from it you were taken; For you are dust, And to dust you shall return" (Gen. 3:19). The ground will receive and then consume man's lifeless remains—a reminder of the fall, in which Adam and Eve subordinated themselves covenantally to an aspect of the creation in preference to the Creator. Having subordinated themselves covenantally to a creature, Adam and Eve delivered their posterity into the less than tender mercies of a now-resistant creation, which receives the inheritance of man's remains.

C. Sin

Point three: ethics. Sin is a violation of God's law. "So for one who knows the right thing to do and does not do it, for him it is sin" (James 4:17). Because of sin, men's actions are now bounded by God's law. This is the major boundary of life.

God's law empowers men. Without it, they fly blind. But this law is also a restriction on men. It is like a clock. A clock reduces the waste of time. This is a great benefit. We can plan our days more precisely. We can become more productive. The clock and then the wristwatch became important tools in the European West.[13] Yet, at the same time, a clock places limits on the person who wears it and abides by it. His schedule reduces his flexibility. He must honor this schedule. If he violates it, there are negative sanctions.

---

13. David S. Landes, *Revolution in Time: Clocks and the Making of the Modern World*, 2nd ed. (Cambridge Massachusetts: Harvard University Press, [1983] 2000).

The Bible is clear on this point: when a majority of members of any society consistently violate biblical law, the society suffers negative sanctions (Deut. 28:15–68). In contrast, obedience brings external blessings (Deut. 28:1–14).[14] So, biblical law is the basis of both positive and negative sanctions.

When societies obey, they get richer. This is supposed to lead them to greater obedience. This in turn produces greater wealth (Deut. 8:17–18).[15] This system is designed to extend the kingdom of God in history. The rule of law extends over an ever-greater domain. The wealth produced by obedience is capital for fulfilling the dominion covenant.

Sin thwarts this process. Negative sanctions thwart it. The reduced rate of capital formation thwarts it. This is an aspect of sanctions, point four of the biblical covenant. But it also has direct implications for the kingdom. People are supposed to become more familiar with God's law. Psalm 119 is the longest chapter in the Bible. It is devoted to praising God's law.

There is internal conflict individually: *righteousness vs. sin*. This extends to the general culture. It is an aspect of conflict. The ultimate conflict is the conflict between God and Satan. This is manifested in history by a conflict between rival kingdoms. Satan and God have the same goal: for their respective kingdoms to inherit the earth in history. Each kingdom extends its spiritual authority at the expense of another. This competition is a form of warfare. Each of them seeks to displace the other in history. Economists call this a zero-sum game. The winner profits at the expense of the loser. This is not a game. It is a war. Yet it is an odd sort of war. Satan is completely dependent on God for everything he controls: time, intelligence, power, and subordinates.[16] He prospers economically in history, building up wrath for himself in eternity. This is a zero-sum contest. It is *winner takes all*. Satan loses everything of value. God wins everything of value. Satan is today unwilling to surrender unconditionally. This guarantees his defeat. Surrender to God must be unconditional.[17]

14. North, *Inheritance & Dominion*, chaps. 69, 70.

15. Ibid., chaps. 21, 22.

16. Gary North, *Dominion and Common Grace: The Biblical Basis of Progress* (Moulton, Alabama: Axehead Press, [1987] 2024), 26–27, 29–30.

17. Gary North, *Unconditional Surrender: God's Program for Victory* (Moulton, Alabama: Axehead Press, [1981, 2010] 2022).

When the Hebrews lived in Egypt prior to the Pharaoh of the persecution, they prospered and grew, attracting large numbers of converts. Three generations did not allow the increase of numbers to 2.4 million people. Converts made up the bulk of the exodus generation.[18] Egypt prospered in this period. Yet the Pharaoh of the persecution saw a threat: the increased numbers of Hebrews (Ex. 1:8). He viewed the transformation covenantally, not economically: a zero-sum conflict of kingdoms, which it was. He enslaved the Hebrews by imposing a top-down tyranny in order to gain the benefits of the division of labor, yet also maintaining covenantal mastery over them (Ex. 1:9–14).[19] He substituted central planning for the free market. Continuing this policy, the Pharaoh of the exodus lost his kingdom and his life. At the exodus, the Hebrews inherited the gold and silver of Egypt's deceased firstborn males (Ex. 12:35–36). This was a zero-sum economic conflict. Central planning and enslavement had made it such. Pharaoh refused to surrender. So, he lost everything.

Sinful men would prefer to extend their power through violence (James 4:1). God has cursed both mankind and nature in such a way that men must suppress their preference for violence in order to prosper economically. This is the price of productive cooperation. The curse of scarcity provides grace.

D. Uncertainty

Point four: sanctions. These are positive and negative. Because of their rebellion, Adam and Eve came under negative sanctions. Before the fall, they did not see clearly into the future. They did not see the nature of God's punishment on them. They had to take His word for it. They refused. So, as part of the curse, God made men even less clear about the future. He has partially blinded them. Even covenant-keepers who are the recipients of God's special grace remain short-sighted. Paul wrote: "For now we see in a mirror dimly, but then face to face;

18. Gary North, *Authority & Dominion: An Economic Commentary on Exodus*, vol. 1, *Part I: Representation & Dominion* (Moulton, Alabama: Axehead Press, [1985, 2012] 2025), ch. 1.

19. Ibid., ch. 2.

now I know in part, but then I will know fully, just as I also have been fully known" (I Cor. 13:12). This blindness imposes limits on our use of resources. I do not even know what I will want to buy in the future or at what prices. Neither do you. The future is clouded. Our efforts are limited. We peer into the future, and we see shadows.

How can a man survive, let alone prosper, under such circumstances? He has responsibilities, yet he does not know how he will be able to meet them. He does not know what the environment will bring. He does not know who will cooperate with him. In the modern phrase, he is flying blind.

We see through a glass, darkly. This is an aspect of the curse. Finitude is not the problem. This was true before the fall: "The secret things belong to the LORD our God, but the things revealed belong to us and to our sons forever, so that we may follow all the words of this Law" (Deut. 29:29). Sin is the problem. "The serpent said to the woman, 'You certainly will not die!'" (Gen. 3:4). Adam decided to test God by testing His word. He learned that God's word was correct. He learned from experience.

From Adam until today, sin blinds men. God has cursed covenant-breaking men with blindness regarding the future. Why? Because of their sin.

> Then I heard the voice of the Lord, saying, "Whom shall I send, and who will go for Us?" Then I said, "Here am I. Send me!" And He said, "Go, and tell this people:
>
> 'Keep on listening, but do not understand;
> And keep on looking, but do not gain knowledge.'
> Make the hearts of this people insensitive,
> Their ears dull,
> And their eyes blind,
> So that they will not see with their eyes,
> Hear with their ears,
> Understand with their hearts,
> And return and be healed."
>
> Then I said, "Lord, how long?" And He answered,
>
> "Until cities are devastated and without inhabitant,

> Houses are without people
> And the land is utterly desolate,
> The LORD has completely removed people,
> And there are many forsaken places in the midst of the land."
> (Isa. 6:8–12)

Jesus repeated this passage in explaining to the disciples why He spoke in parables (Matt. 13:13–14). Paul cited it as his justification for not going to the Jews with the gospel, but to the gentiles instead (Acts 28:25–28).

This blindness affects men's ability to see the future. Nature buffets people. Wars disrupt them. Disasters overwhelm them. Throughout history until about 1800, the unforeseen disasters of life blindsided mankind. Humanity remained poor. Per capita wealth rarely increased for long. The bad things that people could not foresee usually offset the good things that they hoped for, planned for, and saved for.

E. Poverty

Point five: succession. In economics, this means inheritance. The biblical standard is this: *increasing economic prosperity for covenant-keepers*. This is a matter of covenantal confirmation. Moses warned the Israelites against the sin of pretended autonomy regarding God's economic blessings. "Otherwise, you may say in your heart, 'My power and the strength of my hand made me this wealth.' But you are to remember the LORD your God, for it is He who is giving you power to make wealth, in order to confirm His covenant which He swore to your fathers, as it is this day" (Deut. 8:17–18). Covenant-keepers are supposed to leave an inheritance. "A good person leaves an inheritance to his grandchildren, And the wealth of a sinner is stored up for the righteous" (Prov. 13:22).[20] *This is a vision of increasing per capita wealth*. Yet from Moses' day until 1800, the world suffered from severe limits on per capita wealth. Always, population growth ate up any agricultural increase. Poverty was universal.

Poverty in the Bible is presented as a curse, mainly in Deuteronomy 28. Moses warned Israel that poverty would be part of a series of com-

20. Gary North, *Wisdom & Dominion: An Economic Commentary on Proverbs* (Moulton, Alabama: Axehead Press, [2012] 2029), ch. 41.

prehensive setbacks. "The LORD will send against you curses, panic, and rebuke, in everything you undertake to do, until you are destroyed and until you perish quickly, on account of the evil of your deeds, because you have abandoned Me" (Deut. 28:20). Invasion would confiscate their productivity (v. 33). "You will have olive trees throughout your territory but you will not anoint yourself with the oil, because your olives will drop off prematurely" (v. 40). "The cricket [locust] will take possession of all your trees and the produce of your ground" (v. 42). Poverty was not presented here as a permanent condition of humanity. Yet it was for the next 3,100 years. Most people in history consumed about the same amount of food, of the same monotonous type, from childhood, which few survived, until old age, which few reached. Whenever an agricultural society broke out of poverty, its population grew. Then poverty per capita reappeared. This process was a constraint on all societies until about 1750 in English-speaking North America and 1800 in Great Britain.[21]

We do not know what changed in 1800. It is the most important historical question there is. Per capita wealth began to increase without a setback. This was in the range of 2% per year. Why did it happen in Great Britain and English-speaking North America in 1800? Why not in Israel in 1350 BC? No one has offered an agreed-upon explanation. What we know is this: per capita wealth had increased exceedingly slowly throughout history. Any major gains of food production were always eaten up by population growth. When Rev. T. Robert Malthus wrote his anonymous book in 1798, *An Essay on the Principle of Population,* he seemed to have all of history on his side. He predicted that there would be no long-term prosperity. Population growth would erase all economic gains. This was the most erroneous plausible forecast in modern history.

The economic change was already visible in England and the United States. Ben Franklin had seen this in 1751 in his essay, "Observations Concerning the Increase of Mankind." Even more astounding, Rev.

21. By far the best economic history of this transformation is Gregory Clark, *A Farewell to Alms: A Brief History of the World* (Princeton, New Jersey: Princeton University Press, 2007). But the best economic analysis of what could not have caused this process is Dierdre McCloskey, *Bourgeois Dignity: Why Economics Can't Explain the Modern World* (Chicago: University of Chicago Press, 2010).

Ezra Stiles, president of Yale College, preached an election sermon in the year of American independence, 1783: *The United States Elevated to Glory and Honor.* He predicted that there would be 50 million Americans within a century of independence. In 1880, there were 50 million Americans. He continued: "So that before the millennium, the English settlements in America may become more numerous millions than that greatest dominion on earth, the Chinese empire." In his sermon, he estimated the Chinese empire at 250 million people. That was achieved in the United States in 1990, a decade before the millennium. In terms of accuracy, these predictions are unparalleled. Malthus saw none of this. He was blind. But he had economic history on his side.

Conclusion

Scarcity is an inescapable factor in every area of life because of finitude and linear time. Cursed scarcity has amplified original scarcity.

Adam Smith established a tradition which has been followed faithfully by subsequent free market economists. He began his book with a discussion of the division of labor, which is the most important institutional way to overcome scarcity. This was a conceptual error. God's original ownership is primary: creation. Man's stewardship under God is secondary: the dominion covenant. Private property is tertiary: the prohibition against eating from God's tree. Then comes cursed scarcity: the curse of the ground. Finally comes economic growth: the expansion of the kingdom of God, which is visible in the comparative wealth of nations.

Smith's decision to begin with scarcity was also a strategic error. Because Smith did not place private property before scarcity, defending it theologically, morally, and legally, he weakened his theoretical case for the free market. He made a very weak defense of private property. Nineteenth-century socialists therefore had a far easier time evading and denying the implications of free market economics, since free market economists, following Smith's lead, failed to establish the moral case for private ownership.

Socialists were able to occupy the moral high ground when presenting their case against private property. It was not very high ground, but it was the highest ground occupied in the economic debates of the nineteenth century. This appeal to morality made their case against the free market more compelling in their highly moralistic era.[22] It took over a century and a half for academic economists to develop a theoretical framework to explain the comprehensive implications of private property.[23] Even here, their defenses have rarely relied on an appeal to morality. They prefer defenses that rest on arguments for efficiency.

The Bible teaches that the economic curses can be overcome by economic growth. But this growth is not autonomous. It comes in response to the establishment of a particular kind of social order: the private property order.

---

22. Karl Marx was an exception. He did not invoke moral arguments. He regarded all morality as class morality: implements of class warfare. He dismissed morality as pertaining to society's superstructure. He regarded the mode of production as the real foundation of society. He had contempt for those he labeled utopian socialists, who preached a "new social gospel." Marx and Engels, *Manifesto of the Communist Party* (1848), Section III.

23. Tom Bethell, *The Noblest Triumph: Property and Prosperity Through the Ages* (New York: St. Martin's, 1998), ch. 7.

Chapter 5

Overcoming the Economic Constraints on Man

A good person leaves an inheritance to his grandchildren,
And the wealth of a sinner is stored up for the righteous.

Proverbs 13:22

Analysis

Point five of the biblical covenant is succession.[1] In economics, this is inheritance.

The dominion covenant established the general responsibility of mankind as a species. God told mankind to multiply. This is an aspect of extending man's jurisdiction: an aspect of kingdom-building. This means extending man's judicial boundaries. Boundaries are point three of the biblical covenant. "Then God said, 'Let Us make mankind in Our image, according to Our likeness; and let them rule over the fish of the sea and over the birds of the sky and over the livestock and over all the earth, and over every crawling thing that crawls on the earth.' So God created man in His own image, in the image of God He created him; male and female He created them. God blessed them; and God said to them, 'Be fruitful and multiply, and fill the earth, and subdue it;

1. Ray R. Sutton, *That You May Prosper: Dominion By Covenant*, 2nd ed. (Tyler, Texas: Institute for Christian Economics, [1987] 1992), ch. 5.

and rule over the fish of the sea and over the birds of the sky and over every living thing that moves on the earth'" (Gen. 1:26–28).[2]

Part of this requirement is biological: population growth. Part of it is ecological: administering the animal and vegetable worlds. With this responsibility comes the means of achieving the ends. *There is no covenantal responsibility without ability*. So, we know that it was possible for mankind to fulfill this requirement, had mankind's covenantal representatives not rebelled against God. Because this assignment was given again to Noah (Gen. 9:1–3),[3] we know that the means of fulfilling it are available, despite the biological and ecological curses of Gen. 3:17–19.[4]

Ever since the rebellion of Satan, there have been two kingdoms in conflict: the kingdom of God and the kingdom of Satan. Men must choose which covenantal order in which they will serve. There is no neutrality. They must join one or the other. Jesus said: "No man can serve two masters: for either he will hate the one, and love the other; or else he will hold to the one, and despise the other. Ye cannot serve God and mammon" (Matt. 6:24, KJV). Mammon offers man a promise: "More for me in history."[5] So does God. "But seek first His kingdom and His righteousness, and all these things will be provided to you" (Matt. 6:33).[6] The difference between these promises is three-fold: (1) mammon offers only temporal blessings; (2) God offers eternal blessings as well; (3) the blessings of God's kingdom are secondary sanctions for success in seeking the kingdom of God. That is, the kingdom of God is central; the blessings are given to confirm the covenant (Deut. 8:17–18),[7] to motivate people to serve God, and to provide capital for further extending God's kingdom. To whom much is given, much is expected (Luke 12:47–48).[8]

---

2. Gary North, *Sovereignty & Dominion: An Economic Commentary on Genesis* (Moulton, Alabama: Axehead Press, [1982, 2012] 2022), chaps. 3, 4.

3. Ibid., ch. 18.

4. Ibid., ch. 12.

5. Gary North, *Priorities & Dominion: An Economic Commentary on Matthew* (Moulton, Alabama: Axehead Press, [2012] 2030), ch. 14.

6. Ibid., ch. 15.

7. Gary North, *Inheritance & Dominion: An Economic Commentary on Deuteronomy* (Moulton, Alabama: Axehead Press, [1999, 2012] 2028), ch. 22.

8. Gary North, *Treasure & Dominion: An Economic Commentary on Luke* (Moulton, Alabama: Axehead Press, [2012] 2031), ch. 28.

The emphasis in the Bible is on production. It takes production beyond one's immediate needs to extend the kingdom of God. It therefore takes thrift. *Consumption is presented in the Bible as a secondary goal.* It is a motivation to serve God. It is also a means to a greater end: to demonstrate in the sight of men that God is faithful to the laws of His covenant, which are reliable.

> "See, I have taught you statutes and judgments just as the LORD my God commanded me, that you are to do these things in the land where you are entering to take possession of it. So keep and do them, for that is your wisdom and your understanding in the sight of the peoples who will hear all these statutes and say, 'Surely this great nation is a wise and understanding people.' For what great nation is there that has a god so near to it as is the LORD our God whenever we call on Him? Or what great nation is there that has statutes and judgments as righteous as this whole Law which I am setting before you today?" (Deut. 4:5–8)[9]

A. Purpose

Point one: God's sovereignty. The creation week is the primary model for human creativity. God spoke the world into existence in a sequence of days. He was implementing a plan. But behind the plan was a purpose. We know that God looked forward to redemption. The key phrase is this: "before the foundation of the world."

> Blessed be the God and Father of our Lord Jesus Christ, who has blessed us with every spiritual blessing in the heavenly places in Christ, just as He chose us in Him before the foundation of the world, that we would be holy and blameless before Him. In love He predestined us to adoption as sons and daughters through Jesus Christ to Himself, according to the good pleasure of His will, to the praise of the glory of His grace, with which He favored us in the Beloved. (Eph. 1:3–6)

The creation was an extension of purpose. This is man's operational model. There is no escape from it. Man is made in God's image. Purpose reflects a person's understanding of his role in the world. Cove-

9. North, *Inheritance & Dominion*, ch. 8.

nant-keepers are concerned with life beyond the grave. They see what they do in history as affecting their lives beyond the grave. A tiny handful of Christians are postmillennial. They view history as leading up to the defeat of Satan's kingdom. There will be continuity between the final days of history and the final judgment, in which Satan is defeated.[10] They have a sense of destiny. Rival eschatologies, premillennialism and amillennialism, do not view the present era of the church as significantly improving the world prior to the second coming of Christ. They deny ethical and institutional continuity for society. They do not see God's kingdom as a civilization. I have discussed this in my book, *Millennialism and Social Theory* (1990).[11]

Optimism regarding the future is basic to entrepreneurship. Entrepreneurship extends beyond the quest for monetary profits. It extends to such questions as the calling: the most important thing you can do in which you would be most difficult to replace. It has to do with legacy. Will you be remembered? Why? This is the issue of personal destiny, which is always a question of destination.

People set goals. They have purposes that govern these goals. Action is purposeful. This was how Ludwig von Mises began his magnum opus, *Human Action* (1949). Before a person devises a specific plan, he has a goal. His plan reflects his goal. It is based on a concept of cause and effect. This relationship between goal and plan is true in every area of life, not just economics. Here is the rule: *purpose precedes planning.*

Overcoming the economic constraints on man begins with a purpose. Men must first believe in the possibility of systematically overcoming economic limits in their lives. Then the set this as a their purpose. This is basic to the Lord's prayer. "Give us this day our daily bread" (Matt. 6:11).[12] Covenant-keepers must pray in confidence of receiving a positive answer. "But if any of you lacks wisdom, let him ask of God,

---

10. The best introduction to postmillennial theology is David Chilton, *Paradise Restored: A Biblical Theology of Dominion* (Ft. Worth, Texas: Dominion Press, 1985). The most comprehensive presentation is Kenneth L. Gentry, *He Shall Have Dominion: A Postmillennial Eschatology* (Tyler, Texas: Institute for Christian Economics, 1992). For a detailed commentary on the Book of Revelation, see Chilton, *The Days of Vengeance* (Ft. Worth, Texas: Dominion Press, 1987).

11. Gary North, *Millennialism and Social Theory* (Moulton, Alabama: Axehead Press, [1990] 2030).

12. North, *Priorities & Dominion*, ch. 12:B.

who gives to all generously and without reproach, and it will be given to him. But he must ask in faith without any doubting, for the one who doubts is like the surf of the sea, driven and tossed by the wind. For that person ought not to expect that he will receive anything from the Lord, being a double-minded man, unstable in all his ways" (James 1:5–8).

What is the primary biblical purpose associated with increased wealth? Increased wealth is a visible affirmation of God's covenant in history. Beware of the lure of autonomy, God warned. "Otherwise, you may say in your heart, 'My power and the strength of my hand made me this wealth.' But you are to remember the LORD your God, for it is He who is giving you power to make wealth, in order to confirm His covenant which He swore to your fathers, as it is this day" (Deut. 8:17–18).[13]

Purposes guide economic planning. They are guided by some ethical system. There is no neutrality. They are guided by some concept of economic causation. Most people think that honesty is the best policy, in Ben Franklin's aphorism. They believe that righteousness eventually produces success. They do not believe that evil people are forever triumphant. They teach this to their children. This optimism is foundational to overcoming man's constraints. People believe that they are more likely to be successful by seeking righteousness than by seeking evil. They believe in ethical causation, including economics. They see their purpose in life as extending righteousness, not evil. This gives them confidence in the future. This future-orientation is basic to entrepreneurship.

B. Planning

Point two: hierarchy. God is over man. Man is over nature (Gen. 1:26–28). The Bible begins with an affirmation of the Creator/creature distinction. God started on day one with nothing except His own being. "In the beginning God created the heavens and the earth" (Gen. 1:1).[14] Then, day by day, He added new resources by speaking them into existence. Combined with the resources of the previous days, these

13. North, *Inheritance & Dominion*, chaps. 21, 22.

14. North, *Sovereignty & Dominion*, ch. 1.

new phenomena became capital. This capital is to be used by man to increase his productivity as a steward of God.

1. *Value-Added Production*

Insofar as man reflects God in the creation week, he is re-creative. He manifests this creativity through production: increasing the supply of valuable goods and services. The essence of this activity can be described as value-added. Adam started with something morally perfect and not under a curse. He was required to make it better. Today, men start with something flawed and under a curse. They are required to make it better.

During the creation week, God conserved what He had made the previous day. Then He added more, integrating it with what was already in existence. *Original creativity took place in a context of preservation.* This is the nature of all progress: positive change within the context of stability. *Without stability as a means of comparison, there is no measure of progress.* Randomness would rule. Instead of the creation week, God could have spoken the universe into existence in one sentence. Instead, He took time. That was not because He faced a trade-off between time and capital, as men do. He took time because He was establishing a pattern for man's week: six days of work and one day of rest. There was no surrender of something by God in order for Him to obtain something else. Over the first week, the economic value of God's capital increased daily. There was more of it, day by day. *More is better than less at the same price.* Finally, with the creation of man, God's image, the potential value of this capital base was made ready for continuous expansion.

God added value each day. He operated in terms of a hierarchy of values. There was temporal sequence in implementing these values, day by day. Here was the rule: *first things first.* He implemented His own decree. He added value because He acted consistently with His scale of values and His decree for that day's work. He then imputed value retroactively to His work, day by day: "It is good." He made this assessment in terms of the consistency of His work with His decree. He had achieved perfectly what He had decreed. He looked ahead in the morning, worked through the day, and evaluated in the evening. The process of adding value involves all five factors: purposes, standards, a plan, implementation, and evaluation. The value of the work depends on all five factors. *The process of adding value is inherently future-oriented.*

Man was (and is) the capstone of the creation. His creativity, not the raw material of the universe, is the most important created resource. This is because God is more important than the creation. So is His image—something that did not sit well with Satan, who presumably had been created, along with the other angels, shortly prior to man. The immensity of the universe is impressive, but not so impressive as man. *God's imputed meaning for mankind is of far greater value than lifeless matter.* Lifeless matter cannot impute either meaning or value. Man can and does. He does so as a delegated agent of God, thinking God's thoughts after Him in a creaturely fashion.

2. *Representation*

God is represented in history and eternity by man. Angels also represent God, but they are not agents of dominion. Mankind is. This means that men are required to accumulate wealth, including knowledge, on behalf of God. This is the meaning of stewardship. This is seen best in Jesus' parable of the talents (Matt. 25:14–30).[15] This is immediately followed by Jesus' description of the final judgment (Matt. 25:31–46).

Productivity is mandated by God. Men must be productive because this is part of the dominion covenant. *One of the greatest errors of all humanistic economic theory is to regard labor as a net liability.* Specific kinds of labor must be paid for, but labor as such is basic to man. The built-in preference of man is to labor, to be productive. This is why children imitate their parents' work. *Leisure is not man's default preference. Production is.* It is part of the nature of man because it was God's original design for man. We hear this phrase: "I would do this for free if I had to." This is not economically irrational. Labor is cursed because man rebelled. But leisure is also cursed.

3. *Specialization*

Individuals vary. Each person has a specific set of gifts. The doctrine of specialization is taught clearly in Romans 12 and I Corinthians 12: the

15. North, *Priorities & Dominion*, ch. 47.

church is made up of members. Paul used the metaphor of the human body to describe the church. The family is also based on the division of labor. A woman was given to man. She was "fit" for him, meaning designed to complement his work. This reflects the doctrine of the Trinity. The doctrine of the Trinity is two-fold: (1) ontological Trinity, meaning the equality of the persons of the Godhead; (2) economic Trinity, meaning a hierarchy of authority. God the Father is over God the Son in terms of function. The Holy Ghost is under both: "who proceedeth from the Father and the Son."[16] There are differences of function.

Specialization requires economic cooperation. Without cooperation, output per person is minimal. The special gifts of each individual are not able to flourish under such autarky. In the division of labor economy, each person has tasks that he is required to perform as part of a contract of one kind or other, either formal or informal. The more that the division of labor extends, the more that these tasks are spelled out in contracts. The *less personal* the cooperation, the *more formal* these arrangements must become. These arrangements set forth the stipulations of the production process. These are formally enforceable agreements.

4. *Imputation*

This process of imputation is mankind's analogical equivalent of God, who pronounced judgment on His own work at the end of five of the six days of creation. God had a plan. He implemented this plan, day by day. Then He ratified His plan, day by day. This was the exercise of judgment. It was an exercise of evaluation.

We act in the present to deal with our expectations regarding an unknown future. There is no escape from our limited knowledge. We are finite. We are also under a curse, which will someday be removed. "For now we see in a mirror dimly, but then face to face; now I know in part, but then I will know fully, just as I also have been fully known" (I Cor. 13:12). Our productivity begins in the present, based on an

16. This confession is known as the filioque. It marks Western Christianity. Eastern Orthodoxy rejects it. See R. J. Rushdoony, *The Foundations of Social Order: Studies in the Creeds and Councils of the Early Church*, 3rd ed. (Vallecito, California: Ross House, [1968] 1998), ch. 11.

inheritance from the past, to be achieved in the future. The outcome is dependent on the resource inputs, but the economic value of the outcome is dependent on the imputations and decisions of others: buyers. This is consistent with the creation week. "And God saw all that He had made, and behold, it was very good. And there was evening and there was morning, the sixth day" (Gen. 1:31).[17]

Individuals impute economic value to scarce resources. This act of imputation became the cornerstone of the Austrian School of economics with the publication of the book by Carl Menger of the University of Vienna, *Principles of Economics* (1871). Menger argued that economic value does not come from inputs, whether labor or raw materials. Economic value is imputed by consumers, meaning final customers. Their competing bids in an open market establish final prices. These final prices ratify or thwart the output decisions made by producers. Prices in the production process are the result of entrepreneurs who forecast future prices. Then they buy production goods in order to produce final output. Some of these people reap profits. Others reap losses. The production process is future-oriented.

5. *Future-orientation*

God looked to the future during the week of creation. He looked toward the sixth day, when He would make man. This element of future-orientation is important for our understanding of the meaning of the creation. God's plans for the future, as revealed by His words, were central He created the stars on day four so that as-yet uncreated mankind could measure the seasons (Gen. 1:14–16). In other words, the creation sequence was purposeful.[18] Theologians and philosophers call this *teleology*. The essence of Darwinism is its anti-teleological interpretation of the origin of the cosmos.[19]

Successful plans must offer a sequence of appropriate steps. Because production takes place over time, it consumes time. *Time is not a zero-price resource.*[20] We must allocate it: doing one thing rather than

17. North, *Sovereignty & Dominion*, ch. 5.
18. Ibid., ch. 2.
19. Ibid., Appendix A: "From Cosmic Purposelessness to Humanistic Sovereignty."
20. Ibid., ch. 11.

another. We must therefore pay for it by forfeiting the possible benefits from doing the other thing. *Time is the only purely irreplaceable resource in history*. Time does not run back.

C. Cooperation

Point three: ethics. This is related to law. Law is God's means of restraining human evil. This is crucial for the division of labor. Men must cooperate if they are to overcome cursed scarcity. To pursue their goals, they need the cooperation of others. They all pursue their own plans. How can these individual plans mesh?

Planning is both individual and corporate. This is true for God: "Let us." It is also true of mankind. The production process requires a feedback system to reconcile plans rationally and voluntarily. It must therefore reconcile competing goals and values. There must be *agreement* before the plan is completed. There must also be *continuing plan reconciliation* while the plan is implemented. There must be *feedback* from the production process to decision-makers. There must then be plan reconciliation among these decision-makers. This is an aspect of private property. Men have rights of ownership. This means that they have the right to disown property: exchange. They have the right to exclude others. They also have the right to transfer ownership's right to exclude. This is the free market's means of increasing production.

In every cooperative venture, decision-makers have plans regarding the future. They have a vision of a future they prefer. They imagine a future when that which they face today and will face tomorrow is over. How will they like the result? These plans rarely mesh. So, in order to see to it that they do mesh, there must be plan reconciliation.

The most famous example in the Bible of plan reconciliation is the case of Joseph and his brethren. They initially wanted to kill him. Reuben intervened to save him (Gen. 37:21–22). They revised their plans. They sold him to a passing caravan. He was sold into slavery in Egypt, where he prospered under Potiphar. Then Potiphar changed his plans. He had Joseph cast into prison. Joseph prospered, running the prison. Then the head of the prison had to revise his plans when Joseph was elevated to second in command in Egypt. Joseph persuaded Pharaoh to change his plans: store up grain for seven years. Then famine struck the entire region, including Canaan. His brothers had to revise their plans. They came to Egypt to buy food. Joseph initially tricked them by concealing his identity. Later, he revealed himself. Next, he brought his family into Egypt. This was a major plan revision on Jacob's part. Next, his father died, and the brothers expected him to kill them. Only then did he identify God as the great reconciler. "As for you, you meant evil against me, but God meant it for good in order to bring about this present result, to keep many people alive" (Gen. 50:20). The numerous plan revisions in this story were part of a comprehensive plan of God, which was not revised.

The archetype of irreconcilable plans is the conflict between Moses and Pharaoh.[21] It took ten plagues to change Pharaoh's mind and let the Israelites go, but his mind did not stay changed very long. He perished in the Red Sea with his chariots. The matter was settled by violence: God's. This reflected the ultimate irreconcilable plans: God's and Satan's. God's plans are sovereign. Satan's are not.

Here is *the supreme practical question* for all social theory: "Is there a system of predictable plan reconciliation that does not rely on either love, which is in very limited supply, or violence, which most people wish were in very limited supply?" The answer is provided by economic theory: *voluntary exchange*. This answer is an aspect of the social division of labor. People have varying values, goals, and abilities. Sometimes these are in conflict. People also have wide variations of knowledge regarding specific facts and their relationships. To motivate some people to participate in the planning process and others in the plan-implementation process, the economic system must reward cooperation.

What is needed is a system of *mutual feedback* between buyers and sellers, i.e, economic sanctions (point four). This feedback process must convey accurate information to all of the participants. It must also supply motivation for people to respond appropriately to accurate information. It must do all this in a cost-effective manner.

---

21. Gary North, *Authority & Dominion: An Economic Commentary on Exodus*, vol. 1, *Part I: Representation & Dominion* (Moulton, Alabama: Axehead Press, [1985, 2012] 2025), ch. 1.

If the feedback system is to remain voluntary, it must be *self-reenforcing*. For the system to work, it must operate without extensive monitoring by officials who threaten negative sanctions against poor performers. It must operate in terms of criteria that have wide acceptance, thereby furthering self-government. *Self-government lowers society's enforcement costs*.

There is no reference in the Bible to the price system as an economy's primary feedback process (note: not a "mechanism"). This feedback process was first explained in detail by Adam Smith in *The Wealth of Nations* (1776). The Bible mandates the private property legal order through which the pricing system comes into existence through voluntary agreement. The feedback system of free pricing through competitive bidding—buyers vs. buyers, sellers vs. sellers—does its work in producing profits or losses, which serve as feedback indicators: positive and negative sanctions.

The profit-and-loss system is the tool of the discovery process. Those who want to buy some item can determine how scarce it is by looking at its price compared to other goods' prices. This discovery process was the basis of the incident between Elisha and the king of Israel during the siege by the Syrians. "So there was a severe famine in Samaria; and behold, they kept besieging it until a donkey's head was sold for eighty shekels of silver, and a fourth of a kab of dove's dung for five shekels of silver" (II Kings 6:25). The king wanted to know if he should attack the Syrians. Elisha had already told him not to attack, so he did not repeat himself. Instead, he made a prophecy in the form of a forecast. "Then Elisha said, "Listen to the word of the LORD; this is what the LORD says: 'About this time tomorrow a measure of fine flour will be sold for a shekel, and two measures of barley for a shekel, at the gate of Samaria'" (II Kings 7:1). This was his way of saying to wait, for the siege would not only be lifted the next day, but great stores of food would become available. This came to pass (II Kings 7:8). Prices adjusted the next day because people in the city discovered that the Syrians had departed, leaving their food behind.[22]

When prices change, people are encouraged to adjust their plans.

22. Gary North, *Disobedience & Defeat: An Economic Commentary on the Historical Books* (Moulton, Alabama: Axehead Press, [2012] 2029), ch. 26:C.

Price changes open up new opportunities and close old ones. Certainly, the departure of the Syrians opened up new opportunities for food buyers in Samaria. Their departure also closed old opportunities to sellers of food who had operated in a so-called seller's market the day before. Prices fell dramatically. The people of Israel did not know about Elijah's prophecy to the king the day before. If they had, and if the people had believed him, food prices would have begun to fall the day before in expectation of the coming deliverance. The people did not need to know about the previous day's prediction on the day of deliverance. The new array of opportunities was reflected in the new array of prices.

Price competition is a powerful tool of replacement. Producers can replace competitors by cutting sales prices. Buyers often switch allegiance in response to low prices. In the case of Joseph in Egypt, Pharaoh possessed stores of grain when famine struck. So great was the famine that Jacob could not afford to buy food locally in Canaan. So, he sent his sons to Egypt to buy food, where prices might be cheaper (Gen. 42). Local grain salesmen in Canaan lost Jacob's business to the Egyptian government.

D. Profit

Point four: sanctions. In any system of authority, there has to be accountability. This is why point two of the biblical covenant, authority, is closely associated with point four: judgment. There has to be a system of accounting in order for rulers and ruled to evaluate the performance of leaders. There must also be a system of accounting that lets all participants judge the performance of the institution. The model is God's final judgment. This is presented in Matthew 25. This chapter introduces the account of the final judgment with two parables: the parable of the ten virgins and their lamps, and the parable of the talents.

Jesus' parable of the talents tells the story of a rich man who prepared to go on a journey. He distributes money to each of three servants. He gives ten coins to one man, five to a second man, and one coin to a third. Then he leaves. When he returns, he demands an accounting. The man who had been given ten coins doubled the money. The man who had been given five coins doubled the money. The man who had been given one coin buried it. He handed it back. The rich man had made nothing, not even money that a banker would have paid. The two servants were given more money to work with. The third man was cast into outer darkness. What about his coin? "'Therefore: take the talent away from him, and give it to the one who has the ten talents.' For to everyone who has, more shall be given, and he will have an abundance; but from the one who does not have, even what he does have shall be taken away. And throw the worthless slave into the outer darkness; in that place there will be weeping and gnashing of teeth" (Matt. 25:28–30).

This parable is easy to understand. It deals with money. The owner judged performance exclusively in terms of money delegated and money returned. But Jesus' listeners were not fools. They understood that this parable was about lives lived, not money invested. Parables are meant to be simple. Money is easy to understand.

Double-entry bookkeeping was one of the greatest inventions of all time. This was in the mid-1300s. It allowed businessmen to identify more precisely where their money went and what brought money in. The accuracy of accounting made it easier to assess the performance of businesses. This reduced waste. It made businesses more successful. It allowed businessmen to determine what was working. "Do more like this." It allowed them to determine what was not working. "Stop doing this." This increased profits and reduced losses. It conserved capital.

Accounting techniques and their interpretation enable modern businessmen to make more rapid assessments of past performance. They make profits by predicting accurately the financial effects of future economic conditions on the business. Modern accounting enables them to evaluate the success of their forecasts and the implementation of their plans, which they made in terms of net revenues. They require this information. They need this to assess retroactively the success of their plans. This helps them plan for the future. It allows those in authority to hire and fire managers more profitably. That was the message of the parable of the talents.

Jesus told His disciples that all men are unprofitable servants. "Now which of you, having a slave plowing or tending sheep, will say to him after he comes in from the field, 'Come immediately and recline at the table to eat'? On the contrary, will he not say to him, 'Prepare something for me to eat, and properly clothe yourself and serve me while I eat and drink; and afterward you may eat and drink'? He does not thank the slave because he did the things which were commanded, does he? So you too, when you do all the things which were commanded you, say, 'We are unworthy slaves; we have done only that which we ought to have done'" (Luke 17:7–10).[23] This was His way of issuing a warning: people need the soul-saving special grace of God in order to escape the lake of fire after the final judgment (Rev. 20:14–15). If they rely on their own productivity to buy their way into heaven, they are doomed.

E. Accumulation

Point five: succession. Deuteronomy 28:1–14 describes the blessings of God in response to covenantal faithfulness. The passage includes economic output. What is the requirement of covenantal faithfulness? Acknowledgment of God as the source of wealth. "But you are to remember the LORD your God, for it is He who is giving you power to make wealth, in order to confirm His covenant which He swore to your fathers, as it is this day" (Deut. 8:18).[24] This acknowledgment must be manifested in word. "Know therefore that the LORD your God, He is God, the faithful God, who keeps His covenant and His faithfulness to a thousand generations for those who love Him and keep His commandments" (Deut. 7:9).

1. *Labor*

What are the Bible's rules for increasing output? One is to work six days a week. Its companion rule is one day of rest per week. "For six days you shall labor and do all your work, but the seventh day is a Sabbath of the LORD your God; on it you shall not do any work, you, or your son, or your daughter, your male slave or your female slave, or your cattle, or your resident who stays with you" (Ex. 20:9–10).[25]

23. Gary North, *Treasure & Dominion*, ch. 41.
24. North, *Inheritance & Dominion*, ch. 23.
25. North, *Authority & Dominion*, ch. 24.

Work is basic to success. Without it, poverty comes. "How long will you lie down, you lazy one? When will you arise from your sleep? 'A little sleep, a little slumber, A little folding of the hands to rest,' Then your poverty will come in like a drifter, And your need like an armed man" (Prov. 6:9–11).[26] The Book of Proverbs returns to this theme again and again.

2. *Land*

The kingdom of God is geographical. It must be extended. This is a call to accumulate real estate. This is the second rule of expansion. God told Abram: "Arise, walk about in the land through its length and width; for I will give it to you" (Gen. 13:17). Ownership of land in safety is one of God's greatest blessings. "Instead, each of them will sit under his vine And under his fig tree, With no one to make them afraid, Because the mouth of the LORD of armies has spoken" (Mic. 4:4). The Mosaic law announced: "Behold, to the LORD your God belong heaven and the highest heavens, the earth and all that is in it" (Deut. 10:14).[27] The psalmist clarified the nature of the delegation. "The heavens are the heavens of the LORD, But the earth He has given to the sons of mankind" (Ps. 115:16). Covenant-keepers are assigned the task of occupying the land as a way to manifest the comprehensive ownership of all things by God.

3. *Capital*

Capital is the product of land plus labor over time.[28] It is the product of thrift. Thrift is rarely mentioned in the Bible. Thrift is at the center of the proverb about the ant. "Go to the ant, you lazy one, Observe its ways and be wise, Which, having no chief, Officer, or ruler, Prepares its food in the summer And gathers its provision in the harvest" (Prov. 6:6–8).[29] We intuit this in the law of the sabbatical year's rest of the ground. "For six years you shall sow your field, and for six years you shall

---

26. Gary North, *Wisdom & Dominion: An Economic Commentary on Proverbs* (Moulton, Alabama: Axehead Press, [2012] 2029), ch. 12:A; ch. 74, Conclusion.

27. North, *Inheritance & Dominion*, ch. 26.

28. Murray N. Rothbard, *Man, Economy, and State: A Treatise on Economic Principles*, 2nd ed. (Auburn, Alabama: Mises Institute, [1962] 2009), 58, 373.

29. North, *Wisdom & Dominion*, ch. 12.

prune your vineyard and gather in its produce, but during the seventh year the land shall have a Sabbath rest, a Sabbath to the LORD; you shall not sow your field nor prune your vineyard" (Lev. 25:3–4).[30] This law implicitly mandated thrift for six years in order to eat in the seventh. The requirement of consuming less than what you produce was built into the Mosaic land laws. This law was also part of a system of fallow ground, which was an important means of preserving the land's fertility.

Jesus spoke of the present sacrifice of wheat for the sake of future output. "Truly, truly I say to you, unless a grain of wheat falls into the earth and dies, it remains alone; but if it dies, it bears much fruit" (John 12:24). Any agricultural society understands this principle: deferred gratification. There must be thrift—forfeited present consumption—in order to gain increased future output. *To eat your seed corn is to sacrifice your future.* Jesus' warning regarding the rich man who accumulated wealth points to the means of producing increased output: capital formation—in this case, barns. Without barns, agricultural produce is wasted.

> And He told them a parable, saying, "The land of a rich man was very productive. And he began thinking to himself, saying, 'What shall I do, since I have no place to store my crops?' And he said, 'This is what I will do: I will tear down my barns and build larger ones, and I will store all my grain and my goods there. And I will say to myself, "You have many goods stored up for many years to come; relax, eat, drink, and enjoy yourself!"' But God said to him, 'You fool! This very night your soul is demanded of you; and as for all that you have prepared, who will own it now?' Such is the one who stores up treasure for himself, and is not rich in relation to God." (Luke 12:16–21)[31]

Capital formation also includes lending, meaning credit expansion through thrift.

> "The LORD will open for you His good storehouse, the heavens, to give rain to your land in its season and to bless every work of your hand; and you will lend to many nations, but you will not borrow." (Deut. 28:12)[32]

30. Gary North, *Boundaries & Dominion: An Economic Commentary on Leviticus* (Moulton, Alabama: Axehead Press, [1994, 2012] 2026), ch. 24.

31. Gary North, *Treasure & Dominion: An Economic Commentary on Luke* (Moulton, Alabama: Axehead Press, [2012] 2031), ch. 25.

32. North, *Inheritance & Dominion*, ch. 70.

Tools are crucial for economic growth. Tools increase our productivity. Someone has to save to pay for tools. Future-oriented people own more tools and more profitable tools than present-oriented people do.

We have seen the effects of capital accumulation ever since 1800. Except in major wars, the West has not suffered poverty, biblically defined. It takes historical imagination for modern men even to empathize with poverty, biblically defined. The last Western famine was the Irish potato famine of the mid-1840s, when a million people starved or died from famine-related diseases, and a million emigrated, out of a population of 8 million. The best summary of modern poverty was made in the early 1930s by America's greatest humorist, Will Rogers. This was during the last worldwide economic depression. He quipped: "America is the first nation to go to the poorhouse in an automobile."

Beginning in the late eighteenth century in England and the United States, poverty as described in the Bible began to recede. For reasons still unknown, slow, steady economic growth began. London in 1850 did not resemble London in 1800. By 1900, electricity, the internal combustion engine, and cheap oil had begun a transformation of the West that changed everything by 1950. The memory of 1950 remains, if only through television re-runs. Modern men could adjust to 1950. They could not easily adjust to 1900 unless they were very rich, and even then, they would be uncomfortable. Think "air conditioning."

There is still poverty in the West,[33] but it is comparative. It is not absolute, e.g., the threat of starvation. Rather, it is the threat of not having medical insurance, which tens of millions of Americans do not have. Yet, even in this case, the lack of health insurance by the poor means waiting in an emergency room of a hospital for free care. It probably does not mean death. The West has overcome poverty, which existed in familiar forms from pharaonic Egypt until 1800.

---

33. There is one exception: the island nation of Haiti. It is the only nation in the West that has voodoo as its main religion. The economic contrast between Haiti and the Dominical Republic on the other half of the island is the word's best example of the contrast between Christianity and occultism.

Conclusion

God's fundamental command to mankind is to subdue the earth to the glory of God. This establishes man's purpose. But purpose must be implemented by a plan. The plan is governed by economic law. This economic law is inherently ethical. This means using God's rules as our primary tools of dominion. Conclusion: economic theory is not value-free. It is ethical.

In a world of cursed scarcity (Gen. 3:17–19),[34] this means that men must cooperate in the production process. There must be a division of labor. There must also be capital formation: the creation of tools. This requires thrift: greater output than consumption. This places production, not consumption, at the center of economic life.

Production, not consumption, is central because God is sovereign. He is the cosmic Owner. Men are required to serve God. They are subordinate to God. They are required to place God's interests first. They are to consume only after they have served God by transferring to Him what is owed: the tithe. What is true of our dealings with subordinates is also true of God's dealings with us: "Now which of you, having a slave plowing or tending sheep, will say to him after he comes in from the field, 'Come immediately and recline at the table to eat'? On the contrary, will he not say to him, 'Prepare something for me to eat, and properly clothe yourself and serve me while I eat and drink; and afterward you may eat and drink'? He does not thank the slave because he did the things which were commanded, does he? So you too, when you do all the things which were commanded you, say, 'We are unworthy slaves; we have done only that which we ought to have done'" (Luke 17:7–8).

Free market economists, from Adam Smith to modern academic economists, place personal consumption at the center of their economic analysis: individual self-interest. This is because they adhere to the principle of buyer's sovereignty. But the buyer is not sovereign. He is merely an intermediary in God's hierarchy. God is sovereign. A man must first master production in order to be a independent buyer. Without production, he will die unless he is supported by the production of others.

---

34. North, *Sovereignty & Dominion*, ch. 12.

A consistent covenant-keeper lives to work. Work is the goal. Life on cursed earth is not. Paul wrote: "But I am hard-pressed from both directions, having the desire to depart and be with Christ, for that is very much better; yet to remain on in the flesh is more necessary for your sakes" (Phil. 1:23–24). Service to God through service to others is the biblical structure of economic hierarchy. This means that *consumable wealth is a success indicator of profitable service*. To the extent that consumption becomes a person's goal of production rather than merely a success indicator, he has replaced God with mammon in his covenantal structure: "More for me in history."

Man is constrained by his finitude. This means that economic theory is inescapable. There is a universal desire to own more at the same price, either to consume or to conserve. Men cannot create something out of nothing. They are not God. So, they must have purposes: ends. They must also have means, including plans. Man was not created to evolve into God. Man is also constrained by God's curse of man and the ground in response to man's rebellion. The supreme curse is death. That was God's threat from the beginning (Gen. 2:17).

There is economic progress in history. We are told to pray for this: "Give us this day our daily bread" (Matt. 6:11).[35] We should also work for this.

---

35. North, *Priorities & Dominion*, ch. 12.

Conclusion to Part I

The structure of economic theory reflects the structure of God's covenants with mankind. To the degree that economic theory departs from the structure of the biblical covenant model, it will produce erroneous results.

The fundamental covenant is the dominion covenant: "Then God said, 'Let Us make mankind in Our image, according to Our likeness; and let them rule over the fish of the sea and over the birds of the sky and over the livestock and over all the earth, and over every crawling thing that crawls on the earth.' So God created man in His own image, in the image of God He created him; male and female He created them. God blessed them; and God said to them, 'Be fruitful and multiply, and fill the earth, and subdue it; and rule over the fish of the sea and over the birds of the sky and over every living thing that moves on the earth'" (Gen. 1:26–28).[1] This general covenant defines mankind and the earth, which is under man's authority. This covenant is implemented by means of four subordinate covenants: individual, family, ecclesiastical, and civil.

Economic theory must correspond to these four subordinate covenants. If it does not, then it is wrong. Nevertheless, there are degrees of error. Some non-covenantal economic theories are closer to the biblical covenant model than others. Economists who adopt these comparatively superior theories can and do make important insights into the way the world works. But, at bottom, the rival economic theories provide accurate insights only to the extent that the economists do not apply them comprehensively. None of these systems begins with God's creation of the universe out of nothing. None of them accepts the gen-

---

1. Gary North, *Sovereignty & Dominion: An Economic Commentary on Genesis* (Moulton, Alabama: Axehead Press, [1982, 2012] 2022), chaps. 3, 4.

eral dominion covenant and the four subordinate covenants. None of them accepts the doctrine of the Trinity: the ontological Trinity (the equality of being of the three Persons) and the economic Trinity (their hierarchy of function). So, to the extent that economists come up with accurate insights, they do so only by being inconsistent with their fundamental presupposition: the autonomy of both man and the cosmos from the Trinitarian God of the Bible.

The five-point biblical covenant has specific applications in economic practice and therefore economic theory. First, the sovereignty of God establishes God as the cosmic Owner of the creation. He alone is absolutely sovereign. Second, the dominion covenant establishes a system of hierarchical authority under God: trusteeship. Man is responsible upward to God, downward to the creation, outward to other men, and inward. Third, the doctrine of God's Bible-revealed law establishes the principle of private property. This leads to voluntary exchange of ownership claims: the right to disown property. Fourth, this in turn leads to numerical accounting through money prices. This makes possible a system of profit and loss. Fifth, covenantal inheritance produces inter-generational compound economic growth.

There are two separate aspects of God's delegated economic responsibility to men: guardianship (judicial) and stewardship (economic). First, there is the judicial aspect. This refers to God.

1. God owns everything.
2. God delegates ownership.
3. God prohibits theft.
4. God evaluates performance.
5. God mandates growth.

Second, there is the judicial aspect for men: trusteeship, i.e., guardianship.

1. Owners are trustees.
2. Trustees possess authority.
3. Trusts are binding.
4. Trustees are accountable.
5. Trustees designate successors.

Third, there are the implications of the economic responsibilities for man: stewardship.

1. Purpose precedes planning.
2. Priorities structure planning.
3. Ownership involves exclusion.
4. Owners evaluate performance.
5. Owners designate heirs.

Fourth, there are laws governing the world of scarcity. These are inescapable conditions in a world of scarcity, where, at zero price, there is greater demand than supply. These laws relate to the *creational limits* on what men can do with the assets that God entrusts to them. They are what we call the laws of economics. These are the fundamental laws of economics.

1. Owners adopt purposes.
2. Prices provide information.
3. People prefer more.
4. Scarcity imposes costs.
5. Growth reduces scarcity.

The details of this system of covenantal hierarchy must be worked out in terms of the separate covenants: individual, familial, ecclesiastical, and civil. Each has its lawful zone of delegated authority. Each has lawful claims on a portion of men's output. *Economic theory must not begin with the assumption of the autonomy of man.* This includes the doctrine of the autonomy of any one of man's covenantal administrations. To present economic theory as an exclusive outworking of any of these covenants as autonomous and therefore sovereign leads inescapably to an error: the dismissal of the others' lawful claims. Such an assumption justifies unlawful incursions into the delegated domains of God: trespassing. This was the sin of Adam and Eve. They violated God's property rights.

PART II

The Economic Structure of the Individual Covenant

Introduction to Part II

The dominion covenant is the general covenant for all mankind. It defines both the individual and collective mankind. It establishes God's relationship to individuals and to collectives. It defines man in history, and it defines man in eternity. In eternity, covenant-breakers are incapable of fulfilling any aspect of the dominion covenant, but it still defines them, and it still serves as a standard by which God imposes eternal negative sanctions. In eternity, covenant-keepers are capable of fulfilling the dominion covenant without being restricted by sin and its effects. This covenant defines them throughout eternity, and it governs their decision-making forever.

A. Individual Responsibility

The second covenant to consider is the individual covenant. Why not the family covenant? Why not the church covenant? Why not the civil covenant? The main theological reason for placing the individual covenant in the first position after the dominion covenant is because *the individual is made in the image of God*. The family is not, for it involves male and female. God is exclusively male. The church is not, for it also is both male and female. The state is not. Same reason. Because the individual is made in the image of God, responsibility lodges with the individual more than it does in the family, the church, and the state. *Responsibility is always primarily individual*. An individual may participate in a collective group in making a decision, but the individual's ultimate responsibility cannot be shifted to the group. Each person is judged by God in both history and eternity in terms of his or her thoughts, words, and deeds. Any attempt to shift primary responsibility away from the individual and toward a group violates this covenant principle. So, I begin to apply the dominion covenant to the individual covenant rather than another covenant.

There is another reason to place it second. This reason is more practical than theological. The individual covenant governs God's imposition of personal sanctions. It governs the judicial status of the individual: saved or lost. It therefore governs the eternal status of the individual: initially, heaven versus hell; then, after the resurrection and the final judgment, the new heavens and new earth (Rev. 21, 22) versus the lake of fire (Rev. 20:14–15). Because individuals in most situations respond to personal sanctions more strongly than any other kind of sanctions, the individual covenant follows the dominion covenant in terms of covenantal sequence. This is a matter of incentives, which is one of the fundamental teachings of all economic theory, namely, that *people respond to incentives.* They respond so predictably to incentives that economic theory enables an economist to make statistically relevant predictions about people's behavior in response to changing economic incentives.

Men's motivation is usually stronger with respect to the individual covenant than the others. The personal stakes are extremely high. This is why Paul's statement that he was willing to be cursed by Christ for the sake of his brethren in the flesh, the Jews (Rom. 9:3), is unique in history. There is nothing else to match this offer in recorded history. It is analogous to Jesus' decision to sacrifice His life on behalf of the world in general (common grace) and covenant-keepers specifically (special grace).[1]

There is a third reason: methodology. Modern free-market economic theory incorrectly begins with acting man. It should begin with the sovereign God who created acting man. *This is the fundamental difference between Christian economics and humanistic economics.* But, once this distinction is made clear to an aspiring Christian economist, it is time to move to individual analysis. Free-market economics correctly begins with the individual rather than the family or the state or the

1. Gary North, *Dominion and Common Grace: The Biblical Basis of Progress* (Moulton, Alabama: Axehead Press, [1987] 2024).

church as the primary locus of epistemology. By epistemology I mean this: "What can we know, and how can we know it?" We begin with the acting individual because this acting individual is made in the image of God, and also because he is most highly motivated by the quest for positive sanctions and the desire to avoid negative sanctions. To begin with a collective as the primary locus of our understanding of economics would be a major conceptual error.

In saying that free market economics begins with the individual, I am also saying that free market economics applies mainly to the market and the market process. When free market economists discuss families, churches (rare), and civil governments, their methodological tools become far less effective. This is why there is no developed theory of economics as it applies to the family and the church. Public choice economists have made some important discoveries regarding the interrelationships between individual motivation and civil authority, but there is no general economic theory of the state. There is also no economic theory of non-profit organizations. Mises claimed that he had devised a comprehensive theory of human action, but it applies only to the market, which he called catallactics. So, the scope of academic economics is a highly limited. Economic laws apply in very different ways in businesses, families, churches, and states. Regarding churches, states, and families, economists have very little to say. In matters familistic, economists sound more like sociologists than economists. Whenever they sound like economists, they usually sound silly. The more rigorous their theory, the sillier they sound.[2]

B. Adam Smith on Consumption

As soon as the issue of production arises, so does the issue of consumption. Adam Smith announced the central pillar of economic theory: human motivation. He placed individual self-interest, or *enlightened self-interest,* at the center of his economic analysis. This raises the

2. My favorite example is Gary S. Becker, A *Treatise on the Family,* 2nd ed. (Cambridge, Massachusetts: Harvard University Press, [1981] 1991). He won the Nobel Prize in economics in 1992.

question of the supreme motivation in economics. Smith said this is consumption.

> Consumption is the sole end and purpose of all production; and the interest of the producer ought to be attended to only so far as it may be necessary for promoting that of the consumer. The maxim is so perfectly self-evident that it would be absurd to attempt to prove it. But in the mercantile system the interest of the consumer is almost constantly sacrificed to that of the producer; and it seems to consider production, and not consumption, as the ultimate end and object of all industry and commerce.[3]

He was challenging the position of mercantilists, who argued in favor of producers' interests and the state's interests in preference to consumers' interests. He was opposing regulations imposed by the civil government.

> The laudable motive of all these regulations is to extend our own manufactures, not by their own improvement, but by the depression of those of all our neighbours, and by putting an end, as much as possible, to the troublesome competition of such odious and disagreeable rivals. Our master manufacturers think it reasonable that they themselves should have the monopoly of the ingenuity of all their countrymen. Though by restraining, in some trades, the number of apprentices which can be employed at one time, and by imposing the necessity of a long apprenticeship in all trades, they endeavour, all of them, to confine the knowledge of their respective employments to as small a number as possible; they are unwilling, however, that any part of this small number should go abroad to instruct foreigners.[4]

His distrust of producers was grounded in an accurate understanding of their motives. But in order to oppose their interests in getting such legislation passed, he grounded his entire theory on a statement that needed to be proven: *consumption is the sole end and purpose of all production*. These ten words have been adopted by virtually all free market economists ever since. His assertion—he offered no proof—is in direct conflict with Jesus' words: "But seek first His kingdom and His righ-

---

3. Adam Smith, *The Wealth of Nations* (1776), IV:VIII:49.
4. Ibid., IV:VIII:48.

teousness, and all these things will be provided to you" (Matt. 6:33).[5] To the extent that any defense of the free market as an institutional arrangement rests on the assumption that consumption is the sole end and purpose of production, to that extent it is wrong. It is the philosophical foundation of this: "'Come,' they say, 'let's get wine, and let's drink heavily of intoxicating drink; And tomorrow will be like today, only more so'" (Isa. 56:12). It is dead wrong—eternally dead wrong: "Then Death and Hades were thrown into the lake of fire. This is the second death, the lake of fire. And if anyone's name was not found written in the book of life, he was thrown into the lake of fire" (Rev. 20:14–15).

The heart of Christian economics—and every other academic discipline and practical organization—is the dominion covenant: the subduing of the earth on God's behalf (Gen. 1:26–28). *The heart of Christian economics is stewardship*. It calls for compound growth of the kingdom of God in history and eternity. Compound growth is based on thrift: reduced consumption. The other factor is successful entrepreneurship. Consumption is a reward for profitable service. Throughout most of human history, consumption was mainly a tool of production. It just barely kept people alive, so that they could fulfill their share of the dominion covenant. To the extent that consumption replaces production as a man's main lifetime goal, to that extent he has substituted himself for God. He has substituted the kingdom of man for the kingdom of God.

Christian civilization is *value-added* civilization. To add value, we must possess capital. To possess capital, we must save. We must not consume all of our income. But thrift is not to serve primarily as a means of greater future consumption. It is to serve primarily as a means of greater future production. It de-emphasizes leisure. Murray Rothbard summarized the difference between Roman Catholicism's view of leisure and Calvinism's.

> ...But there is, especially in the later Puritans, the idea of success in one's calling as a visible sign of being a member of the elect. The success is striven for, of course, not to *prove* that one is a member of the elect destined to be saved but, assuming that one is in the elect by virtue

5. Gary North, *Priorities & Dominion: An Economic Commentary on Matthew* (Moulton, Alabama: Axehead Press, [2012] 2030), ch. 15.

> of one's Calvinist faith, to strive to labour and succeed for the glory of God. A Calvinist emphasis on postponement of earthly gratification led to a particular stress on saving. Labour or 'industry' and thrift, almost for their own sake, or rather for God's sake, were emphasized in Calvinism much more than in the other segments of Christianity.
>
> The focus, then, both in Catholic countries and in scholastic thought, became very different from that of Calvinism. The scholastic focus was on consumption, the consumer, as the goal of labour and production. Labour was not so much a good in itself as a means toward consumption on the market. The Aristotelian balance, or golden mean, was considered a requisite of the good life, a life leading to happiness in keeping with the nature of man. And that balanced life emphasized the joys of consumption, as well as of leisure, in addition to the importance of productive effort. In contrast, a rather grim emphasis on work and on saving began to be stressed in Calvinist culture. This de-emphasis on leisure of course fitted with the iconoclasm that reached its height in Calvinism—the condemnation of the enjoyment of the senses as a means of expressing religious devotion.[6]

Rothbard was correct. This attitudinal difference between late-medieval Roman Catholicism and early modern Calvinism was grounded on rival views regarding epistemology: Aristotelianism vs. the Bible.

6. Murray N. Rothbard, *Economic Thought Before Adam Smith: An Austrian Perspective on the History of Economic Thought* (Auburn, Alabama: Mises Institute, [1995] 2006), 141.

Chapter 6

Ownership

"For every animal of the forest is Mine,
The cattle on a thousand hills."

Psalm 50:10

"Is it not lawful for me to do what I want with what is my own? Or is your eye envious because I am generous?"

Matthew 20:15

Analysis

Point one of the biblical covenant is the sovereignty of God.[1] With respect to economics, this is original ownership. As the Creator, God established His original ownership. He has delegated limited legal sovereignty to individuals and institutions to speak in God's name. He has also delegated limited ownership to individuals and institutions to act on God's behalf. This has made them legally responsible to Him. They are not autonomous, contrary to humanistic economic theory. Each individual acts as an economic agent of God, whether or not he acknowledges this. This is the message of the parable of the talents (Matt. 25:14–30).[2]

1. Ray R. Sutton, *That You May Prosper: Dominion By Covenant*, 2nd ed. (Tyler, Trxas: Institute for Christian Economics, [1987] 1992), ch. 1.

2. Gary North, *Priorities & Dominion: An Economic Commentary on Matthew* (Moul-

God had a goal before His creation of the world. The New Testament has a unique phrase regarding existence before history began: *before the foundation of the world*. "[J]ust as He chose us in Him before the foundation of the world, that we would be holy and blameless before Him" (Eph. 1:4a). "[B]ut with precious blood, as of a lamb unblemished and spotless, the blood of Christ. For He was foreknown before the foundation of the world, but has appeared in these last times for the sake of you" (I Pet. 1:19–20). He had a goal or a purpose for mankind and each individual before the foundation of the world. He also had a plan. These were consistent with each other. There were no loose ends. There was no element of surprise. God was not bounded by time. In contrast, men are not omniscient. We are bounded by time. So, our plans are extensions of our purposes. *Purpose precedes planning*. There is sequence in our plans.

A. Goals

Point one: God's sovereignty. This related to the creation week. Goal-setting precedes planning. The old line is this: "If you don't know where you're going, you won't know if you have arrived." You should have some idea of what you want to accomplish before you create a plan to achieve it. Goals are extensions of a person's worldview.

Goal-setting also involves imagination. Men are not digital creatures. We think visually. For effective goal-setting, people usually need to have a mental image to guide them. This is the origin of the New Age program known as *visualization*. People are asked to picture a new car or new home. They are told that this is the way to achieve their goals. This confuses cause and effect. The mental image is supposed to provide motivation, not causation. The mental image is a tool in producing a plan of action and then sticking to it. Think of a person who wants to lose weight. He may have a mental image of what he wants to look like. But this mental images is worthless if he spends his time imagining a thinner body while he is eating chips and bean dip. The image of a thinner self may motivate him. It will have no other effect. He would lose

ton, Alabama: Axehead Press, [2012] 2030), ch. 47.

the weight if he adopted a diet and exercise program, with or without the mental image. But the image may help him stick with the program.

For goal-setting to be effective, there has to be a plan that is consistent with the goals. Goal-setting is a useful success technique, but for it to work, there must be feedback. People must review their goals every few months in order to evaluate their progress. If they are falling behind, they must re-evaluate their program. The model for this is the creation week. God reviewed the quality of His output at the end of every day except day two. He pronounced judgment: good.

Goal-setting implies purpose. A goal is a specific end. We have lots of goals in life. But purpose is more inclusive. "What is life's purpose?" This is a common question. More specifically: "What is my purpose in life?" It is focused. People ask about their purpose: singular. They view their specific goals in life, or next year, in terms a primary purpose that they use to define themselves.

Ever since 1963, I have had a single defining purpose in life: to produce a systematic theory of Christian economics. I have had multiple goals related to this. One is book writing, production, and marketing. Another goal, ever since the development of YouTube in the early twenty-first century, is the production of teaching videos. These goals are extensions of my purpose in life.

I have had to do a lot of planning. These plans were extensions of my goals. The goals were extensions of my purpose. *Purpose precedes planning.*

Jesus announced the general purpose: "But seek first His kingdom and His righteousness, and all these things will be provided to you" (Matt. 6:33).[3] People's individual goals are supposed to be guided by, and structured by, this general purpose. This goal is not imposed by the market. It is imposed by God.

B. Planning

Point two: hierarchy. Planning is the task of entrepreneurship. It is closely related to accounting (point four). The planner begins with a

3. North, *Priorities & Dominion*, ch. 15.

series of goals. These are ranked hierarchically. He must now make an assessment of what it will take to achieve these goals with the resources he possesses. He has a limited number of resources. The task of allocating these scarce resources among competing uses, as both a consumer and a producer, is the heart of textbook economics.

A careful planner counts the cost of his plan. Jesus said. "For which one of you, when he wants to build a tower, does not first sit down and calculate the cost, to see if he has enough to complete it? Otherwise, when he has laid a foundation and is not able to finish, all who are watching it will begin to ridicule him, saying, 'This person began to build, and was not able to finish!' Or what king, when he sets out to meet another king in battle, will not first sit down and consider whether he is strong enough with ten thousand men to face the one coming against him with twenty thousand? Otherwise, while the other is still far away, he sends a delegation and requests terms of peace" (Luke 14:28–32).[4] This means counting the cost in the broadest sense. What will be the outcomes of the completion of the plan? This is not always clear to planners. In fact, it is almost never clear. There is a famous "law": *the law of unintended consequences*. Men are not omniscient. But God is. The coherence between God's plan and covenant-keepers' plans is greater than the coherence between God's plans and covenant-breakers' plans. Why? Paul put it this way: "For who has known the mind of the LORD, that he will instruct Him? But we have the mind of Christ" (I Cor. 2:16). Covenant-keepers have access to God's law. Psalm 119 is the longest passage in the Bible with a single theme. The theme is biblical law. Its message is this: men gain wisdom through meditation on God's law, which is a single unit. "I have seen a limit to all perfection; Your commandment is exceedingly broad. How I love Your Law! It is my meditation all the day. Your commandments make me wiser than my enemies, For they are ever mine. I have more insight than all my teachers, For Your testimonies are my meditation. I understand more than those who are old, Because I have complied with Your precepts" (Ps. 119:96–100).

Planning is an aspect of economic stewardship. Men own their assets as economic agents of God. This is the message of the parable of the talents

4. Gary North, *Treasure & Dominion: An Economic Commentary on Luke* (Moulton, Alabama: Axehead Press, [2012] 2031), ch. 35.

(Matt. 25:14–30). A rich man provides capital for his stewards to administer. Then he departs. Each of the stewards has a plan of action. Two are successful. One is not. There is economic responsibility upward to the owner. The stewards are not autonomous. But their responsibility is also outward: to customers. A planner has to keep them happy if he is to profit from selling to them. Then there is downward responsibility to all those under his economic authority, beginning with his household. Finally, there is responsibility inward: conscience and personal goals. Our plans should consider all of these responsibilities. The free market imposes these responsibilities. Monetary profit-and-loss statements govern the planner in the marketplace. Other economic sanctions prevail in non-profit sectors.

C. Standards

Point three: ethics. An individual is a creature of law. He is under limits, ethical and physical. He is not omnipotent. He is not autonomous: *autos* (self) *nomos* (law). He is under God's law-order, both ethical and physical. So, when he considers his purpose in life, he must consider the means by which he can fulfill his purpose. The same applies to goal-setting. He should understand the nature of the limitations that constrain him.

At the same time, God's law helps him make sense of the world around him. If the world were random, he could not make effective plans. He could not implement these plans. The world is predictable to men in a way that it is not predictable to animals. That is because man is made in God's image. So, God's law is a source of liberation from the unpredictable effects of nature. It makes our world more predictable. We can be better stewards of God's resources if we understand God's law. Our understanding of predictable cause and effect in nature is a tool of production. Our understanding of ethical cause and effect is also a tool of production. But it is also a tool of consumption. It tells us what not to do with the resources we possess.

Law is a means to various ends. The ends are supposed to be an aspect of the general purpose of mankind: "But seek first His kingdom and His righteousness, and all these things will be provided to you" (Matt. 6:33). To fulfill this purpose, people must understand God's law and adhere to it. They must apply God's laws to their plans. If they refuse to do this, they are operating in terms of a false view of social causation: autonomous social and personal ethical law.

D. Judgment

Point four: sanctions. All law has sanctions. It is not good enough to know God's laws. We must also apply them to specific circumstances. This is the art of casuistry. James warned: "But prove yourselves doers of the word, and not just hearers who deceive themselves. For if anyone is a hearer of the word and not a doer, he is like a man who looks at his natural face in a mirror; for once he has looked at himself and gone away, he has immediately forgotten what kind of person he was. But one who has looked intently at the perfect law, the law of freedom, and has continued in it, not having become a forgetful hearer but an active doer, this person will be blessed in what he does" (James 1:22–25).

The ability to connect personal ethics and visible historical sanctions is necessary for adopting and then reaching God-pleasing goals in life. This connection is a matter of judgment. It is not innate. It is a developed skill. "Make me walk in the path of Your commandments, For I delight in it. Incline my heart to Your testimonies, And not to dishonest gain. Turn my eyes away from looking at what is worthless, And revive me in Your ways" (Ps. 119:35–37). If a person has only a minimal ability to judge his own actions in terms of ethical causation, then he will be hampered in pursuing any long-term purpose in life. His goals will be out of conformity to God's law. The results will not be what he had thought were appropriate in his life.

E. Legacy

Point five: succession. This is related to inheritance. A person hopes to be remembered favorably by a lot of people. Yet this is impossible for the vast majority. Hardly anyone is remembered by anyone outside his family as his peers die. The Internet is unique in history. It allows records of many people to be available indefinitely. But someone must search for a name. Who will do this a decade after a person's death?

God brings perfect judgment in history at the end of time. He does not forget. He imputes meaning to history as a whole and to every event. "But I tell you that for every careless word that people speak, they will give an account of it on the day of judgment" (Matt. 12:36). The final judgment will bring all things to light. God is omniscient.

What about in history? There is coherence to God's plan. Every event plays a part. Nothing is random. This means that covenant-keepers have hope. They can have confidence that their legacy will prevail through time.

This is an incentive to leave a legacy. This does not guarantee the positive impact of anyone's legacy, but it offers hope. Hope is a crucial motivation for identifying our purpose in life, and then identifying goals that are consistent with this purpose. There is coherence between God's overall plan (the one) and His plans for individuals (the many). He is a Trinity: both one and many.

Every legacy requires capital accumulation. This is capital in the broadest sense: tools of production. This is not just money. It is primarily worldview: a consistent doctrine of sovereignty, authority, law, sanctions, and the future. "Train up a child in the way he should go, Even when he grows older he will not abandon it" (Prov. 22:6). The transmission of this legacy down through the generations is mandatory. But to implement this takes wealth. Therefore, the Bible teaches this: "A good person leaves an inheritance to his grandchildren, And the wealth of a sinner is stored up for the righteous" (Prov. 13:22).[5] This is a goal. To attain a goal takes planning.

Conclusion

Each individual has been granted life. This is an act of grace on God's part. Life is a tool of production. Everyone is held accountable by God for what he achieves in life. There are standards of performance. There

---

5. Gary North, *Wisdom & Dominion: An Economic Commentary on Proverbs* (Moulton, Alabama: Axehead Press, [2012] 2029), ch. 41.

are sanctions in history. There is succession in history: the extension of a worldview.

Individual purpose is crucial for this world and the next. Purpose is what guides people in their forming of a plan for their lives, and then their pursuit of it. *Purpose precedes planning.* Without purpose, people pursue self-destructive paths. Jesus warned: "For what good will it do a person if he gains the whole world, but forfeits his soul? Or what will a person give in exchange for his soul?" (Matt. 16:26).[6] If a man's goal is centered on this world, he will lose his life in the next world. Mammon's creed is simple: "More for me in history." Jesus warned: "No man can serve two masters: for either he will hate the one, and love the other; or else he will hold to the one, and despise the other cannot serve God and mammon" (Matt. 6:24, KJV).[7]

6. North, *Priorities & Dominion*, ch. 35.
7. Ibid., ch. 14.

Chapter 7

Stewardship

"For it is just like a man about to go on a journey, who called his own slaves and entrusted his possessions to them. To one he gave five talents, to another, two, and to another, one, each according to his own ability; and he went on his journey. The one who had received the five talents immediately went and did business with them, and earned five more talents. In the same way the one who had received the two talents earned two more. But he who received the one talent went away and dug a hole in the ground, and hid his master's money. Now after a long time the master of those slaves came and settled accounts with them."

Matthew 25:14–19

Analysis

Point two of the biblical covenant is hierarchy.[1] In law, this is guardianship. In economics, this is stewardship. Each owner is a covenantal agent. The doctrine of the covenant is point two of the biblical covenant. The book of Exodus is said to be the book of the covenant. "Then he took the Book of the Covenant and read it as the people listened; and they said, 'All that the Lord has spoken we will do, and we will be obedient'" (Ex. 24:7). Exodus is the second book in the Pentateuch. *The individual's covenant under God is the legal basis of the Bible's sys-*

1. Ray R. Sutton, *That You May Prosper: Dominion By Covenant*, 2nd ed. (Tyler, Texas: Institute for Christian Economics, [1987] 1992), ch. 2.

tem of private property. An owner is a legally responsible agent because all of his legal authority originates in the covenant. This implies that *covenants possess original authority*. All contracts rest legally on covenantal authority.

Stewardship is the application in economic theory to point two of the biblical covenant: *representation*. Each individual acts as an economic agent of God. This is an application of the principle of the dominion covenant. Jesus used the parable of the talents to illustrate this hierarchical, representative system of ownership. God allocates assets. He holds the recipients accountable for the proper use of these assets (Matt. 25:14–30).[2] But the owner is also an economic agent of other people. He decides whether to sell an asset, keep it, rent it, or give it away. In many cases, the principle of *monetary high bid wins* applies. If an individual does not sell an asset, he thereby becomes the highest bidder for that asset. He outbids the second-highest bidder. He therefore forfeits the use of whatever amount of money the second-highest bidder bid.

There are three aspects of stewardship: guardianship (legal), sharecropping (economic), and auctioneering (economic). I will go though all three.

First, guardianship. Guardianship is judicial. A guardian has the legal authority to act *in the name of* an owner. He is under general legal rules regarding the use of an asset. He must always act legally in the name of the owner on behalf of the owner economically, even if his own interests are placed at risk. His primary task to act as a legal agent of the owner. This may involve economic management, but the guardian usually operates on a minimal percentage payment. His level of legal accountability is far greater than a sharecropper's.

Second, sharecropping. Sharecropping is less legal and more economic in nature. An owner of seeds, land, and tools hires someone to use these capital assets to plant a crop. The owner is guaranteed a percentage of this crop. The sharecropper keeps the rest. The owner establishes rules regarding the use of his capital. These rules are enforceable in a court of law. But because the sharecropper has no capital other than his reputation and labor, the owner is not in a strong position to

2. Gary North, *Priorities & Dominion: An Economic Commentary on Matthew* (Moulton, Alabama: Axehead Press, [2012] 2030), ch. 47.

collect restitution plus damages from a sharecropper who has violated the terms of the contract.

The sharecropper may be granted full authority to decide when to plant, when to harvest, and what to do in between. He exercises judgment regarding the best way to follow the rules. He also decides what to do when the rules are silent. The system operates on this assumption: *the self-interest of the sharecropper leads him to reduce his personal costs.* He keeps the difference between revenues and costs. He has an incentive to keep his personal costs down. This reduces the owner's costs of monitoring him, with this major exception: the sharecropper's misuse of the capital as a way to cut his costs.

Sharecropping is no longer common in the West. What other economic office is comparable? A franchise is not. That is because the person who is buying the franchise must invest his own money as a down payment. He must also borrow the money. He buys equity. The sharecropper owns no equity. He sells labor and management services: self-management.

A lease is not. A lessor offers a person a lease. The lessee promises to pay a fixed money price for the use of the property. He therefore bears most of the uncertainty. The owner knows what he will receive in payment. In contrast to the sharecropper, the lessee begins with an understanding of what he must produce in order to fulfill the terms of the lease. The sharecropper does not. The sharecropper knows what percentage of his crop he will surrender to the owner, but he is not required to produce a specified quantity in order to meet the terms of the contract. He bears less uncertainty than the lessee does. The owner of the capital bears greater uncertainty under a sharecropping arrangement than a leaseholder does.

The urban economic occupation that is closest to biblical stewardship is a commissioned salesman. As with a sharecropper, he receives no salary. He is given a sales contact list, just as a sharecropper is given seeds. He may be given the use of a car, just as the sharecropper is given the use of tools. A salesman, like a sharecropper, does not begin with capital of his own. He has only his skills, just as a sharecropper does. He does not guarantee the employer a rental price or other guarantee. He offers him only a percentage of his sales revenue. The boss has no sure return. He must participate in the successes and failures of his sales force. The uncertainty is shared by both the employer and the employee.

Third, auctioneering. An auctioneer acts economically on behalf of an owner. There is also a legal aspect. He is legally authorized by the owner to sell the goods. But the economic aspect is primary. His task is to sell the owner's assets at the highest prices available. To do this, he adopts a rule: *monetary high bid wins*. He advertises to attract potential buyers to a sale. At the auction, he offers items for sale, one at a time. He uses sales techniques to persuade potential buyers to bid against each other, thereby driving prices higher. To accomplish all this, he must be future-oriented. He must allocate money and time to marketing.

From the standpoint of economic analysis, the bidders are in charge of the auction process. This is because they own the most marketable commodity: money. If no bidders show up at the auction, the auctioneer has wasted his time and money. He is driven by the expectation of monetary profit. His forecast of the outcome of his efforts guides him. This means that the dual economic sanctions of monetary profit and loss guide him. He knows the outcome only retroactively. As a forecaster and then as a planner, he is an entrepreneur.

A. Sovereignty

Point one: God's sovereignty. God possesses absolute sovereignty. Yet He shares sovereignty through delegation. This was manifested in the original dominion covenant (Gen. 1:26–28).[3] This was re-confirmed with Noah (Gen. 9:1–3).[4] It was confirmed ontologically with the Incarnation of Jesus Christ, when God became a man. God has delegated limited sovereignty to man.

This could lead to a false conclusion: this delegation has depleted God of some of His sovereignty. Yet it is clear from such passages as Isaiah 45 and Romans 9 that God still retains full sovereignty. This sounds

3. Gary North, *Sovereignty & Dominion: An Economic Commentary on Genesis* (Moulton, Alabama: Axehead Press, [1982, 2012] 2022), chaps. 3, 4.

4. Ibid., ch. 18.

illogical. But consider another doctrine: the glory of God. Did God lack anything before the creation of the world? No. So, the creation did not add anything to God's glory. The creation did not make Him more glorious. You and I do not make God more glorious. This also sounds illogical. So, the creation added nothing to God's glory.[5] Therefore, by delegating limited sovereignty to man, who is part of the creation, God does not become a loser. That is because He did not become a winner by creating man. He does not surrender anything that He did not possess before man was created. This is basic theology. Any suggestion that has the creation adding to, or subtracting from, God the Creator is heretical.

God has established purposes for the creation. These purposes extend back before the creation week. So does His plan. So does His decree. There was nothing to thwart God before the creation. There is nothing to thwart God after the creation. This is why His plans, including His economic plans, are sovereign. He has not surrendered power to man. He is still as sovereign as He was in Genesis 1. Paul wrote: "For He says to Moses, 'I will have mercy on whomever I have mercy, and I will show compassion to whomever I show compassion.' So then, it does not depend on the person who wants it nor the one who runs, but on God who has mercy. For the Scripture says to Pharaoh, 'For this very reason I raised you up, in order to demonstrate My power in you, and that My name might be proclaimed throughout the earth.' So then He has mercy on whom He desires, and He hardens whom He desires" (Rom. 9:15–18).

This is why God's central planning does not destroy individual plans of men. There is coherence to His plans. This includes moral coherence. Imputations of economic value made by acting men do not disrupt God's overall plan. He is not blind. He is not weak. This means that the overall coherence between individuals' valuations and corporate coherence is supported by God's sovereign and comprehensive planning. His plan is the foundation of men's plans.

5. Cornelius Van Til called the full-bucket paradox.

B. Representation

Point two: hierarchy. In any relation to property, an individual is an owner, either directly or as a member of a legally responsible group. I cover this in the following three parts of this book. *God delegates limited sovereignty to individuals*. God then holds them responsible in history and eternity for how they manage His assets. Limited responsibility from God is also given to groups. God holds them responsible in history for how they manage their assets.

Responsibility is an aspect of point two: hierarchy. But this hierarchy is an extension of the original delegation of sovereignty in the dominion covenant. An individual possesses this delegated sovereignty, which is the origin of his judicial position as a guardian, as well as his economic position as a sharecropper or a commissioned salesman. As a steward, he is entitled—holds title to—the net output of the asset owned. He is therefore entitled to the income generated by the sale of this output. He owns the asset. Ownership has value for him only because he is legally entitled to the output generated by the asset. He owns the stream of future income. He can sell this, or rent it, or give it away. This is because the legal *essence of ownership* is the legal right to *disown* the asset involved.

Ownership is based on legal authority. The individual owns a bundle of rights attached to an asset. By "rights," I mean legal immunities. The owner may lawfully reject other claims on the use of the asset. The asset and its accompanying stream of income are immune from interference by non-owners. The owner has the right to place legal boundaries around the asset. These legal boundaries authorize the owner to place *barriers to entry* around the asset. In other words, he has the right to exclude. This is the meaning of boundaries: the *right to exclude*.[6]

The owner possesses knowledge about how best to use his property, according to his hierarchy of values (point two). He knows the local market. He knows what he could obtain from others who want to buy it or rent it. *There is a close correlation between his knowledge and his responsibility for the use of his assets*. By acknowledging his legal claims of ownership, the court system and the law-enforcement system

6. See Section C.

increase the likelihood that the owner's knowledge of the best use of his assets will be put to the service of those who want to buy the output of his time and capital. *The scarce resource of accurate knowledge is put to the most productive uses by those who possess it.* This is because they are legally responsible for its use. If they misuse it, they suffer losses. They are motivated to use it efficiently to satisfy paying customers.

Legal sovereignty over resources must lodge somewhere if there is not to be constant conflict over ownership. By acknowledging God's system of delegated sovereignty and therefore responsibility, the civil government furthers the spread of accurate knowledge. He who has opinions regarding the best use of specific assets is given a legal opportunity to bid for the use of these assets in order to put them to better uses.

The legal issue is *ownership*. This has to do with *guardianship*. God delegates sovereignty over resources. He then holds the designated owners legally responsible for the use of the assets which He has placed in their hands. He has a claim on the fruits of their labor, in the same way that a land owner has a legal claim on the output of a sharecropper who uses his land, seed, and tools. The claim is established when title is transferred.

The tithe principle establishes the ongoing obligation: 10% of net income. The economics of sharecropping is the model. The sharecropper is supplied with seed. He plants it. He replaces the seed from his output, but he pays no percentage on this. He pays a percentage of the output above the initial seed. The same is true for the owner. He does not owe a tithe on the replacement seed.

A sharecropper or a commissioned salesman receives payment based on what the customers paid for the output of his labor, raw materials, and capital goods. He is dependent on others to establish the economic value of this output. He can announce an initial price for the final output. This does not guarantee that anyone will pay him this price. To maximize his return, he must find a price where supply and demand are equal. After the sales are over, there is no remaining inventory, and there is no one bidding to buy anything else. The price was a *market-clearing* price.

The resource owner must act as a steward for bidders as well as the supreme Owner: God. The bidders want to own the final output of capital, raw materials, and labor. They bid against each other to secure ownership. The free market's allocation principle is this: *monetary high bid wins*. The owner does not know who will offer the highest bids. He guesses. Then he stores the goods until the sales take place. He acts as an economic agent of the high bidders. *He allocates the goods or services in terms of the auction process*.

This is true in a free market. As a legal agent, he also allocates wealth in family, church, or state. Here, the high bid principle is not based on competitive entry and money alone. There are other claims, and these usually supersede money bidding. In the state, there are laws against bribery. Churches do not allocate the sacraments in terms of high monetary bids. Wives are not paid money for services rendered. There is no open bidding for most of these services.

Ownership is a social function.[7] The legal sovereignty over assets does not establish this social function. The *price system* does. The presence of competitive bidding establishes market prices. This array of prices imposes economic costs on owners. They must pay to retain ownership. What do they pay? Whatever they could have received by selling or renting the assets.

So, representation is legal. There is a legal hierarchy. God is the Owner. Representation is also economic. The steward is an economic agent of people who possess property and will make bids to gain access to the existing owner's assets. *Because legal sovereignty is hierarchical, so is economic responsibility*. But this responsibility is also horizontal: accepting or rejecting bids. This is the auctioneering function.

The hierarchy extends downward. Mankind is placed over the creation. The creation is responsible to mankind. Specific sectors of the creation are responsible to specific owners. But this representation is two-way. The owner represents God to the creation, and he represents the creation to God. Paul wrote: "For the eagerly awaiting creation waits for the revealing of the sons and daughters of God. For the creation was subjected to futility, not willingly, but because of Him who subjected it, in hope that the creation itself also will be set free from its slavery to corruption into the freedom of the glory of the children of God. For we

7. Gary North, *An Introduction to Christian Economics* (Moulton, Alabama: Axehead Press, [1973] 2025), ch. 28.

know that the whole creation groans and suffers the pains of childbirth together until now" (Rom. 8:19–22).[8] Nature was placed under a curse because of man's fall (Gen. 3:17–19).[9] It will be progressively delivered by mankind's progressive sanctification.

So, the system of *legal sovereignty* is two-way: upward to God and downward to the creation. God owns the individual. The individual in turn owns property. God owns property in general in a direct manner, but His goal is to exercise this ownership by way of stewards. This is the basis of the dominion covenant.

The system of *economic authority* adds a horizontal element: the steward's responses to competitive bidding for his property by would-be owners and renters. In addition, there is economic authority inward. Owners make allocation decisions in terms of self-interest: "What's in it for me?" So, it is a four-way system of responsibility: upward to God, downward to the creation, outward to others, and inward.

C. Boundaries

Point three: ethics. This is related to law. Law establishes boundaries. All of nature is bounded. God has placed it under rules. Mankind is required to acknowledge the existence of these law-governed boundaries. Mankind is not autonomous, nor is nature autonomous. Mankind reflects the character and being of God, and nature does, too.

A major implication of each person's position as a dominion agent is *a system of property rights* associated with individuals and organizations. They exercise jurisdiction over the created realm, but they do not individually exercise authority over much of it. Men's jurisdiction extends to property which they lawfully own. Within these boundaries of ownership, an individual is told by God to be productive. He is to extend his *personal dominion* by means of whatever resources he lawfully owns or controls. He has authority over specific items, and he is responsible to God for the administration of this property. To the extent that he

8. Gary North, *Cooperation & Dominion: An Economic Commentary on Romans* (Moulton, Alabama: Axehead Press, [2012] 2031), ch. 5.

9. North, *Sovereignty & Dominion*, ch. 12.

extends the division of labor by means of extending the jurisdiction of God in history, he increases his own wealth. There is cause-and-effect in nature, and there is also cause-and-effect in the social order. An individual implements a plan of action, and in doing so, he seeks to extend his jurisdiction in history.

Men must recognize boundaries: geographical and organizational. Certain people have specific spheres of influence and authority. The social order is shaped by the boundaries of these jurisdictions. As we extend our dominion, we encounter limits to our authority. Power politics sometimes establishes these limits. Economics sometimes establishes them: buying and selling. Tradition sometimes establishes them. The point is, these boundaries exist. Someone says, "Do not cross the line." This line may be geographical. It may be legal. It may be social. But it exists. Men guard these boundary lines. Children may be slow to learn the concept of "yours," but they rapidly learn the concept of "mine." They make plans in terms of boundaries.

D. Inequality

Point four: sanctions. The parable of the talents (Matt. 25:14–30) teaches that there are two forms of sanctions: positive and negative. Success in multiplying capital leads to greater authority. Failure leads to destruction. The original grant of capital is withdrawn. The steward who produced no increase is stripped of all capital, which is transferred to the most productive steward. He who produces nothing during his time of testing loses whatever he possesses at the end of the test. He who produces the most—the highest rate of increase on the largest initial capital allocation—receives whatever the failure had possessed. This is biblical ownership. *There is no equality at any point: beginning to end. There is an increase in inequality*. This is the biblical structure of sanctions. It applies to all of life. It includes economics.

The parable of the talents teaches that God transfers control over assets to stewards. He then departs. This means that He does not tell people what to do. This is not a bureaucracy. This is a system of entrepreneurship. The new owners are expected to put this capital to profitable uses. God holds them responsible for multiplying His capital. Then He returns for an accounting. The first steward has multiplied capital two-fold: five talents to ten (Matt. 25:20). The master announces a reward: authority over even greater wealth (v. 21). The second steward also achieved a 100% return on investment. But he did so with less capital (v. 22). The performance was not so good as the first steward's performance. It is easier to multiply a small capital base than a large one. The master rewarded the second steward with somewhat less authority (v. 23). The third steward did not multiply any capital. He had buried his talent. He achieved a return of zero. But this was in fact a loss. The master had not had the use of the talent in the interim. He could have buried his own talent. So, he cursed the third steward. He told him that he could at least have lent the talent to a moneychanger, i.e., a banker (v. 27). This statement reveals Jesus' acceptance of lending at interest.[10]

The parable of the talents is a parable of final judgment. It is the second parable in Matthew 25. The first parable is the parable of the ten virgins. Five are wise; five are not. Five use up their oil. They beg the efficient five for some of their oil. The wise ones refuse. Then comes the judge. The five who failed are cast out. There is a message: those who possess greater wealth at the end of the time of testing receive the reward. They possess this advantage for two reasons. First, they were faithful stewards with what they had begun with. Second, they did not share their wealth with the wasteful stewards. A parable represents a fundamental covenantal truth. What is the fundamental truth? *There is no equality*: not in good judgment and not in the outcomes of good judgment.

The final section of Matthew 25 is not a parable. It describes the final judgment: sheep and goats. There is no equality in the final judgment.

So, final sanctions are in view. The question of *final sanctions* raises the issue of *temporal sanctions*. To what extent do sanctions in history reveal success or progress in eternity? The individual asks: "How am I doing?" He wants to identify success indicators that serve representatively as indicators for the outcome of the final day of reckoning. To use a metaphor of grading in school, he wants his success on his homework assignments and pop quizzes to provide indicators of how he is likely

10. North, *Priorities & Dominion*, ch. 47.

to do on the final exam. If there is no connection, then he has no way to evaluate his efforts. He is looking for signs: "Do more of this, and do less of that." In other words, he wants his successes in history to point to success in eternity. All Christians want this.

This was what Job looked for. This was why he grew resentful when three of his four "comforters" told him that the negative sanctions he had experienced pointed to sin on his part. "Confess," they insisted. He insisted that he had not sinned. The book of Job is about historical sanctions as success indicators. The message of the book is this: *history is representative of eternity, but not at every step*. God rewarded Job at the end of the book, giving him greater wealth than before. But this took time. It took a crisis. He was tempted by his wife to curse God and die (Job 2:9). He refused. But then he insisted that God give him an explanation for his plight. God did, and Job admitted that he had been wrong for demanding an explanation from God. This was the message of the fourth man who had come to talk with him.[11]

God is sovereign. He owes no one anything. Each man is a sinner, deserving only eternal death. But, in His grace, God providentially sustains a predictable world in which success indicators point to the outcome of final judgment. These are complex indicators. They are not mere money. Jesus was clear on that. The rich barn-builder was a fool. He laid up treasure without considering God (Luke 12:15–21).[12]

The individual faces eternal judgment. This is a highly motivating factor, or should be. The power of this expectation generally focuses more on the negative sanction than the positive sanction. Men fear hell and the lake of fire more than they desire blessings in heaven and the new heaven and new earth. This is reflected in the discovery that men fear the loss of wealth more than they expect to delight in an increase in wealth. This is one of the most significant discoveries of what is called behavioral economics.[13]

---

11. Gary North, *Predictability & Dominion: An Economic Commentary on Job* (Moulton, Alabama: Axehead Press, [2012] 2029).

12. Gary North, *Treasure & Dominion: An Economic Commentary on Luke* (Moulton, Alabama: Axehead Press, [2012] 2031), ch. 25.

13. Daniel Kahneman and Amos Tversky, "Choices, Values, and Frames," *American Psychologist* (1984); reprinted in Khaneman and Tversky (eds.), *Choices, Values, and Frames* (New York: Cambridge University Press, 2000), ch. 1.

There is always a paradox in success indicators. It is always possible to miss the mark by selecting false success indicators or, more likely, by assuming that they are the final end rather than means. Example: a student uses grades to evaluate his progress in his knowledge of a subject. But then he starts studying to pass the test. He focuses on the test rather than the overall knowledge. Then he decides to cheat in order to do even better on the test. Now he is not only not using the test as an indicator of progress, he is using it to compensate for a lack of progress. I know of no temporal success indicator that cannot be misused in this way.

So, the selection of success indicators as representatives of the outcome of final judgment requires spiritual wisdom. So does the interpretation of the results of one's preliminary evaluations that are based on these success indicators. A success indicator is never autonomous. (Nothing in the created realm is autonomous.) It is not a valid substitute for progressive sanctification. It is merely a means to an end: an indicator of progress toward a positive final judgment.

E. Accumulation

Point five: succession. The parable of the talents mandates capital accumulation. The focus is on money: a talent or weight, either of gold or silver. This is one of Jesus' pocketbook parables. He spoke in terms of categories that men everywhere relate to: money. He affirmed the moral responsibility of multiplying capital. Capital in this sense encompasses money, but it is not limited to money. It refers to assets in general: scarce resources that can be accumulated.

In Matthew 6, we read: "Do not store up for yourselves treasures on earth, where moth and rust destroy, and where thieves break in and steal. But store up for yourselves treasures in heaven, where neither moth nor rust destroys, and where thieves do not break in or steal; for where your treasure is, there your heart will be also" (Matt. 6:19–21).[14] This indicates that capital in the broadest sense does not refer exclusively to time-bound capital, but also to eternal capital. *There is a trade-off between temporal capital and eternal capital*. So, a wise allocation

14. North, *Priorities & Dominion*, ch. 13.

of capital must include the eternal value of accumulated capital. This eternal component does not change the *analytical category* of capital accumulation. It merely adds a post-temporal factor. The warning implied in the parable appeals to a person's economic self-interest.

Anyone who argues that Jesus did not invoke personal self-interest has an inaccurate understanding of Jesus' teachings on wealth. Specifically, with respect to the accumulation of personal wealth in the form of capital, Jesus was adamant: a person has both a moral responsibility and a legal responsibility to accumulate capital. This is an aspect of the dominion covenant. It involves *redeeming the world*, i.e., buying it back in the name of God. To buy it back requires accumulated capital. The alternative interpretation is that we must re-claim it by force. This is not part of the New Covenant's view of capital accumulation. It only happened once in the Old Covenant: the conquest of Canaan.

The capital accumulated by Abram is praised in Genesis 13:2. He was wealthy in cattle, silver, and gold. These asset categories have maintained their value down through the ages. In the state of Texas, there is a saying: "He is all hat and no cattle." He is a talker, not a doer. But the comparison relies on a positive view of cattle. A man with a large cowboy hat and a lot of cattle is worth listening to, but not because of the hat.

Capital is another word for tools. Capital enables its owner to pursue kingdom-building. Without capital, we cannot build the kingdom. Tools are always required to maximize production. This is why Jesus spoke highly of capital. It enables the owner to pursue his goals. The motives and goals are judged by God's law. Capital is not called into question. It can be used for multiple purposes. Money is the most versatile form of capital. It is the most marketable commodity.[15]

Conclusion

Mankind possesses legal jurisdiction over nature. This jurisdiction is part of the dominion covenant. Nature does not possess legal jurisdiction

15. Ludwig von Mises, *Human Action: A Treatise on Economics* (New Haven, Connecticut: Yale University Press, 1949), ch. XVII, sect. 3

over mankind. Mankind is made in the image of God; therefore, mankind exercises lawful dominion and jurisdiction over the creation. This corporate authority requires each individual to formulate and implement plans. *He must implement his plans within specified boundaries.*

Man the steward acts on behalf of God. This is inescapable. This is an aspect of the dominion covenant. As an agent of God, he must also act as an agent of creation: representing God to the creation and the creation to God. This is judicial in the case of ownership: legal rights over property. These rights allow a person to include or exclude. Judicial boundary markers enforce physical boundary markers.

The steward also represents those who do not yet own the asset. He represents them economically, not judicially. They will bid for ownership. He either holds or sells. But he will bear a cost for refusing an offer to buy: forfeiting whatever he could have bought with the purchase price. In short, he allocates his property. There are many bidders for ownership. He allows some people to buy. He excludes others. This is a social function. This is an inescapable economic function. Every item that has a price has a market. There is bidding for the item. This manifests itself in a price. The price imposes the obligation of an owner to accept or reject the offer. This is an allocation decision. It is therefore a stewardship decision.

The parable of the talents is the most important economic passage in the Bible regarding ownership in the broadest sense. Its message: *there is no equality*. All men are created unequal. They die unequal. The final judgment results in a transfer of assets: from the failures to the winners. This is a biblical judicial principle. It is the story of the covenant in history. Covenant-keepers inherit the earth. Then they inherit eternity.

This is not widely believed or widely preached, but the text is clear. Covenant-breakers are outraged by this parable. They devise systems of political coercion to offset this outcome in history, especially in economics. They preach a rival view: all men are created equal. Yet everyone knows it is not true. There is no area of our lives in which such equality exists or has ever existed. *The hierarchies of life are hierarchies of inequality*. There are superiors and inferiors. There are winners and losers.

Nice guys finish first. Jesus, as the incarnate Son of God who died for His people, is the ultimate nice guy. But His generosity is limited. It is not universal. His saving grace does not apply to all. Neither does His common grace apply equally to all.[16]

16. America's Declaration of Independence (1776) announces: "We hold these truths to be self-evident, that all men are created equal." There is no falsehood to match this one in any nation's founding documents. It was written by a unitarian slave owner who believed in universal salvation and who cut several Bibles into slips of paper in order to paste together his own version of Jesus' sayings: *The Life and Morals of Jesus of Nazareth*. The Declaration was ratified by other slaveholders and by legal representatives of New England ship owners who grew rich by transporting kidnapped Africans to the southern colonies. The hypocrisy was recognized at the time. It was phrased most notably by Samuel Johnson. "How is it that we hear the loudest yelps for liberty among the drivers of negroes?"

Chapter 8

Boundaries

"You shall not take the name of the Lord *your God in vain, for the* Lord *will not leave him unpunished who takes His name in vain."*

Exodus 20:7

"You shall not steal."

Exodus 20:15

Analysis

Point three of the biblical covenant is ethics. It has to do with law.[1] Law imposes boundaries: "Thou shalt" and "Thou shalt not." Boundaries are basic to the concept of property: "mine" and "yours." Boundaries are point three of the biblical covenant. They are associated with names and naming. God named Adam. Adam named the animals. Then Adam named Eve. A name identifies a species or a person. The act of naming *separates* the named entity from other named or unnamed entities. That is, a name places boundaries around a person or object. A name reinforces individuality. It places boundaries around the person named. It says "this person is unique."

1. Ray R. Sutton, *That You May Prosper: Dominion By Covenant,* 2nd ed. (Tyler, Texas: Institute for Christian Economics, [1987] 1992), ch. 3.

There is a book of life (Phil. 4:3). It is filled with names. It is the most important list in the world or outside the world.

God names people in order to identify individual responsibility. This act of naming makes someone legally responsible for his actions. Naming is therefore itself a judicial action.

When Moses asked God who he should say told him to bring the message of liberation to the Israelites, God named Himself: "I AM WHO I AM" (Ex. 3:14a). This could also be translated "I shall be what I shall be." Moses had a good reason to ask God for His name. God was asking Moses to speak covenantally in God's name. Moses wanted to know the name of the God for whom he was speaking judicially. He knew that the Israelites would demand to know. Moses needed proof that he was not speaking autonomously, i.e., on his own authority. God's answer identified Himself as autonomous, self-defined, and self-contained. Theologians call this *aseity*: self-contained. This is an incommunicable attribute of God.

Man is also bounded by other characteristics: genetic, social, historical, and covenantal. All of these features bind him. Yet this binding also provides opportunities. He is a specific person with specific abilities in a specific place at a specific time. His environment binds him, but it also empowers him. Just as a clock binds a person's day, so does it enable him to master his use of time. He is inside boundaries, but he can extend these boundaries. Boundaries are like levers. They establish some limits, but they extend boundaries of different limits.

A. Naming

Point one: God's sovereignty. God is the cosmic Owner. This is because He is the Creator. Before He was the Creator, He had purposes. This is why the element of purpose is basic to understanding the created realm. It is associated with God's sovereignty. God's purposes undergird men's purposes. The heavens were created by God in order to provide calendars for man (Gen. 1:14).[2] This means that built into the cosmos is a

2. Gary North, *Sovereignty & Dominion: An Economic Commentary on Genesis* (Moulton, Alabama: Axehead Press, [1982, 2012] 2022), ch. 2.

purpose: serving mankind. There is no escape from purpose. *Purpose is an inescapable concept.* It is never a question of purpose vs. no purpose. It is always a question of whose purpose.

Purpose underlies naming. It underlies all forms of scientific investigation. The essence of Darwinism is its denial of all purpose prior to the evolution of man.[3] This places man on God's throne: the source of purpose. But this raises a fundamental question: Who determines purpose? Is it individual men or collective mankind?

The naming process marks the origin of purpose in man's history. Naming declares legal limits. The person doing the naming may insist that he does this by discovering the existence of limits, or he may assert his own autonomy: his ability to impose limits. This debate is between subordinate discovery and original sovereignty. But if a man asserts that either he or corporate mankind is at the top of the hierarchy rather than God, even the assertion of the right of discovery is still an assertion of autonomy. Given the fact of some men's denial of God, there is no higher court of appeal to decide whether man's discovery process is in fact a concealed form of an autonomous declaration of limits. "Here is what I have discovered. Show me I am wrong."

The Third Commandment establishes a boundary around God's name. This is the third point of the list of five priestly commandments.[4] It is paralleled by the Eighth Commandment, which is the third commandment in the list of kingly commandments. It forbids theft.[5] *Name and property are linked judicially in the most important covenant document in history.*

Private property begins with a person's name. He is a legally identifiable agent. His name identifies him. It says, "you, not someone else." This is the basis of *judicial responsibility*. It is also the foundation of *economic authority*.

As a parent, God named Adam. God requires parents to name their children. Parents are under His sovereignty. He delegates the authority to parents to name their children, but this does not revoke His position

---

3. Ibid., Appendix A.

4. Gary North, *Authority & Dominion: An Economic Commentary on Exodus*, vol. 2, *Part II: Decalogue & Dominion* (Moulton, Alabama: Axehead Press, [1986, 2012] 2025), ch. 23.

5. Ibid., ch. 28.

as the cosmic Namer. He gives names to all mankind, but He does so through His delegated agents. This is why God had Adam name the animals in the garden. Adam was classifying them. He was evaluating their position in the natural order. Then God gave Adam a wife. Adam named her.

The authority to name things is a God-given authority. The person with the authority to establish names possesses a unique hierarchical position at the top. The question, "Who's in charge here?" can be accurately answered by identifying the person with the legal authority to name people and things. The person who possesses this authority is the source of boundaries. These boundaries mark people, places, and things. The rebels at Babel announced that they would make a name for themselves (Gen. 11:4). When the Communists took over in Russia in October 1917, they re-named cities. They drew new maps. After the fall of the USSR in December 1991, the new rulers in Russia re-established the original names. This was a mark of the transition out of Communism and back to a non-Communist social order. Naming is a serious business.

The creation is finite. To master it, men must first name its parts, i.e., classify these parts. Carl Linnaeus was a Swedish biologist in the eighteenth century. He developed a system of naming that transformed the science of biology. He recognized that until we classify something by naming it, we cannot study it scientifically. We cannot grasp why it is similar to some things, yet also different—continuity and discontinuity. We must know where it fits in the grand scheme of things. The very phrase "scheme of things" implies both order and purpose.

B. Bidding

Point two: hierarchy. Having named a person, God then delegates to him secondary ownership over himself. This applies progressively as a person moves from childhood to adulthood. Parents exercise decreasing authority. At some point, societies determine that people are adults and therefore are legally responsible for their behavior. This is basic to all social orders. A person who is responsible for his actions is legally in control of himself. A man owns himself as a steward owns other forms of property. This is not autonomous self-ownership, but it is *delegated self-ownership*. Name and property are linked legally.

The individual seeks to increase his ownership of goods and streams of future services. He purchases assets. He thereby declares legal sovereignty over them. This is an extension of his name. He is bounded by his name: a person legally responsible before God. He is also bounded by what he owns, beginning with himself. He extends his legal jurisdiction by accumulating property. He does this by extending his economic jurisdiction. He offers services in exchange for money. He owns these services because they are extensions of himself. Because he owns them, he can rent them. Through exchanging what he owns for things he does not own, he extends his legal jurisdiction. This builds his economic authority. He possesses what others want. He possesses bargaining power. His economic bargaining power is an extension of his legal sovereignty.

An individual owns a resource. He has the authority to decide what use is highest on his own value scale. The more versatile the asset, the greater the range of uses to which it can be put. Money is the most marketable commodity.[6]

If the resource has a price, there is demand for it. There is someone bidding for it. The owner has the economic responsibility to decide whether to sell or rent the resource to the highest bidder. If he decides not to sell or rent it, he becomes the highest bidder. This is called *reservation demand*.[7]

The owner decides what to do with the asset in terms of his *hierarchy of values*. The asset or the money it can bring can be used to do several things. The owner ranks these: first, second, or third. He then puts the asset to use.

To maximize his monetary income, he must be ready to sell to the highest bidder. This allows others to register their willingness to own or rent the asset. Through competitive bidding, the owner and the would-be owners register their respective demand. The owner can refuse an

6. Ludwig von Mises, *Human Action: A Treatise on Economics* (New Haven, Connecticut: Yale University Press, 1949), ch. XVII, sect. 3

7. Murray Rothbard, *Man Economy, and State: A Treatise on Economic Principles*, 2nd ed. (Auburn, Alabama: Mises Institute, [1962] 2009), 137, 247, 253, 294, 756.

offer, thereby becoming the highest bidder. But all of this is in response to the respective hierarchy of values of each bidder. The *subjective values* of the participants are manifested through a system of *objective bidding*. This establishes the free market price of the asset. The values are hierarchical and subjective. The bidding process is horizontal and objective.

The bidders are limited by the resources they own. They make objective bids in terms of what they own and how much they are willing to surrender in order to make the purchase. Specific bidders make specific bids in terms of specific values and specific possessions. The Bible's system of private ownership allows individuals to compete for ownership of other people's resources. By specifying individuals who must make these estimates and decisions, the system of private property links responsibility to ownership. Owners make their decisions in terms of their values and their assets. *There is no way for them to segregate responsibility from ownership*. The legal responsibilities of ownership are equated with the economic benefits and liabilities of ownership. The person who owns an asset bears the cost of making an allocation decision that does not maximize his income. It focuses his attention on the market for the asset. He can ignore this market, but only at a price: forfeited income.

The individual asks: "What's in it for me?" This has to do with ownership. In asking this, he has a personal economic incentive to pay attention to bidding for the asset. This system of competitive bidding lets a potential buyer reveal what is in it for the owner. When the existing owner decides there is more in it for him by exchanging the asset for something else, the two owners make an exchange. Each owner believes there will be more in it for him after he makes the exchange.

Because ownership is decentralized widely to individuals, the specialized knowledge that owners possess is put to service of the others. An owner seeks ways of attaining a greater level of satisfaction from the assets he owns. To discover a way to maximize his satisfaction, he must take into consideration the objective bids of others. What they want and are willing to pay affects his ability to pursue his wants with whatever he can pay. *The greater the market value of whatever he owns, the more effectively he can pursue his own values*. So, he seeks ways to maximize the economic value to others of the assets he owns, which includes his knowledge of specific circumstances: his circumstances and also the circumstances of others, as reflected in market prices. He can see what others are willing to pay for the assets he owns.

To increase the accuracy of his bidding, he must gain better knowledge of what others are willing and able to pay for his assets. This imposes search costs on him. Time and searching are not free resources. The purpose of this search process is to gain greater knowledge of what others are willing to pay. As with any other asset with a price, accurate knowledge is not a free resource. People cannot locate it free of charge.[8] They must search for it. They cannot initially know how much knowledge is available at a particular. *The free market is a bidding system for accurate knowledge.* It rewards accurate knowledge. Through bidding, men call forth knowledge that would not otherwise have been available to them.

Knowledge and scarce resources are offered for sale to the highest bidders. This is the result of God's initial distribution of resources. The wealth possessed by individuals is put to the use of others. That which is *owned legally* is put to use for the *highest bidder.* (He who gains or retains ownership is the highest bidder.) No one compels others to share their knowledge, yet this knowledge is brought into the marketplace to be put to better use by others. No compulsion is involved. Individuals are bounded, but through the pursuit of profit on a free market, individuals increase the supply of knowledge available to them. This increases their ability to conserve resources and also maximize the subjective value—objective income—of the assets they own.

C. Specializing

Point three: ethics. Law places boundaries around men. We are bounded, but this gives us opportunities to specialize. We hear of a "Renaissance man." This is someone who conforms to the Renaissance ideal of a man well-versed in many fields. But such a person always faces the problem of deciding what to specialize in. If someone can

8. Thomas Sowell, *Knowledge and Decisions* (New York: Basic Books, 1980).

do many things well, his cost of doing one thing magnificently is high. There are so many pathways that he must give up in order to pursue his job or his calling effectively. He must choose wisely. He must decide what is best for him, as well as for God and others. He needs far better judgment than most people possess.

To specialize profitably, a person must be able to say "this is mine." This applies to his work. It applies to whatever he owns and seeks to improve. Biblical law enables property owners to exclude others from their property. In real estate, this property is identified by landmarks. These landmarks identify the legal zone of responsibility for the use of this property. The property produces income over time in some form. The owner possesses legal control over this stream of income. To private property are attached various legal rights, meaning above all the right to exclude. *The concept of a property right means the right to exclude—a legal immunity*. The archetype was the tree of the knowledge of good and evil in the garden. It was God's property. He did not delegate control to Adam and Eve. He excluded them (Gen. 2:17).[9]

Individuals are bounded by time and place. These are great boundaries on every person. A person is born at a time in a place. He grows up in specific places in a particular era. He becomes familiar with the boundaries of time and place as they apply to him. The narrow focus of time and place in someone's life enables him to specialize. He gains expertise in time and place.

We speak of saving time. But do we save time? There is no bank account for deposits of time. Time cannot be set aside in reserve "for a rainy day." It cannot be purchased for money in any market. Yet it can be purchased with righteousness. "And if you walk in My ways, keeping My statutes and commandments, as your father David walked, then I will prolong your days" (I Kings 3:14). Because of this, there is the phenomenon known as *bargaining for time*. It is a common feature of the response to the news that a person is dying. He bargains with God for more time. He promises to do something important for God, as a person imagines. This is not an irrational response.[10]

---

9. Gary North, *Sovereignty & Dominion: An Economic Commentary on Genesis* (Moulton, Alabama: Axehead Press, [1982, 2012] 2022), ch. 9.

10. Gary North, *Stay of Execution: How to Negotiate With God When You Have Under Six Months to Live* (Moulton, Alabama: Axehead Press, [2015] 2032).

When we say that we save time, we mean this: *we achieve our goals for a reduced expenditure of time.* We allocate less time. We do this by becoming more efficient in our use of time. Time is a scarce resource. Once it passes, it is gone forever. *Time is a nonrenewable resource.* Indeed, it is the archetype of a nonrenewable resource. So, men are cautioned not to waste it. Jesus said: "We must carry out the works of Him who sent Me as long as it is day; night is coming, when no one can work" (John 9:4). In short, we economize. But this raises the question of how to evaluate success objectively.

D. Economizing

Point four: sanctions. In economics, sanctions mean either profit or loss. These accounting concepts are basic to the task of economizing: cutting losses and increasing profits. This procedure is basic to overcoming the limits imposed by scarcity. Scarcity is defined by economists as follows: "At zero price, there is greater demand than supply." This is another way of saying "something commands a price." Scarcity imposes boundaries. Because of scarcity, men must gain control over more scarce assets in order to increase their consumption. They must extend their jurisdiction. There is also a scarcity of time. People die.

Scarcity has been cursed (Gen. 3:17–19).[11] Therefore, it is mandatory that covenant-keepers seek to overcome scarcity progressively in history. The marks of this are rising output and falling prices. We all want to buy things cheaper. We all want more for our money. This is universal. It is not confined to covenant-keepers. So, we search for ways to reduce the cost of maintaining our lifestyles. The dominion covenant was given before the fall and the curse of the ground (place) and the curse of death (time). This covenant is still in force. The evidence that almost all mankind honors it is the universal quest for more. To gain more for ourselves, we must extend our control over more. We must subdue the earth.

Cursed scarcity is a negative sanction. To offset it, there must be positive sanctions. There must be ways of offsetting the curse. The Bible describes this in Deuteronomy 8. After describing God's miraculous

11. North, *Sovereignty & Dominion*, ch. 12.

intervention on behalf of the Israelites in the wilderness, Moses said this. "Otherwise, you may say in your heart, 'My power and the strength of my hand made me this wealth.' But you are to remember the LORD your God, for it is He who is giving you power to make wealth, in order to confirm His covenant which He swore to your fathers, as it is this day" (Deut. 8:17–18). This states emphatically that an increase in wealth is a sign of the covenant. It is evidence of the covenantal structure of economics. The positive economic sanctions confirm the covenant.[12]

There is a long tradition for economics textbooks to begin with scarcity. The most rigorous of the textbooks in the Chicago School tradition, Allen and Alchian's *University Economics* (3rd ed., 1972), may be the only textbook ever written that begins with Chapter 0: "How Much Mathematics and Graphs?" Chapter 1 is titled "Scarcity, Competitive Behavior, and Economics." It begins: "Ever since the fiasco in the Garden of Eden, most of what we get is by sweat, strain, and anxiety. Two villains—nature and other people—prevent us from getting what we want. Nature is niggardly: it provides fewer resources than we could use, and much of what is available is made useful only by hard work. As for other people, the problem stems not from malevolence: their wants and ours simply exceed what is available." Mark Skousen, a Mormon who writes from an Austrian School perspective, begins his textbook, *Economic Logic* (3rd ed., 2009), with a discussion of Adam and Eve after their expulsion from the Garden. They had to work. So do we. This refers back to Genesis 3:17–19: the curse of the ground.[13] Roger Leroy Miller in Chapter 1 of his textbook, *Economics Today* (8th ed., 1994), writes in the Introduction: "Economics is the study of how people make choices to satisfy their wants. Wants are defined as all the things people would consume if they had unlimited incomes." Chapter 2 is titled, "Scarcity and the World of Trade-Offs." Edwin Dolan, in his textbook, *Basic Economics* (2nd ed., 1980), titles Chapter 1, "What Economics Is All About." The first section of the chapter is "Scarcity and Choice in Economics." He writes: "In *economics*, scarcity means that people do not have as much of everything as they want." I could go on, but time is scarce.

12. Gary North, *Inheritance & Dominion: An Economic Commentary on Deuteronomy* (Moulton, Alabama: Axehead Press, [1999, 2012] 2028), chaps. 21, 22.

13. North, *Sovereignty & Dominion*, ch. 12.

Economists never start where the Bible starts: ownership. Why is this? The main reason is their quest for universality. Scarcity is universally recognized. It is acknowledged by every economic theory. In contrast, the question of ownership raises fundamental ethical questions. Who owns something? On what legal basis? On what moral basis? These are questions that cannot be settled by an appeal to ethically neutral logic. *This is because there is no such thing as ethically neutral logic.* But economists usually rest their case on what they assume to be ethically neutral logic. So, they begin with scarcity.

Longevity is one of the few blessings that all economists regard as a universally acknowledged blessing. Economists cite increases in life expectancy as a feature of a society that is experiencing economic growth. At the other end of the age spectrum, an increase in the survival rate of children is universally regarded as a blessing. Nevertheless, an increase in the rate of abortion is also implicitly seen as a blessing by humanists. More dead babies are said to produce more economic growth per capita: fewer mouths to feed. Economists never say this in print, but it is implied by their analysis. They are relying on Malthusian presumptions about food shortages and resource limits. They do not count humans as the most productive resource.[14] Here is their unstated judicial position: "There is greater freedom of choice, as long as we do not count the choice of the infants, which modern abortionists refuse to do. Because no adult other than the mother is allowed to speak representatively on behalf of her unborn child, the child's opinion is not regarded as judicially valid and therefore is not economically relevant." At a child's birth, the courts can and do intervene to speak judicially on behalf of the child, but not before. So, reduced death rates for newborn children are seen as positive in economic literature. Reduced post-natal infant mortality is counted as a positive economic sanction.

The free market's system of profit-and-loss accounting enables resource owners to deal with scarcity in a positive way. Over generations, this leads to compound economic growth. This is the connection between point four of the biblical covenant and point five.

---

14. One economist knew better: Julian Simon. Simon, *The Ultimate Resource* (Princeton, New Jersey: Princeton University Press, 1971).

E. Compounding

Point five: succession. In Christian economics, succession involves expansion through the generations. This expansion is an aspect of the dominion covenant: man's obligation to multiply (Gen. 1:28). This means demographic compounding.

Compounding is also known as positive feedback. Profits are reinvested. The economic base expands at an accelerating rate because the reinvested profits expand along with the original base. Economic growth is the result of net compound economic blessings. Positive economic sanctions overcome specific limits—boundaries—of scarcity over time. The promise of compound economic growth is an affirmation of dominion. As a man accumulates capital, he is better able to extend his dominion. He is also better able to put that property to whatever uses he chooses. His range of actions increases because he possesses more wealth.

This promise of economic growth was unique in the ancient world. Only the Hebrews believed that this is possible. One confirmation of God's covenant with His redeemed people is economic growth (Deut. 8:17–18).[15] This means that covenant-keepers should expect economic growth if they remain faithful. Compounding wealth is promised as a confirmation of *compounding ethical progress*, what theologians call progressive sanctification.[16]

The promise of compound economic growth was a promise to individuals and families that comprised the covenantal community. The promise had to do with individual progressive ethical sanctification: *adherence to biblical law*. Progressive ethical sanctification is rewarded with greater wealth: a reduction of the boundaries imposed by scarcity. This in turn produces national wealth by means of a greater division of labor.

Economic growth is biblically normative. In no other ancient religion was economic growth normative. This outlook was unique to the Hebrews. It could exist only because of the biblical concept of time:

---

15. North, *Inheritance & Dominion*, ch. 22.

16. John Murray, "Progressive Sanctification," *Collected Works of John Murray* (Edinburgh: Banner of Truth, 1982), II, ch. 23

creation, fall, incarnation, redemption, and final judgment. In the biblical account, history is linear. All rival outlooks in the ancient world were cyclical. In a cyclical universe, all progress is either temporary or an illusion. But, in the biblical worldview, because individual progress is at bottom ethical, and because there are positive economic sanctions for personal ethical progress, long-term economic growth is a real possibility. There is no biblical theory of inevitable *ethical* reversion to the mean. There can be permanent ethical progress. There is also a clear doctrine of *covenantal inheritance*. This applies to both ethics and capital. Inter-generational ethical progress is possible. Therefore, so is compound economic growth.

The passage warns against attributing economic growth to autonomous man. This is the essence of ethical rebellion: using the fruits of the covenant to praise autonomous individual productivity or even corporate productivity. But the very possibility of ethical rebellion points to the possibility of long-term ethical progress. Temptation need not be submitted to. "No temptation has overtaken you except something common to mankind; and God is faithful, so He will not allow you to be tempted beyond what you are able, but with the temptation will provide the way of escape also, so that you will be able to endure it" (I Cor. 10:13). There is nothing inevitable about a reversion to the status quo ante, either ethically or economically.

Conclusion

The Third Commandment, which announces God's rule regarding His name—an exclusion law—is law three in the list of five priestly laws. The Eighth Commandment protects property from theft: another exclusion law. It is third in the kingly list of rules. *Name and property are linked covenantally.*

God delegates to parents the legal authority to name their children. When a person reaches adulthood, he becomes a legally responsible agent. He has a name. He has an identity. This legal authority under God is also economic authority. The person is legally responsible primarily to God and secondarily to other people. This includes economic responsibility. By tying legal authority to economic authority by means of private ownership, God establishes a comprehensive system of responsibility. Property rights are ultimately legal categories. Only secondarily are they economic categories. In short, *covenantal authority is superior to economic authority*.

The libertarian doctrine of absolute self-ownership as the foundation of property rights rests on the false doctrine of man's autonomy. The concept of self-ownership is correct in this sense: *self-ownership is delegated ownership*. All ownership is delegated ownership. It begins with delegated self-ownership. The individual is owned by God, not by the state. The adult individual is owned by God, not by the family, until such time as an individual marries. At that point, mutual ownership and obligations begins (I Cor. 7:3). Each partner has legal claims on the other.

Trusteeship (point two) by specific individuals (point three) over specific assets (point three) in terms of fundamental law (point three) is the foundation of property rights. A trustee acts as the legal agent of the owner. He defends the owner's assets from unauthorized use by interlopers, who either assert a superior claim of ownership or else steal it. In doing so, he inescapably acts also as an economic agent of the owner. He must consider objective bids for ownership from other stewards of the same owner. These other stewards may not acknowledge their position as legal and economic agents of the owner. They may assert their ownership of their very being—their "name" in the broadest sense. They may assert a legal claim over the goods under their administration. But this does not change the covenantal structure of ownership.

Chapter 9

Imputation

And God saw all that He had made, and behold, it was very good. And there was evening and there was morning, the sixth day.

Genesis 1:31

Woe to those who call evil good, and good evil;
Who substitute darkness for light and light for darkness;
Who substitute bitter for sweet and sweet for bitter!

Isaiah 5:20

Analysis

Point four of the biblical covenant is sanctions.[1] Sanctions are an aspect of God's court. God applies fixed biblical laws to specific judicial cases. This requires the exercise of judgment. God then announces "guilty" or "not guilty." Then He imposes sanctions: positive or negative. To impute is to render judgment: point four of the biblical covenant.

In Calvinist theology, the doctrine of imputation refers to God's declaration of the guilt or innocence of individuals. It is a judicial act, also called a forensic act. This doctrine plays a unique role in Calvinist the-

1. Ray R. Sutton, *That You May Prosper: Dominion By Covenant*, 2nd ed. (Tyler, Texas: Institute for Christian Economics, [1987] 1992), ch. 4.

ology. It is less important in other theological systems. God is seen as a judge. He imputes Adam's sin to all humanity.[2] He applies an ethical standard to all humanity: the perfect humanity of Jesus Christ. Christ's perfection is assessed in terms of His conformity to God's Bible-revealed law. God assesses all individual ethical performance in terms of this standard. This is the model of all *casuistry*: the application of God's law to historical circumstances. God does this. As creatures made in God's image, so must human beings. Imputation has to do with judicial categories: saved and lost, redeemed and unredeemed. But this concept is not confined to the judicial category of justification. It is also the model for the ethical category of sanctification: the degree of ethical conformity to God's Bible-revealed law. Justification has to do with declaring saved or lost: the ultimate pass-fail final examination. Sanctification has to do with grading on a curve: the degree of individual conformity in history to a fixed ethical standard that was attained by Jesus Christ. It also applies to human institutions: corporate sanctification.

The doctrine of imputation is also central to modern economic theory. Indeed, it is the identifying mark of the transition from classical economics to modern economics. The epistemological revolution in economic theory that took place in the first three years of the 1870s was developed most cogently by Austrian economist Carl Menger in 1871. Menger rejected the classical economists' mutually self-contradictory explanations of economic value: the labor theory of value and the cost-of-production theory of value. Menger argued that economic value is imputed by final customers. They decide which goods and services are highest on their scale of values. Then they bid for ownership in the market place. These competitive bids establish market prices, which are the objective manifestation of imputed subjective value. Imputed value and objective price are linked by way of the free market's auction process.

Why does a capital good possess economic value? Menger called this a *higher-order good*. He denied that this value is the product of the price of prior inputs. A capital good is valuable—commands a price—only because of entrepreneurs' expectations regarding the future value of consumer goods: goods that customers will pay for. He called these

2. John Murray, *The Imputation of Adam's Sin* (Phillipsburg, New Jersey, P&R, [1959] 1977).

lower-order goods. He wrote: "... the *economic character of goods of higher order depends upon the economic character of the goods of lower order for whose production they serve*. In other words, no good of higher order can attain economic character or maintain it unless it is suitable for the production of some economic good of lower order."[3] He made it clear that *expectations* are the key. "We therefore have the principle that the value of goods of a higher order is dependent upon the expected value of the goods of a lower order they serve to produce."[4]

There is no objective value, he concluded. "The value of goods arises from their relationship to our needs, and is not inherent in the goods themselves."[5] Therefore, he wrote,

> It is a judgment economizing men make about the importance of the goods at their disposal for the maintenance of their lives and well-being. Hence value does not exist outside the consciousness of men. It is, therefore, also quite erroneous to call a good that has value to economizing individuals a "value," or for economists to speak of "values" as of independent real things, and to objectify value in this way. For the entities that exist objectively are always only particular things or quantities of things, and their value is something fundamentally different from the things themselves; it is a judgment made by economizing individuals about the importance their command of the things has for the maintenance of their lives and well-being. Objectification of the value of goods, which is entirely *subjective* in nature, has nevertheless contributed very greatly to confusion about the basic principles of our science.[6]

Philosophically, this position rests on nominalism: the power of a person to name, classify, and evaluate. This position rejects realism: value or characteristics that are inherent in a physical object. This debate is as old as philosophy. As I have said in numerous passages, biblical thought is based on a rejection of both autonomous realism and autonomous nominalism.[7] Biblical thought rests on covenatalism.

---

3. Carl Menger, *Principles of Economics* (Auburn, Alabama: Mises Institute, [1871] 2007), 107.
4. Ibid., 150.
5. Ibid., 120.
6. Ibid., 121.
7. Gary North, *Sovereignty & Dominion: An Economic Commentary on Genesis* (Moulton, Alabama: Axehead Press, [1982, 2012] 2022), ch. 5.

There is *covenantal realism*, because God created everything. The creation is objective. It objectively reflects the handiwork of God. There is *covenantal nominalism*, because God imputes meaning and value to His creation. In contrast to biblical thought, Menger held to the autonomy of the creation and the autonomy of man. He therefore self-consciously adopted nominalism.

> Just as a penetrating investigation of mental processes makes the cognition of external things appear to be merely our consciousness of the impressions made by the external things upon our persons, and thus, in the final analysis, merely the cognition of states of our own persons, so too, in the final analysis, is the importance that we attribute to things of the external world only an outflow of the importance to us of our continued existence and development (life and wellbeing). Value is therefore nothing inherent in goods, no property of them, but merely the importance that we first attribute to the satisfaction of our needs, that is, to our lives and well-being, and in consequence carry over to economic goods as the exclusive causes of the satisfaction of our needs.[8]

Modern economic thought is officially nominalistic. But there is no escape from covenantal realism: the doctrine of original creation by God. Humanists who defend realism do not accept covenantal realism, so they adopt autonomous philosophical realism. They sneak philosophical realism through the methodological back door of price indexes and other statistical techniques of aggregation. These indexes require the aggregation of subjective economic value—individuals' subjective imputations—which cannot be done without violating the principle of subjectivism-nominalism.[9] All economic policy-making necessarily rests on an implicit denial of nominalism, for it relies on the assumption that an economist can make objectively valid interpersonal comparisons of subjective utility. So, there is an inherent dualism in humanistic economic thought.

With this as background, I am ready to take up the question of the biblical concept of economic imputation.

---

8. Menger, *Principles of Economics*, 116.

9. North, *Sovereignty & Dominion*, ch. 5.

A. Valuation by God

Point one: God's sovereignty. He is the Creator. He is also the Imputer. He evaluated the quality of His work at the end of each of five of the six days (Gen. 1). On what basis? First, He had spoken the day's work of creation into existence. Second, the creation was objectively real. It was capable of being catalogued, measured, and evaluated. Third, He implemented the creation in terms of pre-creation standards. We presume this, i.e., that He did not make things up as He went along. The New Testament adds that the Second Person of the Trinity was the executor. "[F]or by Him all things were created, both in the heavens and on earth, visible and invisible, whether thrones, or dominions, or rulers, or authorities--all things have been created through Him and for Him" (Col. 1:16). Then He evaluated this work in terms of the faithfulness of the creation to His sovereign creative word.

There are no actions beyond the judgment of God. God evaluates every action. Then He renders judgment. An action is either good or bad. The final judgment will be the overall retroactive assessment (Matt. 25:32–42). This does not mean that God makes no further judgments from the end of the week of creation until the final judgment. God renders constant judgments. He evaluates constantly, just as He evaluated each day of creation. This is the archetype for man's rendering of judgment. Man is made in the image of God. This means individual men and corporate man. Individuals are under a covenantal administration, but so are collectives. Individuals are subject to eternal sanctions. No institution other than the church extends into eternity. Individuals are given the ability to make judgments as judicial agents of God. This ability is built into man's very being. Declaring and executing judgment are aspects of the dominion covenant.

The philosophical dualism between hypothetically unchanging logic and ceaseless change—Parmenides vs. Heraclitus—is resolved biblically by means of a doctrine that is based on metaphysics: the *absolute sovereignty of God over His creation*. This doctrine affirms both His omniscience and His omnipotence. He has laid down His law. All of the creation is under God's providence, from subatomic particles (or are they waves?) outward to a hundred billion galaxies with a hundred billion stars each. *There is predictability in history because God is sovereign over history.* He governs the creation. But in one tiny location in the universe, His providence is seen in linear history: creation, fall, incarnation, redemption, and final judgment. Here, the issues of history are *ethical*—not mechanical and not organic.

The universe is subject to laws. Because men are required by God to exercise dominion, they have been given minds that can render judgments. They can perform the art of casuistry: the application of ethical principles to historical cases. They can also do science: discover laws of nature, and then use these laws to exercise power over nature. *What God does originally, men can and must do secondarily and analogically.* This two-fold ability of *comprehension and application* is objectively inherent in men. God created men to do this on His behalf. The concept of "on His behalf" leads to point two of the biblical covenant: representation.

B. Valuation by Man

Point two: hierarchy. Each individual is under God. This is a judicial matter. He is under God's Bible-revealed law. He acts as a steward under God-delegated ownership. He is required to rule over creation by means of God's law, which includes the predictable regularities of nature. So, hierarchy, law, judgment, and inheritance are all part of an integrated system. The sovereignty of God is the foundation of this system.

Each person is made in the image of God. So is corporate mankind. So, each person is responsible for the administration of assets delegated by God. This means that the decision-maker is *responsible upward* to God. But, because the creation is under man, each person is *responsible downward*: to serve as God's representative agent. Each person is *responsible outward* to other people, who also have their God-given tasks. This is the covenantal foundation of the division of labor. Finally, each person is *responsible inward*: conscience. The person seeks his own goals. He reaps rewards and pays costs.

This is the basis of Christ's warning to count the costs when making plans. We must guess what the objective results of our plans will be. Then we must estimate the net increase in subjective economic value. This is the art of looking into the future, and then estimating retroactively what the outcomes of our plans will be. This requires us to impute value in advance.

> "For which one of you, when he wants to build a tower, does not first sit down and calculate the cost, to see if he has enough to complete it? Otherwise, when he has laid a foundation and is not able to finish, all who are watching it will begin to ridicule him, saying, 'This person began to build, and was not able to finish!' Or what king, when he sets out to meet another king in battle, will not first sit down and consider whether he is strong enough with ten thousand men to face the one coming against him with twenty thousand? Otherwise, while the other is still far away, he sends a delegation and requests terms of peace. So then, none of you can be My disciple who does not give up all his own possessions." (Luke 14:28–33)[10]

Man is made in God's image. He is required by God to imitate God, but as a creature. The phrase "thinking God's thoughts after Him" applies to all casuistry: the interpretation of historical events in terms of God's law. This ability is the covenantal basis of casuistry. How can covenant-keepers do this? By the mind of Christ. "But the one who is spiritual discerns all things, yet he himself is discerned by no one. For who has known the mind of the LORD, that he will instruct Him? But we have the mind of Christ" (I Cor. 2:15–16).

C. Criteria: Individual and Corporate

Point three: ethics. This is related to law. There are laws governing economic value. These are to help us in formulating plans. The crucial criterion of economic value is simple: *the extension of the kingdom of God in history.* Covenant-keepers are supposed to honor this principle. "But seek first His kingdom and His righteousness, and all these things

10. Gary North, *Treasure & Dominion: An Economic Commentary on Luke* (Moulton, Alabama: Axehead Press, [2012] 2031), ch. 35.

will be provided to you" (Matt. 6:33).[11] In contrast, covenant-breakers seek to extend the kingdom of man.

The doctrine of the final judgment has an inescapable economic implication: *kingdom competition is zero-sum.* All of that which is built up in history by the kingdom of man is transferred to the kingdom of God at the final judgment. This inheritance is individual. It begins in history at the time of each covenant-keeper's transition from wrath to grace at conversion. This inheritance is primarily judicial: legal status before God. It is definitive. The person gains a legal share of the inheritance of the kingdom of God. But definitive inheritance is not final inheritance. History is a matter of progressive inheritance (I Cor. 3).[12] It builds up over time. Both the kingdom of God and the kingdom of man can expand their capital bases. One is wood, hay, and stubble. The other is gold, silver, and precious stones (I Cor. 3:12). This is made public by *God's retroactive final judgment,* but it is imputed by God through history. With respect to eternity, the wealth of the sinner is laid up for the just (Prov. 13:22).[13] Postmillennialism teaches that this transfer will begin in history, and this will accelerate as we approach the final judgment. Amillennialism denies this. Premillennialism denies it with respect to the era we live in, meaning prior to Christ's bodily return to set up a thousand-year kingdom.

So, the mutual benefits that market transactions offer are limited to history. Ultimately, this mutuality will prove to have been an illusion for covenant-breakers. Life really is a zero-sum competition. Winners take all. More to the point, winners are awarded all by God.

What has value? Anything that can extend the kingdom of God. But this implies that there must be standards of action. These standards are based on the law of God. They are an ethical extension of His character. He pronounced His work "good" at the end of five of the six days of creation. But this implies the existence of a standard of both process and final output. There was an appropriate means to achieve the end.

---

11. Gary North, *Priorities & Dominion: An Economic Commentary on Matthew* (Moulton, Alabama: Axehead Press, [2012] 2030), ch. 15.

12. Gary North, *Judgment & Dominion: An Economic Commentary on I Corinthians* (Moulton, Alabama: Axehead Press, [2012] 2031), ch. 3.

13. Gary North, *Wisdom & Dominion: An Economic Commentary on Proverbs* (Moulton, Alabama: Axehead Press, [2012] 2029), ch. 41.

The legitimacy of the end is the justification of the process. It shapes the theory of the process. The process then either conforms or fails to conform to the standard.

This raises a question. How are we to discover the standard? The Bible has two legal concepts: the spirit of the law and the letter of the law. The two are consistent in the mind of God. They are also consistent in the work of God. Paul contrasted them in operation. "But now we have been released from the Law, having died to that by which we were bound, so that we serve in newness of the Spirit and not in oldness of the letter" (Rom. 7:6). The letter of the Mosaic law kills. The Holy Spirit of God renews it in the lives of individuals and institutions. This is a basic theme in the epistle to the Romans.

There is an inherent dualism in all autonomous thought between the letter of the law and its spirit. The conflict comes when explaining how the letter reflects the spirit and implements it. There is a conflict between them. A rigorous enforcement of the letter of the law—legalism—can undermine the original intent of the lawmakers. The most famous case in the Bible is Darius' imprisonment of Daniel in the lion's den. The king had been tricked by his counselors into issuing a decree regulating prayer. He could not break his own words (Dan. 6:14–17). The letter of the law was opposed to the spirit of the law. Another famous incident was the deception of the Israelites by the Gibeonites. The leaders of Israel were deceived. They verbally granted the Gibeonites' safety, not knowing the Gibeonites were dwellers in the land. Joshua allowed the decision to stand (Josh. 9). He defended the letter of the law against the spirit of the law. Another famous incident was Solomon's decision to execute his half brother Adonijah, despite Solomon's promise to his own mother (I Kings 2:13–25). He defended the spirit of the law—the orderly transfer of the kingly inheritance—against the implications of the letter of the law: an unlawful transfer of this inheritance.

The criteria of *ethical* value are ethical: the spirit of the law. But they are also *judicial*: the letter of the law. The letter of the law preserves predictability of the courts. It makes judges less arbitrary. The spirit of the law upholds justice. It defends what is *ethically right*, not what is *procedurally predictable*. God enables the mind of man to choose an ethical path of justice without destroying predictability. But sometimes men fail.

A popular phrase is this: "What would Jesus do?" It is clear from the Gospel of John that Jesus confused most of those around Him most of the time. They constantly drew incorrect conclusions about what Jesus wanted to do or was going to do.

God's standards are permanent ethically. They persevere through time. This is the challenge in every judicial and ethical system. The permanence and the applicability of impersonal, autonomous logic (Parmenides), despite the flux of autonomous history (Heraclitus) must be explained by the defenders of every legal or ethical system. Biblically, the answer is the doctrine of God's permanence. "'Then I will come near to you for judgment; and I will be a swift witness against the sorcerers, the adulterers, against those who swear falsely, those who oppress the wage earner in his wages or the widow or the orphan, and those who turn away the stranger from justice and do not fear Me,' says the LORD of armies. 'For I, the LORD, do not change; therefore you, the sons of Jacob, have not come to an end'" (Mal. 3:5–6). Consider Psalm 119, which is devoted to the benefits of biblical law.

> Forever, LORD, Your word stands in heaven.
> Your faithfulness continues throughout generations;
> You established the earth, and it stands.
> They stand this day by Your ordinances,
> For all things are Your servants.
> (vv. 89–91)

> Your commandments make me wiser than my enemies,
> For they are ever mine.
> I have more insight than all my teachers,
> For Your testimonies are my meditation.
> I understand more than those who are old,
> Because I have complied with Your precepts.
> (vv. 98–100)

> Seven times a day I praise You
> Because of Your righteous judgments.
> Those who love Your Law have great peace,
> And nothing causes them to stumble.
> I hope for Your salvation, LORD,
> And do Your commandments.

> My soul keeps Your testimonies,
> And I love them exceedingly.
> I keep Your precepts and Your testimonies,
> For all my ways are before You.
> (vv. 164–168)

Biblical law is the God-given, God-mandated means by which all men are required by God to order their scale of values and their lives. By means of biblical law, all men are required to subdue the earth. By means of biblical law, all men are supposed to evaluate decisions and render judgment.

Biblical law applies to individuals and collectives. Both are under biblical law's historical sanctions. This is true of collectives, contrary to libertarian social theory (Deut. 28).[14] A collective is under temporal sanctions, but not under eternal sanctions. *Eternity trumps time*. So, the temporal realm of personal sanctions elevates individualism over collectivism in history, but not in all cases. With respect to history, the collective is sometimes more important: the survival of nation, family, and church. Individuals often sacrifice their temporal interests for the sake of these larger interests. In doing so, they gain positive sanctions in eternity. Their inheritance (point five) is beyond the grave. "Do not store up for yourselves treasures on earth, where moth and rust destroy, and where thieves break in and steal. But store up for yourselves treasures in heaven, where neither moth nor rust destroys, and where thieves do not break in or steal; for where your treasure is, there your heart will be also" (Matt. 6:19–21).[15]

Ethical value is the foundation of economic value. This conclusion opposes modern economic theory all the way back to the mercantilists.[16] Not only is economic theory not value-free, contrary to what economists insist, it is *value-derived*. The very concept of economic value is undergirded by the concept of ethical value: extending the kingdom of God in history. There is nothing ethically neutral about economic theory.

---

14. North, *Inheritance & Dominion: An Economic Commentary on Deuteronomy* (Moulton, Alabama: Axehead Press, [1999, 2012] 2028), chaps. 69, 70.

15. North, *Priorities & Dominion*, ch. 13.

16. William Letwin, *The Origins of Scientific Economics* (Cambridge, Massachusetts: MIT Press, 1963).

D. Value and Price

Point four: sanctions. This is associated with imputation: judging events in terms of biblical law. The covenant-keeper is required by God to apply God's Bible-revealed law to the decision-making processes in his life. He is under God's authority (point two). His obedience is possible only because he possesses the ability to understand both the law and historical circumstances. He can accurately assess and then apply God's specific laws to historical circumstances (point four). Because of this ability, he can assess the economic value of opportunities, which include multiple uses for capital. He can understand the hierarchy of values in terms of available opportunities. He can also understand God's hierarchy of values. He is required to adopt God's hierarchy of values rather than his own.

Economic valuation is subjective in the sense that God is a person who evaluates things and relationships in terms their potential uses. God declares specific economic value in terms of an asset's comparative importance in the building of God's kingdom in history. The human evaluator is also a person. He is supposed to make his evaluation in terms of the same goal: building the kingdom of God in history. Economic value is inherent in the relationships that exist among imputing agents in a world of scarcity and alternative uses. These relationships may have value in terms of building the kingdom of God. But they may have value in terms of building the kingdom of man. There is therefore competition over the authority of rival economic value systems in history. Biblical economics teaches that economic value is imputed by God (point four), and therefore economic value is subjective. But economic value is also objective. It is objective because human imputations are the outcome of God's objective providence (omnipotence) and the objectivity in history of His original imputation (omniscience).

Christian economists must defend both the doctrine of subjective economic value and the doctrine of objective economic value. Both aspects of economic value must be seen covenantally, not autonomously. In contrast, humanistic economists assert that there is only subjective economic value, but then they smuggle in objective economic value through the methodological back doors of statistical aggregation and policy recommendations. To do this, they must assert, either explicitly or implicitly, their ability to make interpersonal comparisons of subjective utility, which is impossible if utility is only subjective.[17]

Imputation is the source of all value, including economic value. A person declares value. This need not be verbal. It rarely is verbal. He *evaluates*. This verb points to the underlying action: to assess value. He considers his circumstances. These include opportunities. He assesses the competing bids—prices—for temporary control of scarce resources. This tells him what others think specific assets are worth. He may decide to bid higher. This does not mean that he subjectively values ownership of the asset more than others do. He may value it as hardly worth anything, but his wealth enables him to bid far more than competitors do. We cannot measure subjective value. We can measure objective bids. *Monetary high bid wins.*

A little-known example in the Bible makes this clearer. David's first wife Michal later was given by her father Saul to another man (I Sam. 25:44). David in the meantime married lots of wives. After Saul's death, when David was king, he demanded the return of Michal. Abner, who had served Saul, now wanted to serve David. David told him that this would not be possible unless Abner returned Michal to him. Abner told the second husband to surrender his wife. "And her husband went with her, weeping as he went, following her as far as Bahurim. Then Abner said to him, 'Go, return.' So he returned" (II Sam. 3:16). From what we can determine by her second husband's demonstrated sadness at losing her, he loved her more than David did. But David's high bid won. "Your wife or your life."

Humanistic economics cannot scientifically resolve the ancient question of the relationship between economic value (subjective) and price (objective). To do so, a humanistic economist would have to give an account of the origin of economic value in terms of subjective imputation, yet also connect this imputation with objective prices. But he cannot scientifically make interpersonal comparisons of subjective utility.[18] So, he cannot say scientifically that the person who values a scarce resource

17. North, *Sovereignty & Dominion*, ch. 5.

18. Lionel Robbins, *An Essay on the Nature and Significance of Economic Science* (London: Macmillan, 1932), ch. VI.

more highly than other bidders do is the bidder who pays the highest price. There may be little relationship between the comparative "height" of the value scale of the winning bidder vs. those of rival bidders. All that the humanistic economist can say scientifically is this: (1) ownership of this asset was highest on the buyer's scale of values for this particular purchase; (2) ownership of this asset was highest on the individual scales of rival bidders for that particular purchase; (3) the highest bidder won. As with Michal's second husband, a losing bidder may have wanted that item more than anything except life itself. He lost it because his was not the highest bid.

Because of the epistemological separation of value and price in humanistic economics, critics of the free market argue that the rich man who can out-bid a poor man has an unfair advantage. The poor man needs an item more, the interventionist insists. The poor man values it more. He just cannot afford to bid more. The interventionist rejects any suggestion that the allocation of wealth established by the free market is morally correct or even desirable. This allocation lacks legitimacy, he says.

This places the humanistic defender of free market allocation at a rhetorical disadvantage. He insists that economics is value-free. He refuses to invoke morality. He thereby concedes the moral high ground to the critics of capitalism, because he denies that there is any moral ground in economic theory. The public thinks otherwise. The public knows instinctively that ethical neutrality is a myth in social affairs. So, defenders of the free market have always had a problem persuading the public of the benefits of an unhampered free market. The public wants moral reasons for accepting any explanation of economic cause and effect. The humanistic free market economist refuses to provide any moral explanations. He thinks he occupies the epistemological high ground, assuming he thinks about epistemology at all. The public does not care about academic epistemology. It cares about justice. Critics of the free market insist that they are calling for economic justice when they demand state intervention. The Bible rejects the claims of the interventionists in the name of a higher morality, i.e., property rights assigned by God.

E. Value-Added Living

Point five: succession. Jesus said: "The thief comes only to steal and kill and destroy; I came so that they would have life, and have it abundantly" (John 10:10). This applies to every Christian. It applies to all Christian covenantal institutions. This principle applies to kingdom expansion.

The adjective "value-added" refers to increased value as perceived by economic actors. They can consume more than they did before (at the same price). They can also save more (at the same price). *More is better than less at the same price.* Maybe they will do both: consume more and save more.

Can economic value be measured? This is one of the most divisive questions in economic theory. How can economic value be measured in an individual's self-assessment? He cannot measure it. There are no objective units. Therefore, there is no cardinal measurement. There are only comparative assessments: more, less, or the same. These are ordinal, not cardinal. When your wife asks you how much you love her, say, "A lot." Do not say, "Compared to whom?" I hope this is obvious. (This should be obvious.) Next, if she says, "How much is a lot?" you are getting into a danger zone. You have already closed off the ordinal response: "Compared to whom?" But there are no cardinal units of measurement.

Can collective value be measured statistically? If not, then what is the meaning of the Gross Domestic Product statistic? If it can be measured statistically, on what basis can anyone defend this assertion? If we cannot measure our own individual improved conditions by a unit of measurement, how can statisticians measure the increased economic value of a nation's resources? Is economic value being added to the nation? How do we know?

1. *Ideal Prices*

As the expansion of God's kingdom in history renders the reign of sin less extensive, God's economic valuations will increasingly shape the array of objective prices as His kingdom expands. More people will think God's thoughts after Him, and act accordingly. Their subjective valuations and their objective bidding will produce objective prices that are more in conformity to what economic value would be in a sin-free kingdom of God.[19]

As history moves toward the final judgment, the prices of all scarce resources will come closer to what they would be in a world without sin.[20] This will not be a world without scarcity. Scarcity is not the product of sin, even though *cursed* scarcity is (Gen. 3:17–19).[21] There still will be allocation decisions in eternity. Time will still be sequential. A person can be in only one place at one point in time. No man will ever be omniscient, omnipotent, or omnipresent. These are incommunicable attributes of God.

Every system of economic theory has a concept of ideal prices. Economists use this concept as a way to explain pricing in the real world. It is a pricing system that would exist if there were no uncertainty. These would be prices that would prevail under conditions of universal human omniscience: no profits and no losses. This is an unrealistic assumption theologically, because omniscience is not a communicable attribute of God. The assumption of omniscience leads to an inescapable conclusion in economic theory: *money prices would cease to exist.* If everyone were omniscient, there would be no need for money. In a world of omniscient decision-makers, there would be no uncertainty. Money evolves only because there is uncertainty. People hold money—the most marketable commodity—in order to reduce their uncertainty about future exchanges. Without money, there would be no money prices. So, there could be no money-based prices in a world of equilibrium. *The very concept of an equilibrium price is self-contradictory.*[22] Therefore, the use of equilibrium prices to explain pricing in a world of

19. This assumes postmillennialism. Rival views would have to defend the idea that prices will reflect the valuations of the kingdom of man. But people who hold these eschatological views have yet to discuss them in relation to economic theory.

20. This is the assertion of postmillennialism. Amillennialism denies this. Premillennialism denies it with respect to life prior to the second coming of Christ to set up a thousand-year kingdom.

21. North, *Sovereignty & Dominion*, ch. 12.

22. Gary North, *Christian Economics for Teachers* (Moulton, Alabama: Axehead Press, [2017] 2026), ch. 54. Mises did not speak of equilibrium prices, but he did use the concept of the evenly rotating economy to explain the origin of the interest rate, which he called the originary rate of interest. He called this time preference. The evenly rotating economy is exactly the same as an economy in equilibrium. It is an economy in which participants know the future perfectly: no profits and no losses.

uncertainty is illogical. It literally makes no sense. Yet I have never seen this obvious implication of omniscience discussed in any economics textbook or treatise, other than my own.

In contrast to omniscience, sin-free living is a communicable attribute. The proof of this is Jesus Christ, who was fully human and also sin-free. There will be prices in the new heaven and the new earth. There will be scarcity. There will be uncertainty. There will be money. There will be allocation decisions. But there will not be sin.

As people's decisions conform more closely to the economic laws of God, there will be reduced waste. There will be ever-growing accurate knowledge. There will be compound economic growth. In short, *there will be added economic value*. This is an ethical requirement, according to Deuteronomy 8:18. "But you are to remember the LORD your God, for it is He who is giving you power to make wealth, in order to confirm His covenant which He swore to your fathers, as it is this day." Wealth is a form of covenantal confirmation of widespread obedience to the ethical terms of the covenant.[23]

2. *Imputed Wealth and the Image of God*

Deuteronomy 8:18 offers the promised sanction of increased corporate wealth for a covenant-keeping nation. There must be ways for citizens to see if the promise is being fulfilled. Otherwise, the promise was empty: unperceived sanctions. So, the concept of wealth is *objective*, in that it can be *measured*. It is also *subjective*, in that it can be *perceived*. So, in Christian economic theory, increased wealth is a legitimate goal and also a perceivable goal.

There are various statistical measures of increased wealth. All are faulty, in that their defenders cannot give an account of how these measures work in a world of competing subjective values, which change. Because man is made in God's image, God's imputation of increasing objective wealth can be perceived by mankind. *There is a point of contact between God and man: the image of God in man*. So, there is a point of contact between God's imputed value and man's imputed value. There is no way for self-proclaimed autonomous economists to defend

23. North, *Inheritance & Dominion*, ch. 22.

their position in terms of their theory of purely subjective economic value, but a Christian can defend his position. It is internally consistent, although incomplete, as both the Bible and Gödel's theorem teach.

There is no need to seek perfection in establishing the relationship between a statistical theorem (Parmenides) and historical changes in both subjective and corporate value rankings over time (Heraclitus). As we say in America, "It's close enough for government work." Statistical sampling to estimate GDP is government work, in fact, although not in theory.

A rate of 2% per year per capita compound growth is not perceivable day to day or even year to year. But it has been perceivable decade to decade ever since 1800. *Compound growth changes everything,* as we have learned since 1800. The world of 2018 would not have been conceivable to John Tyler at age 20. He was born in 1790, in George Washington's first full year as President of the United States. He became President in 1841. Yet his two grandsons were still alive in 2018.[24]

Conclusion

The main differences between modern free market economic theory and Adam Smith's economics are these: (1) the substitution of philosophical nominalism-subjectivism for philosophical realism-objectivism as the explanation of economic value; (2) a far stronger defense of the concept of private ownership as central, rather than the division of labor.[25]

The concept of economic imputation is nominalist in humanistic economics. In Calvinist systematic theology, imputation is God's judicial act. God declares a person "not guilty." On what basis? This: God imputes the ethically perfect humanity of Jesus to specific covenant-breakers. This act transforms them into covenant-keepers. Imputation is God's judicial declaration. In Christian economics, imputation is also God's act of evaluation. It is ethical. It has to do with value. It is also

24. I interviewed one of them, Lyon Tyler, in December 2010.

25. Tom Bethell, *The Noblest Triumph: Property and Prosperity Through the Ages* (New York: St. Martin's, 1998), chaps. 7, 20.

epistemological: the imputation of coherence and meaning to historical objects and acts. *The biblical criterion of imputation is the kingdom of God.* This doctrine is central to economics. (It is also central to historiography.)[26]

By shifting the explanation of economic value from realism to nominalism, economists have created epistemological dilemmas for themselves. How can they explain the relationship between value (subjective) and price (objective)? How can they defend the legitimacy of policy formation for collectives, when there is no scientific way to make interpersonal comparisons of subjective utility? How can they justify the development and use of statistical aggregates, when there is no scientific way to incorporate changes in subjective taste into the statistics? How can they compare statistical aggregates over time? How can they demonstrate scientifically that there is such a thing as economic growth?

The biblical solution is to affirm subjective economic valuation in the image of God in man. Men can accurately impute value, including economic value, because God did this retroactively, day by day, in the creation week. He will do so retroactively at the final judgment. He does so in between these two events. God tells men to evaluate all things by His laws. This is why we know that men can do this as redeemed creatures. *The judicial art of casuistry is grounded in the image of God in man.*

Men must make economic evaluations in their office as God's stewards. They must evaluate their success or failure, individually and collectively, over time. Men are under God's law, yet they are required by God to rule over His creation, also by law. They are responsible to God for the ethically consistent and economically efficient building of God's kingdom in history. Because men can *impute economic value,* they can *count the costs* of their actions, which God requires of all men (Luke 14:28–30).[27]

God's Bible-revealed laws are men's tools of dominion. They provide the standards of imputation. The judicial art of casuistry must be grounded in God's Bible-revealed laws. A person must enforce the judi-

---

26. This issue is this: Who imputes meaning and relevance to historical incidents? Who imputes authority to historical documents? Whose imputation possesses authority?

27. North, *Treasure & Dominion,* ch. 28.

cial letter of the law in terms of the spirit of the law: its goals for history. The letter of the law makes courts *predictable*, but its spirit must be upheld in order to achieve *justice*. There can be economic justice in history. If people do not believe this, they will lose hope.

Value and price are connected by means of men's subjective imputations. This subjectivism can and does reflect objective reality and objective economic value. The link is the image of God in man. Men are told that corporate obedience to biblical law produces economic growth (Deut. 8:18).[28] Therefore, it is possible to make accurate statistical representations of the underlying reality. This is why we can achieve value-added living. God's historical sanctions produce long-term patterns. These long-term patterns can be perceived by men. Men can evaluate the success of their decisions by means of sanctions, both positive and negative.

The epistemological foundation of analyzing market processes is a theory of price. Christian economics identifies this foundation as ethical. The closer that society gets to the final judgment, the more that progressive sanctification[29] brings the pricing system into relation to the ideal. The ideal is ethical. The array of prices is ultimately ethical. Prices reflect people's individual hierarchy of values.

In contrast, humanistic economics announces that the correct analytical tool is based on man's omniscience: equilibrium pricing. But this is conceptually impossible if humanistic economics is true. There could not be money prices in a world of equilibrium: a hypothetical world in which all people are omniscient. Money is a tool for reducing uncertainty. *If there were no uncertainty, there would be no money.*

---

28. North, *Inheritance & Dominion*, ch. 22.

29. John Murray, "Progressive Sanctification," *Collected Works of John Murray* (Edinburgh: Banner of Truth, 1982), II, ch. 23

Chapter 10

Inheritance

"Blessed are the meek: for they shall inherit the earth."

Matthew 5:5 (KJV)

Analysis

Point five of the biblical covenant is succession.[1] In economic theory, this is inheritance.

The essence of the dominion covenant is adding value. This is what Matthew 25:14–30 is all about: the parable of the talents.[2] Man's God-assigned goal is to increase value in the broadest sense. He who fails to do this will have his inheritance transferred to the more productive members of society in the final judgment (Matt. 25:30). The spiritually rich get richer. The spiritually poor are disinherited. Put differently, the poor in spirit inherit the kingdom of God (Matt. 5:3). So do the meek, i.e., meek before God (Matt. 5:5).[3] This is the fundamental New Testament principle of inheritance.

This inheritance procedure is supposed to be reflected in the economy. Those who subordinate themselves to the demands of customers

1. Ray R. Sutton, *That You May Prosper: Dominion By Covenant*, 2nd ed. (Tyler, Texas: Institute for Christian Economics, [1987] 1992), ch. 5.

2. Gary North, *Priorities & Dominion: An Economic Commentary on Matthew* (Moulton, Alabama: Axehead Press, [2012] 2030), ch. 47.

3. Ibid. ch. 4.

will get richer. Those who do not will get poorer. *The market-based sanctions system of monetary profit and loss rewards those who are efficient servants of customers.* They have subordinated their efforts to the demands of customers. This is how stewards prosper. They accumulate wealth. Then they die.

Inheritance is the legal transfer of wealth at the death of the owner. This transfer is inescapable in the era after the fall of man. The accumulator of wealth cannot maintain control beyond his death. He must take steps to transfer it. This is one of the most daunting tasks of the rich man, Solomon said in Ecclesiastes.[4] This is the covenantal issue of inheritance: point five of the biblical covenant. It applies in two ways: inheritance and disinheritance. These are extensions of economic sanctions in history: profit and loss. These sanctions are both individual and corporate.

Both inheritance and disinheritance apply to individuals. There will be a general resurrection (Matt. 25:31–46). Covenant-keepers will receive their inheritance: an extension of the New Heaven and the New Earth. Covenant-breakers will be cut off eternally: the ultimate disinheritance. They will receive the second death (Rev. 20:14–15).

Inheritance also applies to the kingdom of God in history and eternity. There is a corporate inheritance. The kingdom of covenant-breaking man ceases to operate in eternity. It is disinherited.

Each covenant has a doctrine of the last things. The kingdom of God predicts the future eternal extension of its jurisdiction.[5] The kingdom of man predicts either the heat death of the universe, in which everything dies, energy dissipates completely, and time ends,[6] or else endless cosmic cycles. In each case, meaning dies at the end, either at cosmic end or the end of this cosmic cycle. Death swallows up life. Meaninglessness swallows up meaning. There is no sovereign to impute permanent meaning to the past, present, and future. All meaning is temporal, problematical, and transitory.

---

4. Ecclesiastes 2:18–21; 6:1–2. Cf. Gary North, *Autonomy & Stagnation: An Economic Commentary on Ecclesiastes* (Moulton, Alabama: Axehead Press, [2012] 2030), chaps. 4, 21.

5. Kenneth L. Gentry, *He Shall Have Dominion*, 2nd ed. (Tyler, Texas: Institute for Christian Economics, [1992] 1997).

6. Gary North, *Is the World Running Down? Crisis in the Christian Worldview* (Moulton, Alabama: Axehead Press, [1988] 2029), ch. 2.

A. Purpose

Point one: God's sovereignty. With respect to economics, this refers to original ownership. It is the result of God's creation. He owns the universe. Before the foundation of the world, God had as His long-run purpose for the creation of the universe the redemption of His elect. This is a matter of adoption. It is a matter of inheritance. Paul wrote:

> Blessed be the God and Father of our Lord Jesus Christ, who has blessed us with every spiritual blessing in the heavenly places in Christ, just as He chose us in Him before the foundation of the world, that we would be holy and blameless before Him. In love He predestined us to adoption as sons and daughters through Jesus Christ to Himself, according to the good pleasure of His will, to the praise of the glory of His grace, with which He favored us in the Beloved. In Him we have redemption through His blood, the forgiveness of our wrongdoings, according to the riches of His grace which He lavished on us. In all wisdom and insight He made known to us the mystery of His will, according to His good pleasure which He set forth in Him, regarding His plan of the fullness of the times, to bring all things together in Christ, things in the heavens and things on the earth. In Him we also have obtained an inheritance, having been predestined according to the purpose of Him who works all things in accordance with the plan of His will, to the end that we who were the first to hope in the Christ would be to the praise of His glory. (Eph. 1:3–12)

This purpose structures all of history. Without understanding this and acknowledging this, a person misunderstands history. He begins with a distorted understanding of historical causation. Part of historical causation is economic causation. This means ethical causation: point three of the biblical covenant, biblical law, coupled with point four: predictable historical sanctions.

Redemption means "bought back." This is not man's purchase of salvation on his own behalf. He does not possess sufficient capital for this. Later in his letter to the Ephesians, Paul wrote: "For by grace you have been saved through faith; and this is not of yourselves, it is the gift of God; not a result of works, so that no one may boast. For we are His workmanship, created in Christ Jesus for good works, which God prepared beforehand so that we would walk in them" (Eph. 2:8–10). Yes, we work to honor God, but this is not the basis of our redemption. Christ's death is. Paul wrote: "But God demonstrates His own love toward us, in that while we were still sinners, Christ died for us" (Rom. 5:8).

This fact has economic implications. It teaches that error leads people to imagine that they can successfully strive to buy their souls out of hell. Jesus taught: "For what good will it do a person if he gains the whole world, but forfeits his soul? Or what will a person give in exchange for his soul?" (Matt. 16:26).[7] Error leads to the view that salvation is a matter of a sinner's payment to God or bargaining with God. God's purpose structures the most important of all payments to God. The payment was made by the Son of God to God the Father. It is therefore not a matter of economic planning. It precedes economic planning. This is the theological basis of this conclusion: *purpose precedes planning*.

Individuals reflect God. They are made in His image. Like God, they have general purposes. They also have specific goals that are related to their overall purposes. These purposes guide them in devising plans that they hope will enable them to fulfill their goals.

B. Planning

Point two: hierarchy. Man is under God as God's covenantal agent. This is the meaning of the dominion covenant (Gen. 1:26–28). He must make plans in order to fulfill his assignment. Built into this planning is the multiplication of the species.

1. *Multiplication*

The dominion covenant began with multiplication. "Then God said, 'Let Us make mankind in Our image, according to Our likeness; and let them rule over the fish of the sea and over the birds of the sky and over the livestock and over all the earth, and over every crawling thing that crawls on the earth.' So God created man in His own image, in the image of God He created him; male and female He created them. God

7. North, *Priorities & Dominion*, ch. 35.

blessed them; and God said to them, 'Be fruitful and multiply, and fill the earth, and subdue it; and rule over the fish of the sea and over the birds of the sky and over every living thing that moves on the earth'" (Gen. 1:26–28).[8]

God defines man in terms of this covenantal assignment. The Bible defines man in a three-fold way: (1) the image of God, (2) the dominion covenant, and (3), species multiplication. Multiplication mandates extension in space and time. To the extent that it involves time, it now involves death. This raises the twin issues of death and inheritance.

Population growth is a matter of dominion. It is central to the calling of mankind. The extension of population is a covenantally mandated process. *Individual decisions produce a corporate result.* This corporate result is mandated. Therefore, the means by which it is fulfilled is through sexual bonding within the marriage covenant. Sexual bonding is by far the best example in history of the intensely self-interested decisions of individuals which produce results that are glorifying to God. The division of labor is extended by population growth. The realm of dominion is thereby extended. There is the possibility of increasing wealth per capita. The compound economic growth that began sometime around 1800 in the British Isles, Canada, and the United States has transformed the world more than anything else that mankind has ever done. The defense of the idea of the pursuit of individual self-interest as benefitting society should begin here.

The zero population growth ideology is opposed to the clear teaching of the dominion covenant.[9] So is the zero economic growth movement. They are peas in the same anti-dominion pod.

Multiplication mandates thrift. It costs wealth to raise children. Children are wealth-absorbing creatures. Parents are obligated by civil law, by custom, and by love to care for their children. In some limited sense, children are consumer goods. But grandparents, not parents, are the main beneficiaries of children as consumer goods. Raising a family takes time and money. While parents do gain some returns in the short

---

8. Gary North, *Sovereignty & Dominion: An Economic Commentary on Genesis* (Moulton, Alabama: Axehead Press, [1982, 2012] 2022), chaps. 3, 4.

9. Ibid., ch. 22. Cf. Gary North, *Authority & Dominion: An Economic Commentary on Exodus*, vol. 5 (Moulton, Alabama: Axehead Press, [1985, 2012] 2025), Appendix B: "The Demographics of Decline."

run, children are mostly capital expenditures until they either reach adulthood or graduate from college.

The concept of compound growth raises the question of the exponential curve. At some point, a graph of the compound growth of anything turns upward and begins to approach infinity as a limit.[10] In a world of finite resources, this cannot continue indefinitely. With respect to human population, we will run out of living space in short order. So, this means one of two things: (1) there will be a cessation of compound population growth because of limited physical space; (2) there will be a cessation of economic growth because of limited time: the final judgment.[11] Nothing grows forever. Historical time will end.

2. *Serving the Future*

Men add value to the creation over time. So, point two of the covenant—hierarchy—has to apply to this process of future-orientation. Hierarchical authority in a biblical covenant is supposed to spread outward—across borders—and through time. It takes time to spread this authority across borders. So, time and place are linked in the covenant.

In short, *the dominion covenant is future-oriented.* The process of dominion requires present sacrifice for the sake of children, but this is an indirect sacrifice for the sake of families outside the extended family. Parents train their children to become productive. This means becoming customer-satisfying. The future economic success of their children will be dependent on their efficiency in serving the demands of strangers through the market process.

Biblical stewardship is comprehensive. It involves service to God, service to family members, service to strangers, and service to ourselves as individuals. This service is always future-oriented: the next sale and sales by heirs in the distant future. This is inter-generational service.

Future-orientation is inescapable. It is inherent in the dominion covenant. It takes time for covenant-keepers to extend God's kingdom. This kingdom is comprehensive. It involves all of society, which is a far

---

10. Gary North, "The Theology of the Exponential Curve," *The Freeman* (May 1970). Reprinted in Gary North, *An Introduction to Christian Economics* (Moulton, Alabama: Axehead Press, [1973] 2025), ch. 8.

11. Gary North, *Inheritance & Dominion: An Economic Commentary on Deuteronomy* (Moulton, Alabama: Axehead Press, [1999, 2012] 2028), ch. 2:D.

broader category than the state. The state is a relatively small aspect of society. The family has far greater influence than the state possesses. So does the realm of business. These realms absorb more time and money of individuals than taxes do. Wherever this is not true, the state becomes tyrannical. Then it is replaced by a less tyrannical state. Tyranny is inefficient. It invades too many spheres of life. It bankrupts itself. The classic example is the Soviet Union, from its birth on October 25, 1917 to its death on December 25, 1991.

Service is inherently future-oriented. Entrepreneurial profits are obtained in the future by means of correct forecasting and efficient planning in terms of this forecast. The essence of value-added living is making profits. People add to their capital by reinvesting their profits. Capital is a tool of production.

C. Imitation

Point three: ethics. This is associated with law. Jesus commanded His followers: "Go and do the same." (Luke 10:37b). These words are the foundation of all imitation. *Imitation is a crucial aspect of kingdom expansion over time.*

The best managers know that the best way to learn how to manage any organization is to work under an effective manager. This was the way of American business until the 1970s, when bureaucratic training in graduate schools of business administration began to replace the ancient systems of apprenticeship and mentoring.[12] Here was the old rule: *on-the-job training.* It assumed that management involves far more than what is revealed in ledgers. People are not digital creatures. We learn analogically, not digitally.

Adam had to start without a mentor. He alone in history had this responsibility. He was the first human. But his heirs were to receive training in his household. Then they were to depart from his household as adults, setting up their own households (Gen. 2:24). Having seen how a family is supposed to be managed, they were then to go out and apply whatever they had learned to new circumstances.

12. Kenneth Hopper and William Hopper, *The Puritan Gift: Reclaiming the American Dream Amidst Global Financial Crisis* (New York: I. B. Tauris, [2007] 2009), ch. 13.

This process rested on faith in *judicial continuity in history*. The rules governing one generation apply to the next generation. General rules are applicable to new situations. These new situations are both geographical and temporal. The rules will successfully apply across a geographical boundary and a temporal boundary: from *here and now* to *there and then*. These rules will serve as tools of dominion. This is why Jesus told the man to go and do likewise. Jesus knew that there is judicial continuity in history.

This is why we believe that there are lessons worth learning in history. If there were no judicial and social continuity, lessons would not be worth learning. There would be no likelihood that a lesson learned in one time and place would be relevant in another time and place. Men ask: "What are these lessons? Where is there proof that these lessons are in fact lessons? If the lessons are embedded in one time and place, on what basis can we legitimately expect them to be applicable in another time and place?"

The biblical answer is the *continuity of law* in history. Psalm 119 is the great defense of this answer. God is above the law, yet He rules through law. Man is under law. He rules over the creation by means of law. If there were no continuity of law, there would be chaos. Whirl would be king. But whirl is not king.

The covenant's structure of God, providence, law, sanctions, and time provides answers to the logically irreconcilable issues raised by the two major pre-Socratic philosophers, Parmenides and Heraclitus. The logically unchanging rational categories of Parmenides cannot be shown to interact with the constant flux proposed by Heraclitus. The equivalent of a logical machine cannot deal with organically evolving parts. Change is the enemy of autonomously rational categories, and vice versa. Here is the biblical solution to this dilemma. The Bible teaches that God is sovereign (Prov. 21:1). His decree is absolute (Isa. 45). Logic is personal, for it has its origin in God's mind. Historical causation is cosmically personal.[13] Coherence originates in God. The continuity of law originates in God.

God's covenants are above all ethical. *There is ethical continuity over time and across borders*. A covenant-keeper can extend God's king-

13. North, *Sovereignty & Dominion*, ch. 1.

dom through time and across borders. Why? Because God's law is the covenant-keeper's tool of dominion. God's law applies to the details of history. There is covenantal continuity in history. With respect to the individual and the church, this continuity reaches into eternity.

The division of labor rests on judicial continuity through time. Because of continuity across borders and through time, people can more safely trade with each other. They can understand each other. They can make contracts with each other. They can predict each other's behavior. They can coordinate their plans with each other. This increases the output of cooperating people. It extends their dominion as individuals. It also extends the dominion of cooperating social groups. Both the one and the many are recipients of positive sanctions.

For any *system of imitation* to function properly, there must be a *system of predictable sanctions*, both positive and negative (point four). If people could not predict the outcomes of their own behavior, as well as others' behavior, they could not make accurate plans. They would not know which practices should be adhered to, and which should be abandoned. Only because there are predictable sanctions in history can Jesus' command be trusted: "Go, and do thou likewise." It assumes that if we follow the lead of a successful person, we can expect to enjoy comparable success.

D. Judgment

Point four: sanctions. In economics, judgment has to do with forecasting the outcomes of plans. Outcomes are guided by objective economic sanctions: monetary profit and loss. There is causality in economic affairs. This is why rational economic forecasting is possible.

An entrepreneur in a free market is motivated to maximize profits, mainly monetary profits. There is a planning function in all entrepreneurship. This is related to point two. But the primary guide for economic planning is accounting-based profits. This is why I categorize entrepreneurship under point four rather than point two. Economic results are assessed objectively: monetary profit or loss. They are also assessed subjectively: imputation. Both are aspects of point four: judgment and sanctions. The archetype is God's final judgment at the end of history: point four. This leads to a conclusion: *all creativity is results-oriented.* It was for God in the creation week. It is for man.

Every system of economic theory must provide an answer to two questions. First, what is the source of profits in a competitive economy? Second, if it is true, as free market economists argue, that every resource receives its proper share of the value of its contribution in the production process, what aspect of the process guarantees this?

Ludwig von Mises provided an answer. The free market pays for all factor inputs in terms of *expected future value.* But expectations can be inaccurate. It is possible to pay too much for a factor of production. This will produce either losses or reduced profits. It is also possible to pay less than value added. This produces higher profits. It is the *discrepancy between expectations and reality* that produces either profits or losses. In his discussion of entrepreneurship, profits, and losses in his magnum opus, *Human Action* (1949), he stressed the role of the entrepreneur.

> The entrepreneurial function, the striving of entrepreneurs after profits, is the driving power in the market economy. Profit and loss are the devices by means of which the consumers exercise their supremacy on the market. The behavior of the consumers makes profits and losses appear and thereby shifts ownership of the means of production from the hands of the less efficient into those of the more efficient. It makes a man the more influential in the direction of business activities the better he succeeds in serving the consumers. In the absence of profit and loss the entrepreneurs would not know what the most urgent needs of the consumers are. If some entrepreneurs were to guess it, they would lack the means to adjust production accordingly.[14]

The problem with his exposition in *Human Action* is this: it is not clear where these profits or losses come from. In a speech, "Profit and Loss," delivered in 1951, he made his position clear. First, the primary issue is *forecasting.* Second, there is the development of *plans* to buy low and sell high. This is possible only because competing investors do not see the potential for final sales. Third, the plan must be *implemented.* He wrote:

14. Ludwig von Mises, *Human Action: A Treatise on Economics* (New Haven, Connecticut: Yale University Press, 1949), ch. XV:9, 297.

> If all people were to anticipate correctly the future state of the market, the entrepreneurs would neither earn any profits nor suffer any losses. They would have to buy the complementary factors of production at prices which would, already at the instant of the purchase, fully reflect the future prices of the products. No room would be left either for profit or for loss. Profit emerges from the fact that an entrepreneur estimates the future prices of the products more correctly than his rivals do. He buys some or all of the factors of production at prices which, seen from the point of view of the future state of the market, are low. Thus, his total costs of production—including interest on the capital invested—are lower than what he receives from the sale of the product. This difference is entrepreneurial profit.
>
> On the other hand, the entrepreneur who misjudges the future prices of the products allows for the factors of production prices which, seen from the point of view of the future state of the market, are too high. His total costs of production exceed the prices at which he can sell the product. This difference is entrepreneurial loss.
>
> Thus profit and loss are generated by success or failure in adjusting the course of production activities to the most urgent demand of the consumers. Once this adjustment is achieved, they disappear. The prices of the complementary factors of production reach a height at which total costs of production coincide with the price of the product. Profit and loss are ever-present features only on account of the fact that ceaseless change in the economic data makes again and again new discrepancies, and consequently the need for new adjustments originate.[15]

Here is the heart of the matter: "The activities of the entrepreneur consist in making decisions. He determines for what purpose the factors of production should be employed."[16] He can buy low only because other entrepreneurs do not see this opportunity. He can sell higher only because other entrepreneurs have not brought competing goods to the market. Why not? Because they did not see the opportunity.

The essence of entrepreneurship is forecasting future customer demand. There is continuity over time. But there is also discontinuity. Competing entrepreneurs failed to see the discontinuity: low factor

15. Ludwig von Mises, *Planning for Freedom*, 3rd ed. (South Holland, Illinois: Libertarian Press, [1952] 1974), 108–109.

16. Ibid., 111.

prices that can be bought, reassembled, and sold as customer goods at a price higher than the prices of all of the factors of production, including time (interest rate). The discontinuity is filled by entrepreneurs. As information spreads, the discontinuity—a discrepancy between factor prices and final products' prices—disappears. Mises wrote: "Profits are never normal. They appear only where there is a maladjustment, a divergence between actual production and production as it should be in order to utilize the available material and mental resources for the best possible satisfaction of the wishes of the public. They are the prize of those who remove this maladjustment; they disappear as soon as the maladjustment is entirely removed."[17]

The system of profit and loss is governed by future-orientation: *faith in continuity over time*. To increase his wealth, a producer must meet future customer demand. Not being omniscient, forecasters make experience-based guesses. They take hunches seriously. Some win. Some lose. But the entrepreneurial function is tied to the individual's desire to accumulate wealth by satisfying the future demand of customers. The self-interest of the producer and the self-interest of buyers together produce goods and services that clear the market at some array of selling prices.

E. Dominion

Point five: succession. In economics, dominion requires compound economic growth. This is possible to attain only because there are predictable sanctions in history. These include economic sanctions. This means that there is a possibility to increase production over time. Why? Because *positive sanctions accumulate*. There is economic growth because output increases. This is promised in Deuteronomy 8:18. "But you are to remember the LORD your God, for it is He who is giving you power to make wealth, in order to confirm His covenant which He swore to your fathers, as it is this day."[18] There is positive feedback between covenantal faithfulness and wealth. Increasing wealth confirms the covenant.

17. Ibid., 119.
18. North, *Inheritance & Dominion*, ch. 22.

Mises wrote in *Human Action*, "We call a progressing economy an economy in which the per capita quota of capital invested is increasing."[19] The basis of economic growth is therefore thrift: the reduction of consumption by the investor, who makes available his saved money, which is then used to increase the purchases of raw materials, capital goods, and labor during a period of production. Mises wrote:

> In the progressing economy the range of entrepreneurial activities includes, moreover, the determination of the employment of the additional capital goods accumulated by new savings. The injection of these additional capital goods is bound to increase the total sum of the income produced, i.e., of that supply of consumers' goods which can be consumed without diminishing the capital equipment used in its production and thereby without impairing the output of future production. The increase of income is effected either by an expansion of production without altering the technological methods of production or by an improvement in technological methods which would not have been feasible under the previous conditions of a less ample supply of capital goods.[20]

This of course assumes that the entrepreneurial guidance is accurate. It is always possible to pour money down rat holes. So, increased thrift is necessary, but it may not be sufficient to produce economic growth.

The biblical goal is to build a posthumous legacy, individual and corporate, in the broadest sense. This legacy is part of the kingdom's process of compound growth, which is a moral imperative. To the extent that covenant-keepers obey God's laws, they will experience blessings. These blessings confirm the covenantal connection. The Book of Job reinforces this, but only in the final chapter.[21]

Because the one and the many are coordinated in the covenant, the covenant-keeper's legacy compounds in history, and this extends God's corporate kingdom. The capital base of both the individual and the collective grow. The reinforcing gains of the one (corporate) and

---

19. Mises, *Human Action*, 292.
20. Idem.
21. Gary North, *Predictability & Dominion: An Economic Commentary on Job* (Moulton, Alabama: Axehead Press, [2012] 2029), ch. 6:D.

the many (individuals) are coordinated by the Holy Spirit under God's authority. The French Revolution's cry—liberty, equality, fraternity—was completely wrong about equality, and the guillotine did not secure either fraternity or liberty. But the structure of the biblical covenant does encourage both liberty and fraternity within the covenant. This should be true in the church covenant, the family covenant, and the civil covenant. Whenever it is not true, men's first task is to identify which laws are being broken. The task does not end there. Three of Job's four visitors assumed that the negative sanctions that Job was enduring indicated sin on his part. They were wrong. But if, over several years, a covenant is not bringing greater prosperity to its members in response to their greater self-discipline and greater intra-covenantal cooperation, they should start looking for hidden sins. Covenant-breaking is most likely the cause.

Conclusion

The dominion covenant assigns to all mankind the task of adding value to God's creation. The creation was created perfect, but it was incomplete. Man was created perfect, but he was incomplete. Both man and nature will always remain incomplete. They are not infinite. Man will never understand God's infinitude. Yet an infinite God governs the world. To understand this world perfectly, men would have to understand God perfectly, for God interacts with this world. Hence, man can never comprehend the world. In order for mankind to govern the world, individuals must rely on God as their source of covenantal laws, nature's laws, and their personal insight (judgment) as to the proper management of all things. The division of intellectual labor mandates the cooperation of individuals in this species-wide task.

The process takes time. Thus, there has to be an increase of man's knowledge and jurisdiction over time and space. This means that the improved economic value of the creation over time testifies to man's subordination to God. Economic growth reinforces the covenant. It testifies to God's existence, with man and nature under God by means of God's law. Men are supposed to perceive this added value, interpreting it as creatures under God. There must be continuity of God's law through time. This rests on the continuity of God's decree. Without this continuity of law, there would be no way to improve our knowledge of causation. Without knowledge of causation, we would live in mental chaos as well as cosmic chaos.

The fifth point of the biblical covenant is inheritance. This points to *continuity over time*. It also points to *net added value*. A person is to leave more wealth behind, as evaluated by God, than he received at birth. This means that there must be per capita economic growth. The members of each generation are to have more capital to work with than the preceding generation.

This has been fulfilled for more than two consecutive generations only since about 1800. In Great Britain, Canada, and the United States, compound growth began around 1800. It has not been reversed, except during the Great Depression of the 1930s, which was a worldwide phenomenon. This compound per capita economic growth has transformed human society around the world. The world in 1900 in the United States would not have been recognizable to someone who died in 1800. The world in 2000 would have been almost unrecognizable to someone who died 1900. Electricity had become widely used in cities in 1900. Indoor plumbing was widespread in cities. The internal combustion engine was being used in cars, but cars were rare. There was no voice radio, only telegraphy, then a few years old. Train travel was well developed, as were steamships. There were no airplanes. There were anesthetics, but no sulfa drugs. There were punch cards, but no digital computers. There was no television or Internet. There was no electrical air conditioning.

Value-added living mandates thrift. Capital must be accumulated in order to fund increasing production. *This means that consumption cannot legitimately be the sole end of production*. There must be self-restraint on consumption individually to please God. There must be self-restraint corporately to achieve economic growth.

To assess either economic growth or contraction, there must be value criteria. These criteria must be perceptible to individuals. This means that there are interpersonal comparisons of subjective utility, for individuals are required by God to assess corporate economic growth.

Without the ability to compare subjective utilities, there could be no valid price index numbers. There could be no valid economic comparisons at all. All schools of economics rely on these indexes to discuss history. For example, Austrian School economists argue that monetary inflation produces price inflation. But to say anything verifiable about price inflation requires the use of an index number.

All economists make assessments regarding corporate success. But, given the epistemological presuppositions of all schools of modern humanistic economic theory other than Marxism, they cannot do this, given the pure subjectivism of all nominalism. Marxism is an exception because its adherents still adhere to the objective value theory that preceded the marginalist revolution of the 1870s. Marxist economists do not show how economic realism is possible, but they nonetheless maintain it. In this sense, the Marxists are the last of the philosophical realists in economics. There are not many of them any longer. The suicide of the Soviet Union in December 1991 decimated their already thinning ranks.

Conclusion to Part II

The topics of the individual covenant constitute what is generally designated as economics. There was a time when economics was a branch of moral philosophy. This was how it was developed by Adam Smith. But Smith was truly an intellectual schizophrenic. His *Theory of Moral Sentiments* (1759) laid down the ethics of a mild deism. His *Wealth of Nations* (1776) in no way relied on the moral foundations in the first book. The one common concept in both books was the phrase, "the invisible hand." This hand was not God's.

In the nineteenth century, Smith's disciples moved economics out of moral philosophy into political economy. They tried to deal analytically with the state. But they did not provide a moral framework for the state. Neither did they do so for economics.

In the early twentieth century, economic science emerged from the cocoon of political economy. It achieved its status as a separate academic department and a separate epistemological discipline. It announced its autonomy from ethics: value-free.

The Achilles heel of the discipline has always been the same: the discrepancy between subjective value and objective value. The subjectivists of the 1870s self-consciously abandoned the objective value theories of classical economics, which were themselves incompatible: (1) the labor theory of value, and (2) the cost-of-production theory of value. But the result was analogous to what had happened in the fourteenth century, when philosophical nominalists abandoned realism: the substitution of incompatible individual value judgments for collective value judgments. Humpty Dumpty is a nominalist. He keeps falling off the wall. Then he picks himself up, patches up his cracks with statistical aggregates, and climbs back onto the wall.

I have made the case for imputed economic value, using God's week of creation as the covenantal foundation. He spoke authoritatively. He pronounced His work objectively good. His plan had been executed with perfect precision. He did this as a single Being, but in three persons: the one and the many, unity and diversity. There is both individualism and corporate unanimity in God. There is both equality (ontological Trinity) and hierarchy (economic Trinity).

Man is made in God's image. So is society. Mankind reflects unity and diversity, equality and hierarchy. A man formulates plans and carries them out. So do cooperating individuals.

The individual covenant deals mostly with plans that are not irrevocable. Men can revise plans. They can buy and sell. Smith called this "truck and barter." So it is. The substitution of plans, products, and services is central to the individual covenant. You may legally sell your home. You may not legally sell your children or your wife.

What Mises called catallactics has to do with the sale of goods and services in a social order marked by the division of labor and money prices. The key to this market process is product substitution. Wherever there are moral limits on product substitution, there will be criteria for success other than monetary profit and loss. That is because the following principle does *not* apply: *monetary high bid wins.*

PART III

The Economic Structure of the Family Covenant

Introduction to Part III

A. You Cannot Sell Your Wife

In the previous sections of this book, I used a specific analytical strategy to explain economics. I discussed the free market as an auction. This is what all modern academic economists do, although they do not admit this. It is implied. Somehow, students of economics are supposed to figure this out intuitively. Few students ever do. The market as a gigantic auction is the heart, mind, and soul of economic theory. It has been ever since Adam Smith's *Wealth of Nations* (1776).

I made this point: *ownership implies the right of disownership.* It implies the legal right to exchange goods and services. One New Testament passage above all others affirms this. It appears in the parable of the field owner who hires workers throughout the day. At the end of the work day, he pays all of the workers the same amount of money. This outrages workers who began working at the beginning of the day. They insist that they deserve more money. He replies, "Is it not lawful for me to do what I want with what is my own? Or is your eye envious because I am generous?" (Matt. 20:15).[1] This is a pair of rhetorical questions. Jesus expected His listeners to understand that the employer was in the right, morally speaking. He was surely in the right, legally speaking. The workers had this choice: *take it or leave it.* That had been their choice early in the day: money or nothing. They took the offer of money. That was now their choice at the end of the day: money or nothing. They would be wise to take the offer. But understand this: *the legal framework*

1. Gary North, *Priorities & Dominion: An Economic Commentary on Matthew* (Moulton, Alabama: Axehead Press, [2012] 2030), ch. 40.

of this parable was the free market order. The exchange had to do with individuals' labor time in relation to the employer's money.

From this point on in this book, I abandon the definition of ownership as conveying the right of disownership. The concept of ownership in the covenants of family, church, and state does not imply the right to disown. Husbands cannot legally disown their wives, selling them to the highest bidders. The church cannot legally sell access to the sacraments. Citizens cannot legally sell their votes.

This is why the next three sections of this book break with the familiar approach to economic science, as economists like to refer to the art of economic reasoning. As soon as economic theory departs from individual thought and action, it begins to move in one of two directions: either toward physics or toward sociology. Austrian School economists do not want economics to go down either path, but most economists prefer the path toward physics. I do not. More to the point, the Bible does not allow it. Why does biblical economics move toward sociology when discussing family, church, and state? Because the Bible does not allow unlimited market substitution in family relationships, church relationships, and state relationships. Family, church, and state rest on covenants, not contracts. Contracts are aspects of disownership, i.e., exchange. They are aspects of the auction process. Institutional covenants are superior to market contracts. They possess greater authority. They would be destroyed by a full application of the auction process.

The individual covenant has long constituted the vast bulk of those expositions that we define as economics. This covenant lodges primary responsibility in acting individuals. It focuses on decision-making: the allocation of scarce resources among competing individuals' ends, i.e., the market's auction process. It assumes that owners are profit-seeking individuals and corporate entities that can legally disown property. Competing bids to make exchanges are at the heart of the free market's division of labor. Even if an asset cannot legally be leased or sold, the economist still assesses its value in terms of a market: a black market.

This approach to economic analysis at some point reaches conceptual limits that thwart the logical coherence and practical realism of this analysis. Here is an example of such a limit. Can marriage be accurately analyzed in terms of the free market's auction process of competing bids? Should husbands be allowed by law to rent their wives' services as prostitutes? Could a marriage covenant be preserved under such a market-based social arrangement? Every society in history has the same answer: no. But a trained economist would be hard-pressed to reach this negative conclusion, given these two analytical assumptions: the legal autonomy of the individual marriage partners and the legitimacy of free market exchanges. Similarly, a free market economist has great difficulty to explain plausibly why sex for hire is not as valuable in most men's eyes as sex inside marriage. This preference has to do with a husband's legal right to exclude other men. But the price of this legal right to exclude is the prohibition against product substitution in marriage. Any attempt to equate the two legal arrangements economically will invariably sound strange, far-fetched, and out of touch with real-world decision-making. The legal foundation of marriage denies the legitimacy of market substitution. This undermines all economic analyses of marriage that are based on the categories of the market process as an auction. The legal prohibition of market substitution moves the economic analysis of marriage away from the logic of textbook economics toward sociology.

B. Judicially Separate Categories

The categories of academic economics begin to break down when they are applied to families, churches, and civil governments. These categories produce implausible conclusions. In the absence of the moral right to make exchanges, the legal right to make them ceases to be enforced by custom or the state. In fact, such exchanges are prohibited by custom and the state's criminal law. The free market principle of *monetary high bid wins* is called *bribery* when it is pursued by citizens and politicians. It is also illegal to sell your wife. Any such contract will be overturned in a civil court. Christianity insists that the contract should be overturned. I cannot think of any society or religion that would not agree. Any society that did not agree would not survive.

Humanistic free market economists begin with the idea of the autonomous self-ownership of each individual. Christian economics rejects this individualism, for it rejects all autonomy in any aspect of the creation. The glory of man is subordinate to the glory of God. The glory of the creation is subordinate to the glory of man. God's creativity is above man's. Man's creativity is above nature's. God's productivity is above man's. Man's productivity is above nature's. *Ownership is hierarchical under God.* It is also horizontal across geography and time. It is exclusive. He who owns something has the legal right to exclude access. This must be backed up by negative sanctions. The tree of the knowledge of good and evil is the archetype of this exclusionary aspect of property. God imposed negative sanctions for this violation. The Owner was the Judge.

The structure of the individual covenant is based on property ownership and personal responsibility before both God and man for the administration of this property. This includes property rights in one's own person. This leads to a crucial conclusion: *ownership is not autonomous.* It is delegated by God. It is a matter of stewardship. This crucial presupposition makes Christian economics different from all forms of secular economics. We must start with ownership, but not autonomous self-ownership. We must begin with God's ownership, and then move to covenantal self-ownership under the overall stewardship principle.

A husband and wife do not own each other, but each has obligatons to the other. To evaluate marriage in terms of the division of labor is legitimate. To evaluate it in terms of the principle of *monetary high bid wins* is not. (Prior to marriage, there are many forms of bidding.) There is not supposed to be an auction for all of wives' services, and surely not for sale. So, any attempt to evaluate marriage in terms of the economic categories of an auction produces ludicrous results. Only a few economists are so blind to reality as to attempt such an analysis.

Here is my assertion regarding covenants and contracts. If a contract undermines a covenant, and if a society authorizes this, this continual violation will bring supernatural negative sanctions against the society. The economist who ignores this does not understand the nature of covenantal incentives. But economists are humanists and secularists, analytically speaking. They have no awareness of the differences between covenants and contracts. They surely ignore supernatural sanctions, positive or negative.

Here is a biblical example of a contract that permanently removes freedom of future action. It is biblically legal to sell oneself into covenant-keeping slavery to another family. The Mosaic law had such a provision (Deut. 15:16–18). This is a form of permanent disownership. The individual sold himself to a superior manager: the head of a successful household. This added a layer of authority in between him and God. It reduced his authority. The New Covenant strongly recommends that covenant-keepers exercise greater authority. This is an extension of the dominion covenant. This is an implication of Jesus' prophecy that the meek will inherit the earth (Matt. 5:5),[2] meaning those who are meek before God. The New Testament therefore recommends that a lifetime slave accept manumission if it is offered by his owner (I Cor. 7:21).[3]

A biblically defined institutional covenant possesses greater authority than any individual contract. This is because God is a formal sanctions-bringer in a biblical institutional covenant. He is not in a contract. His name may not lawfully be invoked in a contract. His name has a boundary around it (Ex. 20:7).[4]

C. Open Bidding and Market Substitution

A man is not allowed to exchange his wife for someone he thinks would be more suitable. Neither is a wife allowed to do this with her husband. The now-obsolete practice in England of auctioning off a wife to the highest bidder was not sanctioned in the Bible. It was not legally sanctioned in England, either, but it went on for two centuries.[5] Parents are not allowed to sell their children. *As soon as market substitution is prohibited, the free market cannot establish a price.* Without a way to establish a market price, any discussion of economic value's relation to prices becomes even less tied to economic theory and economic practice than

2. Gary North, *Priorities & Dominion: An Economic Commentary on Matthew* (Moulton, Alabama: Axehead Press, [2012] 2030), ch. 4.

3. Gary North, *Judgment & Dominion: An Economic Commentary on I Corinthians* (Moulton, Alabama: Axehead Press, [2012] 2031), ch. 8.

4. Gary North, *Authority & Dominion: An Economic Commentary on Exodus*, vol. 1, *Part I: Representation & Dominion* (Moulton, Alabama: Axehead Press, [1985, 2012] 2025), ch. 23.

5. "Wife selling (English custom)." *Wikipedia*, Wikimedia Foundation, October 5, 2022.

it is under the assumption of asset substitution and competitive bidding. Without a way to relate these two concepts, economic theory loses its seeming precision.

This formal precision is based on an illusion. Value is exclusively subjective, according to economics after the marginalist revolution of the early 1870s. In contrast, a price is exclusively objective: the product of competitive bidding. The theoretical link between exclusively subjective economic value and objective prices has always been an epistemological contradiction. If value is exclusively subjective, then we do not know what an item's value is for anyone else. We know only the price paid by the highest bidder. We do not know how much value he placed on the item. We know only that he outbid the second-place bidder. Whether the second bidder valued it more than the winning bidder did cannot be determined scientifically, because there is no scientific way to measure interpersonal subjective utilities.[6] The winning bidder cannot say scientifically, "I valued this more than the losing bidder did." All he can say scientifically is this: "The loser decided not to match my bid."

The Bible says that a virtuous woman is more valuable than rubies (Prov. 31:10).[7] But this says nothing about their comparative prices. She is not for sale. The services of a non-virtuous woman are. Humanistic economics can therefore deal far better analytically with whores than wives. This is why biblical economics moves in the direction of sociology when it turns its attention to the family.

When we move from economic reasoning based on open entry, market pricing, and asset substitution, we lose the step-by-step rigor of economic reasoning. The theoretical categories are less definable. There is no system of reasoning that enables us to move logically from the characteristic features of the modern division of labor economy to the economics of family, church, and state. There is no equivalent of the conceptual construct of the free market as a gigantic auction. High monetary bids do not automatically win. They may be illegal. The logic of the auction process is not matched by the logic of the family, the

6. Lionel Robbins, *An Essay on the Nature and Science of Economics* (London: Macmillan, 1932), ch. VI.

7. Gary North, *Wisdom & Dominion: An Economic Commentary on Proverbs* (Moulton, Alabama: Axehead Press, [2012] 2029), ch. 86.

church, and the state. *There is no science of economics, once we depart from the auction process*. This is why the transition is resisted by economists. They do not wish to descend into the conceptually swampy terrains of family, church, and state. They prefer to reside in the mountain tops of market processes, where the atmosphere is thin and the growing season is short.

D. Autonomy and Economics

One of the most conceptually important books in the history of conservatism is Robert Nisbet's *The Quest for Community* (1953). Nisbet was a sociologist. In this book, Nisbet argued for the legitimacy of local institutions, such as churches, families, businesses, and schools. Without local allegiances, a man cannot successfully defend himself against the central state. Liberty requires the support of the individual by social institutions and allegiances. He opposed all political theory that begins with individual rights divorced from social institutions. He also believed that economic theory and practice must not begin with the abstract individual.[8] On the final page of the final chapter of the book, he wrote this. "What we need at the present time is the knowledge and administrative skill to create a laissez faire in which the basic unit will be the social group."[9] On the previous page, he had provided his reasoning. "We need a laissez faire that will hold fast to the ends of autonomy and freedom of choice; one that will begin not with the imaginary, abstract individual but with the personalities of human beings as they are actually given to us in association." He continued: "To create the conditions within which autonomous individuals could prosper, could be emancipated from the binding ties of kinship, class, and community, was the objective of the older laissez faire. To create the conditions within which autonomous groups may prosper must be, I believe, the prime objective of the new laissez faire."[10]

8. I describe such an individual as Parmenidean.

9. Robert A. Nisbet, *The Quest for Community: A Study in the Ethics of Order and Freedom* (Wilmington, Delaware: Intercollegiate Studies Institute, [1953] 2010), 257. This was published originally by Oxford University Press.

10. Ibid., 256.

I studied under Nisbet in classroom settings from 1966 through 1969. He was one of the three readers of my PhD dissertation in 1972. I am probably more familiar with his work than any other scholar. I have relied on his work in my writings. I assure you that he had no idea of how his academic goal could or should be attained: free market economic analysis that rests on the primary authority of social institutions, not the individual. He was a nineteenth-century judicial liberal, despite his verbal defense of conservatism as an ideal. He did not seek to demonstrate how, institutionally speaking, it would be possible to sustain the modern social order in terms of a legal order that does not place the individual in a courtroom before a jury, with no way to defend himself with these words: "I was just following orders." He wrote extensively from 1965 until 1992. He had years to deal with this crucial conceptual issue. He never returned to this issue after 1953.

To a limited degree, Wilhelm Röpke attempted to do this in the 1940s.[11] I do not regard his attempt as methodologically successful, but he asked the right sorts of social questions. I do not know whether my efforts in the final three sections of this book will provide an alternative to the economics of methodological individualism, but I hope they will. One thing is sure: I do not begin with the concept of autonomy—not of individuals or institutions. I begin with the biblical covenant.

11. This is not true of his 1937 book, known in English as *Economics of the Free Society* (Chicago: Regnery, 1963). It is more clearly a treatise written in the Austrian School framework.

Chapter 11

Ownership

Now it came about, when the sun had set, that it was very dark, and behold, a smoking oven and a flaming torch appeared which passed between these pieces. On that day the Lord *made a covenant with Abram, saying, "To your descendants I have given this land, From the river of Egypt as far as the great river, the river Euphrates: the land of the Kenite, the Kenizzite, the Kadmonite, the Hittite, the Perizzite, the Rephaim, the Amorite, the Canaanite, the Girgashite, and the Jebusite."*

Genesis 15:17–21

Analysis

Point one of the biblical covenant is God's sovereignty.[1] In economics, this refers to original ownership. As I have already written, the concept of ownership in the family is radically different from the concept of ownership in the free market. The free market allows the buying and selling of goods and services. Individuals own property. This ownership necessarily involves a bundle of legal rights. Among these rights is the right to dispose of the property in any way, so long as no one else is threatened with violence or fraud.

The right to buy and sell is the legal foundation of the law of supply

1. Ray R. Sutton, *That You May Prosper: Dominion by Covenant*, 2nd ed. (Tyler, Texas: Institute for Christian Economics, [1987] 1992), ch. 1.

and demand. This right establishes the crucial institutional sanctions of monetary profit and loss. These sanctions of economic accounting guide market production. This is the meaning of "monetary high bid wins." Because of numerical monetary sanctions, the market process is independent in a way that no other institutional arrangements enjoy. *There are laws of economics only because of the right of disownership, which is the right of voluntary exchange.* The legitimate claim of economists that economics is a real science rests entirely on the right to buy and sell. Without this, there would be no money, no impersonal prices, and no predictability.

We come now to an institution about which almost everyone throughout history has been agreed: *there are valid judicial limits on buying and selling within the family.* There is no bundle of legal rights that entitles any person to sell a member of his family.

I have argued that Christian economics must begin with ownership. God is the Creator. He is therefore the Owner. He has legally enforceable ownership claims on the creation. He will enforce these claims at the final judgment (Matt. 25). This is why, in my analysis of the economics of the family, I begin with ownership.

Ownership establishes personal responsibility. The Bible is clear on this. The more that someone owns, or the more knowledge that he possesses, the greater his responsibility. Jesus was clear on this. He spoke of the final judgment. The person who has less knowledge but breaks God's law is less responsible than the person who breaks God's law in light of greater knowledge. "And that slave who knew his master's will and did not get ready or act in accordance with his will, will receive many blows, but the one who did not know it, and committed acts deserving of a beating, will receive only a few blows. From everyone who has been given much, much will be demanded; and to whom they entrusted much, of him they will ask all the more" (Luke 12:47–48).[2]

Christian economics should place ownership first in its development of economic theory. Economic analysis is much easier when dealing with individual ownership than corporate covenantal ownership. That is because of the free market's system of monetary prices. Prices allow

2. Gary North, *Treasure & Dominion: An Economic Commentary on Luke* (Moulton, Alabama: Axehead Press, [2012] 2031), ch. 28:B.

accounting, and accounting guides production. With corporate units, there is no way to assess productivity in terms of prices generated inside the organization.

We know this: those who are authorized to make decisions regarding the organization's resource allocation have great responsibility. This fact leads to a conclusion: they function as owners. *There is no way to separate responsibility from ownership*. This works both ways: from ownership to responsibility and from responsibility to ownership.

A. God's Ownership

Point one: God's sovereignty. As with every other academic discipline, Christian economics must begin with the doctrine of God. This governs the first and foremost issue of economics: *ownership*. God owns the world. He created it, so He owns it. He owns it both individually and corporately. He is both one and many.

The New Testament says that the Second Person of the Trinity created everything that was created. Paul wrote:

> ...giving thanks to the Father, who has qualified us to share in the inheritance of the saints in light. For He rescued us from the domain of darkness, and transferred us to the kingdom of His beloved Son, in whom we have redemption, the forgiveness of sins. He is the image of the invisible God, the firstborn of all creation: for by Him all things were created, both in the heavens and on earth, visible and invisible, whether thrones, or dominions, or rulers, or authorities—all things have been created through Him and for Him. He is before all things, and in Him all things hold together. (Col. 1:12–17)

This affirmation reveals that there is *specialization within the Godhead*. There is a division of labor. God the Son is subordinate to God the Father. This is an aspect of the doctrine of the economic Trinity, as distinguished from the ontological Trinity, which affirms the equal ultimacy of the three persons of the Godhead. Christ was the original Creator. In this sense, creation was an aspect of stewardship. The creation remains under the authority of God the Son. He is a trustee for God the Father. He will deliver up the creation to the Father at the end of time. Paul wrote:

> But the fact is, Christ has been raised from the dead, the first fruits of those who are asleep. For since by a man death came, by a man also came the resurrection of the dead. For as in Adam all die, so also in Christ all will be made alive. But each in his own order: Christ the first fruits, after that those who are Christ's at His coming, then comes the end, when He hands over the kingdom to our God and Father, when He has abolished all rule and all authority and power. For He must reign until He has put all His enemies under His feet. The last enemy that will be abolished is death. For He has put all things in subjection under His feet. But when He says, "All things are put in subjection," it is clear that this excludes the Father who put all things in subjection to Him. When all things are subjected to Him, then the Son Himself will also be subjected to the One who subjected all things to Him, so that God may be all in all. (I Cor. 15:20–28)

God has purposes for the future. He makes plans for the future. He decrees the future. He the executes His decree in history. All of this is hierarchical. The Son is the Trustee for the Father. What we see with respect to the economic Trinity in relation to the creation, we see reflected in the family of man. The one and the many are manifested in a hierarchal relationship.

B. Central Planning

Point two: hierarchy. In economic theory, this is manifested in economic stewardship. It is always hierarchical. Stewards place property into service: to God, future buyers, dependent subordinates, and themselves. The model is the parable of the stewards (Matt. 25:14–30).[3]

The phrase "central planning" commonly applies to the state. It means economic planning by state officials. Conceptually, it applies equally well to the family and the church. Someone makes allocation decisions for the family's assets. This is the legal head of the household. The same hierarchical principle is true of the institutional church. This is a matter of economic representation. It is also a matter of guardianship, a legal category.

---

3. Gary North, *Priorities & Dominion: An Economic Commentary on Matthew* (Moulton, Alabama: Axehead Press, [2012] 2030), ch. 47.

1. *Planning and Prices*

The phrase "central planning" refers to socialist planning, also known as the command economy. That is because the state either owns or controls the means of production. But this is too narrow a definition. Central planning refers to planning by the head of any organization that operates internally without a system of competitive bidding in terms of monetary prices. Most organizations operate this way. Prices are derived from outside the organization. Here is an example. An employee finds out that others with his skills and level of responsibility in a rival firm are paid significantly more per hour. Armed with this information, he asks his boss for a raise. If he does not get it, he may quit. His boss now faces competition for the employee's services. In a free market, employers compete against employers. Employees compete against employees. The market's price system is external to a profit-seeking organization. This is exactly how Mises described the socialist economy. Because of its lack of internal pricing, Mises said that socialism is economically irrational.[4] Nevertheless, in a free market social order, organizations are not irrational. They can use prices derived from outside the organization to guide production. They sell their output into a market with open competition. The market is governed by "monetary high bid wins."

These organizations are run by senior management. This is central planning. But the price system enables lower-level experts in the organization to make economically rational decisions. Accurate information of local conditions is mainly located locally. So, within a profit-seeking organization, there is a meshing of plans: top and bottom. Market competition forces this. Prices guide production. *The market system's greatest benefit is the information provided by prices.* Without this, central planners would be irrational. They are not God. They are not omniscient.

I return to my example of the employee. What if an employee could not legally quit? What if he could not be fired? Market pricing would become close to irrelevant inside the organization. *This is the situation in a family.* Central planning in a family has almost no internal feedback based on monetary prices. There is no monetary accounting.

---

4. Ludwig von Mises, *Economic Calculation in the Socialist Commonwealth* (Auburn, Alabama: Mises Institute, [1920] 1990).

There are few objective criteria, and none is measurable. Under these conditions, the senior decision-maker is a central planner.

Central planning by families and churches works. Central planning by the state doesn't. What makes them different?

The first major difference is information. A family is small. A local church usually is. The head of the household is as aware of market conditions after he is married as before. He also has a lot more responsibility. He bears the burden of representative failure. He gains rewards if he succeeds. He is not planning a national economy. The same applies to church officers.

The second major difference is God's delegation of judicial authority to heads of families, usually fathers. I have argued in this book that ownership establishes both judicial and economic responsibility. But it works the other way, too. Legal responsibility establishes functional ownership economically, and usually also legal ownership. God delegates responsibility to heads of households. This means they are owners in His eyes. They possess legal control over family assets. They have the task of allocating capital. They have the task of coordinating household production. They must oversee plan reconciliation among family members.

The third major difference is this: children leave home when they become adults (Gen. 2:24). The family's central planner will not exercise authority over them forever. He will grow old and die. He will not be in charge of his finances if his children must care for him in his old age. He wants such care if required, and this requires children with assets. He therefore wants his children to be responsible owners of capital. This keeps wise family planners humble.

The fourth major difference this: family cooperation is based on love. This means discipline (sanctions) based on love. In a family, there are mutual claims on its members. *This element of mutuality is the very nature of the family*. The New Testament compares Christ's love of His church as the model for a man's love of his wife.

> Wives, subject yourselves to your own husbands, as to the Lord. For the husband is the head of the wife, as Christ also is the head of the church, He Himself being the Savior of the body. But as the church is subject to Christ, so also the wives ought to be to their husbands in everything.

> Husbands, love your wives, just as Christ also loved the church and gave Himself up for her, so that He might sanctify her, having cleansed her by the washing of water with the word, that He might present to Himself the church in all her glory, having no spot or wrinkle or any such thing; but that she would be holy and blameless. So husbands also ought to love their own wives as their own bodies. He who loves his own wife loves himself; for no one ever hated his own flesh, but nourishes and cherishes it, just as Christ also does the church, because we are parts of His body. For this reason a man shall leave his father and his mother and be joined to his wife, and the two shall become one flesh. This mystery is great; but I am speaking with reference to Christ and the church. Nevertheless, as for you individually, each husband is to love his own wife the same as himself, and the wife must see to it that she respects her husband. (Eph. 5:22–33)

2. *Corporate Ownership*

God created the family (Gen. 1:26–28). He designated the family as His agency of dominion. Thus, with respect to dominion, ownership is more corporate than individual. Why? Because *responsibility in history is corporate*. Does this contradict the principle that the final judgment is ultimately personal and individual, so responsibility is primarily personal? No. Why not? *Because each man is responsible to God above all as God's agent*. Adam rebelled. He was more responsible than Eve, Paul wrote (I Tim. 2:14), but Eve also suffered a curse (Gen. 3:16). Her responsibility was to her husband, but they were both involved in rebellion. This was joint rebellion. It was therefore corporate. The family unit was involved. God had assigned tasks to the family jointly. Adam's individual responsibility to God was mediatorial. Adam represented Eve. They both represented the creation to God in the context of the family. Theirs was a joint representation.

This means that they both had ownership claims over the creation. Because both of them were responsible, they both had ownership. It was hierarchical ownership, for it was corporate. Each of them had unique duties. This was reflected in their punishments, which were not the same. She would henceforth have pain in childbirth (Gen. 3:16). He would labor in the sweat of his brow (Gen. 3:17–19).[5] Both would

5. Gary North, *Sovereignty & Dominion: An Economic Commentary on Genesis* (Moulton, Alabama: Axehead Press, [1982, 2012] 2022), ch. 12.

die. The universality of death is the sign of their joint responsibility and joint ownership. *They rebelled as a team.*

The individualism of free market economic theory has led to great insights. Nevertheless, this almost exclusive reliance on individualism is wrong. This is because it is theologically wrong. It assumes that only individuals are responsible before men. In those areas of life in which individuals do bear most of the responsibility before men, economic theory has made great strides. But, at bottom, *modern economic theory cannot deal consistently with corporate responsibility.* It cannot make sense of individuals' decisions—decisions involving such issues as honor, love, and responsibility to and for collectives. When economists explain these decisions, they do not come to grips with individuals' motivation. When an economist discusses a mother's relation to her child as a capital investment that she expects will pay off in her old age, he sounds like a fool. That is because he really is a fool. He begins with the fool's premise: *there is no God.* "The fool has said in his heart, 'There is no God'" (Ps. 14:1a). The rest of his foolishness follows from his assumption.

The essence of the analytical problem and the practical problem is allocating shares of ownership: the share of the profits and the share of the losses. Above all, there is the share of the blame (Gen. 3). This allocation has to be made in terms of the degree of responsibility within a corporate organization whose members cannot legally separate themselves from a lifetime covenant. A covenant is not a contract. It is an oath-bound promise before God. Its degree of authority is far greater than any contract's authority.

Owners impute economic value to assets. They also impute economic value to the family covenant. This imputation is individual. But, as representing God, it is also corporate. So, the decision-makers within a family must come to some sort of agreement on the allocation of family assets. In earlier eras, women had no ownership rights in civil law. That was a defect of civil law. There is nothing explicit in the Bible that would forbid a woman entering into marriage from setting aside a portion of her assets for the use of her children. A drunken husband has no moral authority over the economic assets of his wife. There is nothing inherently immoral with a pre-nuptial agreement.

3. *Hierarchical Planning*

Planning has to do with the allocation of scarce resources. It therefore is based on ownership. God owns everything. He delegates control over assets to individuals. But He also delegates control to collectives. The idea of joint ownership is inherent in the biblical doctrine of the family. Family ownership reflects covenantal hierarchy: God over man over woman over children. It also is reflected in the family's dominion over nature (Gen. 1:26–28).[6] Ownership is not original. It is derived from God's grant of authority. While ownership is point one of the biblical covenant with respect to God, for man, ownership is point two: trusteeship.

Parents are responsible for non-adult children. They possess legal authority over them. This makes them economically responsible for their children. This rule of law always applies: *where there is authority, there is also responsibility*. Individuals must give an account to God for their trusteeship (Matt. 25). This involves giving an account of themselves for their joint authority as members of families. No one is autonomous. Every individual answers to God. Our attitudes and behavior toward others do count, meaning they are counted by God: assessed and evaluated.

There is an assumption in patriarchal societies that the woman surrenders ownership of her property at the time of marriage. But she does not uniquely surrender her body to her husband. She has the same legal claim on his body as he has on hers. This is *mutual submission*. The Old Testament affirms this. The husband owes her "conjugal rights" (Ex. 21:10). As we have seen, the New Testament speaks of mutual claims, husband and wife (Eph. 5:22–33). This verse is explicit: "subject yourselves to one another in the fear of Christ" (Eph. 5:21). The judicial fact of *mutual ownership claims* between persons, husband and wife, is indirect evidence of her legal claim to his property. He must care for her. He must care for her children. He does not possess a unique legal claim on her property that is not offset by her legal claim on his.

She is to defer to his judgment unless she has reason to believe that he is a wastrel. In such a case, she has a legal right to appeal to the church or the civil government for assistance. No one is autonomous.

6. North, *Sovereignty & Dominion*, chaps. 3, 4.

No one is beyond the civil law. No church member is beyond the legal claim of church law. *There are offsetting legal claims.* To imagine that the victimized wife of a drunkard must suffer just because she is a wife is a denial of the biblical foundation of civil government, victim's rights.[7]

Thus, the concept of joint economic planning is inherent in the family's biblical structure. The allocation decisions are individual, in the sense that the decision-makers have reached a reconciliation of their plans. But the outcome affects both parties, as well as children. God holds the adults responsible. They are responsible agents in the judicial context of a covenant. Neither party can escape blame. The attempt by Adam and Eve to blame others did not work. Each of them came under negative sanctions. Yet they participated in their rebellion as family members. The curse was on them and their children. Third parties were involved, despite the fact that third parties were not present in the garden. The concept of responsibility extended forward through time.

Plan reconciliation is basic to the free market. This has its roots in the family, which is a voluntary institution, but which becomes permanent in history by a formal oath. The exchange arrangements within a family are not based on *monetary high bid wins*. In short, *justice trumps profit*. Authority is not based on the purchase of an office. *The planning arrangement reflects the hierarchical structure of dominion.* God rules through families. His transfer of ownership to families is His way to maximize His return. But this return is not primarily monetary. His return on investment is far beyond monetary. It involves such things as ethical faithfulness, biological multiplication, and kingdom extension.

Husbands and wives are involved in constant plan reconciliation. In no other institutional arrangement is plan reconciliation more central. There are more instances of plan reconciliation in business, because negotiations are constant. One negotiation is completed or abandoned. Another takes its place. In a family, negotiations must be minimized in order to achieve peace. But the plans are far more fundamental in families than in businesses. The reconciliations are far more permanent. The stakes are far higher. The judicial bond of marriage is the result of plan reconciliation.

---

7. Gary North, *Victim's Rights: The Biblical View of Civil Justice* (Moulton, Alabama: Axehead Press, [1990] 2029).

Ownership involves asset allocation. This includes the allocation of work and time. This is inherent in any joint venture. Someone must take responsibility for performance. This is the division of labor in action. Family members defer to the head of the family. *This deference is an act of subordination*. The person who does the deferring is transferring responsibility to the other person. He is saying this: "I trust your judgment. I have now become dependent on your performance." This is crucial in any long-term arrangement. *The division of labor is both mutual and hierarchical*. Each of the parties becomes dependent on the other. Each of them exercises authority over the other. This is true in every institutional arrangement. The family is the primary model.

When children reach adulthood, they are under far less family authority. They establish their own households. Their parents let go, or should. Over time, the relationship of authority may reverse. If the parents become infirm, the children must step in and take over. This involves a transfer of economic responsibility. The children must support the parents. This is an aspect of the fifth commandment: honoring parents (Ex. 20:12).[8] In most circumstances, this involves paying attention to parents' wishes. As children mature, they pay less attention because they must focus on their children's needs. This takes time and resources. At the end of the parents' lives, this may mean that their children must take over their finances. Here, plan reconciliation is crucial. It involves a surrender of authority by the parents. They must surrender authority because they are surrendering responsibility.

All of this stems from the fact of the division of labor. There is mutuality. But mutuality always involves dependency. Each party must give up something of value in order to obtain something of value. Mutuality involves a surrender of responsibility. It therefore involves a transfer of authority. "I will do this for you, if you will do that for me." In the market, it is usually easy to substitute a new supplier. This is especially true in the consumer goods markets. There are many competing offers. Loyalty is weaker. *The more specialized the exchange, the more expensive it is to substitute a new supplier for an old one*. There are fewer available

---

8. Gary North, *Authority & Dominion: An Economic Commentary on Exodus*, vol. 2, *Part II: Decalogue & Dominion* (Moulton, Alabama: Axehead Press, [1986, 2012] 2025), ch. 25.

suppliers. Mutual dependence is therefore greater. The disruption of the division of labor is greater. *In marriage, this division of labor is highly specific*. This is why partner substitution is prohibited by the Bible, except for major moral violations.[9] A covenant is more binding than a contract is. It is affirmed by an oath under God.

C. Boundaries

Point three: ethics. This is related to law. Law places judicial boundaries around property. In the family, the primary boundaries are sexual. They establish exclusive access. These boundaries include, but they also exclude. The archetype on this exclusion aspect is the tree of the knowledge of good and evil. God definitively excluded mankind from this tree. The sexual boundaries of marriage mark many other aspects of the family. The rights of exclusion are fundamental.

Property rights are boundaries. These boundaries/rights are clearer in boundaries against intrusion by non-family members. The boundaries around the family are more easily understood and enforced: by individuals, family members, church, and state. Inside the family, these boundaries become less clear. Also, the general boundary of the family reduces the authority of outside agencies to intervene to settle disputes. For example, unless one of the parties is being threatened by serious physical violence, the state should not intervene in family disputes.

The division of labor in a family involves boundaries of responsibility. But because it is not easy to substitute other agents in most important activities within a family, the hierarchy becomes more important in plan reconciliation. Someone with greater authority establishes the boundaries of responsible performance. Voluntary reconciliation is replaced by orders from above.

Inherently, the nature of family authority is personal. The participants are known to each other. There is no system comparable to the free market, with its information system based on price signals. The boundaries of the free market are impersonal in the sense that decision-

9. R. J. Rushdoony, *The Institutes of Biblical Law* (Nutley, New Jersey: Craig Press, 1973), 402.

makers are unknown to each other. Prices establish the boundaries. Anyone who makes decisions without paying attention to prices is going to lose money in most cases. The restraining boundaries of prices are very tight. The market adjusts prices by means of arbitrage: simultaneously buying slightly lower in one market and selling in another.

Boundaries in the family are personal. The quirks of each participant are known to the others in the household. This content of information is fundamentally different from market prices. People make adjustments based on their knowledge of each other's reactions and patterns of behavior. There is much greater flexibility of responses. Appeals based on price changes are not as effective as appeals based on sanctions other than price.

People learn which boundaries not to violate in a family. These boundaries are far more problematical than the boundaries imposed by price. Negotiations are based more on personalities than price. Thus, the outcome of these negotiations is less predictable. *The complexity of negotiations makes the outcomes less predictable*. There is no rule in family negotiations comparable to this familiar law of economics: "At a higher price, less is demanded."

People in a family seek their goals, just as people in a market do. They are self-interested. But love is a factor that is highly personal. It broadens the definition of self-interest. Unlike a price, we cannot calculate love. Love is therefore like economic value. It is subjective. It is ordinal, not cardinal. It is "more than," but not "precisely this much more than." A price is objective. Love is not. The boundaries imposed by love are broader than the boundaries imposed by prices. The predictability of law enforcement in a family is far less than the predictability of the restraints imposed by objective prices.

Economists cannot easily pretend to provide meaningful equations to describe family boundaries. They can and do pretend to provide meaningful equations regarding price relationships. The illusion of scientific precision is more easily adopted with respect to objective prices in open markets than with subjective boundaries inside families.[10]

---

10. The pages of equations in Gary Becker's book, *A Treatise on the Family*, mark the book as one of the most amusing examples of economic science ever written. The utter uselessness of these equations for any practical purpose, other than the pretense of scientific rigor, marks this book as a model of scientism. If any social policy based on the

People are committed to family solidarity far more than they are committed to market solidarity. They defend their families from intervention by government bureaucrats far more vigorously than they defend the free market from intrusion by government bureaucrats.

Plan adjustment in a family is imposed by force on young children. As children mature, techniques of plan adjustment, under parental plan adjudication, become more influenced by mutual bargaining than by the threat of physical sanctions. The currency in a family is less likely to be money than barter. The division of labor is partially established by price competition, but this competition is more likely to be in time exchanges and task exchanges than monetary exchanges.

Families spread across geographical boundaries. Children become productive in society mainly after they leave their parents' homes and start their own families. But economic production always mandates service: (1) serving paying customers; (2) serving the poor or weak, (3) serving their own children. Their service to their children is their primary motivation for serving present customers: earning a living. Their adult children will serve future customers or donors. Parents must educate their children to meet these future demands. This is why family service involves sacrifices in the present. It requires reduced consumption for parents during the years of child-raising. *The parents become investors in the future.* To the extent that they hope their children will support them in their old age, this is a capital investment in their own futures. But the bulk of their children's net output will go toward raising their own children. Parents sacrifice for the sake of their grandchildren. This is a matter of inheritance.

D. Imputation

Point four: sanctions. The application of sanctions is preceded by an active interpretation of historical circumstances in terms of fixed bibli-

---

book has been adopted by any profit-seeking firm, I am unaware of it. Becker won the Nobel Prize in economics in 1992. In his Nobel Prize lecture, "The Economic Way of Looking at Life," he admitted that his theory of the family rested on the idea that altruism is basic to family relationships. This assumption severs the economic discussion of family relationships from a theory of market relationships. But equations fill the book. Yet there are no equations for altruism.

cal law. This is called *casuistry*. The judicial assessment leads to a declaration of judgment: guilty or not guilty. If the declaration is guilty, the court imposes negative sanctions.

In economics, casuistry is a matter of imputation: *reckoning economic value*. I begin with a statement that I made in the Analysis section of Chapter 9 in Part II. Part II deals with the individual covenant. I wrote:

> Modern economic thought is officially nominalistic. But there is no escape from covenantal realism: the doctrine of original creation by God. Humanists who defend realism do not accept covenantal realism, so they adopt autonomous philosophical realism. They sneak philosophical realism through the methodological back door of price indexes and other statistical techniques. These indexes require the aggregation of subjective value—individuals' subjective imputations—which cannot be done without violating the principle of subjectivism-nominalism.[11] All economic policy-making necessarily rests on an implicit denial of nominalism, for it relies on the assumption that an economist can make objectively valid interpersonal comparisons of subjective utility. So, there is an inherent dualism in humanistic economic thought.

Families are covenantal institutions. They are created by public oaths under God. This means that God holds individual members of families accountable for the sins committed by the head of the household. The most obvious example of this in the Bible is the story of Achan, who brought his entire household under covenantal judgment when he committed sacrilege when he hid stolen prohibited goods from Jericho inside his tent (Josh. 7).[12] The family members would have shared in the profits of this theft. They therefore shared in the corporate negative sanction imposed on the family.

The Trinitarian God is both plurality and unity. Therefore, in His capacity as the cosmic Imputer of economic value, He is both plural and individual. The family reflects this combination of plurality and unity. Individual family members impute personal economic value, but the God-sanctioned decision-makers in the family make *representative*

---

11. North, *Sovereignty & Dominion*, ch. 5.

12. Gary North, *Boundaries & Dominion: An Economic Commentary on Leviticus* (Moulton, Alabama: Axehead Press, [1994, 2012] 2026), Appendix A; North, *Disobedience & Defeat: An Economic Commentary on the Historical Books* (Moulton, Alabama: Axehead Press, [2012] 2029), ch. 5.

imputations of economic value. These judgments are judicially binding on the members.

Here is an example. A woman decides that she wants to live in a specific house. Her husband does not veto her decision. He signs the note for the mortgage. He signs the deed. So does she. Then the family moves into the house. All members are beneficiaries. They all impute value to the house. They do this as individuals. But they are corporately bound. If the income-earner loses his job, and the family is evicted from the property because of a default on the mortgage, the members all suffer a loss. They moved in as a corporate unit. They move out as a corporate unit.

Work performed by family members has economic value to each member. This economic value is imputed by each member. To assess this value accurately, members must take into consideration the value to all other members. Economists must do the same. Not to do so would be to ignore the corporate value of the work. But secular economists face an epistemological dilemma. They can argue in favor of the existence of the economic value of work to any family member, but to make a judgment of corporate value mandates the interpersonal comparison of subjective utilities. This is impossible, according to the subjectivism of modern economic theory.[13]

Family ownership brings the owners under special responsibilities. Stewardship is inescapable from ownership. This stewardship is upward to God, outward to other economic bidders, downward to family members, and inward to each individual owner. To say that this office of steward belongs only to the head of the household is to ignore the legal and moral claims to joint ownership by other family members. As members, they benefit personally. They impute economic value to these claims of ownership. But they cannot sell these claims. This is the problem of corporate ownership. *Without a functioning public market for the exchange of family ownership claims, the free market cannot establish a price.* This is why all varieties of humanistic economic theory face conceptual boundaries in analyzing the economics of the family.

The head of the household must decide how to budget. He makes assessments regarding the value to members of the family associated with the ownership of an asset. He makes representative judgments

13. North, *Sovereignty & Dominion*, ch. 5.

regarding individual imputations. These judgments must involve the summing up of the costs and benefits of ownership for each family member. Yet there is no scientific way that he can do this, meaning no methodologically valid way, given the epistemology of subjective economic theory.[14] There is no objective measure of economic value.

The fact that there is no objective economic measure of value is not a valid argument against the necessity of making representative economic value judgments. But these value judgments do not rest on a system of objective pricing established by exchange. The judicial roles of each family member cannot be sold to the highest bidder. Therefore, the individual economic imputations of family members must be taken into consideration by the decision-maker if he is to do justice—legal justice in God's system of imputation of personal responsibility—to other members. He is in a legal position to oppress them. This is an inescapable aspect of his office as head of the household. He is required by God to act representatively. He is required by God to act justly. As Paul wrote: "Fathers, do not provoke your children to anger, but bring them up in the discipline and instruction of the Lord" (Eph. 6:4).

E. Inheritance

Point five: succession. In economics, this refers to inheritance. It applies above all to the family. The family owns property. This property is held in trust by the family. The family's name and reputation are supposed to mark the kingdom of God.

So important was the family's legacy under the Mosaic law that God mandated that a brother who lived on the same land with his childless married brother had to go to his brother's widow and father a child after his brother died. This child would carry the name of his deceased brother. The child's inheritance of land would be whatever his covenantal father owned. The surviving brother would not inherit this land (Deut. 25:5–6).[15] This was the law of what theologians call the levirate

14. Lionel Robbins, *An Essay into the Nature and Significance of Economic Science* (London: Macmillan, 1932), ch. VI.

15. Gary North, *Inheritance & Dominion: An Economic Commentary on Deuteronomy* (Moulton, Alabama: Axehead Press, [1999, 2012] 2028), ch. 64.

marriage. The most famous example of a levirate marriage in the Bible is Ruth's marriage to Boaz, her deceased husband's second-nearest of kin. The nearest of kin had refused to marry her, so Boaz did (Ruth 4:3–4).[16] In my comments on this passage, I wrote:

> This case law was a seed law. As a law governing inheritance, it was also a land law. The firstborn of a levirate marital union inherited the deceased father's name. The inheritance was above all covenantal: part of God's promise to Abraham. The deceased man's name was imputed to the heir by God and by law, even though he was born of the levir. *The imputation of a man's name was the essence of his inheritance*: from his fathers and to his children. God had revealed this to Abraham: "And I will make of thee a great nation, and I will bless thee, and make thy name great; and thou shalt be a blessing: And I will bless them that bless thee, and curse him that curseth thee: and in thee shall all families of the earth be blessed" (Gen. 12:2–3).
>
> What the levirate law tells us is that the imputation of a man's name was more fundamental than either genetic inheritance or family discipline. In the context of the continuing academic debate between "nature" (genetics) and "nurture" (social environment), neither was fundamental in Israel. What was fundamental was *judicial imputation*. The levir performed a redemptive act on behalf of his brother's covenant line. This act was far more judicial than biological or social. He provided biological seed and family discipline, but the decisive factor was judicial-covenantal-eschatological, not biological or social. It was so decisive that the law prohibiting a brother from marrying his sister-in-law was suspended. That law had specifically stated that the negative sanction would be childlessness (Lev. 20:21). The levirate marriage was mandated by God specifically for producing an heir.[17]

This law was annulled when Jesus, as the Kinsman-Redeemer—the nearest of kin—established the foundation of a new marriage. His name is supreme, not the family's name, which was supreme in Mosaic Israel. The tribes of Mosaic Israel are gone. So is family name within the holy commonwealth. But the importance of that name, while no longer a matter of the Mosaic seed laws and land laws, which were annulled by

16. North, *Disobedience & Defeat*, ch. 11.
17. Ibid., ch. 11:B:2.

the New Covenant,[18] is still great. But it is not supreme. A man's grandsons through his daughters do not usually bear his name in the West. But they bear Christ's name if they are part of the church covenant. This name counts most.

"A good person leaves an inheritance to his grandchildren, And the wealth of a sinner is stored up for the righteous" (Prov. 13:22).[19] This has to do with capital of all kinds, including spiritual. But it surely includes economic capital. The biblical focus is on inheritance, which is point five of the biblical covenant. This transfer of ownership across generations is supposed to extend the kingdom of God. The expansion of the kingdom across time and across borders is sustained by the effects of compounding: more children, more capital, and more property brought under God's covenant.

Conclusion

God is both unity and diversity: the Trinity. This aspect of God is reflected in mankind. Specifically, it is reflected most universally by the family, which is found in every society.

God announced the dominion covenant to mankind as a whole, by way of the family: male and female. Adam was the representative head of a family.

God has broad purposes and complementary goals. He then plans. He executes His plans in history. Man is required by God to do the same. Man is corporate as well as individual, as is God. This corporate aspect of mankind appears most clearly in the family. Therefore, planning must be corporate. But because there is a hierarchy of authority in the family, which reflects the *hierarchy of the economic Trinity*—as distinguished from the ontological Trinity—there has to be plan reconciliation. This is perfect in the Trinity. It is not perfect in fallen humanity.

The family is not governed by the commercial principle of *monetary high bid wins*. This is because the value of any participant cannot

18. North, *Boundaries & Dominion*, Conclusion, C1.

19. Gary North, *Wisdom & Dominion: An Economic Commentary on Proverbs* (Moulton, Alabama: Axehead Press, [2012] 2029), ch. 41.

lawfully be capitalized by the free market's pricing process. We are not allowed to sell our children into slavery for a capitalized price. We may be able to rent out their labor services, but not all of their services can be rented. Similarly with the spouses' owed services to each other. So, the *factor-pricing arrangements* of commercial markets do not apply inside a family.

Economic theory must deal with this, but it rarely does. Economic theory rests on a theory of ownership/disownership that is denied by the family and to the family. The family covenant is legally binding and exclusive in a way that market-priced contracts are not. So, the conceptual tools of what Mises called catallactics do not apply well to a family or to any other covenantal institution: church or state. Wives are not harlots. The economics of harlotry does not apply to families.

Family ownership of assets is based on hierarchy far more than equality. The legal equality of market participants to make bids for control over scarce resources does not exist in a family. The division of labor in a family is far more hierarchical than horizontal. Market bids are far more horizontal than hierarchical.

Personal knowledge is central to the family. It is peripheral in a commercial market. Money prices are dominant in a commercial market. They are not dominant in a family. Allocation decisions made by the head of a household are based on personal knowledge. An entrepreneur in a market that is marked by widespread ownership of assets pays little attention to personal knowledge. A wheat farmer is not interested in the moral outlook of a buyer, except with respect to payment. If the buyer pays his bills on time, the farmer will sell his crop to him.

God holds families accountable. The head of a household should factor this into any allocation decisions. God has purposes for every family. God also has plans for every family. The heads of households are supposed to factor this into their purposes and plans.

The family is supposed to extend its legacy through time. The family's name is important. Family capital is important. But the central name in New Testament times is Jesus' name. He is the head of every Christian household.

The joint responsibility of the family makes it imperative that the decision-makers consider each other's imputation of economic value.

The individualism of economic theory's subjectivism makes impossible a theoretical justification for the interpersonal comparison of subjective utilities. Yet this must be done all the time by the head of the household. He must act representatively on behalf of those under his jurisdiction. In terms of the nominalism of modern economic theory, he cannot do this. But God mandates that he do this. God holds him accountable for this representative summing up of multiple imputed economic values inside the family. What every head of every household does constantly, economic theory says is scientifically impossible. This is why pure subjectivist economics is epistemologically naïve.

Chapter 12

Stewardship

Now concerning the things about which you wrote, it is good for a man not to touch a woman. But because of sexual immoralities, each man is to have his own wife, and each woman is to have her own husband. The husband must fulfill his duty to his wife, and likewise the wife also to her husband. The wife does not have authority over her own body, but the husband does; and likewise the husband also does not have authority over his own body, but the wife does.

I Corinthians 7:1–4

Analysis

Point two of the biblical covenant is hierarchy.[1] In economic theory, this is trusteeship. I cover individual stewardship in Chapter 7. Some of the general principles of stewardship that apply to individual stewardship also apply to family stewardship, but others do not. We must understand these differences. We must also understand the economic implications, both in theory and in practice, of these differences.

The most obvious difference is the application of the fundamental principle of pricing: *monetary high bid wins*. Within a family, the high bid is rarely monetary. The bids are in terms of individual characteristics, assignments, and responsibilities. The decision-maker, meaning

1. Ray R. Sutton, *That You May Prosper: Dominion By Covenant*, 2nd ed. (Tyler, Texas: Institute for Christian Economics, [1987] 1992), ch. 2.

the head of the household, allocates scarce resources. As a representative agent of the members of the household, he makes these allocation decisions on behalf of all of the members of the household. He guesses as to costs and benefits of those under his authority. In other words, he makes interpersonal comparisons of subjective utilities.

As with individual stewardship, there are three aspects of family stewardship: guardianship (legal), sharecropping (economic), and auctioneering (economic). First, the head of the household acts as a legal representative agent. He represents God to the members of his household, and he represents them before God. Representation is mediatorial and hierarchical. This representation is corporate.

Second, the sharecropper keeps a percentage of the crop. In the case of the tithe, this is a high percentage: 90%. The family owes the tithe to the local church, which represents God to its members.[2] The head of the household makes this allocation on behalf of the family. This representation is corporate. It is hierarchical. It has to do with the head of the household as a covenantal economic agent.

There is a third aspect of stewardship: allocational. This has to do with the decision to put a resource to work on behalf of other people. This is a horizontal relationship. It is not covenantal. It is contractual. In a free market, it is the role of the auctioneer. He acts on behalf of the legal owner in the owner's quest for a sale. The general principle of free market stewardship is this: *monetary high bid wins*. By inviting other resource owners to bid for ownership, the steward maximizes the income of the owner. He transfers ownership to the person who offers the highest bid.

A. Sovereignty

Point one: God's sovereignty. I begin this paragraph with the words I previously used to begin the parallel paragraph on individual stewardship. Point one of the biblical covenant is sovereignty.[3] God possesses absolute sovereignty. Yet He shares sovereignty through delegation. This

2. Gary North, *The Covenantal Tithe: The Providential Plan for Fruitful Stewardship* (Moulton, Alabama: Axehead Press, [2011] 2026), ch. 10.

3. Sutton, *That You May Prosper*, ch. 1.

was manifested in the original dominion covenant (Gen. 1:26–28).[4] This was re-confirmed with Noah (Gen. 9:1–3).[5] It was confirmed ontologically with the Incarnation, when God became a man. God clearly delegated sovereignty to man.

In both cases, Adam and Noah, God was dealing with families. He spoke to mankind through Adam, but it is clear in Genesis 1:26–28 that God was dealing with the family: male and female. He was dealing with a covenantal unit. It is not just that individual members of a family are judged by God in terms of their adherence to God's law. It is that the family as a corporate unit is the focus of God's concern. Achan's family is the archetype (Josh. 7).[6] It is not sufficient to argue that Achan, unlike us, was under the Mosaic law. Adam was not. Noah was not.

God deals with men by disappearing. He hands over assets, and then goes away. He did this in the garden of Eden. The model is the investor who hands over assets to stewards, and departs (Matt. 25:14–30).[7] He then sees how those under His authority handle their delegated authority. There is an old slogan from farming: "The best fertilizer is the owner's shadow." Crops grow better when the owner is there to watch the sharecropper's actions. More of the crop is collected at the harvest. But in this case, the Owner wants to test people's abilities while they not being actively supervised. He finds out who is productive. He finds out who honors the terms of the lease.

A father's delegation of ownership to children is always conditional. He has the authority to revoke this grant. He can legally override a child's allocation decision. But this authority ends with the departure of the child from his household. In the case of Jesus' parable of the prodigal son, the father granted him a preliminary inheritance (Luke 15:11–24).[8]

---

4. Gary North, *Sovereignty & Dominion: An Economic Commentary on Genesis* (Moulton, Alabama: Axehead Press, [1982, 2012] 2022), chaps. 3, 4.

5. Ibid., ch. 18.

6. Gary North, *Boundaries & Dominion: An Economic Commentary on Leviticus* (Moulton, Alabama: Axehead Press, [1994, 2012] 2026), Appendix A; North, *Disobedience & Defeat: An Economic Commentary on the Historical Books* (Moulton, Alabama: Axehead Press, [2012] 2029), ch. 5.

7. Gary North, *Priorities & Dominion: An Economic Commentary on Matthew* (Moulton, Alabama: Axehead Press, [2012] 2030), ch. 47.

8. Gary North, *Treasure & Dominion: An Economic Commentary on Luke* (Moulton, Alabama: Axehead Press, [2012] 2031), ch. 37.

The son took his money and squandered it. He was an adult.

A father must deal with those under his authority in a way analogous to God's dealing with him as an individual. He must delegate sovereignty. But, unlike God, he surrenders sovereignty when he delegates. This moves the covenantal issue from point one to point two: hierarchy.

There is a temptation to conclude that God has surrendered a portion of His sovereignty through delegation. This would lead to the conclusion that God became poorer after He made His covenant with mankind. Both conclusions are incorrect. The logic of the two positions may seem sound. But this logic was denied by Paul, who asserted the absolute sovereignty of God.

> What shall we say then? There is no injustice with God, is there? Far from it! For He says to Moses, "I will have mercy on whomever I have mercy, and I will show compassion to whomever I show compassion." So then, it does not depend on the person who wants it nor the one who runs, but on God who has mercy. For the Scripture says to Pharaoh, "For this very reason I raised you up, in order to demonstrate My power in you, and that My name might be proclaimed throughout the earth." So then He has mercy on whom He desires, and He hardens whom He desires. You will say to me then, "Why does He still find fault? For who has resisted His will?" On the contrary, who are you, you foolish person, who answers back to God? The thing molded will not say to the molder, "Why did you make me like this," will it? Or does the potter not have a right over the clay, to make from the same lump one object for honorable use, and another for common use? (Rom. 9:14–21)

So, God retains all of His sovereignty, all of His glory, and all of His wealth. Yet He did delegate dominion authority to mankind. This means control over property.

God repeatedly plays the role of an absentee landlord throughout Scripture. He did this in the garden. He disappears from view. He then sees whether men will obey Him despite his absence. This is the setting of the parable of the stewards (Matt. 25:14–30). But He is always present judicially, meaning covenantally. Point one of the covenant is His transcendence, but also His presence.[9]

---

9. Ray R. Sutton, *That You May Prosper: Dominion By Covenant*, 2nd ed. (Tyler, Texas: Institute for Christian Economics, [1987] 1992), ch. 1.

B. Representation

Point two: hierarchy. The head of the household has a responsibility to train his children how to manage wealth. This means that he must delegate authority. He monitors their use of the assets he delegates. In this, he is analogous to God, who also monitors performance. But he must surrender sovereignty over the decisions of his children. He retains a veto, but he puts the asset at risk. If he turns over a tool to his child, the child may break it. The head of the household may lose the asset permanently. This will reduce his wealth. God does not face this threat.

So, in making the decision as to how much authority to delegate, he must count the cost. He must assess the readiness of his child to handle wealth. This is what the father in the parable of the prodigal son did not do well. The wealth subsidized the rebellion of his son. The father could have retained control over the wealth until he died. Instead, he made an early transfer of ownership. As it turned out, this wealth transfer was exactly what his son needed. The son lost the wealth, but gained respect for his father's way of life. The process of losing his wealth, reaching bottom, and returning home was the means of his redemption. But the father had no guarantee that future events would produce this result.

The head of the household must allocate capital within the household on the basis of his trusteeship assignment. He says: "Serve God." He must assess the competing claims of family members to a share in the family's wealth. He is a fiduciary agent.

He must also listen to competing bids of those outside the family. They ask: "Serve me." These bids are mainly offers to exchange money for assets owned by the family. Price bids are most common in a mass-production economy. An asset owner does not have the time or specialized knowledge to hear the case to sell from every bidder. So, he uses price as a means of screening offers. Price bids reduce his obligation to investigate the details of each bidder's situation.

In specialized trades, such as local real estate, an investor can make profits based on his ability to focus on one property, either as a buyer or seller. He listens to individual stories in search of the most profitable way to structure the transaction. There may be special desires of buyers or sellers that will motivate them. In such situations, the high monetary bid is probably not the best bid for either the buyer or the seller. It takes personal knowledge of the other negotiator's desire to arrange the deal to meet his goals. But to the extent that such personal knowledge is expensive to collect, buyers and sellers substitute price for personal knowledge.

In the case of the virtuous wife of Proverbs 31, she is a skilled entrepreneur of real estate deals. "She considers a field and buys it; From her earnings she plants a vineyard" (v. 16). Her husband transfers authority to her. This frees up his time, so that he can serve as a judge. "Her husband is known in the gates, When he sits among the elders of the land" (v. 23). His delegation of authority to her is based on trust. "The heart of her husband trusts in her, And he will have no lack of gain. She does him good and not evil All the days of her life" (vv. 11–12). This delegation of responsibility over capital is to the benefit of the head of the household. But his wife is focused on the needs of the household. She acts as a steward on their behalf. "She watches over the activities of her household, And does not eat the bread of idleness" (v. 27). She pursues her plans in terms of her economic representation of other members in her family.[10]

C. Lease

Point three: ethics. This is related to law. A lease is a long-term contract between an owner and a renter. It also applies to the agreement between a land owner and a sharecropper. A renter commonly pays a fixed monthly fee. A sharecropper pays a percentage of the crop.

The renter and the sharecropper have legal use of property for a period of time. The property is land. The productivity of land is depleted through its productive use. In agriculture, the soil's nutrients pass into the crop, which is then sold. These nutrients must be replaced if the productivity of the land is to be maintained. If these nutrients are not replaced by the user or by nature, then the depletion of the soil is counted as capital consumption. The same analysis applies to the use

10. Gary North, *Wisdom & Dominion: An Economic Commentary on Proverbs* (Moulton, Alabama: Axehead Press, [2012] 2029), ch. 86.

of all property. The second law of thermodynamics is always operating to reduce the value of all property. Things wear out: the effects of entropy.[11] Entropy is a one-way movement toward randomness. The only way to reverse is this is to apply energy to the process. This consumes more energy than it replaces in a closed system. Over eons of time, if there were eons of time, this would produce the heat death of the universe: frozen waste.

A lease specifies the restrictions on the renter's or sharecropper's use of the property. The details of the lease are written to protect the property's value. The renter or the sharecropper must maintain the property as a cost of operation. Otherwise, the rental payment would not cover the preservation of the property's value. The economic value of his payment would be reduced by the economic value of the capital depletion involved in the use of the property. This would reduce the owner's net return on the lease.

Here is the crucial rule of the family's lease. God prohibits adultery (Ex. 20:14).[12] The marriage vows are absolute. This law maintains the integrity of the family unit. It also maintains the integrity of the individuals who make the vows. This law makes it clear to all people that the two parties have mutual obligations, which are legal rights. They possess mutual rights of exclusion. This is the essence of the law governing property. *The right to exclude is the essence of property rights.*

The family's lease prevents the parties from abandoning their covenantal assignments by abandoning each other. There are biblical laws against divorce. A divorce is destructive of family capital. The division of assets is usually an expensive legal battle in which lawyers on both sides prosper. Also, the family's division of labor is destroyed. This means that output is reduced. This is another economic reason for the prohibition of divorce. The anti-divorce laws are not absolute. A good book on this is Rev. Ray Sutton's book in my Biblical Blueprint Series (1986–1988), *Second Chance: Biblical Principles of Divorce and Remarriage* (1988).[13]

11. Gary North, *Is the World Running Down? Crisis in the Christian Worldview* (Moulton, Alabama: Axehead Press, [1988] 2029), ch. 2.

12. North, *Authority & Dominion*, vol. 2, *Part II: Decalogue & Dominion*, ch. 27.

13. Ray Sutton, *Second Chance: Biblical Principles of Divorce and Remarriage* (Tyler, Texas: Dominion Press, 1988).

Rushdoony also provided a list of exceptions.[14] The judicial issue is *covenantal death* through breaking fundamental laws of the marriage covenant. The victim must be protected through physical separation and also by the court's award of all of the marriage's capital to the victim. This is an application of the biblical legal principle of victim's rights.[15] There is no such thing as a biblically justified system of no-fault divorce.

Adult children have the covenantal responsibility of caring for aged, infirm parents. This is an application of the fourth commandment: "Honor your father and your mother, so that your days may be prolonged on the land which the LORD your God gives you" (Ex. 20:12).[16] There is a positive sanction attached to this law. Paul mentioned this fact: "Honor your father and mother (which is the first commandment with a promise), so that it may turn out well for you, and that you may live long on the earth" (Eph. 6:2–3). This law indicates that the family is the primary welfare agency for the aged. To transfer this responsibility to the state undermines the family covenant. It substitutes bureaucratic impersonalism for familistic personalism.

Educating minor children is the responsibility of the family. "Train up a child in the way he should go, Even when he grows older he will not abandon it" (Prov. 22:6). This is a matter of ethics: point three of the biblical covenant. The focus of education must be Bible-revealed law. "Now this is the commandment, the statutes, and the judgments which the LORD your God has commanded me to teach you, so that you may do them in the land where you are going over to take possession of it, so that you, your son, and your grandson will fear the LORD your God, to keep all His statutes and His commandments which I command you, all the days of your life, and that your days may be prolonged" (Deut. 6:1–2). Note: the reward is longer life. Here is another biblical law with the positive sanction of long life. It parallels the fourth commandment. This positive sanction is widely considered to be the

---

14. R. J. Rushdoony, *Institutes of Biblical Law* (Nutley, New Jersey: Craig Press, 1973), ch. VII:12.

15. Gary North, *Victim's Rights: The Biblical View of Civil Justice* (Moulton, Alabama: Axehead Press, [1990] 2029).

16. Gary North, *Authority & Dominion: An Economic Commentary on Exodus*, vol. 2, *Part II: Decalogue & Dominion* (Moulton, Alabama: Axehead Press, [1986, 2012] 2025), ch. 25.

premier positive sanction of life: life extension. This raises the covenantal issue of sanctions.

D. Success Indicators

Point four: sanctions. The individual or the head of a business uses these success indicators: monetary profit and loss. But the concept of profit and loss must extend beyond numbers in a ledger. Sanctions must include evidence of God's approval or disapproval. For the individual, the final judgment is the archetype of historical sanctions. The individual is singled out. So, the focus is on individual benefits. This is not true of the family. The family does not pass through the historical sanction of death into eternity (Matt. 22:30).

Then what is God's goal for the family? *Maintaining the covenant.* This keeps the family's capital inside the kingdom of God. *The confession of faith is central.* It is a matter of oath: point four of the biblical covenant.[17] The extension of the oath through time is sacramental. But the family has no sacraments. So, these must be the church's sacraments: baptism and the Lord's Supper.

Monetary indicators are valid as secondary indicators. If a family sees its capital shrinking, due to losses, the senior decision-maker must pay attention to the market. Why is the capital base declining? What must be done to reverse this? Unless there are adjustments in the allocation of family capital, there will be no inheritance to pass on.

E. Accumulation

Point five: succession. The accumulation of capital is an ethical command. It is not optional. The building of God's kingdom requires capital. It is a redemptive process. The meaning of redemption is "bought back." Covenant-keepers are required to buy back the world on behalf of God. This is why the biblical covenant is governed by Deuteronomy 8:18: "But you are to remember the LORD your God, for it is

17. Sutton, *That You May Prosper*, ch. 4.

He who is giving you power to make wealth, in order to confirm His covenant which He swore to your fathers, as it is this day."[18] Who were the fathers? Abraham, Isaac, and Jacob. They left an inheritance. *The biblical goal is capital accumulation, not capital consumption.* This in an inter-generational assignment. Each generation is supposed to leave more behind than it began with. This is the meaning of value-added living, as applied to capital ownership.

A family head pursues capital accumulation, but on behalf of the family. He is a judicially representative agent. Abram was rich in cattle, silver, and gold (Gen. 13:2). But Abram was not accumulating capital on his own behalf. He was accumulating it for his heir. He did not have an heir. He did not know who his heir would be. His servant (Gen. 15:2)? God told him he would have a son (15:4). Through this son, he would have more heirs. God changed his name to Abraham: father of nations. This story focuses attention on the accumulation of family capital. Abram had accumulated it. He did not know who would inherit it.

What was the economic value of this capital? It was of greater value to Abram if a son would inherit. He did not know who would inherit until God told him. Its value was higher after that because he knew his capital would play an important role in history. His name would be on it in a special way. What he had accumulated would produce fruit more reliably through a family blessed by God than through a servant not singled out by God as the heir, and therefore the recipient of the blessing.

1. *Factors in Inheritance*

As the head of the household, Abram had to make an assessment of the value of his capital in terms of the future. This is true of all capital. Its present value is based on the expected future stream of income. It is also based on the evaluator's degree of future-orientation. If he is future-oriented, his capital is worth more to him than if he were present-oriented. The rate of discount he applies to future income is lower. Hence, the expected future economic value is higher to him.

The longer the estimated time period of the expected stream of net income, the higher the market value to the owner. But the degree of

18. Gary North, *Inheritance & Dominion: An Economic Commentary on Deuteronomy* (Moulton, Alabama: Axehead Press, [1999, 2012] 2028), ch. 22.

time orientation has far greater impact on present economic value than the term of expected income. If the rate of long-term interest doubles, this will depress the present value of the stream of income by almost half. A doubling of the expected period of net income from the asset will not compensate for the doubling of the rate of interest. Why not? Because the extra years are so far out chronologically. The discount applied by the doubled rate of interest will have even more depressing effects on the value of income far out than it has on income that will arrive sooner.

The head of the household makes his economic judgments representatively: *on behalf of*. He makes them on behalf of himself, but within a context: the family. He has legal and moral obligations to heirs. "A good person leaves an inheritance to his grandchildren" (Prov. 13:22a).[19] The longer the line of heirs, the more capital he must accumulate. Far more important, he must educate his heirs in the basics of investing. The capital must grow in order to provide heirs with tools of production. The heirs must know how to use these tools. Otherwise, the capital will be dissipated within a few generations: too many heirs (population growth), not enough capital.

The person who accumulates wealth does not know for sure who will inherit, or what this person will do with the inheritance. This was a continuing theme in the Book of Ecclesiastes.[20] He may be accumulating capital for the sake of a fool. So, he must accumulate capital that his heirs can administer efficiently. He must look to the future in order to decide what kind of capital is appropriate for the long-term accumulation and inheritance. He must make judgments on behalf of God, and then in terms of his circumstances.

The accumulation of family capital must include the worldview he passes to his children. This wordview will be their primary tool of production. It will shape their administration of inherited wealth. It will shape their ability to make decisions on behalf of future generations. There is a law element to consider: ethics. There is a sanctions aspect: causation in history. There is also a time element to consider: the market's rate of interest.

---

19. North, *Wisdom & Dominion*, ch. 41.

20. Gary North, *Autonomy & Stagnation: An Economic Commentary on Ecclesiastes* (Moulton, Alabama: Axehead Press, [2012] 2030), chaps. 4, 21.

A covenant-keeper can inherit wealth beyond the grave.[21] A family cannot. Then how is the economic covenant renewed? By covenant succession. The family's capital is transferred to the next generation of covenant-keepers within the family. *Succession is the biblically mandated means of extending God's kingdom through time.* The time factor is the basis of economic compounding. Parents die. Children inherit the task of extending the kingdom of God in history.

If the heirs keep the terms of the covenant, they will usually be in a position to add value. They will have to increase their productivity. They will then leave more behind than they inherited. *This is the economic aspect of the redemption of the world.* The heirs participate in an inter-generational increase in capital. Ownership of resources progressively is transferred to covenant keepers.

This inter-generational process of inheritance, compound economic growth, and accumulation of capital is the covenantal basis of *economic redemption in history*. The accumulation of capital under a covenantal oath is the economic basis of redemption in every area of life. The covenantal family extends its jurisdiction by means of the process of economic compounding. This process of wealth creation is entirely voluntary. It does not involve the use of force. Historically, the kingdom of God has expanded its jurisdiction primarily in terms of families. Individuals have played a crucial role, especially in the area of invention and innovation, but this was usually within the judicial context of the family. This has begun to change.

A limited liability corporation is the modern economy's substitute for the family. It extends through time. The compounding process builds capital. It also is voluntary. It is not bound by a Trinitarian confession. It is not established by a covenantal oath. It is a contractual institution, not covenantal. It is therefore secular-contractual, not theocentric-covenantal. *It is the most important non-covenantal economic institution in history*. It has been at the heart of the expansion of economic produc-

---

21. "Do not store up for yourselves treasures on earth, where moth and rust destroy, and where thieves break in and steal. But store up for yourselves treasures in heaven, where neither moth nor rust destroys, and where thieves do not break in or steal; for where your treasure is, there your heart will be also" (Matt. 6:19–21). Gary North, *Priorities & Dominion: An Economic Commentary on Matthew* (Moulton, Alabama: Axehead Press, [2012] 2030), ch. 13.

tivity in modern times. In terms of the accumulation of capital, it is the greatest engine of wealth-creation in man's history, other than the family. In today's world, the corporation is far greater in its control of capital than all of the families combined. The Pareto distribution of wealth has placed 80% of the world's capital in the hands of no more than 20% of the world's population. The institutional means of this accumulation has been the corporation. The richest 2,000 corporations own about $100 trillion in assets. This is about two-thirds of the world's assets.[22] But the ownership of corporate shares is mainly held by families or by non-profit foundations controlled by families.[23]

2. *The Super-Rich*

I have at long last arrived at the crucial dividing line between the Bible's explicit teaching on inheritance vs. the statistical reality of inheritance in the modern world. A tiny handful of anti-Christians control most of the world's wealth and power. There are about 6,000 people who are at the top in terms of wealth and power.[24] In other places, Rothkopf has said this elite numbers 6,600. There are about 7.5 billion people. *This elite is fewer than one in a million.* But this is normal. In every era, about one person in a million stands out from all the rest. This has been known for almost a century.[25] Yet Jesus said that few rich people enter the kingdom of God (Matt. 19:24).[26] So, the issue is this: Given the fact of the Pareto 20/80 distribution of wealth, which is close to universal, is Proverbs 13:22 annulled by Matthew 19:24? Is the wealth of the just laid up for the sinner?

The free market benefits customers. *The super-rich serve customers.* Customers spend their money, and the super-rich accumulate capital, but this is a stewardship function on the part of the rich. The super-rich own capital. They cannot spend all of this wealth on personal con-

22. David, Rothkopf, *Superclass: The Global Power Elite and the World They Are Making* (New York: Farrar, Straus and Giroux, 2008), 121.

23. Rothkopf writes: "The world's billionaires, those roughly one thousand individuals, have combined greater wealth than that of the poorest 2.5 billion." Ibid., 66.

24. Ibid., 40.

25. David Stove, *The Enlightenment* (New Brunswick, New Jersey: Transaction, 2003), ch. 3. He called this "the Bateson fact," named after the British geneticist, who wrote about it in 1928.

26. North, *Priorities & Dominion*, ch. 38.

sumption. They can sell their ownership shares, but they cannot consume their wealth fast enough to reverse capital accumulation. Their wealth enables them to buy the trinkets of civilization, but it does not extend their life expectancy by much, nor does it enable them to enjoy their wealth. What is known as the *hedonic treadmill* takes over. People adjust to increasing economic benefits. They are no happier with greater wealth—above subsistence—as a result of their increasing net worth.[27]

Yet there is no question that the truth of Matthew 19:25 remains true. Few rich people enter the kingdom. Then what of Proverbs 13:22? If it is still in force, as I believe it is, it points to a world-transforming Christian revival in the future that will change the theological confessions of the very wealthy. They will inherit from sinners, by being delivered from their prior judicial status as covenant-breakers. In short, *this passage points to the truth of postmillennialism.* For, if postmillennalism is not an option, then the wealth of the just is laid up for the sinner. This is what we have seen on a scale never imagined by earlier generations. A great revival will negate Matthew 19:25. The rich will participate. Here are the theological alternatives. Either Proverbs 13:22 has been negated by Matthew 19:24 on a permanent basis, or else Matthew 19:24 will not be in force at some time in the future.

If we take Matthew 19:24 as fixed throughout man's history, then we must adopt amillennialism: the doctrine of utter failure of the gospel to displace the society of Satan. The wealth of the just is laid up for the sinner. Great wealth will remain the inheritance of covenant-breakers throughout history. Covenant-breakers will provide leadership in all areas of life outside the Christian household and the Christian church, both of which will remain under siege until time ends. Jesus spoke of the defensive gates of hell as being unable to resist the offensive onslaught of institutional church (Matt. 16:18), yet in history, the defensive gates of the church will only just barely be able to resist the offensive cultural onslaught of covenant-breakers.

---

27. Dan Ariely, *The Upside of Irrationality: The Unexpected Benefits of Defying Logic at Work and at Home* (New York: Harper, 2010), ch. 6. This works both ways. People adjust to catastrophes in their lives. A person loses his eyesight or the use of his legs, yet in a few years, he says he is happy.

Conclusion

The economics of the family is inherently vertical: from father to children. The economics of the free market is inherently horizontal: competing bids for the use or ownership of scarce resources. The principle of *monetary high bid wins* governs the free market. This bid is impersonal. The free market is open to new bidders and new sellers. In contrast, the high bid of the family is established by the head of the household. This bidding system is non-monetary and highly personal. It is not open to new bidders and new sellers.

The deciding authority is the head of the household. He has the power and the authority to reject any bid. Society grants him this right, meaning this *legal immunity,* from outside bidding. His word prevails because society holds him legally responsible for the outcome of his allocation of resources. In the language of economics, the head of the household retains ownership of family assets as the highest bidder. He ignores higher monetary bids. This is sometimes called *reservation demand.*[28] The goods that he owns, as an agent of God and also his family, do not enter into exchange. They are used or consumed inside the household. Some things he is not allowed by God's law or man's law to sell: those under his authority. On their behalf, he allocates scarce resources that the family possesses.

The head of the household, as both a legal agent (guardian) of God and an economic agent (sharecropper) of God, can act in terms of either his own hierarchy of economic values or the hierarchy of those under his authority. The drunkard acts mainly in terms of his hierarchy of values. The covenant-keeper acts in terms of what should be the hierarchy of economic values of those under his authority. This hierarchy should conform to God's assessment of this hierarchy. Both God and the head of the household have the ability to compare interpersonally the subjective utilities of those under his authority. Modern economic theory officially rejects the existence of God as a meaningful analytical concept. It also rejects the ability of anyone to make such comparisons scientifically. But as soon as any economist offers a pol-

28. Murray N. Rothbard, *Man, Economy, and State: A Treatise on Economic Principles,* 2nd ed. (Auburn, Alabama: Mises Institute, [1962] 2009), 137, 247.

icy recommendation to the civil government, he does so only on the implicit but rarely stated methodological assumption that he can make such comparisons scientifically, and therefore people in power should adopt his recommendations.

The existence of the household is the greatest testimony against the methodological principle of the exclusive and universal reign of methodological individualism. The original realm of economics—the household—was the center of most economic decision-making until the modern world. Not until around 1875, at least seven decades after compound economic growth appeared as the relentless confirmation of private property, entrepreneurship, and the market economy, did economic theorists adopt the dual nominalism of methodological individualism and subjective imputation as the source of economic value.

The widespread adoption of the limited liability corporation, which was introduced in the United States around 1875, made possible the transfer of primary economic authority from the family to the corporation. The corporation is a legal fiction: an individual which can survive across generations. It is not an economic fiction. It has become the most powerful institutional and economic reality of the modern world. Legally, its model is not the family. Rather, its model is the church: the first limited liability corporation.[29]

29. Gary North, "Rothbard's Defense of Contractual Limited Liability," *LewRockwell .com*, Sept. 28, 2005 lewrockwell.com/2005/09/gary-north/rothbards-defense.

Chapter 13

Boundaries

"You shall not displace your neighbor's boundary marker, which the ancestors have set, in your inheritance which you will inherit in the land that the Lord *your God is giving you to possess."*

Deuteronomy 19:14

Analysis

Point three of the biblical covenant is ethics.[1] This is related to law. Law establishes ethical and judicial boundaries: "Thou shalt" and "Thou shalt not."

The central judicial-covenantal fact of the family is the right to exclude. The marital union is exclusive. This right of exclusion involves every area of the family's operations: property, authority over children, and inheritance.

In Chapter 8, I discussed the relationship between name and boundaries. God announced His defense of His name in the Third Commandment (Ex. 20:7). This is the third law in the list of five priestly laws. He announced the prohibition against theft—a defense of property—in the Eighth Commandment (Ex. 20:5). This is the third in the list of five commandments relating to kingly rule or civil society.[2]

1. Ray R. Sutton, *That You May Prosper: Dominion By Covenant*, 2nd ed. (Tyler, Texas: Institute for Christian Economics, [1987] 1992), ch. 3.

2. On the dual lists, priestly and kingly, of the Ten Commandments, see Gary North, *Authority & Dominion: An Economic Commentary on Exodus*, vol. 2, *Part II: Decalogue & Dominion* (Moulton, Alabama: Axehead Press, [1986, 2012] 2025), Preface B:I.

Families are legally separate judicial social units. They are covenantal units because they are established by a mutual oath under God. They are identified by names. These names establish legal liability before God and man. A name is associated with a legal boundary.

A. Name and Ownership

Point one: God's sovereignty. As I wrote in Chapter 8, private property begins with a person's name. He is a legally identifiable agent. His name identifies him. It says, "you, not someone else." This is the basis of judicial responsibility. It is also the foundation of economic authority. This same analysis applies to a family as well as to an individual. I also went on to write this: "The authority to name things is a God-given authority. The person with the authority to establish names possesses a unique hierarchical position at the top. The question, 'Who's in charge here?' can be accurately answered by identifying the person with the legal authority to name people and things." This analysis also applies to a family.

Abram was a rich man (Gen. 13:2). He was the head of a household. He had a problem. He had no heir. He had a steward, Eleazar (Gen. 15:2). Unless he adopted Eleazar as his son, his family's name would not extend beyond his death. God told him that he would have a biological heir (Gen. 15:4). God established a covenant with Abram at that point (Gen. 15:5–6). His heirs would descend into Egypt. The fourth generation after the descent in Egypt would inherit the land of Canaan (Gen. 15:16).

The head of the family names the children. This usually is the father. He provides his children with legally identifiable boundaries: names. These names identify them as under his judicial authority until they become legal adults. Then their names identify them as judicial authorities. This act of separation marks them as guardians: legal administrators in the name of God. Whatever they own in their names belongs to God.

A married couple is no more married after three decades of marriage than they were at any time after their marriage. But their responsibilities have changed. Similarly, an individual is no more an individual at age 70 than he was on the day he was born. But his responsibilities have changed. The degree of responsibility increases with increased knowledge (Luke 12:47–48).[3] The existence of a name makes clear who is responsible. This has to do with the book of life (Phil. 4:3).

Family property comes under the authority of the head of the household, who is in charge of the family's property. He serves as a trustee, both for God and for those under his authority. *By extending his family's ownership, he extends its jurisdiction.* In the case of covenant-keeping families, this is the process of redemption: buying back the world forfeited by Adam as the trustee for his heirs.

With the decline of family-owned businesses, the economic connection of a family to its name has weakened. The degree of responsibility associated with a family's name has been reduced. Buyers trust names. A family name places the family's reputation on the line. This reputation extends to the family's business. This becomes a prejudice that can give a family an advantage or a disadvantage. The costs associated with a disadvantage make it profitable to avoid a bad reputation.

B. Resource Allocation

Point two: hierarchy. My discussion of resource allocation in Section B of Chapter 12 goes over the basics of subjective value and objective pricing of scarce resources. The free market is governed by the principle of *monetary high bid wins*. This bid is impersonal on well-organized markets. Buyers and sellers do not know each other.

The head of a family acts representatively. He allocates in terms of his judgment regarding the conflicting values of members of the family. Inside the legal boundaries of the family, he treats people differently from those outside these boundaries. He is responsible to God for the administration of family-owned assets. He represents them legally (guardian). He acts as a guardian for family members as individuals, but also as an agent of the family as a covenantal unit.

---

3. Gary North, *Treasure & Dominion: An Economic Commentary on Luke* (Moulton, Alabama: Axehead Press, [2012] 2031), ch. 28.

This allocation is not governed by legal rules based on contract. He can give either more or less to a member in relation to another. If a child suffers from an illness or other handicap, the father allocates more time and money to that child than to a healthy child. This is unequal treatment. The family's resources are not part of a system of equality or even a system of fixed proportional claims. The family cares for the weak member. This is highly personal. A free market-based system of allocation is far more dependent on contracts between strangers.

Children are economic resources as well as liabilities. As they mature, their labor adds to the family's output. The two sons of a prophet who went into debt served as collateral for the loan. "Now a woman of the wives of the sons of the prophets cried out to Elisha, saying, 'Your servant my husband is dead, and you know that your servant feared the LORD; and the creditor has come to take my two children to be his slaves'" (II Kings 4:1).[4]

When children mature and leave the household, the responsibilities of the head of the household are reduced. He represents fewer people. He is no longer required to balance as many conflicting values and goals as he did before. He still has a role as the builder of capital to be passed on to the adult children and their families. This responsibility is less intense and less immediate than it was when the children were under his authority. With reduced authority comes reduced responsibility (Luke 12:47–48).

C. Time and Place

Point three: ethics. This has to do with boundaries: legal limits. Families extend beyond time and place. They begin in a time and a place, but extended families can extend the worldview of the family. This is another reason why fathers are required by God to teach biblical law to their children (Deut. 6:7).[5] The family's boundaries expand beyond its initial time and place.

4. Gary North, *Disobedience & Defeat: An Economic Commentary on the Historical Books* (Moulton, Alabama: Axehead Press, [2012] 2029), ch. 24.

5. Gary North, *Inheritance & Dominion: An Economic Commentary on Deuteronomy* (Moulton, Alabama: Axehead Press, [1999, 2012] 2028), ch. 15.

There is loss involved in such an extension. Competing ideas and experiences threaten to overcome the confessional inheritance of the family. Children who are out from under their parents' geographical authority may not maintain the same degree of confessional rigor as their parents did. This may affect the family inheritance in the broadest sense. But while the rigor of the family's confession can get weaker, the geographical impact of whatever confession remains may be greater. It reaches more people.

This weakening of the family's confession is well known with respect to recent converts to a worldview. The first generation defines itself in terms of the break that it made from the traditional confession. The children grow up in the confessional environment established by their parents. They did not experience the confessional break which their parents did. They did not pay a heavy price or experience negative sanctions. The family's confessional boundaries are familiar to them. These boundaries may be little more than background noise: easily adapted to and ignored. Their children will in turn grow up in a confessional setting, but one far less rigorous than either their parents' confession or their grandparents' confession.[6]

A family should increase its per capita capital over time. This is rarely achieved for four consecutive generations. In the modern world, only one family is legendary for this: the Rothschilds. Were the Sassoons better known, they might receive accolades as long-term builders of capital. In the United States, the Rockefellers are famous, but the founding father of the Du Ponts established his fortune at least 50 years before John D. Rockefeller began to establish his. There is no other American family to match it in terms of manufacturing: growth and innovation for

6. In early colonial American history in New England, 1630 to 1700, this theological decline was accompanied by the invention of a theological doctrine, the halfway covenant. The founding generation, 1630 to 1660, gave verbal testimony of their faith as a requirement to gain church membership in Congregational churches. This requirement was a new doctrine. Continental Calvinism did not require such personal testimony of conversion. The second generation tended not to join churches, not having had their parents' experience. Then what was the legal status of their children, who were not the children of church members? A new doctrine arose: the halfway covenant. The churches decided that they could be baptized lawfully, but they could not take communion or vote in church elections. The main book on this is Edmund S. Morgan, *Visible Saints: The History of a Puritan Idea* (New York: New York University Press, 1963).

over two centuries. But as to their confession of faith, there has been no continuity. The entry on Wikipedia in 2017 did not mention the family's church connection. With 3,500 relatives, the confessions are diverse.

The more skilled the children become in economic affairs, the greater the process of economic redemption. The children are supposed to implement and extend the vision of the parents. This is part of the multiplication process. But we find that children depart confessionally from their ancestors' confessions. Also, large families disperse any inheritance. To maintain this inheritance per capita, the lineal families must achieve economic growth. To increase per capita inheritance down through consecutive he generations is exceedingly rare. Per capita wealth regresses to the mean when families become larger. The law of large numbers asserts itself.

Only through the maintenance of the confession, which includes the Bible's inter-generational postmillennial vision of the future,[7] can a family overcome regression to the mean beyond three or four generations. The Second Commandment says that this is possible to achieve. "You shall not worship them nor serve them; for I, the LORD your God, am a jealous God, inflicting the punishment of the fathers on the children, on the third and the fourth generations of those who hate Me, but showing favor to thousands, to those who love Me and keep My commandments" (Ex. 20:5–6). The word "thousands" applies here to "generations."[8] The observation that this has not been achieved in the past does not prove theologically that the promise of the Second Commandment is null and void under the New Covenant.

The amillennialist necessarily argues as follows. "The promise of the Second Commandment is hypothetical. It is an ideal. It is not connected to historical reality. It never has been. It never will be. Bible prophecy teaches this. History reveals that the blessings of God are showered on covenant-breakers, who down through the ages keep and extend the kingdom of man, which is the kingdom of Satan. God visits the iniquity of the fathers upon the third and fourth generation of

7. Gary North, *Confidence & Dominion: An Economic Commentary on the Psalms* (Moulton, Alabama: Axehead Press, [2012] 2029).

8. Gary North, *Authority & Dominion: An Economic Commentary on Exodus*, vol. 2, *Part II: Decalogue & Dominion* (Moulton, Alabama: Axehead Press, [1986, 2012] 2025), ch. 22:C:3.

those who hate him, and then He rewards this iniquity. The kingdom of man in culture will not be replaced by the kingdom of God. To argue otherwise is triumphalism. This is Constantinianism politically. Here is how covenantal economic sanctions work in the New Testament. God shows lovingkindness to covenant-keepers by placing them at the mercy—the tender mercy—of covenant-breakers. So, the correct way of interpreting the Second Commandment's historical manifestations of blessings and cursings is to reverse the cultural positions of covenant-breakers—thousands of generations of cultural victory—and covenant-keepers: three or four generations of cultural victory, and then defeat through replacement of the confession." Premillennialists hold the same view with respect to the era of the church before Christ's bodily return to set of an international Christian bureaucracy for a thousand literal years. Prior to this, the economic efforts of Christians will be thwarted by covenant-breakers.

D. Scarcity

Point four: sanctions. I wrote this in Section D of Chapter 8, on the individual covenant.

> Scarcity is defined by economists as follows: "At zero price, there is greater demand than supply." This is another way of saying "it commands a price." Scarcity imposes boundaries on men. It means that they must gain more assets in order to increase their consumption. They must extend their jurisdiction. There is also a scarcity of time. People die.

This applies differently to institutions. They need not die. There is replacement: *succession*. Surely this is true of the church. It is somewhat less true of the state. Families extend through time, but their continuity is far less meaningful than the continuity of churches and states. Few people know anything about their ancestors a hundred years previously. They know a great deal about their nations' histories. They can find out a great deal about the history of large denominations. But church history is not a popular field, even within denominations.

Scarcity can be overcome through compound economic growth, but until 1800, it was always reversed. Population growth always led to a reversal of economic growth—what is called the Malthusian trap.[9] Population pushed rapidly to the economic limits of man's social environment. Then the rate of population growth slowed, and per capita wealth stagnated once again. Men have prayed some version of "give us this day our daily bread" down through history. Famines were real threats. So was malnutrition. They no longer are in the industrial West.

Infant mortality and young child mortality were high before 1800. Families buried their children. Adam Smith wrote in 1776,

> But poverty, though it does not prevent the generation, is extremely unfavourable to the rearing of children. The tender plant is produced, but in so cold a soil, and so severe a climate, soon withers and dies. It is not uncommon, I have been frequently told, in the Highlands of Scotland for a mother who has borne twenty children not to have two alive. Several officers of great experience have assured me, that so far from recruiting their regiment, they have never been able to supply it with drums and fifes from all the soldiers children that were born in it. A greater number of fine children, however, is seldom seen anywhere than about a barrack of soldiers. Very few of them, it seems, arrive at the age of thirteen or fourteen. In some places one half the children born die before they are four years of age; in many places before they are seven; and in almost all places before they are nine or ten. This great mortality, however, will every where be found chiefly among the children of the common people, who cannot afford to tend them with the same care as those of better station. Though their marriages are generally more fruitful than those of people of fashion, a smaller proportion of their children arrive at maturity.[10]

Parents burying their children has been uncommon in the era after the development of sulfa drugs in the 1930s. Yet it had been universal throughout recorded history. No greater economic benefit exists—no more universally recognized economic benefit—than this: children bury their parents with far more regularity than parents bury their children.

---

9. Gregory Clark, *A Farewell to Alms: A Brief Economic History of the World* (Princeton, New Jersey: Princeton University Press, 2007), Part I.

10. Adam Smith, *The Wealth of Nations*, Book I, Chapter 8, "On the Wages of Labour."

E. Economic Growth

Point five: succession. In economic theory, this is related to inheritance. There is an intense desire of parents to see their children living as adults in a better world. Mainly, this refers to economic growth. Parents in Western Europe since about 1850 have had legitimate hope in the West that their children would live in a richer world. This was not clear in 1800. It was becoming clear in 1850. The culturally representative turning point was the London exhibition of 1851. Manufacturers came from all over the West to display their products in national pavilions. It was called the Great Exhibition, and great it was. Wikipedia reports: "Six million people—equivalent to a third of the entire population of Britain at the time—visited the Great Exhibition. The average daily attendance was 42,831 with a peak attendance of 109,915 on October 7. The event made a surplus of £186,000 (£18,370,000 in 2015), which was used to found the Victoria and Albert Museum, the Science Museum and the Natural History Museum."

With the arrival of compound economic growth in 1800, the thinking of the Western world began to change. What had been understood in theory as early as 1650 in Holland became a reality in 1800. This was a kind of economic postmillennialism, but without a Christian confession. Before 1800, specific families would grow larger, but at some point, families in general could not, unless some families ceased to grow or there was sufficient economic growth to accommodate new arrivals. This restraint hampered population growth until 1800. Then it was loosened. World population grew from a billion people to seven billion in two centuries. The birth rate increased because of younger marriages, infant mortality decreased, and life expectancy increased. Per capita wealth worldwide increased by at least a factor of 10.[11] It may have increased by a factor of 45 in Norway, and by 40 in the United States.[12] South Korea is the most astounding case. Its per capita wealth increased by a factor of 18 in the four decades after 1953.[13] McCloskey capitalizes this economic growth as the Great Fact of the modern world.

11. Dierdre McCloskey, *Bourgeois Dignity: Why Economics Can't Explain the Modern World* (Chicago: University of Chicago Press, 2010), 2.

12. Idem.

13. Ibid., 50.

This process deserves to be capitalized. We have seen the preliminary conquest of scarcity in the last two centuries. If this growth continues for another three decades, there will be few destitute people in the world,[14] and there will be nine billion people. Two questions arise: (1) Why did this begin in 1800? (2) Why did it begin in Great Britain and the United States? There is no answer as of 2019, although I regard this as the most important historical question there is. The world changed after 1800 as never before in recorded history. It got rich. Economic historians do not know why.

Conclusion

The family is bounded. It is bounded by confession, by the number of children, by the size of its capital, by geography, and by time. But it can extend across borders and through time. It need not die out. The possibility of family growth is basic to the covenantal promises of the Mosaic law.

The absence of long-term family growth until 1800 seemed like a negation of this promise for most of man's history. Families always reached their limits to growth, and did so within a few decades. The death rate then rose for children and adults. Families reached their economic limits. But then, without warning in 1800, this changed in Great Britain and English-speaking North America. The vast lands of Canada and the United States allowed migration westward. The narrow band of about a hundred miles from the Atlantic ceased to be a major barrier to expansion. Families grew.

One man had seen this as early as 1783, the year that the United States signed the treaty of independence from Great Britain. In a long election day sermon, Rev. Ezra Stiles, the president of Yale college, forecasted that the United States might have 300 million residents in 2000. This is almost exactly what it had. "Already for ages has Europe arrived to a plenary, if not declining, population of one hundred millions; in two or three hundred years this second enlargement may cover America with three times that number, if the present ratio of increase continues

14. McCloskey, *Bourgeois Dignity*, 3.

with the enterprising spirit of Americans for colonization and removing out into the wilderness and settling new countries. . . ."[15] This was published 15 years before T. Robert Malthus' then-anonymous book, *An Essay on the Principle of Population*, appeared in print. Malthus argued that population will always reach the limits of its food supply. Then starvation will reappear. He had the weight of history on his side, but he was wrong—at least so far. But this unprecedented expansion of population seemingly had nothing to do with national confession. Politically-judicially, the national confession is adherence to the United States Constitution, an explicitly non-biblical document.[16]

Christian families do not retain their confessions down through the generations. Jews seems to be an exception, but what they maintain is not theological confession. They are identifiable by their commitment to cultural Judaism. Reform Judaism is as liberal theologically as liberal Protestantism. National abandonment of Trinitarian confessions breaks the covenantal promise of Deuteronomy 8:17–18. "Otherwise, you may say in your heart, 'My power and the strength of my hand made me this wealth.' But you are to remember the LORD your God, for it is He who is giving you power to make wealth, in order to confirm His covenant which He swore to your fathers, as it is this day.' "[17] Economic growth seems to have become a matter of common grace, not covenantal special grace. Amillennialists are silent of this matter, but they would argue that these promises did not extend into the New Covenant. But if this is true, then the promises were always nothing more than unattainable ideals, for the theology of the Mosaic covenant was not maintained in Persia by the creators of the oral tradition that became the written Talmud after Bar Kochba's rebellion against Rome in AD 133–135. The confession was not maintained by the Hebrews. Neither was per capita wealth. The Jews in Jesus' time were not known for their wealth.

Either the promise is still in force, or else it was always an unattainable ideal. The theonomic postmillennialist argues that it is still binding. There can still be confessional continuity over generations. There

15. Ezra Stiles, *The United States Elevated to Glory and Honor* (1783).

16. Article VI, Section 3 prohibits religious test oaths. Cf. Gary North, *Conspiracy in Philadelphia: Origins of the United States Constitution* (Moulton, Alabama: Axehead Press, [2013] 2032).

17. North, *Inheritance & Dominion*, chaps. 21, 22.

can be sustained economic blessings based on covenantal faithfulness. Families are economically bounded, but far less so than before 1800.

It is true that economic blessings have accompanied increasing apostasy among the intellectual elite in the United States. The slow but steady secularization of American culture has been accompanied by economic growth. The period of the most rapid economic growth in the United States, 1865 to 1914, was marked by the harnessing of energy: coal, oil, and electricity. It was also marked by huge immigration.[18] It was not marked politically by a Trinitarian confession of faith, but the general culture remained Protestant, although with a large Roman Catholic subculture. The social order defended the free market: property rights, low taxes, free trade inside the nation, and a gold coin standard. These are all biblical principles. From the point of view of common grace, the United States conformed closely to biblical laws governing economics until World War I.

18. Robert Higgs, *The Transformation of the American Economy, 1865–1914: An Essay in Interpretation* (Auburn, Alabama: Mises Institute, [1971] 2011).

Chapter 14

Imputation

How blessed is a person whose guilt the Lord *does not take into account,*
And in whose spirit there is no deceit!

Psalm 32:2

Analysis

Point four of the biblical covenant is sanctions.[1] Imposing sanctions requires the exercise of judgment. In economic theory, this is called imputation. It applies to economic value. My introductory remarks in Chapter 9, "Imputation," covers the connection between the Calvinist doctrine of judicial imputation and the Austrian School's doctrine of economic imputation. Calvin began with the presupposition of God's judicial imputation to each individual regarding his status as either saved or lost. Carl Menger in 1871 began with the autonomous individual who imputes economic value to specific goods and services. Calvin's doctrine of imputation was judicial and theocentric. Menger's doctrine of imputation was economic and anthropocentric. Calvin believed in the sovereignty of God. Menger believed in the sovereignty of the individual.

Calvin's doctrine then moved from God to man: casuistry. Casuistry

1. Ray R. Sutton, *That You May Prosper: Dominion By Covenant*, 2nd ed. (Tyler, Texas: Institute for Christian Economics, [1987] 1992), ch. 4.

is the individual's application of God's law to specific circumstances. An individual can make such imputations only because he is made in God's image. He can think God's thoughts after Him, as a creature. This is an an epistemology of *judicial representation*. In contrast, Menger had no comparable epistemology. He began with the fact of economic imputation. He did not make an epistemological case for the possibility of imputation. He did not ask the crucial question: "What can a man know, and how can he know it?" His follower, Ludwig von Mises, adopted Kant's epistemology. Kant's dualism[2]—phenomenal (ideal of science) vs. noumenal (ideal of personality)—is inherent in Mises' epistemology. The same is true of Mises' disciple, F. A. Hayek.[3] The central philosophical problem with Kantianism is this. *There is no way logically to connect the phenomenal realm and the noumemal realm*. There is no identifiable point of contact. There is no cause-and-effect relationship between Kant's hypothetical impersonal realm of scientifically understandable causation and the hypothetical realm of human freedom and autonomy.

The central institutional question for all economic epistemologies that are based on a theory of individual imputation of meaning, causation, and economic value is this: *How can the imputations of theoretically autonomous individuals explain decision-making by groups?* This is an application of the recurring philosophical problem of the one and the many. If we begin with the autonomy of the individual, we soon must face the fact that he is not autonomous. There are other imputing individuals in this world. He interacts with lots of them. To make sense of our world, we must have a way to assess the relevance of competing imputations. We must assign "weight" to individual imputations, and then "add up" the value of all of them. But no such value scale exists, according to the methodological individualist.[4] If this is true, this makes all representative decision-making on behalf of a group scientifically impossible. It also raises the question of who possesses the lawful

2. Richard Kroner, *Kant's Weltanschauung* (Chicago: University of Chicago Press, [1914] 1956).

3. Gary North, *Sovereignty & Dominion: An Economic Commentary on Genesis* (Moulton, Alabama: Axehead Press, [1982, 2012] 2022), Appendix B.

4. Lionel Robbins, *An Essay on the Nature and Significance of Economic Science* (London: Macmillan, 1932), ch. VI. See also North, *Sovereignty & Dominion*, ch. 5.

authority to make such representative decisions. On what basis? *Every epistemology of autonomous man soon crashes into the rocks of competing men.* No individualist epistemology is known to have survived this crash.

Once a procedure becomes scientifically impossible on its own terms, a humanistic economist is reduced to sociology. This is the fate of all economic theories of individual imputation. The alternative to sociology is either physics or silence. Either the methodological individualist must dismiss the scientific relevance of representative imputations and therefore also representative decision-making, thereby remaining mute with respect to collectives, or else he must lay down the economist's toolkit and pick up the sociologist's knapsack. This is a humiliating experience for an economist, but epistemologically necessary.

A. Valuation by God

Point one: God's sovereignty. God evaluated the results of His daily creative work on all days except day two (Gen. 1). This was an individual's evaluation of His individual work. But Christianity teaches that God is three Persons as well as one God. So, this imputation was also corporate. So was the creation. Only Christianity announces such a doctrine.

There was unity of purpose in the creation. God said "Let Us make mankind in Our image, according to Our likeness" (Gen. 1:26a). God is both singular and plural. Therefore, so is mankind, who as a species is made in God's image. The ability of men to make corporate judgments is inherent in the being of God and the being of man, both individual man and corporate man. This is why Christian economics can deal successfully with the epistemological issue of the one and the many. In the field of economics, the problem of the one and the many begins with epistemology, as it does in all other academic disciplines. The question of epistemology is this: "What can man know, and how can he know it?" It applies to individuals and collectives in every area of thought.

In every area of philosophy there is *axiology*: value theory. The same questions arise. What is value? How can men discover it? Is it independent of men? Is it imputed by men? Are we speaking of individuals or collectives? But in no social science is the question of axiology more important than economic theory. The central issue that the economist deals with is this: "What is the relationship between value and price?" This question has its individualistic side, but more important is its corporate side. If value is imputed individually, how do we know that the outcome of competitive bidding in a free market corresponds to the aggregate valuation of the participants? The socialist denies that it does. He denies that the process of competitive bidding leads to socially beneficial outcomes. He calls for state coercion to establish socially beneficial collective value. *To establish socially beneficial outcomes, a representative state agency must allocate scarce resources.* This is the heart, mind, and especially soul of socialism.

The problem of socialist imputation is an extension of the problem of family imputation. *The process of allocation by the head of the household is the central epistemological issue.* How can the head of the household maximize the value of the scarce resources at his command? He must consider the individual evaluations of family members. Then he must evaluate the accuracy of these judgments in terms of a standard. What standard? His own value scale? Or a composite value scale of all family members? Or a weighted value scale, weighted in terms of the capacities and responsibilities of each family member? Methodological individualism denies the existence of any such scale. But, if this is true, then are the estimates of the head of the household epistemologically irrelevant, an exercise in self-delusion? If there is no Trinitarian God, the answer is yes. There is no judicially authoritative corporate many in any autonomous act of individual economic imputation. There can therefore be no economically authoritative corporate *many* in an autonomous act of individual imputation. So, according to humanistic economic theory, the head of a household cannot represent such a God. He is on his autonomous own. Nevertheless, a person with authority knows that he must make authoritative decisions as the head of a legal entity. He allocates resources as an agent. By what standard?

B. Valuation by Man

Point two: hierarchy. My comments here are extensions of what I wrote in Section B of Chapter 9. They have to do with thinking God's thoughts after Him. This exercise begins with the presupposition of God's Bible-revealed law. This law applies to individuals, who are held responsible by God in history and eternity. But it also applies to corporate entities. The decision-makers must begin with any laws of God that apply to the corporate entity, either through biblical revelation or through the logical extension of biblical revelation. This is Christian casuistry: the application of biblical principles to historical circumstances.

Responsibility is four-way: upward to God, outward toward society—as manifested both in market demand and charitable need—downward toward family members, and inward: ethical conscience and personal needs. The head of the household is required by God to consider this complex array of competing demands on the family's resources. *The allocation is economic, but the responsibility is judicial*. It is stewardship within the legal framework of guardianship.

The head of a household makes valuations on behalf of each of the members of the family. He must take into consideration what God requires of each member. He must also consider God's expectations regarding the family as a covenantal unit. This makes his position as the head of the household highly complex. God holds him responsible for the accurate assessment of the value scales of each member, as well as the potential net output of each member. He must consider short-run net output and long-run. He then must motivate each member to maximize his or her output. He must fund these individual plans.

Because there are sometimes market prices of comparable services outside the household, the decision-maker can substitute market prices. He must discover the prices charged for comparable services, and then assess to what extent these "shadow prices" are relevant inside the household. Maybe he can pay one family member the equivalent of what it would cost to clean the house. But how can he charge this member what room and food would cost? These would be pseudo prices. The exact market value of this family member's living space, shared with siblings, is not available.

C. Criteria: Individual and Corporate

Point three: ethics. In Chapter 8, I explained why economic value is derived from ethical value, an epistemological position that is contrary to the prevailing notions of humanistic economic theory. I stated that the criterion of economic value is this: *the extension of the kingdom of God in history*. Economic theory is not value-free. It is value-derived.

The head of a household is required by God to use the kingdom of God as his standard of economic value in assessing the profitability of any course of action. He is supposed to allocate family capital based on this criterion. He acts as a steward of God, both judicially (authority) and economically (wealth). He acts on behalf of God: extending the kingdom of God. He acts as a steward of his family: extending its inheritance in history. The steward has the middleman aspect of it. It is both judicial and economic. He is judicially responsible before God. The rewards and penalties of stewardship are both judicial and economic. By means of successful stewardship, his responsibilities increase (Luke 12:47–48).[5]

The parable of the talents focuses on economic investment. A resource owner gives capital to three servants. He tells them to administer it until he returns. At his return, he assesses each steward's performance. The details of the parable are different in Matthew and Luke. In Matthew's version, the focus is on economics: investing a total of five coins (Matt. 25:14–30).[6] In Luke's version, the focus is on rulership (Luke 19:12–27).[7] Ten servants get one mina (small coin) each. At the accounting, one man has made ten to one; another man has made five to one. The first man is given rulership over ten cities. The second is given rulership over five cities. The third man in both versions is cast out. Luke's version makes this point: *success in economics is a surrogate for effective rulership*. Why should this be true? Because of the principle of biblical stewardship: it is both judicial and economic. I will consider Luke's version in greater detail in Part V, on the civil covenant.

5. Gary North, *Treasure & Dominion: An Economic Commentary on Luke* (Moulton, Alabama: Axehead Press, [2012] 2031), ch. 28.

6. Gary North, *Priorities & Dominion: An Economic Commentary on Matthew* (Moulton, Alabama: Axehead Press, [2012] 2030), ch. 47.

7. North, *Treasure & Dominion*, ch. 46.

The criteria of family economic success are varied. Parents are to teach their children the law of God (Deut. 6:7).[8] We see this applied in the instruction of a son in Proverbs, chapters 1 through 9. This instruction is based on the assumption that God's law is valid through history and across geographical borders. Second, it assumes that children can be taught the principles of understanding biblical law and then exercising judgment in applying the appropriate laws to historical circumstances. This is the skill of biblical casuistry. This skill begins in the context of the family. *The family, not the church, is the central agency in the transmission of the skill of casuistry.*

The classic example in the New Testament of the transmission of family values is Jesus' parable of the prodigal son (Luke 15:11–24).[9] At his son's request, a father gives his younger son an early inheritance. He squanders it. First, he departs from his home. Second, he departs from his country. Third, he falls into bad company. Fourth, he loses his money. Fifth, penniless in a pig sty, he comes to his senses. Sixth, he correctly evaluates his condition. The pigs live better than he does. Seventh, he devises a plan of action. He will return to his father's house, where he will apply for work as a servant. Eighth, when he returns, penniless, to offer his services as a servant, his father rejoices at his return. "'[F]or this son of mine was dead and has come to life again; he was lost and has been found.' And they began to celebrate" (Luke 15:24). This was *covenantal resurrection*. His judicial condition had been lost. Now it was found. The son had come to his senses, meaning covenantal senses.

The older son was upset. "Why throw a party for the younger son?" He father tells him: his brother's sonship had been restored. But the older brother remains the heir: "all that is mine is yours" (Luke 15:31b). *The restoration of sonship did not change the economics of family inheritance*. The family was restored judicially, but the inheritance of the prodigal son still reflected his squandered capital. It was gone.

The parable is about the gentiles and Israel. The gentiles were being restored, after years of wandering. The Israelites resented this. They did not understand that the judicial restoration of the family of God did

8. Gary North, *Inheritance & Dominion: An Economic Commentary on Deuteronomy* (Moulton, Alabama: Axehead Press, [1999, 2012] 2028), ch. 15.

9. North, *Treasure & Dominion*, ch. 37.

not threaten the Israelites' economic inheritance, assuming that they remained faithful, which meant rejoicing at the restoration of the gentiles. But the Israelites remained hostile. So, they lost their inheritance, as Jesus had prophesied. "Therefore I say to you, the kingdom of God will be taken away from you and given to a people producing its fruit" (Matt. 21:43). The repentant prodigal sons re-claimed their judicial status as sons of God. The Israelites refused. So, God disinherited Israel in AD 70: the fall of Jerusalem.[10]

The parable is also about judicial imputation. It is also about the role of repentance. Its context is the family. The younger brother had evaluated poorly, and then came to his senses. The older brother had evaluated wisely, but then faced a choice: to uphold his own righteousness or to rejoice with his father. *The issue was the judicial restoration of the family.* "But we had to celebrate and rejoice, because this brother of yours was dead and has begun to live, and was lost and has been found" (Luke 15:32). The father rejoiced, the younger son rejoiced, but the older brother hesitated. Jesus was making a point: rejoice with God the Father regarding the restoration of covenantal sonship to the gentiles.

D. Value and Price

Point four: sanctions. The parable of the prodigal son is about judicial imputation. This judicial imputation is based on the father's announcement of the son's judicial status as a son. But this is different from economic imputation. The prodigal son was not made richer than he was before he departed. But he was richer than he was in the pig sty. He had correctly imputed his economic condition then, which is why he returned to his father's house.

The father was the owner of the resources that remained after the prodigal son departed, inheritance in hand. The father told the older brother that all that he possessed belonged to the older brother. Why did he say this? Because he understood his role as a trustee of the family's capital. He held it in trust judicially for the future heirs. The heir would be the older brother.

10. David Chilton, *The Days of Vengeance* (Ft. Worth, Texas: Dominion Press, 1987).

The older brother—Israel—so resented the feast put on by the father to celebrate the return of the younger brother that he was threatening his own inheritance. By breaking covenant with his brother through his resentment, he displayed envy. He was willing to put his inheritance at risk by resisting the celebration of the return of his brother. He regarded his father's celebration as an affront. He imputed greater value to the feast his father had never celebrated for him than he imputed to his inheritance. He wanted to be honored for his steadfastness. He was willing to risk disinheritance by refusing to attend the feast. If his father disinherited him, the younger brother would become the heir.

This is the pattern in the Bible. *The younger brother inherits because of the sin of the older brother.* Seth is the first example; he replaced Cain. Isaac is another; he replaced Ishmael. Jacob is another; he replaced Esau. Jesus is the central example: the second Adam (I Cor. 15:45–47), not the first. The sin of Israel was the sin of the older brother in the parable of the prodigal son. He relied on his own works. His younger brother relied on his father's mercy.

The younger brother imputed greater economic value to his father's house than to the pig sty. His older brother imputed greater economic value to his own economic steadfastness than to his father's mercy. *These were competing economic imputations within the household.* Jesus warned His listeners not to side with the leaders of Israel. He sent the disciples to the cities of Israel, but He acknowledged that the great examples of faith in His day were the Roman centurion (Matt. 8:10) and the Canaanite woman (Matt. 15:28). This was a warning to Israel, the older brother. The gentiles were more concerned with receiving Jesus' mercy than with receiving the inheritance, which they could not legally claim. Yet Jesus told the Jewish leaders that God's kingdom would be removed from them and given to a new people (Matt. 21:43). This new people was the gentile church.

When the inheritance is transferred from the older son to the younger son because of the repentance of the younger son, there are rival imputations of economic value. The older brother places greater value on his own external obedience—self-righteousness—than on his need for submission and repentance. God the Father places greater value on submission and repentance. In the parable of the prodigal son, the prodigal son evaluates the comparative value of the income stream from feeding pigs vs. the income stream from working as a servant back home. His evaluation is correct. The price is his return home. He pays this price. The older brother evaluates the income stream from separating himself from his father's celebration vs. his own disinheritance. He seems ready to choose disinheritance. This is what Israel did choose.

Imputation economically reflects imputation judicially. The meek will inherit the earth (Matt. 5:5).[11] But this imputation is based on faith. It is not always clear in history that covenant-keepers have an advantage economically over covenant-breakers. Indeed, history seems to testify to the opposite. But history is not over. This same anomaly initially bothered the author of Psalm 73. He changed his mind later.[12]

E. Value-Added Living

Point five: succession. Jesus said: "The thief comes only to steal and kill and destroy; I came so that they would have life, and have it abundantly" (John 10:10). This applies to every Christian. It applies to all Christian covenantal institutions. This principle applies to kingdom expansion. *More is better than less at the same price.*

Individuals impute economic value. Individuals are responsible for the accuracy of these imputations, case by case. This ability is grounded in God's economic imputation.[13]

There is no possibility of a cardinal scale of value: numerical designations. There is only an ordinal value scale: first, second, third. This is because man is an analogical being. He is not digital. He is made in God's image. *God is personal, not digital.*

The act of imputation is always representational. Man imputes economic value on behalf of God: the cosmic Owner. He also imputes it on behalf of any subordinate owners of the assets involved. This act of economic imputation is always governed by the judicial category of ownership. *Economic ownership is always an extension of judicial own-*

11. North, *Priorities & Dominion*, ch. 4.

12. Gary North, *Confidence & Dominion: An Economic Commentary on the Psalms* (Moulton, Alabama: Axehead Press, [2012] 2029), ch. 17.

13. Chapter 8:E.

ership. It is not autonomous. Nothing in the creation is autonomous. Ownership is covenantal under God.

The head of a household makes estimates of the value of future potential streams of income. He then allocates resources under his control to buy or lease control over these income streams. He estimates in terms of *the present economic value of future legal ownership*. Imputed economic value drives legal ownership, but legal ownership secures future economic value. If there were no possibility of securing ownership, the division of labor would contract. The range of cooperative ventures would shrink. The ability to make estimates influences the array of assets owned, but this ability is valuable only because of the possibility of securing ownership.

The art of estimating future economic value presupposes economic cause and effect: sanctions. It also assumes linear history. There is causation over time. If there were not, our ability to estimate future economic value could not exist. We would be overwhelmed by randomness. The individual could not plan for an objective outcome. This outcome is in part legal and in part economic. Legal: "Will I still own it?" Economic: "What will it be worth?"

The head of the household acts in the name of others. This is the *guardian* function. Second, he also acts in terms of expected future value. He may have no present legal relationship with future customers, but at some point, there will be a legal exchange of ownership. Third, he acts as a *steward for future owners*, who will pay him to gain ownership. He is not a legal guardian for these people, but he is an economic agent: an auctioneer. *This is why ownership is a social function.*[14]

Abram was a trustee of family assets. He was a trustee for heirs to come, God told him (Gen. 15, 17). This was a covenantal promise. God told him that he would have many heirs. God changed his name to Abraham: father of nations. This mandated a stewardship function. He would have to leave an inheritance. It would have to increase in order to match the increase in heirs. He had to plan for an objective outcome: biological heirs. He had to make resource allocation decisions in terms of this objective outcome. The numerical units were analogical: like

14. Gary North, *An Introduction to Christian Economics* (Moulton, Alabama: Axehead Press, [1973] 2025), ch. 28.

the stars above and the sand of the sea. That is, they were objective. What was not objective was the future capital value per capita. That would have to be imputed.

Part of this inheritance was collected by the Israelites at the time of the exodus. They borrowed from the Egyptians. They would not repay, for they were leaving Egypt. This was a *transfer of inheritance* from the families of the dead firstborn sons. It was also a *restitution payment* from the entire population on behalf of the line of Pharaohs, who had enslaved them.[15]

Economic growth is the product of accurate forecasting coupled with objective resource allocation. These activities assume a system of private ownership. They also assume a world of economic causation: predictable sanctions. If there were no sanctions—profit and loss—there could not be economic rationality. These twin sanctions must be enforced by customers in a free market order. *There must be decentralized private ownership.* Without this, central planners are flying blind. This was Ludwig von Mises' point in his 1920 essay, "Economic Calculation in the Socialist Commonwealth."[16]

Conclusion

The biblical explanation of economic imputation rests on the biblical system of private ownership. An owner is a legal guardian (vertical-judicial), an economic steward (vertical-economic), and an auctioneer who acts on behalf of high bidders (horizontal-economic). The head of a household is the biblical model of this arrangement. He acts legally in the name of God, himself, and his heirs. He acts economically on behalf of all these, plus future customers: the resource-bidding public.

Subjective economic imputation undergirds the system of competitive bidding, which is objective. People with resources make estimates of future economic value. Then they enter the market and make bids

15. Gary North, *Authority & Dominion: An Economic Commentary on Exodus*, vol. 1, *Part I: Representation & Dominion* (Moulton, Alabama: Axehead Press, [1985, 2012] 2025), chaps. 6, 12.

16. Ludwig von Mises, *Economic Calculation in the Socialist Commonwealth* (Auburn, Alabama: Mises Institute, [1920] 1990).

for legal control over scarce resources. This produces prices on capital markets. These markets assume the existence of a system for transferring ownership. It is governed by this economic principle: *monetary high bid wins*.

Economic planning is an extension of the practice of casuistry: the application of unchanging principles to changing historical circumstances. These are moral principles, according to the Bible. Humanistic economics denies this. It treats these unchanging ethical principles as evolving and technical. It treats them as value-free. But it suffers from the dualism that afflicted Greek philosophy: there is no point of contact between the unchanging logical principles (Parmenides) and historical flux (Heraclitus). The conceptual models are separated from history.[17]

The skill of economic casuistry is to be taught to one's heirs. This is an aspect of the teaching of God's law (Deut. 5:4–8). God's law encompasses the realm of economic theory resource allocation. So does covenantal instruction.

17. Mises was less vulnerable to this criticism, but by invoking the evenly rotating economy as a substitute for neoclassical equilibrium, he exposed his system to this criticism.

Chapter 15

Inheritance

A good person leaves an inheritance to his grandchildren,
And the wealth of a sinner is stored up for the righteous.

Proverbs 13:22

Analysis

Point five of the biblical covenant is succession.[1] In economic theory, this is inheritance. Its focus is the family. The family is under the terms of the dominion covenant. God's assignment to the family has to do with mankind's dominion under God and over nature.

There is a strong element of future-orientation associated with inheritance. The future for covenant-keepers is supposed to be prosperous. They are to pass down an inheritance to their children. This includes a worldview. This worldview is supposed to be capitalized with assets. "A good man leaves an inheritance to his children's children, but the sinner's wealth is laid up for the righteous."[2] Over generations, this inheritance compounds. When sustained, economic compounding creates great wealth. This is God's ethical criterion for covenant-keepers. It is not optional. The next generation is supposed to be more prosperous

1. Ray R. Sutton, *That You May Prosper: Dominion By Covenant*, 2nd ed. (Tyler, Texas: Institute for Christian Economics, [1987] 1992), ch. 5.

2. Gary North, *Wisdom & Dominion: An Economic Commentary on Proverbs* (Moulton, Alabama: Axehead Press, [2012] 2029), ch. 41.

than the previous one. This is a crucial motivation for dominion. The desire to pass along an inheritance within a family produces long-term economic growth that benefits people outside a family's boundaries.

A. Purpose

Point one: God's sovereignty. Purpose precedes planning. This fact is analogous to the even more fundamental fact that God's absolute sovereignty is the judicial basis of man's delegated authority. God's purposes establish the boundaries of His plans. God then uses His original purposes to judge the degree of success or failure of the outcomes of men's plans. Sometimes God's pre-creation purposes are revealed by the Bible. Usually, they are not. We must infer them from the Bible's revelation of God's stated plans and also His judgments on individuals and institutions because of the outcomes of their plans.

God's purposes for the family are revealed in the words of the dominion covenant: to exercise dominion and to multiply (Gen. 1:26–28).[3] This appears in the account of the creation week: day six. On day four, God created the heavenly orbs. He did this in order to provide a means of creating calendars to mark the seasons (Gen. 1:14). That was future-oriented planning. Man had not yet been created. So, what we know about the purposes of the family before the foundation of the world must be inferred from the planning stage. The family alone is authorized by God for this task of multiplication. This is its unique purpose. It is shared with no other institution. Each covenant has a unique purpose that defines it. The church's unique purpose is preaching and administering the sacraments. The state's unique purpose is the suppression of certain kinds of public evil by the threat of legal violence.

B. Central Planning

Point two: hierarchy. The head of a household looks to the future of his nuclear family. He sacrifices present income for better education, both

3. Gary North, *Sovereignty & Dominion: An Economic Commentary on Genesis* (Moulton, Alabama: Axehead Press, [1982, 2012] 2022), chaps. 3, 4.

for his children and himself. He seeks to avoid becoming an economic liability in his old age. Paying for education is a way to transfer capital to his heirs on a tax-free basis. He does not consume all of his capital. His children's finances are not drained by the cost of supporting parents.

Long-term forecasting is different from short-term. The head of a household may try to estimate the market value of family capital several generations in the future, but this is rare. The unknown is too great a barrier. He has no control over the confession of faith of each succeeding generation in his family. He knows that his ability to establish institutional means of preserving wealth is limited. The size of future inheriting families is also beyond his control. Therefore, per capita wealth in his family is beyond his control. Entrepreneurship is wasted on the long run for most investors.

Because conditions change, and because people's responses to these changing conditions also change, it is close to impossible to specify far in advance how family capital should be used. The general principles will become subject to conflict among heirs. This conflict may be taken into the civil courts. The outcome of these disagreements is unknown to the head of the household. After he dies, his influence wanes. So, his focus is medium-term. It relates to his own lifetime and the lifetime of his children. It cannot extend to the adulthood of his grandchildren.[4]

The head of a household can train his children in a craft, but will this craft match the skills of his children? Probably not. The division of labor is so great that specialization grows ever greater. The skills required for mastery in a craft become more specialized. Sons do not often follow in their father's craft. We see few companies named "Jones and Son" today. The sons depart from more than their fathers' households.

In Section B of Chapter 7, I discussed future-orientation and population growth. My basic point was that having a large family is an assertion of low time-preference. The costs of children today are seen as worthwhile, given the increased output of adult children in the future. So, a large family is a capital investment.

---

4. John Tyler (1790–1861) served as President of the United states from 1841 to 1845. There was no way that he could have foreseen the economics of the early twenty-first century. Yet his two grandsons were still alive in 2018. One of them lived on his grandfather's estate in Virginia. For a 2012 television interview of him, see: CBS, "President Tyler: The VP who became President", YouTube, February 19, 2012, youtube.com/watch?v=Svwg0j19KGI.

When the service aspect of a growing population is seen as extending beyond the family, birth rates are less likely to fall below replacement rate. Parents who view large families as a means of extending their worldview have a greater incentive to have large families. They see the return on investment in terms of the benefits to a future society. They see the family in terms of production as well as consumption. This reveals a service mentality. It reveals a dominion mentality.

This service-oriented outlook is in no way a denial of personal self-interest. Jesus told His disciples to lay up treasure in heaven. "[F]or where your treasure is, there your heart will be also" (Matt. 6:21).[5] This principle of long-term investing applies to the costs associated with large families. Parents experience reduced net personal income in their child-rearing years. If they understand the ethical imperatives of the dominion covenant, they see this as a kingdom-building activity. They rely on Jesus' promise of greater rewards beyond the grave. *This is not self-denial. It is low time-preference. It is high future-orientation.* It is what Edward Banfield called the upper-class mentality.[6] It is focused on post-resurrection economic status.

For those who affirm postmillennialism, this willingness to accept lower net income in the present for the sake of the future refers also to history. The postmillennialist does not believe, as the premillennialist does, that Christian capital in the aggregate will suffer a discontinuity prior to the time when Jesus comes back in person to set up a thousand-year earthly kingdom.[7] He sees continuity. He does not believe, as the amillennialist does, that Satan inherits in history through his earthly disciples. He does not believe, as the amillennialist does—but refuses to say in public—that the wealth of the just is laid up for the sinner. He believes in the compound economic growth of the kingdom of God in history. The wealth of the sinner is laid up for the just (Prov. 13:22b).

---

5. Gary North, *Priorities & Dominion: An Economic Commentary on Matthew* (Moulton, Alabama: Axehead Press, [2012] 2030), ch. 13.

6. Edward Banfield, *The Unheavenly City Revisited* (Boston: Little, Brown, 1974), 57–59.

7. The historic premillennialist believes in a future "great tribulation," which will immediately precede Christ's bodily return. The non-postribulational dispensational premillennialist believes that the church will be raptured out of history before the great tribulation, but Christian capital will be destroyed during this tribulation period.

C. Imitation

Point three: ethics. Fathers are to teach their sons the Bible-revealed law of God (Deut. 6:7; Prov. 4:3–4). This is an aspect of covenantal continuity in history. The law of God is supposed to bind the generations. The family is the chief agency of this binding. This continuity is supposed to be a continuity of word-and-deed evangelism.[8] The children are to see that the law of God produces success in history. They are supposed to see what pagan nations also are supposed to see (Deut. 4:5–8).[9]

Success has imitators. This concept is basic to economic theory. Economists believe that a competitive advantage in the free market that produces an above-average rate of return will be imitated. Entrepreneurs want to appropriate a share of these above-average profits. So, they seek to discover what advantage a competitor possesses, and then they imitate it. When they do, their output increases. The prices of resources associated with this line of production increase, at least until a new innovation emergences. Thus, the spread between costs and revenues narrows. The original competitive advantage disappears. This process of competition brings benefits to customers. They are the long-term beneficiaries of the entrepreneurs' continual quest for profits.

This imitation process is always limited by *ceteris paribus*: "other things remaining equal." When covenant-breakers grow weary of copying successes that are based on adherence to biblical law and its implications, they eventually rebel. They refuse to continue to imitate covenant-keepers. They cannot tolerate their increasing conformity to the terms of biblical law. This resentment is the basis of the final rebellion of Satan at the end of history (Rev. 20:7–9).[10] He rebels against the success of God's kingdom, not its failure.

To the extent that the legal and moral foundations of capitalism are based on biblical norms, it can and will prosper. If private property is upheld by custom and civil law, capitalism can and will flourish. If

8. George Grant, *In the Shadow of Plenty: The Biblical Blueprint for Welfare* (Ft. Worth, Texas: Dominion Press, 1986), ch. 1.

9. Gary North, *Inheritance & Dominion: An Economic Commentary on Deuteronomy* (Moulton, Alabama: Axehead Press, [1999, 2012] 2028), ch. 8.

10. Gary North, *Dominion and Common Grace: The Biblical Basis of Progress* (Moulton, Alabama: Axehead Press, [1987] 2024), ch. 9.

future-orientation becomes widespread, an outlook that is the result of optimism concerning history, then the rate of investment will increase. If a rejection of envy is widely adopted, then cooperation across economic classes will increase. If taxes remain lower than Samuel's warning figure of 10% (I Sam. 8:14, 17),[11] economic growth will be maintained. If wealth gained through entrepreneurship is upheld by the people who influence public opinion, there will be economic growth. Societies can adopt the fruits of a biblical worldview, but without adopting Christianity.

D. Entrepreneurship

Point four: sanctions. Entrepreneurship is the art of forecasting the future in terms of a set of subjective and objective goals, and then organizing production to meet these goals at the lowest cost. It is inherently future-oriented. This is mostly an aspect of planning: point two. But it is also a matter of feedback: sanctions. They cannot be separated. This is why point two and point four are tightly connected.

In the free market, the primary sanctions are monetary profit and loss. These are objective criteria. Prices are set by competitive bidding: buyers vs. buyers, sellers vs. sellers. This is not the case in the family covenant. There is no product substitution. There are rarely competing bids. There is no objective set of criteria for success and failure, other than this: divorce. That brings product substitution into play, which is a violation of the family covenant.[12] The monetary costs are high: lawyers and asset allocation.

Parents have long-term economic goals: retirement, old age expenses, and inheritance to children. They are required by God to recognize this principle: "A good person leaves an inheritance to his grandchildren, And the wealth of a sinner is stored up for the righteous" (Prov. 13:22). To achieve this goal, they must save money throughout the marriage. They must invest wisely: a postive rate of return compounded. One or both must earn high incomes. Retirement in a rural society involved

11. Gary North, *Disobedience & Defeat: An Economic Commentary on the Historical Books* (Moulton, Alabama: Axehead Press, [2012] 2029), ch. 14.

12. Ray R. Sutton, *Second Chance: Biblical Principles for Divorce and Remarriage* (Tyler, Texas: Dominion Press, 1988).

living with children. The family farm would usually go to the child who cared for the parents, normally a son. When families moved to urban locations, they tried to become home owners. By the 1920s, at least half of white families in the United States owned homes.

If a culture is secretive regarding family wealth, as the culture in the United States is, children are kept in the dark about who will inherit what, and on what terms. They usually do not find out the details until the executor of the written will or trust reads the document at a post-mortem gathering of the children of the deceased. This makes forecasting family-owned capital difficult for the prospective heirs. This was not the case in Jesus' parable to the prodigal son and his stay-at-home older brother (Luke 15:11–24). Both sons knew the terms of their inheritance. The younger son disinherited himself economically. But he restored himself covenantally. The older brother did not disinherit himself economically, but he risked being disinherited covenantally because of his resentment against his newly repentant brother.[13] This degree of openness regarding inheritance is the biblical standard.

E. Accumulation

Point five: succession. The increase in family capital in the narrow sense—tools of production—is the same as it is for an individual's capital. The difference is this. An individual can benefit from any expansion of personal capital by means of personal consumption. He then dies on the day be runs out of wealth. He has no biological heirs and no causes to support. He leaves no inheritance. A Christian family must avoid such an end. It must extend God's kingdom in history.

The family's time perspective must be long-term. The head of a family is supposed to act on behalf of future generations. While he can know little of what future generations will require, he can make guesses. Gold holds value through the ages. It is recognized in most societies in most eras. But Jesus was clear that the accumulation of gold for an individual involves a trade-off between capital in this life and capital in the

13. Gary North, *Treasure & Dominion: An Economic Commentary on Luke* (Moulton, Alabama: Axehead Press, [2012] 2031), ch. 37.

next life: more here, but less there. So, this form of inter-generational wealth transfers has a major limitation. A wise man does not accumulate large quantities of gold except in times of potentially great social disruptions. The gold is capital for use on the far side of the disruption. It can be sold. The money generated from the sale can be used to buy growth-producing tools. Gold's advantage is the advantage of money: it is highly marketable. It therefore is a way to protect capital value against unexpected changes in market demand.

Personal capital is easier to manage, for its value need be increased in only one lifetime. An individual specializes in dealing with the trials and tribulations of his time period and geography. This specialization enables him to make better allocation decisions. But inter-generational forecasting of future capital value, aside from gold, is an exercise in futility. If men cannot intelligently impute value to future capital, due to their lack of specialized knowledge about future economic conditions, then the accumulation of capital for wealth transfer mandates the use of independent trustees. The capital must be transferred to trustees. But this problem arises: appointing a trustee who will act as a fiduciary for the heirs rather than as an agent of his own self-interest.

I knew a woman who was the heiress of a fortune. Her father had founded a national chain of what used to be called five[14]-and-dime[15] stores: low-cost goods for the masses. The chain long ago succumbed to market forces. It disappeared. He designated a trustee for this fortune. The woman was a wise and well-educated woman. She told me that the trustee was a large bank. The bank gave her 2% of the earnings of the invested pool of capital every year. The bank kept the rest in reserve. It collected management fees for decades. When she died, the bank no doubt went on serving as the family trustee. That was working capital for the bank: an inter-generational source of management fees. That was the bank's inheritance. The rich man had disinherited his daughter. His heir was a bank.

For capital to multiply over generations, the heirs must be trained in the principles of wealth-creation and inheritance. They also must accept the parents' vision, and then have the foresight and competence

14. Five pennies. The penny is lowest-value American coin: one one-hundredth of a dollar.

15. Ten pennies.

to implement it. This involves a confession of faith of some kind. Any confession of faith is easily abandoned by any heir. Furthermore, in most communities, there is no awareness of any link between theological confession and wealth accumulation. If anything, this link is rejected on the basis of a rejection of worldliness. Within certain subcultures there is a link. Among Jews and Armenians, there is at least a cultural link. Their theological confessions have not been maintained in the post-1900 world. We sometimes see this connection in small business cultures. Again, Jews and Armenians are examples. But those Jews who have become enormously wealthy have not generally maintained the theological confession of Orthodox Judaism.

Families are not effective instruments for the creation of inter-generational wealth. Corporations are. Corporations have only one major goal: to make a profit. All other goals are eventually sacrificed to the goal of profit. A firm may begin with a mission statement, but a century later, that mission statement will be a museum piece. Families launch small businesses that occasionally become successful medium-size businesses. These businesses do not become conglomerates. At some point, they cease to be family enterprises. The knowledge required to continue to expand them cannot be found within one family.[16] In the United States at the end of the twentieth century, about 80% of American businesses were family-owned. But only one-third of them survived into the second generation. By the third generation, most surviving companies had passed into the hands of professional managers.[17] In contrast, Chinese businesses rarely survive into the third generation. Family bonds make it difficult to trust professional managers.[18]

Conclusion

As an institution, the family can either add economic value or reduce it. If a family is covenantally established by oath as an agency in the kingdom of God, it adds value by extending the kingdom through produc-

16. Francis Fukuyama, *Trust: The Social Virtues and the Creation of Prosperity* (New York: Free Press, 1995), 64–65.

17. Ibid., 78.

18. Ibid., 78–82.

tivity. It does this by biological multiplication or multiplication through adoption. It does this by educating children: a way to extend the worldview of the covenant. It can do this by a family business that serves customers in a free market. It can do this by serving individuals outside the family through unpaid charitable service.

Unlike the covenanted individual, the family does not extend into eternity (Matt. 22:29–30). So, it is not possible for a family to build capital in eternity by foregoing the use of wealth in history. This is possible for individuals, who can forfeit present wealth in exchange for permanent wealth beyond the grave (Matt. 6:21–23). The family is temporally limited. But, unlike the individual, the family extends in history through future generations. So, the trade-off is consumption now vs. increased capital in the future. The effects of individual saving and wealth-building today extend posthumously by means of the family. Participation in a family adds a degree of future-orientation to individual decision-making.

This element of future-orientation gives an incentive for wealth-creation in societies that place the family at the center of society. But wealth-creation is limited by the capacities and vision of a limited group: the family. Apart from the intervention of the Holy Spirit, this limitation eventually overcomes long-term wealth-creation by a family. The confessions of faith, the visions of the future, and the creativity of future members have been limited in the past by the law of large numbers, which includes the phenomenon known as *regression to the mean*. Genetics limits the productivity of family members. The family has a limited gene pool. This is why successful family enterprises must recruit workers and managers from outside the family. The businesses must broaden the pool of available talent. The only way that this can be done while maintaining the family structure is by the adoption of managers into the family. Operationally, this can be done only through arranged marriages. This raises a problem. How can good managers be retained after divorces? The family is not the proper institution for running successful growing businesses down through the generations. The Rothschilds have succeeded. They are the great exception. Not until 2010 did the family hire a non-family member for a senior position.[19] This was 198 years after the founder died.

19. Julia Werdigier, "Rothschild Leadership Moves Outside Family," *New York Times* (March 30, 2010).

The family is an effective institution for creating businesses, but it is not an effective institution for extending them by long-term growth. The requirements of running the business exceed the capabilities of family members. Wealth-creation has been limited historically by this limitation. The development of the limited-liability corporation in the late nineteenth century in the United States gave the United States a huge advantage. It allowed the accumulation of capital through the generations, for the corporation is legally immortal. Corporations can reinvest profits. They can focus the talents of senior managers and employees on a limited goal: making a profit. This concentration of capital and the narrowing of vision have led to compound economic growth, both for corporations and for societies.

The corporation is more like a church than a family in this respect: limited liability. Members of a church are not legally liable for the debts of the church. Neither are investors in a corporation personally liable for the debts of the corporation. In a family, members of the nuclear family suffer losses when a family-run business suffers losses. The head of the household places his spouse and children at risk by starting a business. The head of a corporation places the value of the shares of ownership at risk, which a family may own, but he does not place at risk the investors' personal assets. This makes the corporation ideal for long-term wealth creation. But it is clearly a liability with respect to preserving a confession of faith, other than this one: "More for me in history." This is the confession of faith of the religion of mammon (Matt. 6:24).[20]

A corporation is not a living creature. It is not threatened by eternity in the lake of fire (Rev. 20:14–15). Yet corporations are excellent arrangements for wealth creation. Individuals are the beneficiaries of this wealth, both as investors and customers. So are families. Corporations specialize in profit-seeking activities. They profit from selling goods and services to customers. Economically, they are auctioneers. They serve buyers who are not usually owners of the corporation. They sell on this basis: *monetary high bid wins*. They are market institutions, not covenantal institutions. They are based on written contracts, sometimes unavailable to the public. They are not based on public self-maledictory covenantal oaths before God and men. Families are.

---

20. North, *Priorities & Dominion*, ch. 14.

There are *fundamental judicial distinctions* between families and corporations. The main two are these: the corporation's limited liability legal status and the absence of a covenant oath. There are also *fundamental economic distinctions*. The main one is this: a corporation's auction process for serving customers vs. a family's mutual oaths of lifetime mutual service. The corporation is a market organization with a social function: allocating capital to its highest uses by paying customers. Monetary high bid wins. The family is a social institution with an economic function: covenantal inheritance to build one of two kingdoms: the kingdom of God or the kingdom of mammon. God's kingdom wins ...according to postmillennialism.[21]

21. Kenneth L. Gentry, *He Shall Have Dominion*, 2nd ed. (Tyler, Texas: Institute for Christian Economics, [1992] 1997).

Conclusion to Part III

The family is universal. It is established in every culture by a public oath, as far as I can determine. This oath is enforceable institutionally: by family, church, and state. To this oath are attached sanctions: positive and negative (for violation).

The family as an institution has a future until the end of time. But the confessional continuity of the family is weak. Any adult can renounce the confession, defy it, or ignore it. Over time, some family branches depart from it. Some maintain it. The historical archetypes were Cain and Seth. There were Ishmael and Isaac. There were Esau and Jacob. Ultimately, there are Adam and Jesus. Note: in all these cases, the younger brother inherited, due to a superior confession and superior ethics. The older brother was disinherited.

A head of household is a judicial agent: a guardian. He acts in the name of God to family members, and in the name of family members to God. This is hierarchical-judicial. There is also economic stewardship: the sharecropper function. It is also hierarchical. The mandated payment is the tithe. Finally, there is the auctioneer function: service to other society members. The general rule is *monetary high bid wins*. But this can also be a charitable function. It is horizontal. It looks outward.

The family is a judicial unit. It is therefore responsible to God, to other covenantal institutions, and to those who trade with it. This responsibility is corporate. Family members sink or swim with the family. Responsibility in the family is to a corporate entity. Thus, methodological individualism does not logically apply to the family. The family is more than the participants. God holds it responsible. The classic example is Achan's theft of the valuable assets from Jericho (Josh. 7).

Wealth and poverty apply to the family, not to individual members. All economic approaches that rely on methodological individualism as the sole tool of explanation fail to make sense of the operations of family, church, and state.

The economic time horizon of a family unit is limited. This is because death removes each generation from responsibility. The ability of any generation to specify the use of family capital from beyond the grave is highly limited and fades rapidly. The Book of Ecclesiastes refers to this fact.

Because the head of the household must make economic decisions on behalf of family members, he must make interpersonal comparisons of subjective utility. He must "balance" or "weigh" the goals and aspirations of multiple members. He must also make estimates regarding God's assessment of these aspirations. So, in order to make accurate assessments of multiple subjective valuations, he must rely on his ability to assess God's assessments. He acts as God's fiduciary agent in his allocation of family capital. But he also acts as his family's fiduciary agent with God and with the world outside the family. There are multiple acts of economic imputation.

This must be done mostly without reference to money prices. The family is an agency that implements the division of labor. But this process is not marked by a money economy. This division of labor is far more personal than impersonal. Money has a peripheral role as a way to compensate children for work performed inside the family: "chores." But money is geared to voluntary exchange, so most services performed in a family cannot be out-sourced. If children are to learn how to work, they can be paid in terms of the going rate outside the family. But the use of outside prices is for purposes of establishing fairness, not for threatening the family member with replacement by a price-competitive non-family member. The family member must learn how to work.

In a covenantal unit, pricing is not based on substitution. So, the logic of exchange that applies to a free market does not apply in a covenantal unit. There is no substitution allowed by law. This is why that which Mises called catallactics is highly limited. This is why he never attempted to apply the science of human action outside the market, the realm in which monetary high bid wins.

A family is supposed to add economic value. So is an individual. This is the basis of compound economic growth. The extension of a family's influence is by means of capital accumulation. But the law of large numbers reasserts itself over time. Families do not seem to be able to increase the per capita wealth of its members over many generations. The performance of the members, especially heads of households, reverts to the mean. Confessions revert to the mean. The more influential that a family has in extending God's kingdom, the more this performance over the generations reverts to the mean. New families appear.

God's challenge to Christians is to improve their performance in every area of life. This is the meaning of progressive sanctification. In economics, this means greater thrift and entrepreneurship. Children must be taught to increase their responsibility, not avoid it. The replacement process inevitably continues. This is true of families, churches, and states. But it is most obvious in families. Covenant-keeping families must teach the theology of dominion to their children. If they refuse, reversion to the mean is inevitable.

PART IV

The Economic Structure of the Church Covenant

Introduction to Part IV

A. You Cannot Sell That Pew

It is clear that the modern church is involved in the economy. Churches own real estate. They have bank accounts. They are legal entities that are responsible for the administration of property. Yet any suggestion that the church ought to be run as a profit-seeking business is correctly greeted with skepticism. People understand that the church is not a business. The suggestion that the church should sell access to the sacraments would be rejected outright by Christians, and it would be ridiculed by non-Christians. Yet there was a time, not so long ago, when some churches in the United States rented prime pews to the highest bidders. A pew is a long bench in the church's sanctuary. Renting pews was sufficiently common for Wikipedia to devote a section to it in the entry for "Pews."[1]

There is a scene in the autobiographical book, Broadway play, and movie, *Life With Father* (1947), in which the father in a financially successful New York City household around 1900 confronts the pastor of his Episcopal Church. The father is a not a member. He attends only because his wife, Vinnie, pressures him. He works on Wall Street. He understands investing.

Rev. Dr. Lloyd: After considerable thought, we voted that our supporting members should each contribute a sum equal to the cost of their pew.

Father: I paid $5,000 for that pew.

1. "Pew." *Wikipedia*, Wikimedia Foundation, October 15, 2020.

VINNIE: Yes, Clare, that makes our contribution $5,000.

FATHER: That's robbery. Do you know what that pew is worth today? $3,000. That's what the last one sold for. I've taken a dead loss on that pew of $2,000 already. Frank Bags sold me that pew when the market was at its peak. He knew when to get out. And I'm warning you, Vinnie. If the market ever goes up, I'm going to unload that pew![2]

The audience laughed. What great fun! It is less amusing when we consider that $5,000 in 1900 would be $125,000 today. At $3,000, it would be $75,000. Had he waited, he would have saved $50,000.[3] Yet the incident, or something like it, really did happen. The irony of this scene is this: the father had a far better sense of the economics of pew-selling than the minister did.

This simple example raises a crucial organizational issue: the nature of success indicators for managing a church. They are clearly not monetary profit and loss. That is because the market principle of *monetary high bid wins* does not apply in matters eternal. We do not buy our way into heaven. Christ paid this representatively for His people. His people do not pay it. Even the salesmen of indulgences in Luther's day did not claim that anyone could buy his way into heaven. The indulgence was said merely to offer a way to reduce penalties in purgatory.

The moment that the principle of product substitution no longer applies, "monetary high bid wins" no longer applies. Yet there can be product substitution in church membership. This was a basic principle of the Protestant Reformation. People can and do leave. When they leave, they seek out other ways to use their time and money than attending a particular congregation. We assume that the principle of "high monetary bid" should not apply. But the free market principle of "monetary high bid wins" in theory is not limited to monetary exchange. It applies to individual satisfaction: subjective utility. "What's in it for me?" So, why don't the market principles of product substitution and

---

2. If you understand the doctrine of sunk costs, you recognize the error of his thinking. He had already sustained the loss. His number-one investment issue was this: what to invest in to regain the lost wealth.

3. It is possible that Clarence Day revised the figures to reflect price inflation in 1947 I hope so. Even so, the sums are huge. In 1947, $5,000 would be $57,000 today.

"monetary high bid wins" apply to churches? We sense that they don't, but it is difficult to specify why not.

B. The Priestly Function

The closer we come to life and death, the less we trust the price system to solve our problems. We understand that money can at best buy extra time. We apply this understanding to market exchange.

A physician who comes across a seriously injured person may bargain with the person for payment. He may demand a very high price. He may get the person to sign a contract to this effect. But no court will enforce it. A jury will not force the victim to pay. The medical guild or the state might even revoke the physician's license to practice. *The ethics of saving lives imposes limits on the price charged.* The public understands this.

The church deals with issues of eternal life and death. Therefore, access to church care is supposed to be open. But this is in fact a myth. Because of the high price of real estate in large cities, the number of churches is limited. Membership is not available to all who might receive the gospel's message of salvation. There is not enough church space to accommodate a mass revival. The way around this is the World Wide Web. Sermons, Sunday school courses, and singing can be delivered to any place that has access to the Web. But churches resist this. They deny that such meeting places are real churches. So, price competition in rents—"home church"—is resisted by traditional church hierarchies.

In Massachusetts before 1834, Congregational churches received tax subsidies. In Europe, state churches still receive state funds. But these churches are liberal, poorly attended, and barely functional. They are being replaced by mosques attended by North African immigrants, and by Pentecostal congregations attended by sub-Saharan African immigrants. *There is constant product substitution going on.*

The market's principle of "monetary high bid wins" is modified for churches. The element of priestly authority substitutes quality competition for price competition. Because the church is a covenantal institution, it is not governed by the market's principle of "monetary high bid wins." Neither is the family. Neither is the state. These are not investor-owned, profit-seeking corporations in a market with open entry and price competition. But a congregation can die off. Its building will be sold to a more successful congregation. But it probably will not house a commercial enterprise. Aging members may decide that a replacement church should take possession, not a commercial enterprise.

At the corner of Wall Street and Broadway in New York City there is a church. It has been there for over three centuries. It will come as no surprise that it is an Episcopal Church. The value of that real estate is immense. It is not taxed by the city. It is Trinity Wall Street. Its URL is www.TrinityWallStreet.org. It is not .com. We understand this. No one would expect it to become .com.

The members of the congregation have made a decision: keep the property and thereby forfeit the money that it could be sold for. This is a "monetary high bid wins" decision. The church retains ownership. Economists call this "reservation demand." The church is the highest successful bidder. The decision is based on a higher principle than money. At least the members believe it is a higher principle. But the members must pay for that decision: forfeited projects that the money could be used to support.

The church has a gift shop. It is online. There, you can buy an Alexander Hamilton doll.[4] Hamilton was the main American proponent behind the First Bank of the United States (1791–1811), the precursor to the Federal Reserve System. He surely deserves recognition on Wall Street. But not in a church, I think. And especially, not in a church gift shop.

Sometimes the lines between the market and the priestly function grow vague.

C. Conserving Scarce Resources

The issues of corporate ownership and stewardship are much the same in the church as in the family. Thus, there is an opportunity for me to

4. Gary North, "Alexander Hamilton Doll—Trinity Church Wall Street Gift Shop," *GaryNorth.com*, March 12, 2014, garynorth.com/public/12213.cfm.

conserve resources: time and effort. Where the issues are the same, I extract text from the chapters on the family. Why not? Why not use good arguments wherever they apply equally well? Word processing makes this easy: cut and paste. A good argument is like a good friend. Spend more time with both.

Chapter 16

Ownership

"And that slave who knew his master's will and did not get ready or act in accordance with his will, will receive many blows, but the one who did not know it, and committed acts deserving of a beating, will receive only a few blows. From everyone who has been given much, much will be demanded; and to whom they entrusted much, of him they will ask all the more."

Luke 12:47–48

Analysis

Point one of the biblical covenant is sovereignty.[1] Ownership is an aspect of creation. God owns the cosmos because He created it. This serves as the model for human creativity. This is why someone who physically creates something owns it.[2]

Ownership establishes personal responsibility. The Bible is clear on this. The more that someone owns, or the more knowledge that he possesses, the greater his responsibility. Jesus spoke of the final judgment. The person who has less knowledge but breaks God's law is less

1. Ray R. Sutton, *That You May Prosper: Dominion By Covenant*, 2nd ed. (Tyler, Texas: Institute for Christian Economics, [1987] 1992), ch. 1.

2. If someone builds something, it is his permanently. The state must defend his property right. This does not mean that someone who comes up with a new idea owns it. If it did mean this, then state-enforced patents and copyrights should be perpetual, not limited to a few years. Either copyrights and patents should be abolished, or else the laws should be changed to grant perpetual ownership. The present laws are clearly inconsistent.

responsible than the person who breaks God's law in light of greater knowledge (Luke 12:47–48).[3]

Christian economists are duty-bound to place ownership first in the development of economic theory. Economic analysis is much easier when dealing with individual ownership than corporate covenantal ownership. That is because of the free market's system of monetary pricing. Prices allow accounting, and accounting guides production. Inside corporate units, there is no way to assess productivity in terms of prices generated from within the organization.

Those who are authorized to make decisions regarding the organization's resource allocation have great responsibility. This fact leads to a conclusion: they function as owners. *There is no way to separate responsibility from ownership*. This works both ways: from ownership to responsibility, and from responsibility to ownership.

The church is different from the family and the state. It has different responsibilities. Therefore, its structure of ownership is different. God's relationship to the church is unique. The family derives its authority from the original creation and the dominion covenant (Gen. 1:26–28).[4] The church derives its authority from the fact that it is the bride of Christ. This position is gained through adoption, not creation. There is general ownership, which is based on creation. There is special ownership, which is based on adoption. This theological difference structures my analysis of the church.

The church has a mission statement. Christ announced it after His resurrection. "And Jesus came up and spoke to them, saying, 'All authority in heaven and on earth has been given to Me. Go, therefore, and make disciples of all the nations, baptizing them in the name of the Father and the Son and the Holy Spirit, teaching them to follow all that I commanded you; and behold, I am with you always, to the end of the age'" (Matt. 28:18–20).[5] This is the Great Commission.[6] This mission

3. Gary North, *Treasure & Dominion: An Economic Commentary on Luke* (Moulton, Alabama: Axehead Press, [2012] 2031), ch. 28:B.

4. Gary North, *Sovereignty & Dominion: An Economic Commentary on Genesis* (Moulton, Alabama: Axehead Press, [1982, 2012] 2022), chaps. 3, 4.

5. Gary North, *Priorities & Dominion: An Economic Commentary on Matthew* (Moulton, Alabama: Axehead Press, [2012] 2030), ch. 48.

6. Kenneth L. Gentry, *The Greatness of the Great Commission: The Christian Enterprise in a Fallen World*, 2nd ed. (Tyler, Texas: Institute for Christian Economics, [1990] 1992).

statement is to supposed govern every aspect of the institutional church. It is the church's unique service proposition.

A. God's Ownership

Point one: God's sovereignty. Consider the family and the church. God owns the family because of the dominion covenant. He has delegated to the family primary responsibility for dominion. The family is the primary institution for production, especially the production of human beings: multiplication. But it is strictly an agency of history. Jesus said that there is no marriage in heaven (Matt. 22:30). The family is a temporal institution.

It is different with the church. The church extends into eternity. The New Testament refers to the church as the bride of Christ. Christianity has always taught that the church has replaced Israel as the bride. Paul referred to the church as "the Israel of God" (Gal. 6:16). The institutional church is referred to in the Bible as a bride. This was Israel's position under the Mosaic covenant. This is clearly presented in Ezekiel 16. The New Testament applies this designation to the church, as we shall see. By picturing the church as a bride, the New Testament points our attention to the issue of exclusion. Exclusion is basic to marriage. The partners are bound by oath to each other. Similarly, Christ is bound to the church in the same way. Christ has the right of exclusion. *The right of exclusion is fundamental to ownership.*

Ezekiel 16 is not a familiar passage. It is God's announcement of His ownership of Israel. The context is not the six-day creation. That was the judicial basis of God's general ownership. The context is marriage: God's special ownership. In the context of biblical law, this was a matter of adoption, not purchase.

> Then the word of the LORD came to me, saying, "Son of man, make known to Jerusalem her abominations, and say, 'This is what the Lord GOD says to Jerusalem: "Your origin and your birth are from the land of the Canaanite; your father was an Amorite and your mother a Hittite. As for your birth, on the day you were born your navel cord was not cut, nor were you washed with water for cleansing; you were not rubbed

> with salt or even wrapped in cloths. No eye looked with pity on you to do any of these things for you, to have compassion on you. Rather you were thrown out into the open field, for you were abhorred on the day you were born. When I passed by you and saw you squirming in your blood, I said to you while you were in your blood, 'Live!' Yes, I said to you while you were in your blood, 'Live!' I made you very numerous, like plants of the field. Then you grew up, became tall and reached the age for fine jewelry; your breasts were formed and your hair had grown. Yet you were naked and bare. Then I passed by you and saw you, and behold, you were at the time for love; so I spread My garment over you and covered your nakedness. I also swore an oath to you and entered into a covenant with you so that you became Mine," declares the Lord GOD. "Then I bathed you with water, washed off your blood from you, and anointed you with oil. I also clothed you with colorfully woven cloth and put sandals of fine leather on your feet; and I wrapped you with fine linen and covered you with silk. I adorned you with jewelry, put bracelets on your wrists, and a necklace around your neck. I also put a ring in your nose, earrings in your ears, and a beautiful crown on your head. So you were adorned with gold and silver, and your dress was of fine linen, silk, and colorfully woven cloth. You ate fine flour, honey, and oil; so you were exceedingly beautiful and advanced to royalty. Then your fame spread among the nations on account of your beauty, for it was perfect because of My splendor which I bestowed on you," declares the Lord GOD.'" (Ezek. 16:1–14)

This was a matter of God's economic sacrifice for the sake of the bride-nation. This was the context of Ezekiel's covenant lawsuit against Israel (Ezek. 16:15–63).

Now consider the New Testament.

> For I am jealous for you with a godly jealousy; for I betrothed you to one husband, to present you as a pure virgin to Christ. (II Cor. 11:2)

> Husbands, love your wives, just as Christ also loved the church and gave Himself up for her (Eph. 5:25).

> "Let's rejoice and be glad and give the glory to Him, because the marriage of the Lamb has come, and His bride has prepared herself." (Rev. 19:7)

> And I saw the holy city, new Jerusalem, coming down out of heaven from God, prepared as a bride adorned for her husband. (Rev. 21:2).

> Then one of the seven angels who had the seven bowls, full of the seven last plagues, came and spoke with me, saying, "Come here, I will show you the bride, the wife of the Lamb." (Rev. 21:9)

This relationship is therefore one of personal love. The church is uniquely loved by God. So, the ownership relationship is that of a bridegroom for his bride. He does not buy or sell her. He cares for her. She is subordinate to him. She is dependent on him. She can trust him. She is bound to him by an oath. But this refers to an institution, not to individuals. There is no other institutional relationship to match this.

Christ's name is on the church. "[A]nd when he had found him, he brought him to Antioch. And for an entire year they met with the church and taught considerable numbers of people; and the disciples were first called Christians in Antioch" (Acts 11:26). A name is a matter of ownership. The third commandment has to do with God's restriction on the use of His name (Ex. 20:7).[7] This is the third commandment in the list: priestly. The eighth commandment prohibits theft (Ex. 20:15).[8] This is the third commandment in the second list: kingly. These are parallel verses. They both deal with ownership.

Market pricing has nothing to do with this. The relationship is legal, not economic. There is no open entry. It was the error of Adam and Eve to assume that there could be open entry. Open entry was the serpent's offer (Gen. 3:5). No rival bid for the affection of the bride was to be tolerated. Adam and Eve refused to seal the marriage covenant of the church with God. They did not go to feast at the tree of life: the communion meal. They went to the forbidden tree. They established a rival marriage covenant. They created a rival church with a harlot. This was spiritual whoredom.

God calls to people to join the bride through faith in Christ as Savior. He calls them to subordinate themselves to the bridegroom by means of membership in the church. He offers them a communion meal, but only on His terms (I Cor. 11). We must avoid the false communion meal with demons. "What do I mean then? That food sacrificed to idols is

---

7. Gary North, *Authority & Dominion: An Economic Commentary on Exodus*, vol. 2, *Part II: Decalogue & Dominion* (Moulton, Alabama: Axehead Press, [1986, 2012] 2025), ch. 23.

8. Ibid., ch. 28.

anything, or that an idol is anything? No, but I say that things which the Gentiles sacrifice, they sacrifice to demons and not to God; and I do not want you to become partners with demons. You cannot drink the cup of the Lord and the cup of demons; you cannot partake of the table of the Lord and the table of demons" (I Cor. 10:19–21).

B. Central Planning

Point two: hierarchy. As I explained in Part B of Chapter 11, the concept of central planning applies outside the state covenant. It applies to the family. Someone makes allocation decisions for the family's assets. This is the legal head of the household. The same hierarchical principle is true of the institutional church. This is a matter of economic representation. It is also a matter of guardianship, a legal category.

God has purposes for the future. He makes plans for the future. He decrees the future. He the executes His decree in history. All of this is hierarchical. The Son is the Trustee for the Father. What we see with respect to the economic Trinity in relation to the creation, we see reflected in the family of man. The one and the many are manifested in a hierarchal relationship. In a family, there is mutual ownership. Members have legal claims on each other. The same principle applies to the institutional church. There are mutual claims on its members. Paul speaks of the church as a body. A body is composed of members. The body functions properly only when all of the members are functioning individually.

> For the body is not one part, but many. If the foot says, "Because I am not a hand, I am not a part of the body," it is not for this reason any less a part of the body. And if the ear says, "Because I am not an eye, I am not a part of the body," it is not for this reason any less a part of the body. If the whole body were an eye, where would the hearing be? If the whole body were hearing, where would the sense of smell be? But now God has arranged the parts, each one of them in the body, just as He desired. If they were all one part, where would the body be? But now there are many parts, but one body. (I Cor. 12:14–20)[9]

---

9. Gary North, *Judgment & Dominion: An Economic Commentary on I Corinthians* (Moulton, Alabama: Axehead Press, [2012] 2031), ch. 16.

An institutional church may own property. In most Western societies, church buildings are common. This was not true in the early church. It is not true in times of persecution. But as the church gains influence, individual congregations begin to purchase land. They build buildings. They become responsible for the administration of property, including money.

The church is a separate legal institution. Its members have claims against each other within a congregation. These claims are moral rather than legal. The church does not threaten negative sanctions against members who do not participate in charitable activities.

In his two epistles to the church at Corinth, Paul spoke of fund-raising. He was raising money to support the church at Jerusalem. He cajoled them. He unquestionably attempted to humble them into giving more. He referred back to the congregation's corporate promise of support. "But take care that this freedom of yours does not somehow become a stumbling block to the weak. For if someone sees you, the one who has knowledge, dining in an idol's temple, will his conscience, if he is weak, not be strengthened to eat things sacrificed to idols? For through your knowledge the one who is weak is ruined, the brother or sister for whose sake Christ died. And so, by sinning against the brothers and sisters and wounding their conscience when it is weak, you sin against Christ" (I Cor. 8:9–12). The congregation had made a commitment. Paul was asking them to fulfill that commitment. There had been a corporate plan. There had been a corporate promise. Now he reminded them of their obligation. He appealed to individuals. "And so, by sinning against the brothers and sisters and wounding their conscience when it is weak, you sin against Christ" (I Cor. 8:12). But this was in the context of a joint commitment.

In Acts 5, we have the story of Ananias and Sapphira. They had sold a property. They had pledged that they would donate the proceeds to the congregation. But they held back some of the purchase price. Peter challenged Ananias on this. He asked him if he had received a specific amount of money. Ananias said that he had. Peter announced this. "But Peter said, 'Ananias, why has Satan filled your heart to lie to the Holy Spirit and to keep back some of the proceeds of the land? While it remained unsold, did it not remain your own? And after it was sold, was it not under your control? Why is it that you have conceived this deed in your heart? You have not lied to men, but to God.' And as he heard these words, Ananias collapsed and died; and great fear came over all who heard about it. The young men got up and covered him up, and after carrying him out, they buried him" (Acts 5:3–6). Peter repeated this exercise with Ananias' wife. She also lied. The results were identical. "And great fear came over the whole church, and over all who heard about these things" (Acts 5:11). This was a matter of ownership. The church had a legal claim on all of the money. The two had made a pledge to the church. God enforced the terms of this pledge. They had made a transfer of wealth to the church. They owed even more. The church had an ownership claim on whatever money they had set aside. This claim originated with the initial pledge of a family. But Peter acknowledged that each party was responsible. He interrogated both of them separately. God imposed sanctions separately.[10]

The church is not governed by the commercial principle of "monetary high bid wins." This is because its economic value to any participant cannot lawfully be capitalized. Economic theory must deal with this, but it rarely does. The church covenant is legally binding and exclusive in a way that market-priced contracts are not. So, the conceptual tools of what Mises called catallactics do not apply well to a church or to any other covenantal institution.

Personal knowledge is central to the church. It is peripheral in a commercial market. Money prices are dominant in a commercial market. They are not dominant in a church. Allocation decisions are made by the elders based on personal knowledge. An entrepreneur in a market that is marked by widespread ownership pays little attention to personal knowledge. A wheat farmer is not interested in the moral outlook of a buyer, except with respect to payment. If he pays his bills on time, the farmer will sell his crop to him.

God holds churches accountable. God has plans for every church. The elders are supposed to factor these plans into their plans.

Christian theology undergirds the doctrine of hierarchical authority. Christian theology is Trinitarian. God is both unity and diversity. So,

10. Gary North, *Sacrifice & Dominion: An Economic Commentary on Acts* (Moulton, Alabama: Axehead Press, [2012] 2031), ch. 4.

this aspect of God is reflected in mankind. Specifically, it is reflected in the church. God plans. He executes His plan. Man is required by God to do the same. But man is corporate as well as individual, just as the Trinity is. This corporate aspect of mankind appears most clearly in the family. Therefore, planning must be corporate. But because there is a hierarchy of authority in the church, which reflects the *hierarchy of the economic Trinity*—as distinguished from the ontological Trinity—there has to be plan reconciliation. This process is perfect in the Trinity. It is not perfect in fallen humanity.

Church ownership of assets is based on hierarchy far more than equality. The division of church labor is far more hierarchical than horizontal. Market bids are far more horizontal than hierarchical. Church ownership reflects covenantal hierarchy. Church officers possess authority over church property. Ownership is not original. It is derived from God's grant of authority. While ownership is point one of the biblical covenant with respect to God, for man, ownership is point two: trusteeship.

Church officers are responsible for the spiritual care of church members. They possess authority. There is a charitable element in this authority. This makes them economically responsible for members. This rule of law always applies: *where there is authority, there is also responsibility*. Individuals must give an account to God for their stewardship, as we learn from the parable of the talents (Matt. 25:14–30).[11] This involves giving an account of themselves for their joint authority as members of churches. No one is autonomous. Every individual answers to God. Our attitudes and behavior toward others do count, meaning they are counted by God: assessed and evaluated.

All of this stems from the fact of the division of labor. There is mutuality. *Mutuality involves dependency*. Each party must give up something of value in order to obtain something of value. Mutuality involves a partial surrender of responsibility. It therefore involves a partial transfer of authority. "I will do this for you, if you will do that for me." In the market, it is usually easy to substitute a new supplier. This is especially true in the consumer goods markets. There are many competing offers. Loyalty is weaker. *The more specialized the exchange, the more expensive*

---

11. North, *Priorities & Dominion*, ch. 47.

it is to substitute a new supplier for an old one. There are fewer available suppliers. Mutual dependence is therefore greater. The disruption of the division of labor is greater. A covenant is more binding than a contract is. It is established by a public oath under God.

Planning has to do with the allocation of scarce resources. It therefore is based on ownership. God owns everything. He delegates control over assets to individuals. But He also delegates control to collectives. The idea of joint ownership is inherent in the biblical doctrine of the church.

Plan reconciliation is basic to the church. The exchange arrangements within a family, a church, or a state are not based on "monetary high bid wins." *Justice trumps profit.* Authority is not based on the purchase of an office. *The planning arrangement reflects the hierarchical structure of dominion.*

God rules through churches. His transfer of ownership to churches is His way to maximize His return. His return on investment is far beyond monetary. It involves such things as ethical faithfulness. It involves the extension of membership through biological multiplication and evangelism: *kingdom extension.*

Every plan necessarily involves six factors. These are the familiar six factors that historians use to assess what happened in the past. Historians ask five questions: who, why, what, where, when, and how? So do economists. *Who* identifies the primary responsibility for the plan's launching and its fulfillment. It identifies responsible agents needed to implement the plan. *Why* identifies the motivation of the stewards' plan. Both of these are aspects of part two of the biblical covenant: representation. *What* and *where* identify legal and geographical boundaries: the scarce economic resources required to implement the plan. To gain access to these resources, men must ask permission or buy control. *When* identifies temporal limits. A plan must begin at a point in time and end in a point of time. The process of creation takes time. Time must be paid for. It must be allocated. When you do one thing, you cannot do another. Time is in strict fixed supply. It is an irreplaceable resource. Once spent, it cannot reclaimed. It does not move backward. The implementation of the plan begins somewhere and ends somewhere. It does not operate in a geographical vacuum. It involves dominion over nature.

The sixth question is this: *how?* Causation is associated with point four of the covenant: sanctions. The missing first point is God. The traditional list of five questions does not begin with God. It begins with the individual.

Churches cannot escape these obligations, any more than families can. But churches are under an additional set of restraints. They are part of a larger covenantal association. The church as a whole is the bride of Christ. As such, it extends into eternity. A family has limited temporal responsibility. Parents cannot plan much beyond the inheritance of grandchildren. But a church must look to eternity. It has a far longer temporal limit than a family does.

C. Boundaries

Point three: ethics. This is an aspect of law. Law, in turn, establishes boundaries.

The division of labor is an aspect of specialization. There is an inherent responsibility of specialized function: mutuality. Specialization of function is closely associated with ownership. Therefore, it is associated with boundaries. Within the church, there is specialization. This is taught clearly in Romans 12 and I Corinthians 12. Paul described the church as a body. A body has specialized members. This is metaphorical: members as bodily parts. We call church members *members* because of Paul's teaching.

The primary church boundaries are sacramental: the sacraments. These judicial boundaries include, but they also exclude. The archetype on this exclusion aspect is the tree of the knowledge of good and evil. God definitively excluded mankind from this tree. The sacramental boundaries of the church mark other aspects of the church. The rights of exclusion are fundamental.

Property rights are boundaries. These boundaries/rights are clearest in boundaries barring intrusion by non-family members. The boundaries around a family are more easily understood and enforced: by individuals, family members, church, and state. Inside the church, these boundaries become less clear. Also, the general boundary around a church reduces the authority of outside agencies to intervene to settle disputes.

The division of labor in a church involves *boundaries of responsibility*. The hierarchy becomes important in plan reconciliation. Someone with greater authority establishes the boundaries of responsible performance. Voluntary reconciliation is replaced by orders from above. But the officers have very limited initiating authority over church members. This means that they have very little initiating responsibility. With reduced authority comes reduced responsibility.

Inherently, the nature of church authority is personal. The participants are known to each other. There is no system comparable to the free market, with its information system based on price signals. The boundaries of the free market are impersonal in the sense that decision-makers are unknown to each other. Prices establish the boundaries. Anyone who makes decisions without paying attention to prices is going to lose money in most cases. The restraining boundaries of prices are very tight. The market adjusts prices by means of arbitrage: simultaneously buying slightly lower in one market and selling in another. None of this is true in a church. Boundaries in a church are personal. People make adjustments based on their knowledge of each other's reactions and patterns of behavior. But intimacy is limited. There is much greater flexibility of responses.

Church members learn which boundaries not to violate. These boundaries are far more problematical than the boundaries imposed by price. Negotiations are based more on personalities than price. Thus, the outcome of these negotiations is less predictable. *The complexity of negotiations makes the outcomes less predictable*. There is no rule in church negotiations comparable to this familiar law of economics: "At a higher price, less is demanded."

Church members seek their goals from membership, just as they do in a commercial market. They are self-interested. But there is a crucial factor in a church that is not a major factor in commerce: love.

> "I am giving you a new commandment, that you love one another; just as I have loved you, that you also love one another. By this all people will know that you are My disciples: if you have love for one another." (John 13:34–35)

> "This is My commandment, that you love one another, just as I have loved you." (John 15:12)
>
> "This I command you, that you love one another." (John 15:17)
>
> Be devoted to one another in brotherly love; give preference to one another in honor (Rom. 12:10).

Love is a factor that is highly personal. It broadens the definition of self-interest. Unlike a price, we cannot calculate love. Love is therefore like economic value. It is ordinal, not cardinal. It is "more than," but not "precisely this much more than." A price is objective. Love is not. The boundaries imposed by love are broader than the boundaries imposed by prices. The predictability of law enforcement in a church is far less than the predictability of the restraints imposed by objective prices.

Economists do not pretend to provide meaningful equations to describe church boundaries. They can and do pretend to provide meaningful equations regarding price relationships. The illusion of scientific precision is more easily adopted with respect to objective prices in open markets than with subjective boundaries inside churches.

People are committed to church solidarity far more than they are committed to market solidarity. They defend their churches from intervention by government bureaucrats far more vigorously than they defend the free market from intrusion by government bureaucrats.

D. Imputation

Point four: sanctions. Churches are covenantal institutions. They are economic. Church leaders decide where money should be spent. Sometimes, this money is used to support causes that may be anti-biblical. This was the case in the first half of the twentieth century, when most mainline Protestant denominations went liberal theologically, but their members remained. Their donations supported their theological enemies.

The Trinitarian God is both plurality and unity. Therefore, in His capacity as the cosmic Imputer of economic value, He is both plural and individual. The church reflects this combination of plurality and unity.

Individual church members impute economic value, but the God-sanctioned decision-makers in the church make representative imputations of economic value. These judgments are judicially binding on the members.

The joint responsibilities of the church's members make it imperative that the decision-makers consider members' imputation of value. The individualism of economic theory's subjectivism makes impossible a theoretical justification for the interpersonal comparison of subjective utilities. Yet this must be done all the time by church elders. They must act representatively on behalf of those under his jurisdiction. In terms of the nominalism of modern economic theory, they cannot do this scientifically. But God mandates that they do it. God holds them accountable for this representative summing up of multiple imputed economic values inside the church. What every elder does constantly, economic theory says is scientifically impossible. This is why subjectivist economics is epistemologically naïve.

Church ownership brings the elders under special responsibilities. Stewardship is inescapable from ownership. This stewardship is upward to God, outward to non-members, downward to church members, and inward to each individual member. To say that this office of steward belongs only to church officers is to ignore the moral claims to ownership by non-ordained church members. As members, they benefit. They impute economic value to these claims of ownership. But they cannot sell these claims. This is the problem of corporate ownership. *Without a functioning public market for the exchange of church ownership claims, the free market cannot establish prices*. This is why economic theory has trouble in analyzing the economics of a church.

The elders must decide how to budget. They must make assessments regarding the economic value of the outcomes of their plans for members of the church. They must make representative judgments regarding individual imputations. These judgments must involve the summing up of the costs and benefits of ownership for each church member. Yet there is no scientific way that elders can do this, meaning no methodologically valid way, given the epistemology of subjective economic theory.[12] There is no objective measure of economic value.

12. Lionel Robbins, *An Essay into the Nature and Significance of Economic Science* (London: Macmillan, 1932), ch. VI.

The fact that there is no objective measure of economic value is not a valid argument against the necessity of the elders' making representative economic value judgments. But these value judgments do not rest on a system of objective pricing established by exchange. The judicial roles of each church member cannot be sold to the highest bidder. Therefore, the individual economic imputations of church members must be taken into consideration by the decision-maker if he is to do justice—legal justice in God's system of imputation of personal responsibility—to other members. He is in a legal position to oppress them. This is an inescapable aspect of his office as an elder. He is required by God to act representatively.

E. Legacy

Point five: succession. A local church owns property. This property is held in trust by the elders. The church's name and reputation are major aspects of the kingdom of God. A name conveys information. In markets, brand loyalty is an important aspect of marketing.

In families, children's names provoke specific responses. So does a family's reputation. This is especially true in "old" circles: old money and old families.

A church's name is associated with a confession of faith. Specific church traditions are associated with certain beliefs. The name also has to do with liturgy. A name often has to do with social positioning in a community. "First Baptist" and "First Methodist" still have meanings in small towns in the United States. Legacy families belong to these churches because their grandparents did. Churches own buildings in specific locations. But church capital extends beyond real estate. It includes a bank account. A church also has a reputation, which is an aspect of its name. All of this constitutes legacy. The church is supposed to extend its legacy through time. Its name is important. The central name in New Testament times is Jesus' name. He is the Bridegroom of the church (Matt. 25:5–15).

Church officers are supposed to pay attention to long-term effects of their decisions. They must be future-oriented. They must assess present costs in terms of future returns. They must bear responsibility in the future for the outcomes of their present decisions. Their activities will have effects in the long run. Their ownership is limited temporally, but the results of their decisions will have repercussions after they are no longer owners.

Because of the doctrine of the final judgment, Christianity has a long-term perspective. This perspective is personal, not impersonal. It is enforced judicially. This is an aspect of guardianship. Church authorities will be held accountable by God. The fact that they will no longer be held accountable in a human court is not the whole story.

Conclusion

Who owns the church? God does. This is simple to understand if you are a Christian. It is central to your faith, or it should be.

Church members do not own it. Members come and go. So, when we speak of ownership in relation to the church, it is plain to any Christian that the church's officers are not the primary owners. The church may have been launched by an energetic church-planting pastor, but in all likelihood, today's officers are late-comers. They have been invested with judicial and economic authority, either by a bishop or by the members who voted for them. Members understand that the officers are *judicially representative agents* of God. Officers have the right to control the budget. Nevertheless, it is clear to all concerned that if lots of members leave, the church's budget will shrink. Members possess the power of the purse. They are not forced to donate to the church by a threat of excommunication for a failure to pay. They do not purchase individual personal services by means of these payments. They understand that neither they nor the officers are owners of the church's assets in the way that they are owners of money, homes, furniture, and investment goods. They have no legal title.

There is another major judicial factor: the members are not legally liable for the decisions made by the officers. The church is a separate legal entity. Members enjoy what is called *limited liability*. Actually, they are not in any way liable. They do not own the assets of the church.

Churches do not sell pews any longer. Having no legal claim of ownership over the assets of the church, members are separated completely from legal liability. They may have invested emotional capital in the church, but there is no market for emotional capital. No one can buy it or sell it. It has no objective price. It is exclusively subjective. There is no bull market in emotional capital. There also is no bear market.

The officers are also not legally liable personally in most cases. If they violate a zoning law or a building code, the church may be required to pay a fine. The officers do not pay out of their own assets. If there is any personal legal liability, it is only for the commission of illegal acts. In such cases, individual officers are liable, not the institutional church. Only in rare cases, such as the lawsuits brought against the Roman Catholic Church in the United States for priests who seduced teenagers, meaning almost always young men, are the assets of the church at risk. In this sense, the church was the first limited liability corporation.

There is a fundamental separation between ownership and responsibility in the institutional church. Officers who make poor decisions may upset God, or the decisions may upset members, which could lead to a crisis in the church. This could have a serious negative economic impact on the church. But from an institutional standpoint, The separation of ownership from economic responsibility is greater in the case of the institutional church than with any other institution.

Church ownership is fundamentally different from individual ownership. It is also different from family ownership. However, with respect to investing, it is remarkably similar to the post-1870 limited liability corporation. The main difference between the church and a limited liability corporation is the market for corporate shares. Investors have a legal claim against corporate management. They also have ways of profiting economically from the operations of a corporation. This is not true of church members' relationship to the churches they belong to.

Ownership is an inescapable concept. It is never a question of ownership vs. no ownership. It is always a question of whose ownership.

Ownership establishes sovereignty. The owner is the initiating entrepreneur. He deals with uncertainty. Only God is omniscient.

Churches own property in the broadest sense: real estate, bank accounts, and reputation. Ordained leaders exercise ownership as economic stewards (point two). They are oath-bound (point four). The church alone among institutions extends into eternity. It is the bride of Christ. So, stewardship of church property is more important than the stewardship of any other kind of property.

The church is under the general market principle of "monetary high bid wins" with respect to property held in terms of economic stewardship. There are bids for its property: land, bank accounts, and similar market assets. This stewardship is horizontal: society at large. But, far more important, this economic stewardship is vertical: on behalf of God, but also on behalf of members. This vertical stewardship is clear to church members in ways that family stewardship and state stewardship is not. That is because members understand the church as divinely appointed for eternity.

Chapter 17

Stewardship

Now when they had finished breakfast, Jesus said to Simon Peter, "Simon, son of John, do you love Me more than these?" He said to Him, "Yes, Lord; You know that I love You." He said to him, "Tend My lambs." He said to him again, a second time, "Simon, son of John, do you love Me?" He said to Him, "Yes, Lord; You know that I love You." He said to him, "Shepherd My sheep." He said to him the third time, "Simon, son of John, do you love Me?" Peter was hurt because He said to him the third time, "Do you love Me?" And he said to Him, "Lord, You know all things; You know that I love You." Jesus said to him, "Tend My sheep."

John 21:15–17

Analysis

Point two of the biblical covenant is hierarchy.[1] In law, this is guardianship. In economics, this is stewardship. Some of the general principles of stewardship that apply to individual stewardship apply to church stewardship. Others do not. We must understand these differences. We must also understand the implications, both in theory and in practice, of these differences.

The most obvious difference is the application of the fundamental principle of pricing: *monetary high bid wins*. Within a church, there are

1. Ray R. Sutton, *That You May Prosper: Dominion By Covenant*, 2nd ed. (Tyler, Texas: Institute for Christian Economics, [1987] 1992), ch. 2.

no lawful monetary bids. The bids are in terms of individual characteristics, assignments, and responsibilities. The decision-makers, meaning the elders or the pastor, make the allocation of scarce resources. As representative economic agents of the members of the church, they make these allocation decisions on behalf of all of the members. They guess as to costs and benefits for those under their authority. In other words, they make interpersonal comparisons of subjective utilities.

The elders act as representative economic agents: stewards. They represent God to the members of the church, and they represent the members before God. Representation is mediatorial and hierarchical. This representation is corporate. Second, the church gets tithes and donations. The families owe their tithes to the local church, which represents God to its members.[2] There is a third aspect of stewardship: allocational. This has to do with the decision to put a resource to work on behalf of other people. Sometimes, this relationship is vertical: needs within the congregation. Sometimes it is horizontal. The church is involved in evangelism: bringing the good news to people outside the church. Churches have charitable programs and missions. These tasks absorb resources.

A. Sovereignty

Point one: God's sovereignty. God possesses absolute sovereignty. There are three aspects to this regarding human history. First, God has purposes for history. Second, He has a comprehensive plan for history. This plan is perfectly consistent with His purposes. Third, He has issued a decree for history. This is providence. This decree guarantees God's perfect attainment of His plan. These three aspects of God's sovereignty are clearly seen in Joseph's declaration to his brothers about the decree of God regarding their decision to sell him to the slave traders. "As for you, you meant evil against me, but God meant it for good in order to bring about this present result, to keep many people alive" (Gen. 50:20). God's priorities are sovereign. Men's are not.

God holds people responsible for their actions: the final judgment

2. Gary North, *The Covenantal Tithe: The Providential Plan for Fruitful Stewardship* (Moulton, Alabama: Axehead Press, [2011] 2026), ch. 10.

(Matt. 25). But, as I have argued, responsibility always brings with it ownership in the broadest sense. This leads to a conclusion: *people own resources*. God holds them responsible for the use of these resources. Joseph's brothers were thieves. They sold him into slavery. It looked as though they stole his future. They did not have the authority to do this. But this was far better than killing him, which is what they planned to do until Reuben persuaded them to seek a profit from Joseph's convenient disappearance. That saved Joseph's life. It later saved their lives.

B. Representation

Point two: hierarchy. God shares sovereignty through delegation. This was manifested in the original dominion covenant (Gen. 1:26–28).[3] This was re-confirmed with Noah (Gen. 9:1–3).[4] It was confirmed ontologically with the Incarnation, when God became a man.

> Have this attitude in yourselves which was also in Christ Jesus, who, as He already existed in the form of God, did not consider equality with God something to be grasped, but emptied Himself by taking the form of a bond-servant and being born in the likeness of men. And being found in appearance as a man, He humbled Himself by becoming obedient to the point of death: death on a cross. For this reason also God highly exalted Him, and bestowed on Him the name which is above every name, so that at the name of Jesus every knee will bow, of those who are in heaven and on earth and under the earth, and that every tongue will confess that Jesus Christ is Lord, to the glory of God the Father. (Phil. 2:5–11)

God clearly has delegated limited sovereignty to man. In both cases, Adam and Noah, God was dealing with families. Both men were also household priests. They had ecclesiastical authority. They were judicially the equivalent of church elders. The church has always been a covenantally independent agency. It was never an extension of the family. It existed within the family. Circumcision and Passover were administered within families, but the two agencies were different covenant-

---

3. Gary North, *Sovereignty & Dominion: An Economic Commentary on Genesis* (Moulton, Alabama: Axehead Press, [1982, 2012] 2022), chaps. 3, 4.

4. Ibid., ch. 18.

ally. This became visible with the creation of the Levitical priesthood after the golden calf incident (Ex. 32).

Elders must deal with those under their authority in a way analogous to the state's system of courts. They decide cases. They must not initiate programs that invade the legitimate and broad authority of families.

Elders have a responsibility to train members in the basics of how to manage wealth. Why? Because members who get into economic difficulty may insist that they have a moral claim on the assets of the church. That claim depends on whether they acted foolishly. In contrast, the church has no legal or moral claim on family wealth beyond the tithe. The church's authorities do not make decisions regarding the budgets of families and individuals, except in rare cases of judicial issues brought to the elders by families. So, elders must train heads of households on the basics of money management. They rarely do. They do not require families to buy insurance as a condition of receiving charity when something that could be insured against strikes them. Elders thereby place the income of the church at risk.

The question of charity is basic to church asset allocation. The apostles appointed deacons as a way to use the division of labor to their advantage. They were spending too much time deciding who deserved what. The institution of the diaconate was their solution (Acts 6:1–4).[5]

So important is their authority over the church's money that elders must be screened in terms of their generosity. "An overseer, then, must be above reproach, the husband of one wife, temperate, self-controlled, respectable, hospitable, skillful in teaching, not overindulging in wine, not a bully, but gentle, not contentious, free from the love of money" (I Tim. 3:2–3).[6]

C. Lease

Point three: ethics. I have discussed the general economic function of the lease in Chapter 12, "Stewardship," Section C: "Lease."

5. Gary North, *Sacrifice & Dominion: An Economic Commentary on Acts* (Moulton, Alabama: Axehead Press, [2012] 2031), ch. 5.

6. Gary North, *Hierarchy & Dominion: An Economic Commentary on I Timothy* (Moulton, Alabama: Axehead Press, [2012] 2032), ch. 4.

The most important aspect of a church's lease is its confession of faith. Paul wrote: "He made known to us the mystery of His will, according to His good pleasure which He set forth in Him" (Eph. 1:9). "Just as I urged you upon my departure for Macedonia, to remain on at Ephesus so that you would instruct certain people not to teach strange doctrines . . ." (I Tim. 1:3) "If anyone advocates a different doctrine and does not agree with sound words, those of our Lord Jesus Christ, and with the doctrine conforming to godliness . . ." (I Tim. 6:3).

Then there is the charitable function of the church. By giving away wealth, the church increases its standing before God and men. Acts 6 is devoted to the charitable ministry of the church. This makes the church a model for non-profit institutions. The free market's lease is designed to keep the renters from siphoning off wealth through capital consumption: wearing out the property. The church is different from a profit-seeking business. God requires the church to transfer some of the wealth under the control of the church to the deserving poor. It maintains its favorable standing before God by depleting its economic resources. This runs counter to economic reasoning. This policy is analogous to Jesus' statement that the way to accumulate wealth beyond the grave is to give away wealth in history. "Do not store up for yourselves treasures on earth, where moth and rust destroy, and where thieves break in and steal. But store up for yourselves treasures in heaven, where neither moth nor rust destroys, and where thieves do not break in or steal; for where your treasure is, there your heart will be also" (Matt. 6:19–21).[7] It is even more analogous to the warning of Haggai. "Now then, the LORD of armies says this: 'Consider your ways! You have sown much, only to harvest little; you eat, but there is not enough to be satisfied; you drink, but there is not enough to become drunk; you put on clothing, but there is not enough for anyone to get warm; and the one who earns, earns wages to put into a money bag full of holes'" (Hag. 1:5–6).[8] A church that does not give away money to the poor is like a church member who withholds his tithe from the church. He puts his money in a bag with holes. It dribbles away. Malachi had God's

7. Gary North, *Priorities & Dominion: An Economic Commentary on Matthew* (Moulton, Alabama: Axehead Press, [2012] 2030), ch. 13.

8. Gary North, *Restoration & Dominion: An Economic Commentary on the Prophets* (Moulton, Alabama: Axehead Press, [2012] 2030), ch. 31.

answer. It applies to an individual. It also applies to a church. "'Bring the whole tithe into the storehouse, so that there may be food in My house, and put Me to the test now in this,' says the LORD of armies, 'if I do not open for you the windows of heaven and pour out for you a blessing until it overflows. Then I will rebuke the devourer for you, so that it will not destroy the fruit of your ground; nor will the vine in the field prove fruitless to you,' says the LORD of armies. 'All the nations will call you blessed, for you will be a delightful land,' says the LORD of armies. 'Your words have been arrogant against Me,' says the LORD. 'Yet you say, "What have we spoken against You?"'" (Mal. 3:10–13).[9]

The church's lease is designed to extend the kingdom of God. It keeps the church faithful to its confession. It also keeps the church as a light among men. "You are the light of the world. A city set on a hill cannot be hidden; nor do people light a lamp and put it under a basket, but on the lampstand, and it gives light to all who are in the house. Your light must shine before people in such a way that they may see your good works, and glorify your Father who is in heaven" (Matt. 5:14–16).[10]

D. Feedback

Point four: sanctions. The individual uses these success indicators to guide his planning: monetary profit and loss. But the concept of profit and loss must extend beyond numbers in a ledger. The idea of profit must include evidence of God's approval or disapproval. For the individual, the final judgment is the archetype of historical sanctions. The individual is singled out. So, the focus is on individual benefits.

What is God's primary purpose for the church? Baptizing and discipling God's elect (Matt. 28:18–20).[11] To do this, it must maintain its confession of faith. The confession of faith must govern the allocation of church capital. This keeps its capital within the kingdom of God. *The confession of faith is central.* This is a matter of maintaining the church's oath: point four of the biblical covenant.[12] The extension of the

9. Ibid., ch. 33.
10. North, *Priorities & Dominion*, ch. 6.
11. Ibid., ch. 48.
12. Sutton, *That You May Prosper*, ch. 4.

oath through time is sacramental. The family has no sacraments. These are the church's sacraments: baptism and the Lord's Supper.

Secondary goals of the church are these. First, extending its influence in society. This has to do with ethics: the enforcement of church laws on members. This is point three of the biblical covenant. This goes back to biblical law's function in Israel. It had to do with evangelism. "Now, Israel, listen to the statutes and the judgments which I am teaching you to perform, so that you will live and go in and take possession of the land which the LORD, the God of your fathers, is giving you" (Deut. 4:1). "See, I have taught you statutes and judgments just as the LORD my God commanded me, that you are to do these things in the land where you are entering to take possession of it. So keep and do them, for that is your wisdom and your understanding in the sight of the peoples who will hear all these statutes and say, 'Surely this great nation is a wise and understanding people.' For what great nation is there that has a god so near to it as is the LORD our God whenever we call on Him? Or what great nation is there that has statutes and judgments as righteous as this whole Law which I am setting before you today?" (Deut. 4:5–8).[13]

Second, there must be peace among members. This is a matter of justice: point four of the covenant. Paul said that members should not take each other in front of pagan civil magistrates (I Cor. 6:2–9).[14] Third, there must be church growth: the Great Commission (Matt. 28:18–20).[15] This is point five of the covenant.

Numerical indicators are valid as secondary indicators. If a church sees its capital shrinking due to losses, the decision-makers must pay attention to the market. Why is the capital base declining? What must be done to reverse this? These traditional standards of profit and loss must not replace the sacramental sanctions, but unless there are adjustments in the allocation of church capital, there will be no legacy to pass on.

---

13. Gary North, *Inheritance & Dominion: An Economic Commentary on Deuteronomy* (Moulton, Alabama: Axehead Press, [1999, 2012] 2028), ch. 8.

14. Gary North, *Judgment & Dominion: An Economic Commentary on I Corinthians* (Moulton, Alabama: Axehead Press, [2012] 2031), ch. 7.

15. North, *Priorities & Dominion*, ch. 48.

E. Accumulation

Point five: succession. The accumulation of capital is an ethical command. It is not optional. Building God's kingdom requires capital. It is a redemptive process. The meaning of *redemption* is *buy back*. Covenant-keepers are required to buy back the world on behalf of God. This is why the biblical covenant is governed by Deuteronomy 8:18: "But you are to remember the LORD your God, for it is He who is giving you power to make wealth, in order to confirm His covenant which He swore to your fathers, as it is this day."[16] Who were the fathers? Abraham, Isaac, and Jacob. They left an inheritance.

Abram was the head of a household. He was also a household priest. He circumcised male children in his household. This was a sacrament. As the priest of the household, Abram had to make an assessment of the value of his capital in terms of the future. This is true of all capital. *Its present market price is based on its expected future stream of income.* It is also based on the evaluator's degree of future-orientation. If he is future-oriented, his capital is worth more to him than if he were present-oriented. The rate of discount he applies to future income is lower. Hence, the expected value of the outcome is higher.

The longer the estimated time period of the expected stream of net income, the higher its market value to the owner. But the degree of time-orientation has far greater impact on present economic value than the term of expected income. If the rate of long-term interest doubles, this will depress the present value of the stream of income by almost half. A doubling of the expected period of net income from the asset will not compensate for the doubling of the rate of interest. Why not? Because the extra years are so distant chronologically. The discount applied by the doubled rate of interest will have even more depressing effects on the value of additional income that far distant than it has on income that will arrive sooner.[17]

The elders of a church make economic judgments representatively: *on behalf of.* They make these judgments on behalf of church members, but also the corporate church.

16. Ibid., ch. 22.

17. If the expected income stream is 50 years, the value to anyone of the income from 51 years to 100 years is minimal. Life is too short.

The biblical goal is capital accumulation, not capital consumption. This in an inter-generational assignment. Each generation is supposed to leave more behind than it inherited. This is the meaning of value-added living, as applied to capital ownership.

The accumulation of church capital must include the worldview that the church passes to members. This will be their primary tool of production. This will shape their administration of inherited wealth. It will shape their ability to make decisions on behalf of future generations. There is a law element to consider: ethics. There is a sanctions aspect: causation in history. There is a time element to consider.

The individual inherits beyond the grave. So does the church. But the church's inheritance is not said to be economic. The church's inheritance is the marriage supper of the lamb (Rev. 19:6 9) and everything that follows. Then what about economics? How is the church's economic covenant renewed in history? By covenant succession. The church's capital is transferred to the next generation of covenant-keepers within the church. This is the biblically mandated means of extending God's kingdom through time. The time factor is the basis of economic compounding. Members die. Baptized children inherit the task of extending the kingdom of God in history.

If the heirs keep the terms of the covenant, they will usually be in a position to add value. They will have to increase their productivity. They will then leave more behind than they inherited. *This is the meaning of the redemption of the world.* The heirs participate in an inter-generational increase in capital. Ownership of resources progressively is transferred to covenant-keepers. "A good person leaves an inheritance to his grandchildren, And the wealth of a sinner is stored up for the righteous" (Prov. 13:22).[18] This process includes churches. Why? Because family capital produces income, and churches receive tithes.

In the first half of the twentieth century, most mainline Protestant denominations in the United States went liberal theologically. Covenant-breakers inherited the assets: denominational name identification and church buildings. In the final third of the century, liberal mainline denominations began to shrink in membership. They struggled

18. Gary North, *Wisdom & Dominion: An Economic Commentary on Proverbs* (Moulton, Alabama: Axehead Press, [2012] 2029), ch. 41.

for financial support. Conservative denominations grew. *Inheritance shifted away from the liberals.*

This inter-generational process of inheritance, compound economic growth, and accumulation of capital is the covenantal basis of economic redemption in history. The accumulation of capital under a covenantal oath is the economic basis of redemption in other spheres. *The covenantal church extends its jurisdiction in part by means of the process of economic compounding.* This process of wealth creation is entirely voluntary. It does not involve the use of force. The kingdom of God expands its jurisdiction primarily in terms of families, but covenant-keeping family members are members of churches.

Conclusion

The economics of the church begins with the guardian function, which is judicial. But the economics of the church is inescapably horizontal: competition for members, which means keeping existing members and recruiting new ones. The church competes against covenant-breaking society for new members. This is the battle for the souls of men.

The economics of the free market is also inherently horizontal: competing bids for the use or ownership of scarce resources. The principle of *monetary high bid wins* governs the free market. The bidding process is impersonal. It is open to new bidders and new sellers. In contrast, the high bid of the church is established by the church officers. This bidding system is non-monetary and highly personal. The church competes in terms of its worldview, as well as the sanctions associated with the two rival worldviews: heaven or hell.

The deciding authority is the individual. He or she operates under God's overall sovereignty. He or she decides which voice of authority to listen to. He or she decides which kingdom to live under: the kingdom of God or the kingdom of man. The judicial mark of this decision is church membership, delineated by the sacraments.

Chapter 18

Boundaries

Your boasting is not good. Do you not know that a little leaven leavens the whole lump of dough? Clean out the old leaven so that you may be a new lump, just as you are in fact unleavened. For Christ our Passover also has been sacrificed. Therefore let's celebrate the feast, not with old leaven, nor with the leaven of malice and wickedness, but with the unleavened bread of sincerity and truth.

I Corinthians 5:6–8

Analysis

Boundaries are aspects of point three of the biblical covenant: ethics.[1] Ethical boundaries are associated with law. Law imposes negative sanctions on certain acts. The central judicial-covenantal fact of the church is its right to exclude. The church is bounded by its judicial status: the bride of Christ.[2] She is not for sale. No one but Christ has lawful access to her. This exclusion is reflected by the sacraments. The sacraments are bounded covenantally. Those who are not members of an institutional church do not have lawful access to baptism, unless they are declaring their membership by consenting to baptism. Non-members do not have lawful access to the Lord's Supper (I Cor. 5, 11).

1. Ray R. Sutton, *That You May Prosper: Dominion by Covenant*, 2nd ed. (Tyler, Texas: Institute for Christian Economics, [1987] 1992), ch. 3.

2. John 3:29; II Corinthians 11:2; Ephesians 5:25–27; Revelation 19:7–9; 21:2, 9.

Churches are legally separate judicial social units. They are covenantal units because they are established by a mutual oath under God. They are identified by names. These names establish legal liability. A name is associated with a legal boundary.

A. Name and Ownership

Point one: God's sovereignty. In Chapter 8, I discussed the relationship between name and boundaries. God announced His defense of His name in the Third Commandment. "You shall not take the name of the LORD your God in vain, for the LORD will not leave him unpunished who takes His name in vain" (Ex. 20:7).[3] This is the third law in the list of five priestly laws. He announced the prohibition against theft—a defense of property—in the Eighth Commandment. "You shall not steal" (Ex. 20:15).[4] This is the third in the list of five commandments relating to kingly rule or civil society.[5]

In Chapter 8, I wrote that private property begins with a person's name. *He is a legally identifiable agent*. His name identifies him. It says, "you, not someone else." This is the basis of judicial responsibility. It is also the foundation of economic authority. This same analysis applies to a family, a church, and an individual. I also wrote this: "The authority to name things is a God-given authority. The person with the authority to establish names possesses a unique hierarchical position at the top. The question, 'Who's in charge here?' can be accurately answered by identifying the person with the legal authority to name people and things." This analysis also applies to a church.

A local congregation also has a name. This act of separation identifies it as a guardian: a legal administrator of God's property. Whatever it owns in its name belongs to God. Church property comes under the elders, who are in charge of the church's property. They serve as guardians, both for God and for those under their authority. By extending the church's ownership, elders extend its jurisdiction.

---

3. Gary North, *Authority & Dominion: An Economic Commentary on Exodus*, vol. 2, *Part II: Decalogue & Dominion* (Moulton, Alabama: Axehead Press, [1986, 2012] 2025), ch 23.

4. Ibid., ch. 28.

5. On the dual lists, priestly and kingly, of the Ten Commandments, see ibid., Preface B:I.

B. Central Planning

Point two: hierarchy. My discussion on resource allocation in Section B of Chapter 7 goes over the basics of subjective value and objective pricing of scarce resources. The free market is governed by the principle of *monetary high bid wins*. Bidding is impersonal in large, well-organized markets. Buyers and sellers do not know each other. None of this is true of a local church.

The elders of a church act representatively. They allocate time and money in terms of their judgment regarding the conflicting values of members of the congregation. Inside the legal boundaries of the church, elders treat people inside differently from those outside these boundaries. They are responsible to God for the administration of assets. They represent members legally (guardianship). They act as guardians for church members as individuals, but also as agents of the church as a covenantal unit.

This allocation is not governed by legal rules based on contract. Elders can devote more or less time to one member in relation to another. This is unequal treatment. The church's resources are not part of a system of equality or even a system of fixed proportional claims. The church cares for the weak members. This is highly personal. A free market's system of allocation is far more dependent on contracts between strangers.

The members are economic resources as well as liabilities. As they mature spiritually, their donated labor adds to the church's income. So do their tithes.

As a church grows, it increases its influence. This is an aspect of the dominion covenant. Expansion is basic to the dominion covenant. In the New Testament, this is the Great Commission (Matt. 28:18–20).[6] This means that church leaders are required to be future-oriented. They must find ways to attract visitors and serve new members. This is an aspect of point two: service outward.

6. Kenneth L. Gentry, *The Greatness of the Great Commission: The Christian Enterprise in a Fallen World*, 2nd ed. (Tyler, Texas: Institute for Christian Economics, [1990] 1992).

C. Time and Place

Point three: ethics. This is related to law, which establishes boundaries. Churches extend beyond time and place. They begin in a time and a place, but church growth extends the worldview of the church.

There is loss involved in such an extension. Competing ideas and experiences threaten to overcome the confessional inheritance of the church. Confessions of faith change over time, either officially or unofficially. This may affect the church's inheritance in the broadest sense. But while the rigor of a church's confession can get weaker, the geographical impact of whatever confession remains may be greater. It reaches more people.

This weakening of the church's confession is well known with respect to recent converts to a worldview. The first generation defines itself in terms of the break that it made from the traditional confession. The children grow up in the confessional environment established by the elders: ecclesiastical and parental. When a new denomination is born of a split, the issues are clear. But clarity fades over time. The next generation of members did not experience the confessional break which their parents did. They did not pay a heavy price or experience negative sanctions. The church's confessional boundaries are familiar to them. These boundaries may be little more than background noise: easily adapted to and ignored. Their heirs will in turn grow up in a confessional setting, but one far less rigorous than the founders' confession.

Only through the maintenance of the confession can a church overcome spiritual regression to the mean beyond three or four generations. The Second Commandment says that this is possible to achieve. "You shall not worship them nor serve them; for I, the Lord your God, am a jealous God, inflicting the punishment of the fathers on the children, on the third and the fourth generations of those who hate Me, but showing favor to thousands, to those who love Me and keep My commandments" (Ex. 20:5–6). The word "thousands" applies here to "generations."[7] The observation that this has not been achieved in the past does not prove theologically that the promise of the Second Commandment is null and void under the New Covenant.

---

7. North, *Authority & Dominion*, vol. 2, *Part II: Decalogue & Dominion* ([1986, 2012] 2025), ch. 22:C:3.

D. Scarcity

Point four: sanctions. I wrote this in Section D of Chapter 8 on the individual covenant.

> Scarcity is defined by economists as follows: "At zero price, there is greater demand than supply." This is another way of saying "it commands a price." Scarcity imposes boundaries on men. It means that they must gain more assets in order to increase their consumption. They must extend their jurisdiction. There is also a scarcity of time. People die.

Institutions need not die. There is replacement: *succession.* Surely this is true of the church. It is somewhat less true of the state. Families extend through time, but their continuity is far less meaningful than with churches and states. Few people know anything about their ancestors a hundred years previously. They know a great deal about their nations' histories. They can find out a great deal about the history of large denominations. But church history is not a popular subject, not even denominational history.

Scarcity is a major factor in limiting church growth in urban societies. The price of land is bid up by buyers. Businesses generate income from buildings for at least five days a week, and possibly seven. This enables them to buy land. Churches generate income by donations. The building is used only on Sundays, possibly only in the morning. Churches therefore are not successful bidders for property. Also, churches have land requirements for parking. In the United States, a church needs one acre of paved parking for every 100 people. Businesses do not need this much land. Their customers do not all show up in the parking lot at the same time.

Churches can grow without purchasing real estate. First, they can do this by adding worship meetings all day Sunday. Second, they can adopt a house church model. This can be done through the World Wide Web. A common sermon can be broadcast live or posted online as a video. Each home church has a large television that is hooked up to the Internet. This can be done for at least the adult Sunday school. But it would take multiple television sets and rooms for all Sunday schools. Churches can also run day care centers. They charge full-cost fees. This will more than pay the monthly mortgage bill. There should be no subsidies at the expense of church members. A related strategy: rent space to a privately run day care. Either approach generates substantial income five days a week, 52 weeks a year. Then churches can buy property.

A major restriction on church growth is the scarcity of qualified church officers. Most churches in the West demand leadership training. There are few members ready to serve. The cost of this training is high: the value of invested time. This basic economic law is true: when cost rises, less is demanded, other things being equal.

E. Dominion

Point five: succession. The dominion covenant was given to all mankind. It defines man. Adam and Eve broke the law associated with this covenant. They did not take a communion meal at the tree of life. They ate from the forbidden tree. This necessitated a new covenant of special, soul-saving grace. God created the church. Jesus Christ fulfilled the terms of the law. He therefore announced His lordship of the new covenant. "And Jesus came up and spoke to them, saying, 'All authority in heaven and on earth has been given to Me. Go, therefore, and make disciples of all the nations, baptizing them in the name of the Father and the Son and the Holy Spirit, teaching them to follow all that I commanded you; and behold, I am with you always, to the end of the age'" (Matt. 28:18–20). This is the Great Commission. It provides covenant-keepers with their marching orders. The goal is the fulfillment of the dominion covenant by covenant-keepers. It is a call to worldwide dominion.[8]

The church extends its dominion through evangelism. It consolidates its dominion through the sacraments, baptism and communion. Baptism is an oath-sign of a person's subordination to the legal terms of the church covenant. Communion is an oath-sign of covenant renewal.[9]

---

8. Gentry, *Greatness of the Great Commission*.

9. Meredith G. Kline, *By Oath Consigned: A Reinterpretation of the Covenant Signs of Circumcision and Baptism* (Grand Rapids, Michigan: Eerdmans, 1975).

The primary task of church officers is to train church members to be active participants in the Great Commission. This is how the church's authority is extended in history and across geographical borders. The officers are comparable to commanding officers in the military, with this difference: voting church members can fire them. This is basic Protestant doctrine: *the priesthood of all believers*. It separates Protestantism judicially and theologically from Roman Catholicism and Eastern Orthodoxy.

Conclusion

A congregation is bounded by confession, by the number of members, by the size of its capital, by geography, and by time. It can extend across borders and through time. It need not die out. The possibility of church growth is basic to the covenantal promises of the Mosaic law. Church growth is required by the Great Commission.

Chapter 19

Imputation

"Bring the whole tithe into the storehouse, so that there may be food in My house, and put Me to the test now in this," says the LORD *of armies, "if I do not open for you the windows of heaven and pour out for you a blessing until it overflows. Then I will rebuke the devourer for you, so that it will not destroy the fruit of your ground; nor will the vine in the field prove fruitless to you,"* says the LORD *of armies. "All the nations will call you blessed, for you will be a delightful land,"* says the LORD *of armies.*

Malachi 3:10–12

Analysis

Point four of the biblical covenant is sanctions: positive and negative.[1] God threatened Israel with negative sanctions for having robbed Him. But He offered positive sanctioins for paying the tithe.

Church officers have a responsibility to allocate resources belonging to the church. This responsibility means that they are God's stewards. They are also stewards for church members. They must allocate assets rationally. What does "rational" mean? It means making asset allocations without producing above-average waste. How can they do this? For items purchased in a free market, there are prices. But there are no

1. Ray R. Sutton, *That You May Prosper: Dominion By Covenant*, 2nd ed. (Tyler, Texas: Institute for Christian Economics, [1987] 1992), ch. 4.

prices associated with personal relationships. This same problem confronts families.

Mises argued that socialist economic calculation is inherently irrational. There are no market-clearing prices in a socialist commonwealth. Prices do not convey accurate information about consumer demand of production goods. There are no capital markets.[2] But this criticism does not apply to families and churches. They are not irrational ownership arrangements. Stewards in both institutions make rational decisions without capital markets inside these covenantal units. Decision-making in families and churches are based on *casuistry*: the application of general ethical rules to specific cases. They are also based on *empathy*: the ability to understand other people's motives.

There is an institutional problem: the larger the church, the more difficult it is to reconcile the plans of members. How do the officers know what to do? This is the problem of epistemology: "What can we know, and how can we know it?" This is a major problem for establishing boundaries: local church growth. It is also a major problem for exercising judgment. The central question for all epistemologies that are based on a theory of individual imputation of meaning, causation, and value is this: *How can the imputations of theoretically autonomous individuals explain decision-making by groups*? This is an application of the recurring philosophical problem of the one and the many. If we begin with the autonomy of the individual, we soon must face the fact that he is not autonomous. There are other imputing individuals in this world. He interacts with lots of them. To make sense of our world, we must have a way to assess the relevance of competing imputations. We must assign "weight" to individual imputations, and then "add up" the value of all of them. But no such value scale exists, according to the methodological individualist.[3] If this is true, then this makes all representative decision-making on behalf of a group scientifically impossible. It also raises the question of who possesses the lawful authority to make such representative decisions. On what basis?

---

2. Ludwig von Mises, *Economic Calculation in the Socialist Commonwealth* (Auburn, Alabama: Mises Institute, [1920] 1990).

3. Lionel Robbins, *An Essay on the Nature and Significance of Economic Science* (London: Macmillan, 1932), ch. VI. See also Gary North, *Sovereignty & Dominion: An Economic Commentary on Genesis* (Moulton, Alabama: Axehead Press, [1982, 2012] 2022), ch. 5.

A. Valuation by God

Point one: God's sovereignty. God evaluated the effects of His daily creative work on all days except day two (Gen. 1). Who was the Creator? In terms of the doctrine of the economic Trinity, this was the Second Person of the Trinity.

> ...giving thanks to the Father, who has qualified us to share in the inheritance of the saints in light. For He rescued us from the domain of darkness, and transferred us to the kingdom of His beloved Son, in whom we have redemption, the forgiveness of sins. He is the image of the invisible God, the firstborn of all creation: for by Him all things were created, both in the heavens and on earth, visible and invisible, whether thrones, or dominions, or rulers, or authorities—all things have been created through Him and for Him. He is before all things, and in Him all things hold together. (Col. 1:12–17)

Therefore, the day-by-day evaluation was made by the Second Person. This was an individual's evaluation of His individual work. But Christianity teaches that God is three Persons as well as one God. So, this imputation was also corporate. So was the creation. Only Christianity announces such a doctrine.

The church is Christ's bride. I have covered this in Chapter 16, Section A. This means that God imputes supreme value to the church. The church is analogous to wisdom in Proverbs 3, which is presented as a wife: "She is more precious than jewels, And nothing you desire compares with her" (Prov. 3:15).[4] This is a corporate judgment regarding a corporate covenantal institution.

God's valuation includes the value of each congregation's assets in relation to the international church's mission statement, the Great Commission of Matthew 28:18–20. I covered this in the Analysis section of Chapter 16. God assesses the rate of return on all of the church's assets. This is best pictured in the letters to seven churches in Revelation 3.

Heads of churches can and do make decisions about allocating scarce church resources. The reason they can do this is that they are made in God's image. God has delegated sovereignty to them. In this

4. Gary North, *Wisdom & Dominion: An Economic Commentary on Proverbs* (Moulton, Alabama: Axehead Press, [2012] 2029), ch. 9.

sense, as stewards, they must take on the role of sovereigns. They are not autonomous sovereigns. They are delegated sovereigns.

B. Valuation by Man

Point two: hierarchy. My comments here are extensions of what I wrote in Section B of Chapter 9. They have to do with thinking God's thoughts after Him. This exercise begins with the presupposition of God's Bible-revealed law. This law applies to individuals, who are held responsible in history and eternity. But it also applies to corporate entities. The decision-makers must begin with any laws of God that apply to the corporate entity, either through explicit biblical revelation or else through the judicial extension of biblical revelation. This is Christian casuistry: the application of biblical principles to historical circumstances.

Responsibility is four-way: upward to God, outward toward society—as manifested both in market demand and charitable need—downward toward church members, and inner: ethical conscience and personal needs. Elders are required by God to consider this complex array of competing demands on the church's resources. *The allocation is economic, but the responsibility is judicial.*

The elders make valuations on behalf of each of the members of the church. They must take into consideration what God requires of each member. They must also consider God's expectations regarding the congregation as a covenantal unit. This makes the elders' position highly complex. God holds them responsible for the accurate assessment of the value scales of each member, as well as the potential net output of each member. They must consider short-run net output and also long-run. They then must motivate each member to maximize his or her output. This is not primarily economic output. It is spiritual output, but with economic implications.

Because there are comparable services outside the local congregation, the decision-makers must offer a superior message and program. There is competition for allegiance. Elders must discover information about comparable ecclesiastical programs, and then assess to what extent these programs are relevant inside the congregation.

The mixture of market prices, pseudo-market prices, and no market prices confronts decision-makers in every corporate organization. The exact economic value of a church member is difficult to assess. It has something to do with replacement value. But it also has something to do with the market value of loyalty, the market value of understanding the unwritten rules, and the market value of ecclesiastical inertia. Elders are loosely restrained by the church's budget, but they are rarely sure which institutional arrangements should be left alone, which should be restructured, and at what cost. This calls for intuitive judgment, i.e., judgments where economic cause and effect are not strictly numerical. *No economic judgments are strictly numerical.* Man is personal. Accounting numbers are impersonal.

C. Criteria: Individual and Corporate

Point three: ethics. This has to do with law. Law is associated with standards. In Chapter 9, I explained why economic value is derived from ethical value, an epistemological position that is contrary to the prevailing notions of humanistic economic theory. I stated that the biblical criterion of economic value is this: *the extension of the kingdom of God in history*. Economic theory is not value-free. It is value-derived.

Church leaders are required by God to use the kingdom of God as their standard of economic value in assessing the profitability of any course of action. They are supposed to allocate church capital based on this criterion. They act as a trustees of God, both judicially (guardianship) and economically (stewardship). They act in the name of God: extending the kingdom of God. They act as stewards of the church: extending its inheritance in history. They are judicially responsible before God. The rewards and penalties of stewardship are both judicial and economic. By means of successful stewardship, his responsibilities increase (Luke 12:47–48).[5]

The criteria of church success are varied. One is membership growth. Another is confessional continuity. The problem is this: congre-

5. Gary North, *Treasure & Dominion: An Economic Commentary on Luke* (Moulton, Alabama: Axehead Press, [2012] 2031), ch. 28.

gations that stress confessional rigor tend to be small. Churches that are growing generally do not stress preaching based on theology. There is a trade-off. The pastor decides what to preach. He does so as God's agent. Other important goals are stability and peace. These are not matters of "monetary high bid wins."

D. Value and Price

Point four: sanctions. This is related to judgment. Individuals impute economic value subjectively. Individuals are responsible for the accuracy of these imputations, case by case. This ability is grounded in God's economic imputation.[6] The act of imputation is always representational. Man imputes value on behalf of God: the cosmic Owner. He also imputes it on behalf of any subordinate owners of the assets involved. This act of economic imputation is always governed by the judicial category of ownership. *Economic ownership is always an extension of judicial ownership.* It is not autonomous.

Church elders act on behalf of others. This is the stewardship function. They act in terms of expected future value. This is the allocation or the auctioneer function. They act as stewards for future members, who will join to secure the benefits. Elders are economic agents for these people. This is why *ownership is a social function.* This includes the ownership of churches.

Visitors and members ask themselves this about attendance at a specific congregation: "What's in it for me?" They are self-interested. They do not agree on the criteria of greatest value. The church's leaders must decide what a local congregation is equipped best to offer. This requires representational valuation. If some members are not satisfied with the leaders' performance, they can leave. This means that there is constant competition among congregations. Members decide what membership is worth. The covenantal tithe is neither preached nor enforced.[7] So, members decide how much to donate. This is a way for them to impose

---

6. Chapter 8:E.

7. Gary North, *The Covenantal Tithe: The Providential Plan for Fruitful Stewardship* (Moulton, Alabama: Axehead Press, [2011] 2026).

sanctions on the leadership. No one mentions this in public, but this is universal in Protestant churches. With greater mobility, families can drive to competing congregations. Congregations are becoming less like local parishes and more like businesses.

In business, there is the concept of the lifetime net value of the customer. How much money is a typical customer likely to spend? For how long? What is the expected profit rate? Add up these figures. The sum must then be discounted by the prevailing rate of interest for this estimated time period. The result is the expected lifetime value. The cost of acquiring the customer must be kept below this figure.

In church matters, there is a similar concept. Churches never make this calculation officially. They also do not estimate the monetary and institutional cost of gaining a new member. This would be considered crassly commercial. Yet churches cannot escape from these figures. Over time, if the number of new members does not equal the losses due to death, transfer of membership, and dropping out, a church will shrink. It will eventually disappear. This is the feedback system. Every organization has feedback systems. They should be used to guide policy. They surely affect outcomes. These are sanctions imposed by the targeted group of potential members. They vote by means of donations of time and money.

Elders make estimates of the value of future potential streams of income in the broadest sense. They then allocate resources under their control. They estimate what to pay now in terms of the the expected economic value of future legal ownership. The art of estimating future economic value presupposes cause and effect: sanctions. It also assumes linear history. There is causation over time. If there were not, the ability to estimate future value could not exist. It would be overwhelmed by randomness.

E. Value-Added Living

Point five: succession. Jesus said: "The thief comes only to steal and kill and destroy; I came so that they would have life, and have it abundantly" (John 10:10). This applies to every Christian. It applies to all

Christian covenantal institutions. This principle applies to kingdom expansion. *More is better than less at the same price.*

Church growth is the product of accurate forecasting coupled with efficient resource allocation. These activities assume a system of private ownership. They also assume a world of economic causation: predictable sanctions.

Churches are not profit-seeking institutions. Competition between churches is not based on a profit-and-loss monetary accounting system. The concept of value-added living has to do with objective criteria, but also subjectively imputed value. Individuals impute value. If they are happy with value received, God asks them to invite others to church. They are to work and pray for expansion of a local congregation. The is the Great Commission in action (Matt. 28:18–20).[8] On the other hand, if they are not satisfied, they are to seek out another congregation. This is basic to Protestant theology.

Officers must mobilize the members. This is part of the division of labor. It is basic to church growth. Officers must try to find out which members have which talents. Then they must equip the members for evangelism. The goal is to reduce the boundaries of Satan's kingdom. *This is zero-sum competition.* A gain for one kingdom is made at the expense of the other. This is a process of kingdom replacement. *This is special grace expansion.*

There is also common grace expansion. When God-fearing people conform themselves to biblical law in their dealings, the community is benefitted. When a covenant-breaker, by God's grace, is transformed into a covenant-keeper, he becomes more honest and more reliable, or should. The cost of cooperation falls. Here is a fundamental economic law: when price falls, more is demanded. This increases the division of labor. Output per unit of resource input rises. People get richer. *This is common grace expansion.*[9] It is not a zero-sum competition.

The church is God's monopolistic agency of preaching, the sacraments, and discipline. It has a crucial role to play. This role is related

8. Gary North, *Priorities & Dominion: An Economic Commentary on Matthew* (Moulton, Alabama: Axehead Press, [2012] 2030), ch. 48.

9. Gary North, *Dominion and Common Grace: The Biblical Basis of Progress* (Moulton, Alabama: Axehead Press, [1987] 2024).

to economic growth (Deut. 8:18).[10] *Economic growth confirms the biblical covenant.* The church is the central institution in establishing the theology of growth. This idea historically was uniquely Christian. It was an extension of postmillennialism into economic life. The eschatological view was developed systematically in seventeenth-century Holland.[11] That was the period of economic growth for Holland. "The Dutch Economy in the Golden Age lasted from roughly 1580, when the Dutch proved themselves successful in their fight with the Spanish, to about 1670, when the Republic's economy experienced a down-turn. Economic growth was very fast until about 1620 when it slowed, but continued to grow steadily until the end of the Golden Age."[12] That was in 1648: the end of the war of secession from Spain.

Conclusion

The church is not a profit-seeking institution. It is not governed by the free market's allocation principle: monetary high bid wins. It has nothing to sell, other than real estate. Therefore, its principle of allocation is strictly hierarchical. It is not governed by objective prices. This means that the criteria of institutional success and failure are mainly non-monetary. No one comes to church expecting to pay a specific amount of money for a specific service.

Church officers represent God both judicially and economically. They must make their evaluations in terms of spiritual criteria. Only indirectly do monetary criteria become significant, e.g., not being able to pay the mortgage or the pastor.

---

10. North, *Inheritance & Dominion: An Economic Commentary on Deuteronomy* (Moulton, Alabama: Axehead Press, [1999, 2012] 2028), ch. 22.

11. In the spring of 2011, I wrote to Prof. Francis Nigel Lee. I asked him to identify postmillennial Dutch theologians in the seventeenth century. He replied on May 1 (Australia). Here is his list: De Bres, Gellus, the Dordt Dutch Bible, Maresius, Voetius, Leusden, Huernius, Cocceius, Calovius, d'Outrein, Van der Kamp, Witsius, the two Vitringas, Hoornbeek, Essenius, Groenewegen, Koelman, Lampe, Hoekendijk, Brakel, and á Marck.

12. Donald J. Herrald, "The Dutch Economy in the Golden Age (16th–17th Centuries)," *EHNet*, eh.net/encyclopedia/the-dutch-economy-in-the-golden-age-16th-17th-centuries (accessed October 15, 2022).

In a free market, competition is based on this structure: sellers vs. sellers, buyers vs. buyers. Out of this bidding process emerges an array of monetary prices. There is no array of monetary prices in church competition. Church competition is based on this structure: churches vs. churches. There is no competition among prospective members. The principle of monetary high bid wins does not apply. Few churches experience filled seats and pews at the main worship service. If they do, they add another worship service or build a larger sanctuary. There are rarely prospective visitors waiting outside, hoping to get in. While this did happen in the ministries of Charles Haddon Spurgeon in London in the 1880s and Peter Marshall in Atlanta in the 1930s and Washington, D.C. in the 1940s, the competition to get in was based on a bureaucratic principle: *first come, first served.* People lined up at least 30 minutes before the scheduled service.

Church officers are responsible before God not to waste God's resources. Officers must therefore impute value, including economic value, in order to allocate the scarce resources of time and money. Time is money, Ben Franklin said. It is not a free good. The pastor is paid a salary in exchange for his time. But congregation members do not pay for his sermons on a piece-rate basis. It is not a market transaction, unlike attending a movie theater for two hours. (Most members do not want to sit through two-hour services. No visitors do.)

Officers and attendees impute value. They decide in terms of the same structure of stewardship that prevails in the market: upward toward God, outward toward others, downward for those under their authority, and inward toward themselves. But their allocation decisions are only peripherally based on objective prices. There is an auction process, and it is governed by "high bid wins"—just not "monetary high bid wins."

Chapter 20

Legacy

Analysis

Point five of the biblical covenant is succession.[1] In every social theory, there is a doctrine of succession. In economics, this is the doctrine of inheritance. It is inherently the issue of eschatology. Every social theory has a concept of eschatology: the last things. It may be concealed, but there always is one. The Marxists had one. It was highly optimistic. They preached inevitable world domination through proletarian class revolution. All social institutions will be transformed. There will be a new humanity in which class conflict will cease. My friend F. N. Lee wrote the definitive book on this: *Communist Eschatology*.[2] The book is huge: over 1,300 pages. Similarly, cosmic evolutionists have an eschatology: the heat death of the universe, where all things are dead; there is no more change.[3] Some varieties of Eastern mysticism teach the doctrine of karma. There will be eons of personal reincarnation after bodily death. At the end of this process, the liberated soul is absorbed back into the cosmic *one* from which it came. Personal history ends,

1. Ray R. Sutton, *That You May Prosper: Dominion By Covenant*, 2nd ed. (Tyler, Texas: Institute for Christian Economics, [1987] 1992), ch. 5.

2. Francis Nigel Lee, *Communist Eschatology: A Christian Philosophical Analysis of the Post-Capitalistic Views of Marx, Engels and Lenin* (Nutley, New Jersey: Craig Press, 1974).

3. Gary North, *Is the World Running Down? Crisis in the Christian Worldview* (Moulton, Alabama: Axehead Press, [1988] 2029), ch. 2.

self-awareness ends, and change ends. This outlook is hostile to history. The material world is regarded as an illusion: maya.

The central issue of eschatology is the future. Where are individuals headed? Where is history headed? A person's doctrine of history influences his doctrine of responsibility toward future generations. If it is pessimistic regarding progress, this undermines personal commitment and sacrifice to work for long-term social transformation.

There is always the question of winners and losers in history. Men ask this: "To what extent does success in history reflect ethics?" Was Ben Franklin right? Is honesty the best policy in history? Is it the best policy for individuals? What about institutions? How do we know? Is there plausible historical evidence for the correct answer? If there is no correlation between success in history and success in eternity, of what benefit is commitment to future generations? The outcomes are random, after all. Sacrifice today will not make any difference in the corporate transition from history to eternity.

This is not what the Bible teaches. The Old Testament announces: "But the humble will inherit the land And will delight themselves in abundant prosperity" (Ps. 37:11). The Psalmist continued:

> The wicked borrows and does not pay back,
> But the righteous is gracious and gives.
> For those blessed by Him will inherit the land,
> But those cursed by Him will be eliminated.
> The steps of a man are established by the LORD,
> And He delights in his way.
> When he falls, he will not be hurled down,
> Because the LORD is the One who holds his hand.
> I have been young and now I am old,
> Yet I have not seen the righteous forsaken
> Or his descendants begging for bread.
> All day long he is gracious and lends,
> And his descendants are a blessing.
> Turn from evil and do good,
> So that you will dwell forever.
> (Ps. 37:21–27)[4]

4. Gary North, *Confidence & Dominion: An Economic Commentary on the Psalms* (Moulton, Alabama: Axehead Press, [2012] 2029), ch. 6.

It is clear that this prophecy was historical. Sinners will still sin. In contrast, there will be no wicked people living alongside covenant-keepers after the final judgment. The amillennialist spiritualizes this passage. He denies that the prophecy was ever intended to be fulfilled literally in history. In fact, the opposite will take place. Covenant-breakers will inherit in history. They will disinherit covenant-keepers. Calvinist philosopher Cornelius Van Til was adamant on this.[5]

The New Testament's prophecy regarding inheritance is taken directly from Psalm 37:11. "Blessed are the meek: for they shall inherit the earth" (Matt. 5:5, KJV). This refers to meekness before God. It is an aspect of subordination.[6] This passage is interpreted differently in terms of rival eschatologies. Premillennialists say that this inheritance will be during the thousand-year earthly reign of Christ after His second coming, but before final judgment. There is a fundamental discontinuity between history's social order and the millennial social order. Nothing that Christians build institutionally today will have any predictable effect on the millennial kingdom. Amillennialists say that this reign refers exclusively to the world after the final judgment. There is no continuity between today's efforts and the development of a Christian nation, let alone a civilization. There is continuity in history. But there will be no earthly kingdom of God that transforms societies. Postmillennialists say that this passage refers to a long era of visible blessings in history prior to the second coming/final judgment. Efforts today can and will produce significant social benefits in the future.

A. Purpose

Point one: God's sovereignty. God's purposes for the institutional church are restrictive. First, it must preach the gospel. Here is the key passage on preaching. This constitutes the institutional church's mission statement. It is correctly called the Great Commission. "But the eleven disciples proceeded to Galilee, to the mountain which Jesus had designated to them.

5. Gary North, *Political Polytheism: The Myth of Pluralism* (Moulton, Alabama: Axehead Press, [1989] 2029), ch. 4.

6. Gary North, *Priorities & Dominion: An Economic Commentary on Matthew* (Moulton, Alabama: Axehead Press, [2012] 2030), ch. 4.

And when they saw Him, they worshiped Him; but some were doubtful. And Jesus came up and spoke to them, saying, 'All authority in heaven and on earth has been given to Me. Go, therefore, and make disciples of all the nations, baptizing them in the name of the Father and the Son and the Holy Spirit, teaching them to follow all that I commanded you; and behold, I am with you always, to the end of the age'" (Matt. 28:16–20).[7] This is the ecclesiastical application of the dominion covenant, which was given to all mankind (Gen. 1:26–28).[8] The Great Commission was given only to covenant-keepers. It is a command to extend the kingdom of God into every area of life in which sin exists, which means every area of life.[9]

Second, the church administers the sacraments. *This is the church's defining covenantal authority*. The sacraments are exclusive to the institutional church. These are positive sanctions. Third, the church must exercise discipline in order to defend the integrity of its sanctions (Matt. 18:15–18). The church is supported by the tithe, which is morally required by God but is judicially voluntary for the church.[10] Jesus warned: "Woe to you, scribes and Pharisees, hypocrites! For you tithe mint and dill and cumin, and have neglected the weightier provisions of the Law: justice and mercy and faithfulness; but these are the things you should have done without neglecting the others" (Matt. 23:23). Tithing is not enough. There must also be justice, mercy, and faithfulness.

The church is not a profit-seeking institution. It cannot lawfully sell the sacraments for money. This is why it is entitled to the tithe. It prospers when its members prosper.

B. Multiplication

Point two: hierarchy. Church elders must plan for expansion. The call to multiplication comes in the dominion covenant. "God blessed them;

7. Ibid., ch. 48.
8. Gary North, *Sovereignty & Dominion: An Economic Commentary on Genesis* (Moulton, Alabama: Axehead Press, [1982, 2012] 2022), chaps. 3, 4.
9. Kenneth L. Gentry, *The Greatness of the Great Commission: The Christian Enterprise in a Fallen World*, 2nd ed. (Tyler, Texas: Institute for Christian Economics, [1990] 1992).
10. Gary North, *The Covenantal Tithe: The Providential Plan for Fruitful Stewardship* (Moulton, Alabama: Axehead Press, [2011] 2026).

and God said to them, 'Be fruitful and multiply, and fill the earth, and subdue it; and rule over the fish of the sea and over the birds of the sky and over every living thing that moves on the earth'" (Gen. 1:28). It was repeated with Noah: "Then God blessed Noah and his sons, and said to them, 'Be fruitful and multiply, and fill the earth'" (Gen. 9:1).[11] There is no question that this is an ethical mandate given to all mankind.

The church grows through the preaching of the gospel: recruiting non-members. This is spiritual multiplication. It also grows through the expansion of family members. To this extent, the church benefits from biological multiplication. There are more candidates for redemption: inside the church and outside.

In Section B of Chapter 7, I discussed future-orientation and population growth. Future-orientation is what Edward Banfield called the upper-class mentality.[12] For those who affirm postmillennialism, this willingness to accept lower net income in the present for the sake of the future refers also to history. The postmillennialist does not believe, as the premillennialist does, that Christian capital in the aggregate will suffer a discontinuity prior to the time when Jesus comes in Person to set up a literal thousand-year earthly kingdom.[13] He sees ecclesiastical continuity. He does not believe, as the amillennialist does, that Satan inherits in history through his earthly disciples. He does not believe, as the amillennialist does—but refuses to say in public—that the wealth of the just is laid up for the sinner. He believes in compound economic growth of the kingdom of God in history. The wealth of the sinner is laid up for the just (Prov. 13:22b).[14]

C. Imitation

Point three: ethics. Success should have imitators. This imitation process is always limited by *ceteris paribus*: "other things remaining equal."

---

11. North, *Sovereignty & Dominion*, ch. 18.

12. Edward Banfield, *The Unheavenly City Revisited* (Boston: Little, Brown, 1974), 57–59.

13. The historic premillennialist believes in a future "great tribulation," which will immediately precede Christ's bodily return. The non-postribulational dispensational premillennialist believes that the church will be raptured out of history before the great tribulation, but Christian capital will be destroyed during this tribulation period.

14. Gary North, *Wisdom & Dominion: An Economic Commentary on Proverbs* (Moulton, Alabama: Axehead Press, [2012] 2029), ch. 41.

When covenant-breakers grow weary of copying successes that are based on adherence to biblical law and its implications, they eventually rebel. They refuse to continue to imitate covenant-keepers. They cannot tolerate their increasing conformity to the terms of biblical law. This resentment is the basis of the final rebellion of Satan at the end of history.[15] He rebels against the success of God's kingdom, not its failure.

The covenantal rivalry between the kingdom of God and the kingdom of man leads to disagreements over what practices should be imitated. The two kingdoms have rival views of God, man, law, sanctions, and the future. They have different views of historical causation. So, the more consistent that people are with their worldview, the more different will be their interpretation of the evidence. As Christian philosopher Cornelius Van Til taught, there are no brute facts. There are only interpreted facts. The question arises: "Which successes will be imitated by members of each kingdom?" This in turn raises a series of questions. How will historical causation be interpreted? What if the social benefits that Christianity associates with one set of ethical rules are no longer recognized by covenant-breakers as the result of these rules? What if there is widespread abandonment of these rules in a society? What if the corporate negative consequences of this abandonment are not blamed by most people on the abandonment of the previously dominant ethical system? What if these negative consequences are explained as outcomes of Christianity? What if humanistic social theorists and representatives of the policy-making groups identify as the sources of the negative consequences what are in fact the sources of the positive consequences and also barriers against the negative consequences? What if men call good evil, and call evil good? The Bible speaks of such a situation. It calls for an ethical transformation of such a society. It calls for redemption. "No longer will the fool be called noble, Or the rogue be spoken of as generous. For a fool speaks nonsense, And his heart inclines toward wickedness: To practice ungodliness and to speak error against the LORD, To keep the hungry person unsatisfied And to withhold drink from the thirsty. As for a rogue, his weapons are evil; He devises wicked schemes To destroy the poor with slander, Even though the needy one speaks what is right" (Isa. 32:5–7).

---

15. Gary North, *Dominion and Common Grace: The Biblical Basis of Progress* (Moulton, Alabama: Axehead Press, [1987] 2024), ch. 9.

The foundations of capitalism are based on biblical ethical and judicial norms. Whenever and wherever private property is upheld by custom and civil law, capitalism can and will flourish. If future-orientation becomes widespread, an outlook that is the result of optimism concerning history, then the rate of investment will increase. If a rejection of envy is widely adopted, then cooperation across economic classes will increase. If taxes remain lower than Samuel's warning figure of 10% (I Sam. 8:14, 17),[16] economic growth will be maintained. If wealth gained through entrepreneurship is upheld by the people who influence public opinion, there will be economic growth. Societies can adopt the fruits of a biblical worldview, but without adopting Christianity. Conversely, Christian societies have adopted non-Christian attitudes toward time and wealth. Fertility rates have then declined.

D. Entrepreneurship

Point four: sanctions. Entrepreneurship is the art of forecasting the future in terms of a set of subjective and objective goals, and then organizing production to meet these goals at the lowest cost. It is inherently future-oriented. This is mostly an aspect of planning: point two. But it is also a matter of feedback: sanctions. They cannot be separated. This is why point two and point four are tightly connected.

In the free market, the primary sanctions are monetary profit and loss. These are objective criteria. Prices are set by competitive bidding: buyers vs. buyers, sellers vs. sellers. This is not the case in the church covenant. There is no competition among buyers. Access to the worship services and to church membership is open to all comers. There is competition among sellers. They compete for visitors. But this competition is not monetary. There can be competition in terms of physical facilities, such as family life centers, i.e., free gymnasiums for members. Large Southern Baptist congregations are famous for these centers. There can be competition through advertising. But usually there is neither.

Elders must look to the future. There is such a thing as ecclesiastical

16. Gary North, *Disobedience & Defeat: An Economic Commentary on the Historical Books* (Moulton, Alabama: Axehead Press, [2012] 2029), ch. 14.

entrepreneurship. This is called missions. The Great Commission is the church's mission (point one). There must be a plan to implement this mission (point two). The plan must be based on Bible-revealed ethical standards (point three). It rests on a concept of cause and effect (point four). It has a theory of sanctions: positive and negative (point four). It looks to the future: short run and long run (point five).

The entrepreneur must devise a plan. This involves the allocation of resources. Long-term entrepreneurship is different from short-term entrepreneurship. Elders may imagine the capital value of the local congregation several generations in the future, but this is rare. The unknown factors are too great. Elders have no control over the confession of faith of each succeeding generation. They know that the their ability to establish institutional means of preserving wealth is limited. Because conditions change, and because people's responses to these changing conditions also change, it is close to impossible to specify in advance how church capital should be used. Any general principles of resource allocation will become subject to debate among heirs.

Elders know this much: if the church grows, donations will increase. Increased donations are a nearly universal goal for church leaders. Money is the most marketable commodity. Extra money can be used for increases in pastoral salaries. It can be used for advertising, or building a larger sanctuary, or buying a larger church in a better location. So, even though the church is not a profit-seeking institution, elders focus on money. They want more money coming in each week than goes out. They want to expand the church's influence, not shrink it. This is what the Great Commission requires.

E. Accumulation

Point five: succession. Adam and Eve began their joint task of dominion after their ejection from the garden. There is no record or even hint of any activity in between day six, meaning their half-day one, and the fall. Their biological heirs extended man's dominion. Population grew. Wealth grew. Men learned. They developed tools. This expansion was now a covenantally competitive effort: *the kingdom of God vs. the* *kingdom of autonomous man*. Both kingdoms benefitted from economic expansion, but their competition was zero-sum with respect to saved vs. lost. This remains true. Every soul won to God is a soul lost to Satan. The default setting for mankind is covenant-breaking. This is the covenantal effect of original sin. This is Adam's grim inheritance to his heirs.

God's mission for the church is for the church to oversee the training of covenant-keepers to achieve this goal: *the progressive disinheritance of Satan in history*. Each of Christianity's three major eschatological theories has its own explanation of how this will or will not be done.

The Great Commission requires capital. The increase in church capital in the narrow sense—tools of production—is not the same as it is for individuals' capital. The difference is this. An individual can benefit from any expansion of personal capital by increasing his consumption. Paid officers in a church can get raises, but they do not benefit directly from an expansion of the church's capital. They do not have ownership claims on the church's capital. They allocate it, but not to themselves. They control it only as economic stewards.

The church's time perspective should be long-term. The ordained representative of a church is supposed to act on behalf of future generations. While he can know little of what future generations will require, he can make some guesses. In contrast, personal capital is easier to manage, for its value need be increased in only one lifetime. An individual specializes in dealing with the trials and tribulations of his time period and geography. This specialization enables him to make better allocation decisions. But inter-generational forecasting of future capital value is an exercise in futility. If men cannot intelligently impute economic value to future capital, due to their lack of specialized knowledge about future economic conditions, then the accumulation of capital for wealth transfer mandates the use of guardians. The capital must be transferred to guardians. This is what ordination helps to establish. So do training programs. For capital to multiply over generations, the heirs must be trained in the principles of wealth-creation in the broadest sense. They also must accept this vision, and then have the foresight and competence to implement it.

This involves a confession of faith of some kind. This raises a problem. In most Christian churches, there is no self-conscious link between theological confession and wealth accumulation. If anything, this link is rejected on the basis of a rejection of worldliness. Within certain subcultures there is a link. Among Jews and Armenians, there is at least a cultural link. Their theological confessions have not been maintained in the post-1800 world. We sometimes see this connection in small business cultures. Again, Jews and Armenians are examples. But those Jews who have become enormously wealthy have not generally maintained the theological confession of Orthodox Judaism.

Churches are not effective instruments for the creation of inter-generational wealth. Corporations are. Corporations have only one major goal: to make a profit. All other goals are eventually sacrificed to the goal of profit. A firm may begin with a mission statement, but a century later, that mission statement will be a museum piece. A church whose mission statement becomes a museum piece is doomed. It may cease to be a church.

Conclusion

As an institution, the church can either add value or reduce it. Because a church is covenantally established by public oath as an agency in the kingdom of God, it adds value by extending the kingdom through productivity. It does this through biological multiplication of its members and by evangelism. The church also does this by educating children in church dogma: a way to extend the worldview of the covenant.

Conclusion to Part IV

The church is established by an oath. To this oath are attached sanctions: positive and negative.

The church as an institution has a future beyond the end of time. It must maintain its old confessions, but it must adjust to new responsibilities. Any adult can renounce the confession, defy it, or ignore it. Over time, some congregations depart from the confession. Others maintain parts of the confession—possibly most of it. There must be progressive sanctification for church confessions. History progresses. Church confessions must reflect this.[1]

An elder is a judicial agent: a guardian. He acts in the name of God to church members, and in the name of church members to God. This is hierarchical-judicial. There is also economic stewardship: the tithe. This is hierarchical. Finally, there is the service function: service to non-church members. This can also be a charitable function. It is horizontal. It looks outward.

The church is a judicial unit. Responsibility in the church is to a corporate entity. Thus, methodological individualism does not apply well to the church. The church is more than the participants. God holds it responsible. Wealth and poverty apply to the church. All economic approaches that rely on methodological individualism as the sole tool of explanation founder on family, church, and state.

The time horizon of a church should be long. The church extends judicially in time. In contrast, people die.

1. Example: no church confession declares the legal sanctity of unborn children. In the modern world, where abortion is legal, this is an intolerable omission. It promotes murder without remorse.

Because elders must make decisions on behalf of church members, they must make interpersonal comparisons of subjective utility. They must "balance" or "weigh" the goals and aspirations of multiple members. They must also make estimates regarding God's assessment of these aspirations. So, in order to make accurate assessments of multiple subjective valuations, elders must rely on their ability to assess God's assessments. They act as God's fiduciary agents in his allocation of church capital. But they also act as God's church's fiduciary agents with baptized members and with the world outside. There are multiple acts of economic imputation.

This must be done without reference to church-generated money prices, for there are none. The church is an agency that implements the division of labor. But this is not marked by a money economy internally. This division of labor is far more personal than impersonal. Money is geared to voluntary exchange, so most services performed in a church cannot be outsourced.

In a covenantal unit, pricing is not based on product substitution. So, the logic of exchange that applies to a free market does not apply in a covenantal unit. There is no substitution allowed by law. This is why that which Mises called catallactics is highly limited. This is why he never attempted to apply the science of human action outside the market.

A church is supposed to add value. So is an individual. This is the ethical basis of compound economic growth. *The extension of a church's influence is by means of capital accumulation.* But the law of large numbers reasserts itself over time. No church seems to be able to increase per capita wealth of its members over generations. The performance of the members, especially heads of households, reverts to the mean. Confessions historically have also reverted to the mean in terms of enforcement. The more influential that specific churches are in extending God's kingdom, the more their performance has reverted to the mean. The solution has been the creation of new congregations and denominations. This is a form of market-testing. Ultimately, individuals are responsible on judgment day. Individuals decide what they are willing to believe. They choose where to belong as church members. There is a form of customer authority in church membership. Churches may choose to ignore this, but they will not grow. That is the cost of maintaining original orthodoxy. The church grows rigid. It no longer deals authoritatively with the fundamental challenges of each new generation. The art of casuistry fades: applying the Bible, the creeds, and the confessions to specific cases.

There is always a need for more reform. In a world of sin, things always need more sanctification. This is the meaning of progressive sanctification.[2] What is the proper motivation for church reform? The extension of the kingdom of God in history. Are there positive sanctions associated with this? Yes. Church growth is the main one. But there is also the extension of the kingdom by means of enforcing God's Bible-revealed law.

> "See, I have taught you statutes and judgments just as the LORD my God commanded me, that you are to do these things in the land where you are entering to take possession of it. So keep and do them, for that is your wisdom and your understanding in the sight of the peoples who will hear all these statutes and say, 'Surely this great nation is a wise and understanding people.' For what great nation is there that has a god so near to it as is the LORD our God whenever we call on Him? Or what great nation is there that has statutes and judgments as righteous as this whole Law which I am setting before you today?" (Deut. 4:5–8)[3]

> "Only be careful for yourself and watch over your soul diligently, so that you do not forget the things which your eyes have seen and they do not depart from your heart all the days of your life; but make them known to your sons and your grandsons. Remember the day you stood before the LORD your God at Horeb, when the LORD said to me, 'Assemble the people to Me, that I may have them hear My words so that they may learn to fear Me all the days that they live on the earth, and that they may teach their children.'" (Deut. 4:9–10)[4]

The system of church authority is bottom-up: monetary and judicial. Funding is through donations. Judicial authority is through voting for

2. John Murray, "Progressive Sanctification," *Collected Works of John Murray* (Edinburgh: Banner of Truth, 1982), II, ch. 23.

3. Gary North, *Inheritance & Dominion: An Economic Commentary on Deuteronomy* (Moulton, Alabama: Axehead Press, [1999, 2012] 2028), ch. 8.

4. Ibid., ch. 9.

church officers in Protestant churches without bishops. This transfer of money and authority places church officers in control of financial allocations and church discipline. The market's principle does not apply: high monetary bid wins. Officers must guide the churches in terms of vision and forecasting. This is the task of covenantal leadership.

PART V

The Economic Structure of the Civil Covenant

Introduction to Part V

A. You Cannot Sell Your Citizenship

No democratic or republican civil government allows citizens to sell their citizenship or their votes. There is no organized market for either citizenship or votes. We see the same principle in votes on juries. It is illegal to sell your vote on a jury.

The free market acknowledges no such principle. If someone can gain more money, he can buy more of whatever is offered for sale. He can offer more money than a poorer customer can offer. High monetary bid wins. In civil affairs, the principle of competition is this: *high electoral bids win*. Groups of citizens cooperate in order to elect a representative. Each citizen is allowed one vote. This is the principle of individual equality. But, corporately speaking, inequality is the ruling principle. Elections are not based on the principle of equality of outcomes.

The principle of ownership is radically different from the free market's principle. There is no property right regarding citizenship. Citizenship is inalienable. It cannot be disowned. It cannot be transferred. It can be surrendered. It can be removed by civil magistrates. Convicted felons in the United States do not have the right to vote.

The state is not a profit-seeking entity. It is a ministry of justice (Rom. 13:1–7). It has the God-delegated authority to impose negative physical sanctions. The free market does not. The church does not.

The concept of one man, one vote came out of the Protestant Reformation. Luther preached this principle: every man a priest. During the Congregational-Presbyterian revolt in England, 1642–1659, this principle began to be extended from the church to the state. The revolutionaries were opposed to the top-down control by bishops of the state church of England. They wanted local control over their churches: voting by members. At the exactly same time in New England, Puritan Congregationalists extended this voting principle to civil government. It took hold in America's Northern colonies and Canada in the eighteenth century. It was adopted in Western Europe in the immediate aftermath of World War I, beginning in 1919.

As a covenant, the state has the equivalent of the church's sacrament of the Lord's Supper: voting. Voting, as with the Lord's Supper, is an act of covenant renewal. This concept of voting as the judicial equivalent of a sacrament comes from Protestant church government. The vote imposes political sanctions. This is an aspect of point four of the covenant: *covenant renewal*. This is also the basis of *judicial continuity*: point five. The judicial principle is this: those who are under state sanctions have the legitimate authority to determine who will hold office and impose civil sanctions. Every covenant is oath-bound. There is a civil oath of allegiance. This oath is presumed to have been taken by the adult children of citizens. It is taken publicly by naturalized citizens. There is no open entry into citizenship. The state has the right to exclude those who do not meet confessional standards. *Inclusion implies exclusion*. This applies to citizenship.

Chapter 21

Ownership

Every person is to be subject to the governing authorities. For there is no authority except from God, and those which exist are established by God. Therefore whoever resists authority has opposed the ordinance of God; and they who have opposed will receive condemnation upon themselves. For rulers are not a cause of fear for good behavior, but for evil. Do you want to have no fear of authority? Do what is good and you will have praise from the same; for it is a servant of God to you for good. But if you do what is evil, be afraid; for it does not bear the sword for nothing; for it is a servant of God, an avenger who brings wrath on the one who practices evil. Therefore it is necessary to be in subjection, not only because of wrath, but also for the sake of conscience. For because of this you also pay taxes, for rulers are servants of God, devoting themselves to this very thing. Pay to all what is due them: tax to whom tax is due; custom to whom custom; respect to whom respect; honor to whom honor.

Romans 13:1–7

Analysis

Point one of the biblical covenant is the transcendence of God, yet also His presence with the creation.[1]

1. Transcendence/presence is point one of the biblical covenant. Ray R. Sutton, *That You May Prosper: Dominion By Covenant*, 2nd ed. (Tyler, Texas: Institute for Christian Economics, [1987] 1992), ch. 1.

The state is exclusively confined to the era of sin. There will be no need for the state beyond the final judgment. The state is an agency of coercion. It is not an option in society. It exists in every society. It is an inescapable concept in the era of sin. God created it to serve His purposes. The primary purpose is to restrain specified public sins.

There is no market process that governs the state. There is no open entry. It is a closed system. It is close to a monopoly within its geographical jurisdiction. It shares jurisdiction with local civil governments. So, the principles of ownership apply to the state in very different ways from those that apply to the individual, the family, and the church. The state does not operate in terms of "monetary high bid wins." It also does not operate in terms of personalism, unlike the family and the church, except in cases where men's lives are at risk: military and police. In these cases, a form of brotherhood exists: insiders vs. outsiders. This has to do with formal oaths of allegiance to the state.

A. Power

Point one: God's sovereignty. God owns the state corporately. He also owns the state through His control over its officers.

> "But I will harden Pharaoh's heart, so that I may multiply My signs and My wonders in the land of Egypt. When Pharaoh does not listen to you, I will lay My hand on Egypt and bring out My armies, My people the sons of Israel, from the land of Egypt by great judgments." (Ex. 7:3–4)

> The king's heart is like channels of water in the hand of the LORD;
> He turns it wherever He pleases.
> (Prov. 21:1)

> This is what the LORD says to Cyrus His anointed,
> Whom I have taken by the right hand,
> To subdue nations before him
> And to undo the weapons belt on the waist of kings;
> To open doors before him so that gates will not be shut:
> "I will go before you and make the rough places smooth;
> I will shatter the doors of bronze and cut through their iron bars.

> I will give you the treasures of darkness
> And hidden wealth of secret places,
> So that you may know that it is I,
> The LORD, the God of Israel, who calls you by your name."
> (Isa. 45:1–3)

> For He says to Moses, "I will have mercy on whomever I have mercy, and I will show compassion to whomever I show compassion." So then, it does not depend on the person who wants it nor the one who runs, but on God who has mercy. For the Scripture says to Pharaoh, "For this very reason I raised you up, in order to demonstrate My power in you, and that My name might be proclaimed throughout the earth." So then He has mercy on whom He desires, and He hardens whom He desires. You will say to me then, "Why does He still find fault? For who has resisted His will?" On the contrary, who are you, you foolish person, who answers back to God? The thing molded will not say to the molder, "Why did you make me like this," will it? Or does the potter not have a right over the clay, to make from the same lump one object for honorable use, and another for common use? (Rom. 9:15–21)

It could not be any clearer. God owns the state. God owns the representatives of the state. He is in charge. He answers to no one.

B. Planning

Point two: hierarchy. As with economic planning in the family and the church, state planning mandates central planning. Because these three covenants are not governed by the auction's principles of *open entry* and *monetary high bid wins*, there must be a chain of command based on top-down planning by a designated legal agent. He possesses ownership of the office. He therefore possesses the authority to buy and sell assets as a representative of the covenant members under his jurisdiction. Ownership is point one of the biblical covenant with respect to God. For man, delegated ownership is point two: stewardship.

State officials are responsible for the maintenance of civil order. They possess authority over residents and citizens. This rule of law always applies: *where there is authority, there is also responsibility*. Individuals must give an account to God for their stewardship: final judgment (Matt. 25). This involves giving an account of themselves for their joint authority as members of civil jurisdictions. No one is autonomous. Every individual answers to God.

A state owns property. It owns real estate. It owns weapons. It owns highways. The extent of state ownership in the twenty-first century is too enormous to list. No one knows all that the United States government owns. Its land holdings have been immense ever since the ratification of the Constitution.[2]

State officials are involved in constant plan reconciliation. In a state, negotiations must be minimized in order to achieve peace. Plans are far more fundamental in states than in businesses. The reconciliations are far more permanent. The stakes are far higher: life and death.

The judicial bond of citizenship is the result of plan reconciliation. Planning has to do with allocation of scarce resources. It therefore is based on ownership. God owns everything. He delegates control over assets to individuals. But He also delegates control to collectives. The idea of joint ownership is inherent in the biblical doctrine of the state.

Exchange arrangements within a state are not based on "monetary high bid wins." *Justice trumps profit.* Authority is not based on the purchase of an office. *The planning arrangement reflects the hierarchical structure of dominion.* God rules through states. His transfer of ownership to states is His way to maximize His return. But this return is not primarily monetary. It is the suppression of certain kinds of evil acts.

Families are small. They are governed by love. Churches are also small, although larger than families. They also are to be governed by love. Both institutions are marked by personal relationships. Central planning is limited in range. This is not true of the state. States are sometimes huge. Without explicit constitutional limitations, the state can claim the need to impose comprehensive planning. This planning

2. Here are estimates in the states with the greatest percentages of federal land. Nevada, 84.5%; Alaska, 69.1%; Utah, 57.4%; Oregon, 53.1%; Idaho, 50.2%; Arizona, 48.1%; California, 45.3%; Wyoming, 42.3%; New Mexico, 41.8%; Colorado, 36.6%. The huge exception is Texas. Texas came into the Union in 1845 as a separate nation. The federal government owns 1.9% of Texas. These figures, plus an informative U.S. map, are found on the *Strange Maps* site: Frank Jacobs, "Just How Much Land Does the Federal Government Own—and Why?," *Big Think*, July 23, 2010, bigthink.com/strange-maps/291-federal-lands-in-the-us.

is not based on love. It is based on numerical criteria: meeting written rules. To limit the power of state officials, the rules must control their access to the state's money. The money must go only for authorized purposes. Therefore, state agencies are on fixed budgets. The legislature is in control of resource allocation. This means that the system of economic planning is inherently bureaucratic: politics at the top, with executive agencies implementing laws. Bureaucratic management is fundamentally different from profit management. Because the systems of financing are different, the procedural structures are different.[3] This was Ludwig von Mises' profound insight in his little book, *Bureaucracy* (1944).[4]

States cannot escape these obligations to plan, any more than families and churches can. But states are under an additional set of restraints. They are part of a larger covenantal association. The state has a ministerial function (Rom. 13:4). Because of the monopolistic power of the state to coerce, it must be placed under strict limits by law. If this is not done, states will expand their jurisdictions at the expense of people's liberties.

C. Boundaries

Point three: ethics. Ethics is related to law, which establishes boundaries. The primary boundaries of civil government are geographical. These are jurisdictional boundaries. Other states announce "no trespassing." These geographical boundaries include, but they also exclude. The archetype on this exclusion aspect is the tree of the knowledge of good and evil. God definitively excluded mankind from this tree. Geographical boundaries are easily understood and can be enforced technologically. The general boundary of a state reduces the authority of outside agencies to intervene to settle disputes. This is usually identified as an aspect of sovereignty. State sovereignty is by far the most widely

3. Gary North, "Statist Bureaucracy in the Modern Economy," *The Freeman* (Jan 1970). Reprinted in North, *An Introduction to Christian Economics* (Moulton, Alabama: Axehead Press, [1973] 2025), ch. 20.

4. Ludwig von Mises, *Bureaucracy* (New Haven, Connecticut: Yale University Press, 1944).

accepted version of sovereignty in the modern era. Boundaries and state sovereignty are intimately related in modern social theory.

Geographical boundaries reveal an inescapable aspect of civil government. The state uses a zero-sum system of allocating authority. What do I mean, "zero-sum"? When a national government expands its jurisdiction geographically, it does so at the expense of another national government. Shared jurisdictions are rare. They do not survive long. One nation asserts final sovereignty. It says that it is the final court of appeal. It is easy to understand this aspect of political boundaries. The principle governs all of civil government.

Inside a nation, there are overlapping jurisdictions, but the system is hierarchical. It is an appeals court system. The tendency is for the central government to usurp regional governments. Some court declares final jurisdiction. This used to be called the divine right of kings: no appeal to anything above the king. But there was always a final earthly sovereign: the people. They could revolt. Of course, it was not "the people." It was some group of people whose spokesmen announced the revolt in the name of some higher sovereignty than the king. In seventeenth-century England, this happened twice: 1642–1649 (Civil War) and 1688 (Glorious Revolution). The symbol of the transfer of sovereignty in the Civil War took place in 1649: the decapitation of the king. Parliament literally cut off the top of the government. This happened again in the French Revolution in 1793. These were zero-sum transfers of power from the executive to the legislature.

The division of labor within a state involves boundaries of responsibility—jurisdictions. There are competing jurisdictions on a scale not fully understood. Rival agencies declare authority over acts and places. The complexity of these rival claims dwarfs the complexity of medieval feudalism. Medieval feudalism had highly personal loyalties and responsibilities. Modern jurisdictions overlap administratively. Legally, there is no personal loyalty. Operationally, there is. We call these agencies fiefdoms, which acknowledges their feudal-like nature. Because of this administrative complexity, hierarchy becomes more important in plan reconciliation in state matters than in family matters or church matters. In churches and families, personal authority counts for far more than in state matters. In state matters, someone with greater written authority establishes the standards of responsible performance. Voluntary plan reconciliation is replaced by orders from above.

The state's officers have very limited initiating authority, according to biblical law. This means that they have very little initiating responsibility. *With reduced authority comes reduced responsibility.* But modern political theory does not acknowledge the legitimacy of Bible-based concepts of "sphere sovereignty," meaning sphere authority.

Inherently, the nature of state authority is impersonal. The participants are not usually known to each other. Boundaries within the state are judicial. People learn which boundaries not to violate in a state. But these boundaries are far more problematical than the boundaries imposed by price. Negotiations are based more on lawyers than price. Thus, the outcome of these negotiations is less predictable. *The complexity of negotiations makes the outcome less predictable.*

Civil rulers seek their goals, just as people in a market do. They are self-interested. But they are only rarely money-seekers. They are power-seekers. They use state power to extend their personal agendas. They have a vision of what a good society should be. This is why it is wrong-headed to argue that the self-interest in civil government is driven primarily by personal economic gain. Such a hypothesis will lead to misleading analyses of how the state functions. The desire to play God is rarely if ever economically driven. The state is about power.

Bureaucratic functionaries are promoted in terms of how many employees are under them. This creates a relentless demand within state agencies to expand the agencies' jurisdiction. This phenomenon is called mission creep. It is universal in civil government.

Economists cannot easily pretend to provide meaningful equations to describe state boundaries. They can and do pretend to provide meaningful equations regarding price relationships. The illusion of scientific precision is more easily adopted with respect to objective prices in open markets than with subjectively interpreted judicial boundaries inside states. A subdivision of economics, called *public choice theory,* is an attempt to apply the principle of personally self-interest to the civil government. These attempts have had limited success. The main problem is this: these categories cannot deal with altruism: the desire to reform people "for their own good." This is a powerful impulse. To apply to the reformers the categories of personal self-interest in a monetary or career framework is to ignore too much of their psychological makeup. But three generations after the reforms, the motivation of occupational self-interest applies far more effectively to the bureaucracies that were founded by the reformers. This may take only two generations.

People are committed to civil solidarity far more than they are committed to market solidarity. They defend their nations from intervention by foreign officials. This is why nations go to war.

D. Justice

Point four: sanctions. The state is God's agency of physical sanctions. It arrests, tries, and sentences criminals. Then it applies negative sanctions

The biblical system of civil sanctions does not include positive sanctions, except in cases of theft and negligence. The convicted criminal is requited to make a multiple restitution payment to his victim. "If someone steals an ox or a sheep and slaughters it or sells it, he shall pay five oxen for the ox and four sheep for the sheep" (Ex. 22:1). Verses 4–12 deal with other cases of theft and negligence.[5] The state does not fund this re-distribution of wealth. The criminal does. There was a specified restitution payment: usually double the value of whatever was destroyed. The criminal did not pay more if he was rich. He could not escape the same penalty if he was poor. If he was too poor to repay his victim, he was sold into slavery. The victim collected the sale price, up to the limit owed. "A thief shall certainly make restitution; if he owns nothing, then he shall be sold for his theft" (Ex. 22:3b).

A general principle of biblical law is the rule of law. "The same law shall apply to the native as to the stranger who resides among you" (Ex. 12:49).[6] With respect to cases that come berore a civil court, there must be no respect for persons. "You shall not do injustice in judgment; you shall not show partiality to the poor nor give preference to the great, but

5. Gary North, *Authority & Dominion: An Economic Commentary on Exodus*, vols. 3–4, *Part III: Tools of Dominion* (Moulton, Alabama: Axehead Press, [1990, 2012] 2025), chaps. 43–46.

6. Ibid., ch. 14.

you are to judge your neighbor fairly" (Lev. 19:15).[7] This is a principle of civil justice. This principle bans the graduated income tax, which forces high-income taxpayers to pay a larger percentage of their income than poorer people. In the United states, half of taxpayers pay no income tax. This is a flagrant violation of Leviticus 19:15. Defenders of the so-called social gospel refuse to comment of this verse. They implicitly deny that it is still binding on the state. They adopt this version of the eighth commandment: "Thou shalt not steal, except by majority vote." *The graduated income tax is a violation of the rule of law.*

There are no cases in the Bible of state-enforced redistribution of income from one income group to another. *Wherever biblical law is enforced there can be no welfare state.* This is denied by defenders of the social gospel. When I debated three of them in 1984, not one of them responded to my assertion. All three had an opportunity to respond. I began my essay by citing Leviticus 19:15. Later, I wrote:

> The Bible instructs a nation's rulers not to respect persons when administering justice (Deuteronomy 1:17). Both the rich man and the poor man, the homeborn and the stranger, are to be ruled by the same law (Exodus 12:49). Biblical law is a form of God's grace to mankind; it is to be dispensed to all without prejudice. This is the implication of Leviticus 19:15, which introduced this chapter. The predictability of the judicial system is what God requires of those in positions of authority.[8]
>
> The Bible says, "Thou shalt not steal." It does not say, "Thou shalt not steal, except by majority vote." A society which begins to adopt taxation policies that exceed the tithe—ten per cent of income—thereby increases economic uncertainty, as do other types of theft, both public and private. This increase in uncertainty may be even more disrupting, statistically, than losses from burglary or robbery, because private insurance companies can insure against burglary and robbery. After all, who can trust a civil government which claims the right to take more of a person's income than God requires for the support of his kingdom? What kind of protection from injustice can we expect from such a civil government? The next wave of politically imposed wealth redistribution

---

7. Gary North, *Boundaries & Dominion: An Economic Commentary on Leviticus* (Moulton, Alabama: Axehead Press, [1994, 2012] 2026), ch. 14.

8. Gary North, "Free Market Capitalism," in *Wealth and Poverty: Four Views on Economics*, ed. Robert G. Clouse (Downers Grove, Illinois: InterVarsity Press, 1984), 37.

> is always difficult to predict, and therefore difficult to prepare for, so the costs of production increase.[9]

One year later, the Christian evangelical publisher ceased selling the book, despite the fact that it was selling well. The authors received royalty payments. I had my Institute for Christian Economics buy all of the remaining copies at 25 cents each. I used them as premiums to reward donors to the ICE.

The hostility of the academic evangelical community to biblical law is intense. One of the authors, a Keynesian, responded contemptuously:

> That the author is strong on "biblical law" is apparent. The essay provides us with thirty-nine Old Testament citations, of which twenty-three are from the book of Deuteronomy. Alongside these imposing Old Testament references the reader is given only nine New Testament citations, of which only four come from the mouth of Jesus. Notwithstanding one of North's concluding statements that we need "faith in Jesus Christ," this essay might more properly be entitled "Poverty and Wealth according to Deuteronomy." The teachings and parables of Jesus are rich with references to wealth, poverty and justice. Why has the author chosen to ignore these? Can it be that the words of the Master are an embarrassment to the advocates of a free-market system?[10]

He put the words biblical law in quotation marks, as if there were no such thing as biblical law. Virtually all evangelical academics wish that this were true, but it isn't. Biblical law established judicial principles that make the humanist welfare state impossible. Evangelical academic have baptized the welfare state with platitudes.

E. Stability

Point five: succession. The state exists in order to provide residents and citizens with stability. Men fear violence and theft. The state is designed by God to suppress both. The state also defends its territory from invasion. Every nation has a defense program to provide safety.

---

9. Ibid., 41.
10. Ibid., 67.

Then there is the threat of domestic revolution. Every states has agencies to reduce the likelihood of revolution. But revolutions occur occasionally in the face of tyranny. The most famous revolution in the Bible is Jeroboam's revolt against King Rehoboam, Solomon's son. He listened to bad counsel and increased taxes. Ten of the 12 tribes revolted successfully (I Kings 12). Israel was never again united under a Hebrew king.

All of this has to do with stability. The essence of stability is peace. Peace is one of the most familiar goals of mankind. The Bible speaks of it often.

> "The LORD bless you, and keep you;
> The LORD cause His face to shine on you,
> And be gracious to you;
> The LORD lift up His face to you,
> And give you peace."
> (Num. 6:24–26)

> Turn from evil and do good;
> Seek peace and pursue it.
> (Ps. 34:14)

> "Stop striving and know that I am God;
> I will be exalted among the nations, I will be exalted on the earth."
> (Ps. 46:10)

> Those who love Your Law have great peace,
> And nothing causes them to stumble.
> (Ps. 119:165).

> How delightful on the mountains
> Are the feet of one who brings good news,
> Who announces peace
> And brings good news of happiness,
> Who announces salvation,
> And says to Zion, "Your God reigns!"
> (Isa. 52:7)

> First of all, then, I urge that requests, prayers, intercession, and thanksgiving be made in behalf of all people, for kings and all who are in authority, so that we may lead a tranquil and quiet life in all godliness and dignity. (I Tim. 2:1–2)

A nation-state that predictably upholds justice, refrains from taxation above 10%, imposes a flat income tax, and leaves men free to pursue their goals, start enterprises, accumulate capital and consumer goods, and leave an inheritance to their children will not suffer a violent revolution. It will preserve the peace. This is a state that is under judicial restraints imposed by a constitution, a system of courts, and regular elections in which voters can replace incumbent politicians. It will gain continuity through time. It will be like Switzerland.

Conclusion

God created the state after the fall. He therefore owns it. He exercises control over it. The state's God-assigned task is to reduce specified evil acts by means of negative sanctions. The state is God's representative. It has power that reflects God's power. The model of this power is the day of final judgment (Matt. 25; Rev. 20:14–15).

God sits on a throne. "Your throne, God, is forever and ever; The scepter of Your kingdom is a scepter of justice" (Ps. 45:6). This throne is a symbol of power. So is the scepter. God is the supreme judge in the final court of appeal. Covenant-keepers can appeal to God to intervene and deliver them, just as the Hebrews did in Egypt's bondage.

The political doctrine known as the divine right of kings was an assertion of man's autonomy and state sovereignty. It was anti-biblical. The king who proclaimed it most vehemently, James I of Great Britain (1603–1625), was succeeded by his son Charles I, who ended his days on a scaffold in 1649. The Puritan Revolution and Civil War (1642–1649) demonstrated that he and his father had been incorrect about the divine right of kings. The old doctrine was not restored in 1660 when Charles I's son Charles II returned to the throne. The term "divine right" refers to the absence of any court of appeal higher than the state. When it is defended by the state, it produces tyranny. It is the doctrine of the autonomy of the state. There is no autonomy in the creation. God exercises ultimate power. The state that proclaims its divine right is messianic.

Chapter 22

Stewardship

And He said to them, "Whose image and inscription is this?" They said to Him, "Caesar's." Then He said to them, "Then pay to Caesar the things that are Caesar's; and to God the things that are God's."

Matthew 22:20–21

Analysis

Point two of the biblical covenant is hierarchy/authority.[1] Within a civil government, the auction's principle of "monetary high bid wins" does not operate, at least not legally. Power is not officially available to someone who bids the most money. The bids are in terms of individual characteristics, assignments, and responsibilities. The decision-makers, meaning the politicians, make the allocation of scarce resources. As representative agents of the voters, they make these allocation decisions officially on behalf of all of the citizenry. They guess as to costs and benefits of legislation to those under their authority. In other words, they make interpersonal comparisons of subjective utilities.

As with individual stewardship, there are three aspects of civil stewardship: guardianship (legal), taxation (economic), and auctioneering (economic). First, the magistrates act as legal representative agents.

1. Ray R. Sutton, *That You May Prosper: Dominion By Covenant*, 2nd ed. (Tyler, Texas: Institute for Christian Economics, [1987] 1992), ch. 2.

They represent God to the citizens, and they represent citizens to God. *Representation is mediatorial and hierarchical. State representation is corporate*. Second, the state collects taxes. Citizens and businesses owe taxes to the state, which represents God to them. There is a third aspect of stewardship: allocational. This has to do with the decision to put a resource to work on behalf of other people. This is a horizontal relationship. In a free market, it is the role of the auctioneer. He acts on behalf of the legal owner in his quest for a new owner. The general principle of free market stewardship is this: "Monetary high bid wins." In civil government, "high bid wins" applies to voting: one citizen, one vote.

Votes function as the currency of the realm. Politicians seek votes at elections. Voters elect politicians based on how they expect an elected politician to vote. In contrast, someone in a free market surrenders money in exchange for a specific product. He takes it home or else uses it immediately. In contrast, a voter participates as part of a special-interest group. He expects an indirect payoff: an elected politician's voting that follows a predictable pattern. A voter may not get this, but he hopes that he will. The voter trades his vote for expected votes by the politician he elects. For political parties, the currency is votes.

A. Sovereignty

Point one: God's sovereignty. Point one of the biblical covenant is sovereignty.[2] God possesses absolute sovereignty. Yet He shares sovereignty through delegation. This was manifested in the original dominion covenant (Gen. 1:26–28).[3] This was re-confirmed with Noah (Gen. 9:1–3).[4] It was confirmed ontologically with the Incarnation, when God became a man. God clearly delegated sovereignty to man. In both cases, Adam and Noah, God was dealing with families.

Magistrates must deal with those under their legal authority through the state's system of courts. Politicians pass laws. Bureaucrats enforce these laws. Judges decide cases. This reflects God's activity as both king

2. Ibid. ch. 1.

3. Gary North, *Sovereignty & Dominion: An Economic Commentary on Genesis* (Moulton, Alabama: Axehead Press, [1982, 2012] 2022), chaps. 3, 4.

4. Ibid., ch. 18.

and judge. God declares laws. He enforces His laws indirectly and directly in history. He serves as a judge. He applies His law to specific historical cases. He administers justice.

God delegates sovereignty, but He does not surrender it. He does not lose control. What applies to men does not apply to God. *Sovereignty among men is a zero-sum arrangement.* A man gains authority at the expense of someone else. His jurisdiction expands at the expense of someone else. This is most obvious in the case of geographical boundaries. This does not apply to God. He was not less glorious before He created the world. The creation did not add anything of value to Him. He is autonomous. He is not dependent on the creation for anything. So, when He delegates sovereignty, He does not lose anything.

B. Representation

Point two: hierarchy. The magistrates have a responsibility before God to administer justice impartially. "You shall not do injustice in judgment; you shall not show partiality to the poor nor give preference to the great, but you are to judge your neighbor fairly" (Lev. 19:15). This law, when enforced, makes impossible both socialism and the welfare state.[5] Within the context of the tribal system of pre-exilic Israel, it decentralized civil government.[6] The focus of the law is on the neighbor. Local information is more accurate. It is less expensive to collect. Local habits are also better known. The application of biblical judicial principles to specific cases should begin locally. This is why Moses set up a decentralized, hierarchical system of courts (Ex. 18).[7]

State representation is vertical upward: representing the people to God. It is vertical downward: representing God to the people. It is temporal: representing people in the future. It is inward: representing the consciences of the magistrates. This has to do with judicial representation.

5. Gary North, *Boundaries & Dominion: An Economic Commentary on Leviticus* (Moulton, Alabama: Axehead Press, [1994, 2012] 2026), ch. 14.

6. Ibid., ch. 15.

7. Gary North, *Authority & Dominion: An Economic Commentary on Exodus*, vol. 1, *Part I: Representation & Dominion* (Moulton, Alabama: Axehead Press, [1985, 2012] 2025), ch. 19.

This is representation *in the name of*. This is guardianship. The same four-way system of representation governs economic representation: *on behalf of*. This is stewardship. This dual system of representation governs all five covenants: dominion, individual, family, church, and state.

Stewardship always involves economic planning. Economic planning is an extension of the practice of casuistry: the application of unchanging principles to changing historical circumstances. These are moral principles, according to the Bible. Humanistic economics denies this. It treats the unchanging principles as autonomous. It treats them as value-free. But it suffers from the dualism that afflicted Greek philosophy: there is no explainable point of contact between the unchanging logical principles (Parmenides) and historical flux (Heraclitus). In contrast, Christian economic theory attributes to image of God in men their ability to plan.

C. Lease

Point three: ethics. This is related to law. The economics of the lease is found in Chapter 11, "Stewardship," Section C.

To keep the state within bounds, so that citizens will not de-capitalize the social order by means of state power, there are biblical limits on the state. First and foremost is the principle of the rule of law. "The same law shall apply to the native as to the stranger who resides among you" (Ex. 12:49).[8] This involves the refusal to pass laws favoring one group of citizens against another. As part of this general principle is its application with respect to income. "You shall not do injustice in judgment; you shall not show partiality to the poor nor give preference to the great, but you are to judge your neighbor fairly" (Lev. 19:15). The economic principle of this rule denies the legitimacy of seeking to redistribute income through tax policy, especially the graduated income tax, which was universally adopted in the West in the twentieth century, beginning immediately before the outbreak of World War I in 1914. The graduated income tax violates the principle of the tithe: a flat rate of taxation for all citizens. Sales taxes honor this principle with respect

8. Ibid., ch. 14

to a flat rate. But all jurisdictions violate the principle of the tithe by exempting certain favored goods and services.

The next restriction on the state is the level of taxation allowed. The rate of taxation for all jurisdictions combined must not reach 10%. Samuel warned Israel about this.

> So Samuel spoke all the words of the LORD to the people who had asked him for a king. And he said, "This will be the practice of the king who will reign over you: he will take your sons and put them in his chariots for himself and among his horsemen, and they will run before his chariots. He will appoint for himself commanders of thousands and commanders of fifties, and some to do his plowing and to gather in his harvest, and to make his weapons of war and equipment for his chariots. He will also take your daughters and use them as perfumers, cooks, and bakers. He will take the best of your fields, your vineyards, and your olive groves, and give them to his servants. And he will take a tenth of your seed and your vineyards and give it to his high officials and his servants. He will also take your male servants and your female servants, and your best young men, and your donkeys, and use them for his work. He will take a tenth of your flocks, and you yourselves will become his servants. Then you will cry out on that day because of your king whom you have chosen for yourselves, but the LORD will not answer you on that day." (I Sam. 8:10–18)[9]

They did not listen. The nation of Israel split in the reign of King Rehoboam. He decided to hike taxes. Ten tribes revolted (I Kings 12).[10] Israel did not come together again until after the Babylonian captivity. The nation never ruled itself again. It was always under foreign kings.

It is a mark of moral depravity when any society does not cry out to God for deliverance from a system of taxes that extracts as much as a tithe: 10% of income. The modern world has been depraved in this regard for more than a century. This depravity has led to two world wars that could only have been financed by taxation at levels on average four or more times as high as the tithe. God imposed negative sanctions. There will be more before men repent and abide by the economic terms of God's lease for the civil covenant.

---

9. Gary North, *Disobedience & Defeat: An Economic Commentary on the Historical Books* (Moulton, Alabama: Axehead Press, [2012] 2029), ch. 14.

10. Ibid., ch. 20.

D. Feedback

Point four: sanctions. In economics, these are profits and losses. But the concept of profit and loss must extend beyond numbers in a ledger. It must include evidence of God's approval or disapproval. For the individual, the final judgment is the archetype of historical sanctions. The individual is singled out. So, the focus is on individual benefits. This is not true of the family and the state. The family and the state do not pass through the negative sanction of death into eternity. Then what is God's goal for the Christian state? *Maintaining the covenant.* This keeps the capital within the kingdom of God. The confession of faith is central. It is a matter of oath: point four of the biblical covenant.[11] The extension of the oath through time is judicial. The state has sacraments: the initial oath of citizenship, either implicit or public, and repeated voting (covenant renewal).[12]

Another success indicator for the nation-state is military victory. When pursued, this leads to empire. Empires always self-destruct in bankruptcy. The costs of central planning always overwhem empires. The most notable example in history is the Soviet Union. It shut down without a revolt or a *coup* on December 25, 1991. It ran out of money. It ran out of time. It ran out of hope.

State central planners must forecast the outcomes of their actions. In an institution that possesses monopoly authority over the administration of negative sanctions for disobedience, this means that the officials are in control judicially. Those who foresee bad outcomes cannot do much to offset the decisions of the central planners.

The planners have no access to prices that are set inside the state by voluntary exchange. They can copy market prices, but these do not indicate what prices would have been or ought to be inside the government, where there is no personal ownership of assets, and also no counter-offers by sellers of the services.

State officials must decide how to budget. They make assessments regarding the economic value to members of the body politic associated with the ownership of some asset. They make representative judgments

11. Sutton, *That You May Prosper*, ch. 4.
12. North, *Authority & Dominion*, ch. 19.

regarding individual imputations. These judgments must involve the summing up of the costs and benefits of ownership for each person under the state's jurisdiction. Yet there is no scientific way that anyone can do this, meaning no methodologically valid way, given the epistemology of subjective economic theory.[13] There is no objective measure of economic value.

The fact that there is no objective economic measure of value is not a valid argument against the necessity of making representative economic value judgments. But these value judgments do not rest on a system of objective pricing established by exchange. The judicial roles of each citizen cannot be sold to the highest bidder. Therefore, the individual economic imputations of citizens must be taken into consideration by the decision-maker if he is to do justice—legal justice in God's system of imputation of personal responsibility—to other citizens. He is in a legal position to oppress them. This is an inescapable aspect of his office as a magistrate. He is required by God to act representatively.

Every system of allocation is governed by a system of feedback. This is the system of sanctions. The state has several. One is the political system: the voters. Another is war. Another is monetary: inflation, deflation, and the ability to borrow at low rates. Another is the court system. Those officials who are involved in allocation must pay attention to these potential vetoes of their policies. They cannot achieve their goals at zero price. There are no free lunches.

E. Accumulation

Point five: succession. The accumulation of capital is an ethical command. It is not optional. Building God's kingdom requires capital. It is a redemptive process. The meaning of *redeem* is *buy back*. Covenant-keepers are required to buy back the world on behalf of God. This is why the biblical covenant is governed by Deuteronomy 8:18: "You shall remember the LORD your God, for it is he who gives you power to get wealth, that he may confirm his covenant that he swore to your fathers,

13. Lionel Robbins, *An Essay on the Nature and Significance of Economic Science* (London: Macmillan, 1932), ch. VI.

as it is this day."[14] Who were the fathers? Abraham, Isaac, and Jacob. They left an inheritance.

The magistrates must defend private property. In doing so, they allow individuals, churches, and families to accumulate wealth. But the state is not under the same command to accumulate wealth. On the contrary, it is to limit its accumulation of wealth (Deut. 17).[15]

Magistrates make judgments representatively: in the name of. They make economic plans on behalf of citizens: present and future.

The biblical goal is capital accumulation, not capital consumption. This in an inter-generational assignment. Each generation is supposed to leave more behind than it inherited. This is the meaning of value-added living, as applied to capital ownership. This mandates a system of private property.

The accumulation of state capital is based on the worldview which the biblical state enforces: the principle of victim's rights.[16] This principle of law must be the state's primary administrative guide. This principle shapes the extent of inherited wealth. It shapes their ability of owners to make decisions on behalf of future generations. There is a law element to consider: *ethics*. There is a *sanctions* aspect: causation in history. There is a *time* element to consider.

The individual inherits beyond the grave.[17] So does the church. The state does not.

Then what about economics? How is the state's economic covenant renewed in history? By covenant succession. The state's capital in the form of *law and voluntary obedience* by citizens and residents is transferred to the next generation of covenant-keepers within the boundaries.

If the heirs keep the terms of the biblical state covenant, they will

---

14. Gary North, *Inheritance & Dominion: An Economic Commentary on Deuteronomy* (Moulton, Alabama: Axehead Press, [1999, 2012] 2028), ch. 22.

15. Ibid., ch. 42.

16. Gary North, *Victim's Rights: The Biblical View of Civil Justice* (Moulton, Alabama: Axehead Press, [1990] 2029).

17. "Lay not up for yourselves treasures upon earth, where moth and rust doth corrupt, and where thieves break through and steal: But lay up for yourselves treasures in heaven, where neither moth nor rust doth corrupt, and where thieves do not break through nor steal: For where your treasure is, there will your heart be also" (Matt. 6:19–21, KJV). Gary North, *Priorities & Dominion: An Economic Commentary on Matthew* (Moulton, Alabama: Axehead Press, [2012] 2030), ch. 13.

usually be in a position to add economic value. This means they will have to increase their productivity. They will then leave more behind than they inherited. *This is the meaning of the redemption of the world.* The heirs participate in an inter-generational increase in capital. Ownership of resources progressively is transferred to covenant-keepers. "A good person leaves an inheritance to his grandchildren, And the wealth of a sinner is stored up for the righteous" (Prov. 13:22).[18] This process includes states. Why? Because family capital produces income, and states collect taxes.

This inter-generational process of inheritance—thrift, wise investing, compound economic growth, and accumulation of capital—is the covenantal basis of *economic redemption in history*. The accumulation of capital under a covenantal oath is the economic basis of redemption in other spheres. The covenantal state should not extend its jurisdiction by means of war. This process of wealth creation is entirely voluntary. It does not involve the use of force. The kingdom of God expands its jurisdiction primarily in terms of families, but covenant-keeping family members and individuals are citizens.

Conclusion

The economics of the state is inherently vertical. It is a pyramid of power. Special-interest groups compete for votes. This is the battle for the allegiance of men. The economics of the free market is inherently horizontal: competing bids for the use or ownership of scarce resources. The principle of *monetary high bid wins* governs the free market. This bidding process is overwhelmingly monetary. It is impersonal. It is open to new bidders and new sellers. In contrast, the high bid of the state is established by the rule of civil law. This bidding system is non-monetary. It, too, is impersonal when conducted legally.

The deciding authority is the individual. He operates under God's overall sovereignty. He decides which voice of civil authority to listen to. This civil authority possesses power. Its symbols are the badge and

18. Gary North, *Wisdom & Dominion: An Economic Commentary on Proverbs* (Moulton, Alabama: Axehead Press, [2012] 2029), ch. 41.

the gun. There is no open entry into its jurisdiction. There is no system of legal competitive bidding for its favors: bribery. There are negative sanctions. To the extent that bureaucratic independence from politics has been established by law, meaning Civil Service laws, the state is removed from the direct influence of politics. The primary sanctions are then indirect: new rules and reduced departmental budgets. Reduced budgets almost never occur, and never occur as public manifestations of political reprisal. The system favors bureaucracy over both politics and the free market.[19]

19. By far the finest book on bureaucracy is C. Northcote Parkinson's book, *Parkinson's Law: The Pursuit of Progress* (London: John Murray, 1958). It is presented in a humorous format, but it is accurate. See "Parkinson's Law," *The Economist* (Nov. 19, 1955).

Chapter 23

Boundaries

"See, I have taught you statutes and judgments just as the Lord my God commanded me, that you are to do these things in the land where you are entering to take possession of it. So keep and do them, for that is your wisdom and your understanding in the sight of the peoples who will hear all these statutes and say, 'Surely this great nation is a wise and understanding people.' For what great nation is there that has a god so near to it as is the Lord our God whenever we call on Him? Or what great nation is there that has statutes and judgments as righteous as this whole Law which I am setting before you today?"

Deuteronomy 4:5–8

Analysis

Point three of the biblical covenant is ethics.[1] This is related to law.

The central judicial-covenantal fact of the state is the right to impose negative physical and monetary sanctions. Because the state possesses the God-given authority to use violence against evil-doers (Rom. 13:1–7),[2] it must be placed under restraints. It must not invade areas of life which God has granted lawful immunity from violence. *Civil liberty begins*

1. Ray R. Sutton, *That You May Prosper: Dominion By Covenant*, 2nd ed. (Tyler, Texas: Institute for Christian Economics, [1987] 1992), ch. 2.

2. Gary North, *Cooperation & Dominion: An Economic Commentary on Romans* (Moulton, Alabama: Axehead Press, [2012] 2031), ch. 11.

with lawful immunity from coercion by the state. So, to place boundaries on state action, we must define those areas protected by God's law from invasion: individuals, families, churches, and lower units of civil government. The best example of an attempt to specify these limits on state action is the United States Constitution. In other traditions, courts provide this function. As it has turned out, no formal constitutional restraints have been successful in limiting the nation-state's extension of its jurisdiction. The loss of liberties that began in August 1914 with the outbreak of World War I has continued, at varying rates, in the West.

A state has a confession of faith. This establishes the terms of the oath. Every civil government is established by an oath. This distinguishes a covenant from a contract. This civil confession establishes the covenantal limits on state legitimacy and hence on state power. Religion undergirds all power, all culture. Religion is revealed and enforced through a confession of faith.

Only through a systematic defense of a confession can a state overcome regression to the mean beyond three or four generations. The Second Commandment says that this is possible to achieve. "You shall not worship them nor serve them; for I, the LORD your God, am a jealous God, inflicting the punishment of the fathers on the children, on the third and the fourth generations of those who hate Me, but showing favor to thousands, to those who love Me and keep My commandments" (Ex. 20:5–6). The word "thousands" applies here to "generations."[3] The observation that this has not been achieved in the past does not prove theologically that the promise of the Second Commandment is null and void under the New Covenant.

A. Name and Ownership

Point one: God's sovereignty. States are legally separate judicial social units. They are covenantal units because they are established by an oath under God. They are identified by names. These names establish legal liability.

---

3. Gary North, *Authority & Dominion: An Economic Commentary on Exodus*, vol. 2, *Part II: Decalogue & Dominion* (Moulton, Alabama: Axehead Press, [1986, 2012] 2025), ch. 22:C:3.

A name is associated with a legal boundary. In Chapter 8, I discussed the relationship between name and boundaries. God announced His defense of His name in the Third Commandment (Ex. 20:7). This is the third law in the list of five priestly laws. He announced the prohibition against theft—a defense of property—in the Eighth Commandment (Ex. 20:15). This is the third in the list of five commandments relating to kingly rule or civil society.[4] The eighth commandment is the judicial foundation of property rights. Private property begins with a person's name. A person is a legally identifiable agent. His name identifies him. It says, "you, not someone else." This is the basis of judicial responsibility. It is also the foundation of economic authority. This same analysis applies to a family, a church, and a state. I also wrote this: "The authority to name things is a God-given authority. The person with the authority to establish names possesses a unique hierarchical position at the top. The question, 'Who's in charge here?' can be accurately answered by identifying the person with the legal authority to name people and things."

A state has a name. This act of judicial separation marks it a guardian: a legal administrator in the name of God. Whatever the state owns in its name belongs to God. State property comes under the authority of those ordained (sanctioned) magistrates who are in charge of the state's property. They serve as stewards, both for God and for those under their authority.

The extension of the state's property must not come as the product of theft. Therefore, the boundaries surrounding private property establish the jurisdictional limits of state property. These are contiguous boundaries. The old slogan that defines the growth of empire applies here. The king announces: "I am not greedy. I want control over only land that is contiguous to mine." The civil covenant and social ethics must place legal boundaries against this impulse.

B. Central Planning

Point two: hierarchy. Magistrates exercise power. This puts them in a position to substitute the threat of violence for a monetary bid. In the words of Don Corleone in *The Godfather*: "I will make him an offer he

4. On the dual lists, priestly and kingly, of the Ten Commandments, see ibid., Preface B:I.

cannot refuse." If boundaries do not restrain such offers, the realm of liberty will shrink. Property will be transferred to the state.

This extension of state power can be done through taxation, inflation, and debt. The state extracts wealth from those under its jurisdiction. Then it uses this wealth to enhance state power. It buys compliance. This centralizes power. This is best represented graphically in terms of a pyramid. At the top of the hierarchy are the agents who possess (or secretly direct) state power.

The magistrates act representatively. They allocate time and money in terms of their judgment regarding the conflicting economic values of citizens. Inside the legal boundaries of the state, they treat people differently from those outside these boundaries: aliens. They are responsible to God for the administration of assets. They represent citizens legally (guardian). They act as economic stewards for citizens as individuals, but also as agents of the state as a covenantal unit.

With respect to boundaries and central planning, the most important economic boundaries are the limits on each individual's knowledge. Individuals have knowledge of their own local situations. They have little knowledge about the facts of the economy as a whole. This makes detailed economic planning impossible for the state. No committee has sufficient knowledge to coordinate the factors of production in society, especially specific knowledge. This was Ludwig von Mises' point in his 1920 essay, "Economic Calculation in the Socialist Commonwealth."[5] The planners need prices to guide them, but in a socialist society, there is no private property. So, there cannot be prices, especially for capital goods. F. A. Hayek made a similar point with respect to the coordination of dispersed economic knowledge in his 1945 essay, "The Use of Knowledge in Society."[6] The attempt of state planners to coordinate the factors of production leads to coercion. In order to direct production, the planners must compel property owners to use their resources in state-mandated ways. This includes their labor. They must obey or else suffer negative sanctions. Hayek wrote the premier book on this in 1944: *The Road to Serfdom*.

5. Ludwig von Mises, *Economic Calculation in the Socialist Commonwealth* (Auburn, Alabama: Mises Institute, [1920] 1990).

6. F. A. Hayek, "The Use of Knowledge in Society" (1945), reprinted in Hayek, *Individualism and Economic Order* (Chicago: University of Chicago Press, 1948), ch. 4

C. Time and Place

Point three: ethics. This is related to law, which establishes boundaries. States are bounded by geography through time. They begin at a time and a place. There must be an oath of some kind, meaning a loyalty oath. This is point four of the covenant. But this oath is made at a point in time and in a place. There are time lines and maps associated with the establishment of every state.

A state is defensive toward other states. It has boundaries. It must defend these boundaries against invasion and subversion. Every state has a definition of treason. For a biblical commonwealth, the supreme treason is treason against God. The modern humanist world officially rejects this, but this rejection is a delusion. The modern state declares a new god: itself. The state is the source of law. The source of law in any society is the god of that society. Treason against the state is regarded as treason against the only god that possesses original power.

Biblically, empire is prohibited. There are always economic losses that are involved in such an extension. Empires are costly to establish, defend, and administer. When they extend their boundaries geographically, they are forced to pay for defense and administration. They tax the voters in order to maintain the empire.

There is a slogan in business: "Pay me now, or pay me later." The Roman Empire grew through warfare. It was able to extract wealth from the conquered lands. But every empire faces this problem: after the conquered lands and populations are integrated into the empire, their taxes go to the central government. What had been spoils of war at the beginning of the process become costs of administration after the boundaries of the empire have extended to the far edges of the conquered nations. These costs are borne from inside the empire. The more that the empire absorbs and integrates these foreigners, the more the empire must be supported by resources extracted from within the empire. *Outside funding becomes internal funding over time*. The empire ceases to grow. The costs of conquests at a distance become too great. The empire starts to contract when outsiders invade.

The British Empire in North America was surrendered to the American revolutionaries because of the attempt of the British Parliament in

1765 to impose taxes inside the geographical boundaries of the colonies to pay for about 20% of the costs of keeping troops in North America. The taxes were minimal, but the attempt to impose them created political resistance in 1765, and this resistance grew for a decade, when the revolution began. Taxpayers in Great Britain had paid for the expansion of the empire, which culminated with the defeat of the French Empire in North America and also in India in the Seven Years War, 1755–1763. As soon as the British Empire in North America reached its geographical limits, Parliament's quest for new tax revenues led to its contraction. "Pay me now, or pay me later" received an answer: "We will not pay you at all."

There are no free lunches. There are no free empires.

D. Scarcity

Point four: sanctions. Scarcity existed prior to the fall. Men still had to allocate their time and assets.

People overcome scarcity through better investing and through technological innovation. They overcome it through peace. They overcome it through self-government.

The state has a legitimate function in overcoming scarcity. It imposes negative sanctions against criminal behavior. This increases peace. It increases justice. This allows people to invest more money in innovation. So, there is an increase in positive economic sanctions in the social order because of the state. This reduces scarcity.

Taxation is required to finance civil government. The state must threaten tax evaders with negative sanctions in order to collect taxes. But self-government is crucial in the enforcement of all laws, including tax laws. Taxpayers must be willing to cooperate. Otherwise, tax collection will get more expensive. It will then take additional state resources to enforce the tax laws. Taxation should therefore be structured in terms of equity, meaning fairness. The Bible is nearly silent on taxation, except to identify a 10% tax by the king as a form of tyranny (I Sam. 8:14, 17).[7] The state's extraction of wealth from citizens and its

7. Gary North, *Disobedience & Defeat: An Economic Commentary on the Historical Books* (Moulton, Alabama: Axehead Press, [2012] 2029), ch. 14.

subsequent dispersal of this wealth are not governed by legal rules based on voluntary contracts.

The state administers justice. This should be impersonal, meaning impartial. "You shall not do injustice in judgment; you shall not show partiality to the poor nor give preference to the great, but you are to judge your neighbor fairly" (Lev. 19:15).[8] In the name of justice, it establishes a legal claim on scarce economic resources. To keep the state from misusing the threat of negative sanctions against some groups, and the promise of positive sanctions for other groups, the state must be bounded. To restrain the state in its confiscation of resources from the private sector, voters must be diligent in restriction the state's collection of taxes, either directly or through monetary inflation. Voters must also restrict the state's level of debt. This is a matter of political resistance. The state should not be allowed to expand without a reason based on the administration of justice, i.e., its imposition of negative sanctions for crimes.

The state is unlike any other institution. The better it is doing its job, the less that the public should reward it through higher payments. This is counter to the logic of all other institutions. Other institutions are encouraged to do a better job by being awarded positive sanctions. Why is the state different? Because the state is not an agency that imposes positive sanctions. The church is. The family is. Therefore, the state's success in reducing crime is not a biblically legitimate justification for expanding its budget. Why not? Because, in an ethical society, God's positive economic sanctions increase. This result is not primarily because of the state. It is the result primarily of the increase in self-government. The larger the state gets, the more likely that it will impose negative sanctions beyond what is required by biblical justice. It will seek to become messianic: an agency of healing. When the state plays God, justice decreases.

E. Economic Growth

Point five: succession. The state is not an agency of wealth creation. It is supported by taxation. When individuals, families, and businesses

8. Gary North, *Boundaries & Dominion: An Economic Commentary on Leviticus* (Moulton, Alabama: Axehead Press, [1994, 2012] 2026), ch. 14.

grow wealthy, this allows the state to grow. Unlike the other covenantal arrangements, the state is not supposed to expand its jurisdiction as a result of economic growth. Its function is the administration of justice. If the number of crimes is not increasing, or if the percentage growth in crime is lower than overall economic growth, while is difficult to measure, the state's budgets should not increase.

Unless citizens actively resist the expansion of the state's jurisdiction, the state will expand its jurisdiction whenever its tax revenues increase. This is an important reason for lower tax rates when the economy grows. *The more productive the society, the smaller the percentage of the nation's wealth that should be absorbed by the state.*

The fact that the economy is growing is not a reason for the state to expand its borders. The general rule of national civil government is this: there should be no increase in the geographical boundaries of the state. Consider Switzerland. It never expands geographically, yet it one of the most productive economies in history. Switzerland remains neutral. This has kept Switzerland out of wars ever since the Napoleonic wars of the early nineteenth century, when Napoleon invaded. This has kept Switzerland's military costs minimal.

Conclusion

The state is bounded. It is bounded by confession, by the number of citizens, by the size of its capital, by geography, by tradition, and by time.

At the heart of every civil government is a confession of faith, either explicit or implicit. This is the fundamental boundary. There can be confessional continuity over generations. There can also be sustained economic blessings based on covenantal faithfulness. Every state has a confession, either formal or (more likely) informal. This may be in the form of a written constitution. It may be in the form of legal principles that govern civil courts. But there must be general principles of ethics that govern the administration of civil law. The source of this ethical system is the god of the society.

Chapter 24

Imputation

And King Rehoboam consulted with the elders who had served his father Solomon while he was still alive, saying, "How do you advise me to answer this people?" Then they spoke to him, saying, "If you will be a servant to this people today, and will serve them and grant them their request, and speak pleasant words to them, then they will be your servants always." But he ignored the advice of the elders which they had given him, and consulted with the young men who had grown up with him and served him. He said to them, "What advice do you give, so that we may answer this people who have spoken to me, saying, 'Lighten the yoke which your father put on us'?" And the young men who had grown up with him spoke to him, saying, "This is what you should say to this people who spoke to you, saying: 'Your father made our yoke heavy, now you make it lighter for us!' You should speak this way to them: 'My little finger is thicker than my father's waist! Now then, my father loaded you with a heavy yoke; yet I will add to your yoke. My father disciplined you with whips, but I will discipline you with scorpions!' "

I Kings 12:6–11

Analysis

Point four of the biblical covenant is sanctions: positive and negative.[1] God imputed value, day by day, in the creation week: "It is good." He

1. Ray R. Sutton, *That You May Prosper: Dominion By Covenant*, 2nd ed. (Tyler, Texas: Institute for Christian Economics, [1987] 1992), ch. 4.

applied His judgment to His plan of creation. He did a good job while working. He declared His satisfaction at the end of each day, except day two. So, His acts of imputation were objective, meaning public, and also subjective, meaning the product of His personal judgment. Man does the same. Man is made in God's image. He imputes value. This includes economic value.

God imputed value as a Trinity: one God, three Persons. This was individual imputation. It was also corporate imputation. Man does the same. Mankind is both unified and plural. This is the solution to the otherwise unsolvable problem of epistemology in a world of competing and autonomous imputers. The central question for all epistemologies that are based on a theory of individual imputation of meaning, causation, and value is this: *How can the imputations of theoretically autonomous individuals explain decision-making by groups?* This is an application of the recurring philosophical problem of the one and the many. If we begin with the autonomy of the individual, we soon must face the fact that he is not autonomous. There are other imputing individuals in this world. He interacts with lots of them. *To make sense of our world, we must have a way to assess the relevance of competing imputations.* We must assign "weight" to individual imputations, and then "add up" the value of all of them. But no such value scale exists, according to the methodological individualist.[2] If this is true, then this makes all representative decision-making on behalf of a group scientifically impossible. It also raises the question of who possesses the lawful authority to make such representative decisions. On what basis?

The state is an agency of coercion. Therefore, disputes over the correct imputation given by state officials is more divisive than in the family or the state. There are vastly more people involved. There is a far wider range of standards. The difficulty of imputing accurately, according to God's standards, increases with the size of the state and the authority of the state. There is a problem: how to gain widespread acceptance of these standards. Without this, there will be less self-government under law.

---

2. Lionel Robbins, *An Essay on the Nature and Significance of Economic Science* (London: Macmillan, 1932), ch. VI. See also Gary North, *Sovereignty & Dominion: An Economic Commentary on Genesis* (Moulton, Alabama: Axehead Press, [1982, 2012] 2022), ch. 5.

A. Valuation by God

Point one: God's sovereignty. God is the cosmic Imputer. Consider the week of creation (Gen. 1). He passed verbal judgment on His own work: "It is good." What God can do definitively, men can do provisionally. Man is the image of God. He is responsible to God. If he could not impute, God would not hold mankind liable for evil judgment.

1. *God the Imputer*

God evaluated the effect of His daily creative work on all days except day two (Gen. 1). This was an individual's evaluation of His individual work. But Christianity teaches that God is three persons as well as one God. So, this imputation was also corporate. So was the creation. Only Christianity announces such a doctrine.

There was unity of purpose in the creation. But God said "Let Us make mankind in Our image" (Gen. 1:26a). The image of God is both singular and plural. Therefore, so is mankind, who as a species is made in God's image. The ability of men to make corporate judgments is inherent in the being of God and the being of man, both individual man and corporate man. This is why Christian economics can deal successfully with the epistemological issue of the one and the many. In the field of economics, the problem of the one and the many begins with epistemology, as it does in all other academic disciplines. The question of epistemology is this: "What can man know, and how can he know it?" It applies to individuals and collectives in every area of thought.

2. *Value Theory*

In every area of philosophy there is *axiology*: value theory. The same questions arise. What is value? How can men discover it? Is it independent of men? Is it imputed by men? Are we speaking of individuals or collectives? But in no social science is the question of axiology more important than economic theory. The central issue that the economist deals with is this: "What is the relationship between value and price?" This question has its individualistic side, but more important is its corporate side. If value is imputed individually, how do we know that the outcome of competitive bidding in a free market corresponds to the aggregate valuation of the participants? The socialist denies that it does. He denies that the process of competitive bidding leads to socially beneficial outcomes. He calls for state coercion to establish socially beneficial collective value. To establish socially beneficial outcomes, a representative state agency must allocate scarce resources. This is heart, mind, and especially soul of socialism.

The problem of socialist valuation is the problem of state valuation. The outcome of allocation by the magistrate is the central epistemological issue. How can the magistrates maximize the value of the scarce resources at their command? They must consider the individual evaluations of citizens. Then they must evaluate the accuracy of these judgments in terms of a standard. What standard? Their own value scales? Or a composite value scale of all citizens? Or a weighted value scale, weighted in terms of the capacities and responsibilities of each citizen? Methodological individualism denies the existence of any such scale. But if this is true, then are the estimates of the magistrates epistemologically irrelevant, an exercise in self-delusion? If there is no Trinitarian God, the answer is yes. There is no judicially authoritative corporate many in any act of economic imputation. There can therefore be no economically authoritative corporate many in the act of imputation. So, the magistrates cannot represent such a God. They are on their autonomous own. Nevertheless, they must make decisions. They allocate resources. By what standard?

At this point, I apply what I have written here to state decision-making.

3. *Justice*

In the biblical framework, the state is uniquely an agency of justice. This is the assessment of the state's function in most social philosophies. The main exceptions to this rule are these: the anarchist (zero-state) view and the Marxist view, but only after Communism is fully established. Marx's state supposedly must wither away under Communism. But Communist states never arrived at that day of deliverance. Communist states were powerful and highly centralized.

There are four kinds of civil justice in today's political theory: procedural, restorative, retributive, and distributive. Each has its defenders.

Procedural justice refers to the process of justice. For example, does the defendant have access to a lawyer? Is there cross-examination? Is the system fair? Restorative justice is also called restitution. Is the victim of crime compensated by the convicted perpetrator? Retributive justice has to do with the reduction of future crimes. Does the penalty send fear into the hearts of would-be criminals? Finally, there is distributive justice. This has to do with wealth redistribution by state power. It has to do with the fair share, not a fair trial (procedural justice).

Biblical law offers no defense of distributive justice. Biblical law is hostile to such a concept of justice. It promotes impartiality by judges with respect to the wealth of an individual or organization. "You shall not do injustice in judgment; you shall not show partiality to the poor nor give preference to the great, but you are to judge your neighbor fairly" (Lev. 19:15).[3] There must be equality before the law. This negates the possibility of a judicial goal of equality of economic outcomes. No one has put it better than F. A. Hayek. "From the fact that people are very different it follows that, if we treat them equally, the result must be inequality in their actual position, and that the only way to place them in an equal position would be to treat them differently. Equality before the law and material equality are therefore not only different but are in conflict with each other; and we can achieve either the one or the other, but not both at the same time. The equality before the law which freedom requires leads to material inequality."[4]

Biblical law does not speak of procedural justice. It sets no courtroom procedures. But it does make perjury unlikely. If a false witness is discovered, whatever penalty would have been imposed on the victim is imposed on the perjurer (Deut. 19:15–21).[5]

With regard to retributive justice, Deuteronomy 19:20 is clear: "And the rest of the people will hear and be afraid, and will never again do such an evil thing among you." Biblical law is retributive.

There is also restorative justice. This concept of justice rests on res-

3. Gary North, *Boundaries & Dominion: An Economic Commentary on Leviticus* (Moulton, Alabama: Axehead Press, [1994, 2012] 2026), ch. 14.

4. F. A. Hayek, *The Constitution of Liberty* (Chicago: University of Chicago Press, [1960] 2011), 150.

5. Gary North, *Inheritance & Dominion: An Economic Commentary on Deuteronomy* (Moulton, Alabama: Axehead Press, [1999, 2012] 2028), ch. 45.

titution. The fundamental judicial principle of biblical law is victim's rights.[6] The victim of a crime is to be restored to his position before the crime. He is also entitled to a penalty payment (Ex. 22:1, 4).[7] This is not wealth redistribution in the sense of distributive justice. It is the restoration of the *status quo ante*.

B. Valuation by Man

Point two: hierarchy. My comments here are extensions of what I wrote in Section B of Chapter 9. They have to do with thinking God's thoughts after Him. This exercise begins with the presupposition of the authority of God's law. This law applies to individuals, who are held responsible in history and eternity. But it also applies to corporate entities. The decision-makers must begin with any laws of God that apply to the corporate entity, either through biblical revelation or through the extension of biblical revelation. This is Christian casuistry: the application of biblical principles to historical circumstances.

People act as representative agents. They are responsible agents. Responsibility is four-way: upward to God, outward toward citizens, downward toward citizens and residents, and inner: ethical conscience and personal needs. The magistrates are required by God to consider this complex array of competing demands on the state's resources. The allocation is economic, but the responsibility is judicial.

The magistrates make economic valuations on behalf of voting citizens and non-voting residents. They must take into consideration what God requires from each citizen and resident. They must also consider God's expectations regarding the state as a covenantal unit. This makes the magistrates' position highly complex. It is impossible for them to assess the value scales of each resident, as well as the potential net output of each resident. Yet they must consider net output, both short-run and long-run. Laws involve sanctions. There will be unintended con-

6. Gary North, *Victim's Rights: The Biblical View of Civil Justice* (Moulton, Alabama: Axehead Press, [1990] 2029).

7. Gary North, *Authority & Dominion: An Economic Commentary on Exodus*, vols. 3–4, *Part III: Tools of Dominion* (Moulton, Alabama: Axehead Press, [1990, 2012] 2025), ch. 43.

sequences. "You can't change just one thing." When they pass tax laws or regulatory laws, they act on behalf of the citizens, yet there is almost no way for them to know for sure what is best. The citizens rarely are unified on this. So, magistrates guess. Then they wait and see. So do voters. If the outcomes are sufficiently negative, a majority of voters will replace those who voted for the particular law. They will pressure the new magistrates to change the law or reverse it. This change in political representation is the primary negative sanction possessed by the electorate. The profit-and-loss system in politics has to do with votes. The "currency of the realm" of politics is the vote.

To depart geographically from the jurisdiction of any nation-state is expensive. The larger the nation-state is, the more expensive it is to depart. There is competition for political allegiance in the modern world. But the number of people who emigrate from a nation is always very low. Thus, every nation-state has an operational monopoly of justice. There are few effective methods of appeal beyond a nation's highest civil court: revolution, political change, etc. This takes time. It is highly unlikely that anyone who has suffered a defeat in a court will see this reversed. So, the nation-state has a near monopoly. This is the opposite of a free market, where the substitution of services is possible at some price. Without substitution, there is no array of money prices. This is why the economic theory of the market, what Mises called catallactics, barely applies to the nation-state.

Magistrates are loosely restrained by the nation-state's budget, but they are rarely sure which institutional arrangements should be left alone, which should be restructured, and at what cost. This calls for *intuitive judgment*, i.e., judgments where economic cause and effect are not strictly numerical. But economic judgments are never strictly numerical.

C. Criteria: Individual and Corporate

Point three: ethics. This is related to law, which establishes standards, i.e., criteria. In Chapter 9, I explained why economic value is derived from ethical value, an epistemological position that is contrary to the prevailing notions of humanistic economic theory. I stated that the criterion of economic value is this: *the extension of the kingdom of God in history*. Economic theory is not value-free. It is value-derived.

Magistrates are required by God to use the kingdom of God as their standard of economic value in assessing the profitability of any course of action. "But seek first His kingdom and His righteousness, and all these things will be provided to you" (Matt. 6:33).[8] They are supposed to allocate state capital based on this criterion. They act as a stewards of God, both judicially (authority) and economically (wealth). They act on behalf of God: extending the kingdom of God. They act as stewards of the residents. Stewardship has a middleman aspect. It is both judicial and economic. They are judicially responsible before God. The rewards and penalties of stewardship are both judicial and economic. By means of successful stewardship, his responsibilities increase (Luke 12:47–48).[9]

The biblical criteria of state success are varied. Above all, there is justice (Lev. 19:15). There is the defense of the realm (Judg. 4, 5). There is peace.

In economic theory, beginning with Adam Smith, defenders of the free market have argued that individual self-interest, when pursued in a free market, increases the wealth of individuals and nations. This is why Smith's book was titled *The Wealth of Nations* (1776). Socialists have always denied this. Economic interventionists have denied it as a universal principle. They have called for politicians to pass laws that alter the consumption patterns of consumers and also alter the production plans of producers. They see the state as the final reconciler of plans. The Bible is generally on the side of Smith. But there are exceptions. The Bible is opposed to greed. Smith's theory has long been used to defend the social productivity of greed, when greed is pursued in the context of a private property social order.

Here is the single most important difference between Smith's view of economic causation and the Bible's teaching. *There is nothing in the Bible that indicates a cause-and-effect relationship between the pursuit of personal gain and the reduction of poverty in society*. Yet this is the most important insight of Smith and all schools of free market economics.

8. Gary North, *Priorities & Dominion: An Economic Commentary on Matthew* (Moulton, Alabama: Axehead Press, [2012] 2030), ch. 15.

9. Gary North, *Treasure & Dominion: An Economic Commentary on Luke* (Moulton, Alabama: Axehead Press, [2012] 2031), ch. 28.

The Bible mandates private property, the rule of law, low taxes (I Sam. 8:14, 17),[10] and a judicial system based on victim's rights (restitution). But it nowhere makes the connection between the pursuit of profit and the reduction of collective poverty. It nowhere praises greed. Yet free market economists make the case that greed is beneficial whenever it is channeled institutionally by means of free market competition. Greed can and does benefit customers, meaning consumers, they say. Biblically speaking, no one should ever declare that greed is good. But greed can and does have positive consequences in a free market social order. So does discontent with one's present situation. Yet we are told to be content (Phil. 4).[11]

D. Value and Price

Point four: sanctions. Imputation economically reflects imputation judicially. The meek shall inherit the earth (Matt. 5:5).[12] But this declaration is based on faith. It is not clear in history that covenant-keepers have an advantage economically over covenant-breakers. Indeed, history seems to testify to the opposite. But history is not over. This same anomaly initially bothered the author of Psalm 73. He changed his mind later.[13]

This issue is at the heart of the debate over social cost. Social cost has been a hot topic ever since the socialist economist A. C. Pigou wrote *The Economics of Welfare* (1912). Pigou argued as follows. Each additional unit of income is less valuable to the recipient than the previous unit. This is an implication of the law of diminishing returns. This is taught by the subjective value theory of economics: marginal value and marginal pricing. He drew a conclusion: the state can increase total economic welfare by taxing the rich and transferring the money to the poor.

---

10. Gary North, *Disobedience & Defeat: An Economic Commentary on the Historical Books* (Moulton, Alabama: Axehead Press, [2012] 2029), ch. 14.

11. Gary North, *Ethics & Dominion: An Economic Commentary on the Epistles* (Moulton, Alabama: Axehead Press, [2012] 2032), ch. 23.

12. North, *Priorities & Dominion*, ch. 4.

13. Gary North, *Confidence & Dominion: An Economic Commentary on the Psalms* (Moulton, Alabama: Axehead Press, [2012] 2029), ch. 17.

The rich man will hardly miss that last bit of income, while the poor man will be able to purchase necessities. This argument established a strong theoretical case for the graduated ("progressive") income tax.

It was answered by Lionel Robbins two decades later. Robbins argued that it is impossible to make interpersonal comparisons of subjective utility. There is no common scale of economic value.[14] This argument has proven to be irrefutable, but hardly any economists accept it. Even Robbins abandoned it in 1938. Why? Because the argument, while true in theory, leads to an unacceptable but inevitable conclusion: it is impossible for economists, as scientists, to recommend policies of any kind to civil government. To offer such recommendations, economists would have to be able to make scientific estimates of total social utility, estimates based on subjective valuation by all participants. Then economics ceases to be useful. When Roy Harrod pointed this out in a debate with Robbins in *The Economic Journal*, Robbins capitulated. But he never said how his capitulation was logically consistent with his original critique.[15] So, the entire economics profession has lived in implicit epistemological schizophrenia ever since 1938.

The argument was re-examined by R. H. Coase in 1960 in what has become overwhelmingly the most frequently cited article in American legal journals: "The Problem of Social Cost."[16] He won the Nobel Prize in 1991 based on this article and one other, "The Nature of the Firm" (1937). I challenged "The Problem of Social Cost" in an appendix in *Tools of Dominion* in 1990.[17] I revised this slightly to produce *The Coase Theorem: An Essay in Economic Epistemology* in 1992. A short version appeared in a 2002 article in *The Journal of Libertarian Studies.*[18]

Coase argued that judges should decide who owes whom damages by deciding what the highest social value is for society. Using an example supplied by Pigou, if a train emits sparks that can set a field on fire, the judges may decide that the field's owners should pay for any fires

14. Robbins, *Nature and Significance*, ch. VI.

15. I discuss this in Chapter 5 of *Sovereignty & Dominion: An Economic Commentary on Genesis* (Moulton, Alabama: Axehead Press, [1982, 2012] 2022).

16. Fred R. Shapiro and Michelle Pearce, "The Most-Cited Law Review Articles of All Time," *Michigan Law Review*, 110 (2012), 1503.

17. North, *Authority & Dominion*, Appendix H.

18. Gary North, "Undermining Property Rights: Coase and Becker," *Journal of Libertarian Studies*, XVI (Fall 2002).

started by the train, if this will produce the greatest net social value. Or perhaps the farmers should be required to pay the railroad firm to install spark-retardation devices. I argued that the judges cannot make any such determination on a scientific basis. They cannot make interpersonal comparisons of subjective utility. Furthermore, such arbitrary power on the part of judges would undermine private property rights. I cited Exodus 22:5–6. "If a man causes a field or vineyard to be grazed, and lets loose his animal, and it feeds in another man's field, he shall make restitution from the best of his own field and the best of his own vineyard. If fire breaks out and catches in thorns, so that stacked grain, standing grain, or the field is consumed, he who kindled the fire shall surely make restitution."[19] I sent him a copy of *The Coase Theorem* as soon as it was published in 1992. He was 80 years old. He never replied, although he lived to the age of 102. He was still writing at age 101. He died in 2013.

Hayek wrote an entire book on what he called the mirage of social justice.[20] He denied that there can be such a thing. The state cannot achieve that which is impossible, he argued. But his position was based on a denial of transcendent law.[21] He was a social and legal evolutionist. He did not believe in permanent economic or moral laws of any kind. This is not acceptable, epistemologically speaking, as I argued in 1982.[22]

E. Value-Added Living

Point five: succession. Jesus said: "The thief comes only to steal and kill and destroy; I came so that they would have life, and have it abundantly" (John 10:10). This applies to every Christian. It applies to all Christian covenantal institutions. This principle applies to kingdom expansion. More is better than less at the same price.

Individuals impute economic value. Individuals are responsible for

19. North, *Authority & Dominion*, ch. 45.

20. F. A. Hayek, *Law, Legislation, and Liberty*, Vol. 2, *The Mirage of Social Justice* (Chicago: University of Chicago Press, 1976).

21. Ibid., p, 60.

22. Gary North, *Sovereignty & Dominion: An Economic Commentary on Genesis* (Moulton, Alabama: Axehead Press, [1982, 2012] 2022), Appendix B.

the accuracy of these imputations, case by case. This ability is grounded in God's economic imputation.[23]

There is no possibility of a cardinal scale of value: numerical designations. There is only an ordinal value scale: first, second, third. This is because man is analogical being. He is not digital. He is made in God's image. God is personal, not digital.

The act of imputation is always representational. Man imputes value on behalf of God: the cosmic Owner. He also imputes it on behalf of any subordinate owners of the assets involved. This act of economic imputation is always governed by the judicial category of ownership. *Economic ownership is always an extension of judicial ownership.* It is not autonomous. Nothing in the creation is autonomous.

The magistrates make estimates of the value of future potential streams of income in the broadest sense. They then allocate resources under their control to buy or lease control over these income streams. In other words, they estimate in terms of the economic value of future legal ownership. *Imputed economic value drives legal ownership, but legal ownership secures future economic value.* If there were no possibility of securing ownership, the division of labor would contract. The range of cooperative ventures would shrink. The ability to make estimates influence the array of assets owned, but this ability is valuable only because of the possibility of securing ownership.

The art of estimating future economic value presupposes cause and effect: sanctions. It also assumes linear history. There is causation over time. If there were not, the ability to estimate future value could not exist. It would be overwhelmed by randomness. The individual could not plan for an objective outcome. This outcome is in part legal and in part economic. Legal: "Will I still own it?" Economic: "What will it be worth?"

Conclusion

The biblical explanation of economic imputation rests on the idea that God imputes economic value to the world around Him. Mankind is made in God's image: both corporate and individual.

---

23. Part II, ch. 3:E.

The biblical covenant model establishes a legal connection between subjective imputation and objective prices: a system of private ownership. An owner is a legal guardian (vertical-judicial), an economic steward (vertical-economic), and an auctioneer who acts on behalf of high bidders (horizontal-economic). In the case of civil government, the auctioneer function is political. The trustees do not own the state's assets, but they can benefit from them. They make allocation decisions that benefit their supporters. They can legally make these decisions in terms of the coin of the realm: votes, not bribes. They look outward to the power of future voters to impose positive and negative sanctions at the next election. They impute value to these outcomes.

In the free market, subjective economic imputation undergirds the system of competitive bidding, which is objective. People with resources make estimates of future economic value. Then they enter the market and make bids for legal control over scarce resources. This produces prices on capital markets. These markets assume the existence of a system for legally transferring ownership. This arrangement is governed by this economic principle: *monetary high bid wins*. All participants understand this.

This is not the case in the state covenant. In affairs of the state, politicians impute economic value to future political outcomes. The politicians' bids are objective: so much money for this or that project. There will be future losers and winners: contractors and voters. The bids are legally for common projects, not personal gain. Personal gain is implied: re-election.

Chapter 25

Predictability

When all Israel saw that the king had not listened to them, the people replied to the king, saying, "What share do we have in David? We have no inheritance in the son of Jesse; To your tents, Israel! Now look after your own house, David!" So Israel went away to their tents. But as for the sons of Israel who lived in the cities of Judah, Rehoboam reigned over them. Then King Rehoboam sent Adoram, who was in charge of the forced labor, and all Israel stoned him to death. And King Rehoboam hurried to mount his chariot to flee to Jerusalem. So Israel has broken with the house of David to this day. And it came about, when all Israel heard that Jeroboam had returned, that they sent word and called him to the assembly, and made him king over all Israel. None except the tribe of Judah alone followed the house of David.

I Kings 12:16–20

Analysis

Point five of the biblical covenant is succession.[1] King Rehoboam, Solomom's son, undermined predictability in Israel. He imposed unexpected high taxes. Jeroboam led a revolt of ten tribes. The nation of Israel was never again united under a king who was an heir of the conquest generation. This was a major discontinuity.

1. Ray R. Sutton, *That You May Prosper: Dominion By Covenant*, 2nd ed. (Tyler, Texas: Institute for Christian Economics, [1987] 1992), ch. 5.

This chapter is also a major discontinuity. It departs from the five-point structure of the family covenant and the church covenant. In the previous four chapters in Part V, I adopted the same categories that structure the first four chapters of the family covenant and the church covenant: ownership, stewardship, boundaries, and imputation. In Part III and Part IV, the fifth point is legacy. Here, I substitute predictability. The concept of legacy is not foreign, but is not equally appropriate as predictability. Succession is the fifth point of the biblical covenant model. There is covenantal continuity. Predictability is more judicial than economic. Legacy is more economic than judicial. Predictability is more a matter of covenantal guardianship than covenantal stewardship. It is more a matter of acting *in the name of* rather than acting *on behalf of.*

In the chapters on point five in Part III and Part IV, I adopted this structure: redemption (buying back), dominion, imitation, entrepreneurship, and accumulation. These are inherently economic categories. They are therefore not appropriate categories for state succession. *The fundamental aspect of the state covenant is coercion. It is not production.* The state is not an agency to make men ethically better. It is an agency to place negative sanctions on those who violate specific laws. Its task is to reduce evil, not increase righteousness. *The state is not an agency of redemption.* In God's social order, the role of civil law is exclusively negative, not positive. The best example in the Bible is the garden of Eden. There was only one prohibition: a tree. There were no negative sanctions against anything else. Mankind's access to everything except the tree was lawful. The prohibition was an act of exclusion: property rights. It was a test of mankind's acceptance of God's unique ownership of that tree. There was no other test.

It is a mark of a free society that almost everything is legal. It is like the trees in the garden. Here is the governing rule of a free society: "Everything that is not prohibited explicitly is allowed." This is different in a tyranny. There, the rule is this: "Everything is prohibited that is not explicitly allowed."

In the biblical worldview, civil government is not an agency of positive economic sanctions. So, its legacy is positive only in the sense that magistrates and judges maintain the civil government as an agency exclusively of negative sanctions. It is not quite a night-watchman state, but it is very close. Its function is to place judicial boundaries around specific acts. The legacy it is supposed to build is liberty. But this is *liberty by default*. Such liberty develops out of the private sector, meaning the voluntary sector. The state is not to become an agency of distributive justice, which inevitably means re-distributive justice: "Thou shalt not steal, except by majority vote." That is injustice, biblically speaking.

A. Purpose

Point one: God's sovereignty. The state did not exist before the fall. There was no sin. It would have had no purpose. Why not? Because its purpose is to restrict specific sins, not sins in general.

> Every person is to be subject to the governing authorities. For there is no authority except from God, and those which exist are established by God. Therefore whoever resists authority has opposed the ordinance of God; and they who have opposed will receive condemnation upon themselves. For rulers are not a cause of fear for good behavior, but for evil. Do you want to have no fear of authority? Do what is good and you will have praise from the same; for it is a servant of God to you for good. But if you do what is evil, be afraid; for it does not bear the sword for nothing; for it is a servant of God, an avenger who brings wrath on the one who practices evil. Therefore it is necessary to be in subjection, not only because of wrath, but also for the sake of conscience. For because of this you also pay taxes, for rulers are servants of God, devoting themselves to this very thing. Pay to all what is due them: tax to whom tax is due; custom to whom custom; respect to whom respect; honor to whom honor. (Rom. 13:1–7)[2]

The state will not exist beyond the final judgment because there will be no sin to restrain. The state is an institution confined exclusively to post-fall history.

The state is fundamentally different from the family with respect to sanctions. The state possesses the right to impose sanctions. These sanctions are *exclusively negative*, unlike the family's sanctions. Why is this?

---

2. Gary North, *Cooperation & Dominion: An Economic Commentary on Romans* (Moulton, Alabama: Axehead Press, [2012] 2031), ch. 11.

Because God's purpose for the state is exclusively negative: to reduce evil-doing by the threat of negative sanctions. The family has a different purpose: multiplication. It is creative. It owns capital. This capital is to be used for economic entrepreneurship. It is a source of production. In contrast, the state is not to become a source of production. Why not? Because it possesses a monopoly of violence. This violates a fundamental principle of the auction: *peaceful bidding*. God authorizes a family to create a business because it does not possess a legal right to impose negative physical sanctions outside of the boundaries of the family.

God's purpose shapes every covenantal institution. God has different purposes for each. Because His purposes are different for each, their economic operations are different from each other. The state's purposes are the most restrictive. Therefore, God does not call on it to run businesses. He calls on it to enforce justice.

The argument of the social gospel that one of the state's legitimate purposes is to redistribute wealth through taxation or regulation in order to increase a specific group's wealth is contrary to what the Bible teaches about justice. Here is the crucial biblical rule: "You shall not do injustice in judgment; you shall not show partiality to the poor nor give preference to the great, but you are to judge your neighbor fairly" (Lev. 19:15).[3] This is a manifestation of the biblical principle of the rule of law. "The same law shall apply to the native as to the stranger who resides among you" (Ex. 12:49).[4] I keep citing these passages for this reason: Christians who tell us that the welfare state is legitimate are inescpably denying the binding nature of these passages. They deny the biblical principle of the rule of law. They do it in the name of Jesus.

B. Central Planning

State officials are intermediaries between God and residents. They act as God's legal guardians. They act *in God's name* judicially. But this

3. Gary North, *Boundaries & Dominion: An Economic Commentary on Leviticus* (Moulton, Alabama: Axehead Press, [1994, 2012] 2026), ch. 14.

4. Gary North, *Authority & Dominion: An Economic Commentary on Exodus*, vol. 1, *Part I: Representation & Dominion* (Moulton, Alabama: Axehead Press, [1985, 2012] 2025), ch. 14.

necessarily involves economic stewardship. They act *on God's behalf* as stewards.

Corporately, all intermediaries must allocate resources in terms of a plan. This plan must extend through future generations. This is the issue of inheritance. This requires the planners to estimate future economic conditions. They must pass laws and collect taxes in order to preserve private property. The most capable forecasters and planners are the residents inside the nation's borders. They possess the specialized information that is required to allocate resources efficiently, i.e., without excessive waste. This is a stewardship function.

The state's time perspective should be long-term. A magistrate is supposed to act on behalf of future generations. While he can know little of what future generations will require, he can make some guesses. Personal capital is easier to manage. An individual specializes in dealing with the trials and tribulations of his time period and geography. This specialization enables him to make better allocations. Here is the problem: *the time perspective of state planners*. This begins with elected officials. Their time perspective is short: the next election. If they are not re-elected, they lose their authority as intermediaries. So, their primary goal is to get re-elected. They vote for state-funded projects that please a majority of the voters in their districts between the time of vote and the next election.

A father plans as an intermediary between the present and the future. He considers his inheritance to his children. What will it be worth at his death? How can his children extend this inheritance? His perspective is long-term. The same is true of church officers. This is not true of politicians.

Bureaucrats are protected by employment laws that keep a newly elected government from firing them. They have a longer-term perspective than politicians have. They seek the security of their careers. They want the agencies they work for to survive at least until their retirement. So, they seek to maintain and extend the jurisdiction of their agencies. They have an economic incentive to replace the intermediary authority of the family and the church. They have a shorter time perspective than productive accumulators of capital. They also are almost immune to economic feedback from their decisions. They do not spend their own money. They do not face a competitive price system. They cannot be easily fired. So, they do not face career-threatening sanctions for failure.

This is not true of market-based entrepreneurs. They are intermediaries between the present and the future. They can lose their wealth through poor planning. If they leave their wealth to adult children who do not have the ability to expend capital, they put their inter-generational legacy at risk. Compared to the incentives for accurate inter-generational planning, the family is superior to the state. This is the case against allowing the state to extract wealth from families in order to create new wealth. This capital will not be put to uses as productive as those selected by heads of households.

C. Ethics

Point three: ethics. The fundamental principle of biblical law enforcement is this: *self-government under biblical law*. The individual will face God on judgment day. He has an incentive to obey. In the division of judicial labor, he knows more about his actions than anyone else. He has an incentive to obey. He acts as God's agent. If he fails, then he will suffer the eternal consequences.

Institutional law enforcement in the family and the church is personal. They are small organizations. The head of the household knows more about what his children are doing than church elders do. Church elders know more about these children than the police do, unless the police are conducting an investigation. The state enforces the law only rarely in any normal person's life. The police cannot monitor everyone. Only a messianic state attempts to do this. This was George Orwell's warning in his dystopian novel, *Nineteen Eighty-Four* (1949): "Big Brother is watching you." The resources required to implement such a state are beyond the ability of any state to collect from taxpayers and bond-buyers. It would bankrupt any state that attempted this.

How can people govern themselves by law? Only when laws are general and limited in number can the common man know what he is not allowed to do. This is why God required the priests to read the Mosaic law publicly every seven years (Deut. 31:9–13).[5] This kept the legal code

---

5. Gary North, *Inheritance & Dominion: An Economic Commentary on Deuteronomy* (Moulton, Alabama: Axehead Press, [1999, 2012] 2028), ch. 75.

short enough to be read at a public assembly. The public could understand this code. The Mosaic state was highly restricted. Bureaucrats could not justify their exercise of arbitrary power by means of an enormously complex, mutually conflicting legal code. The United States Code is so detailed that no one knows how many federal crimes it designates. A low estimate is 3,000. Higher estimates range to 4,500. The compilation is huge: 23,000 pages, if a page has 60 lines to a page. Most books have under 40 lines.

When the politicians and bureaucrats attempt to devise laws governing the details of the economy, they defeat the principle of family inheritance. The principle of inheritance is based on ethics. The law of inheritance is governed by this principle: *do not subsidize evil.* Biblical law teaches that covenant-keepers inherit in history. Covenant-breakers are disinherited. Parents are required by God to honor this principle. They are to disinherit evil children. The inheritance must go to righteous heirs. To evaluate this, parents must be familiar with their children's ethical principles and their behavior. Yet even when they know, the responsibility of leaving an inheritance is daunting.

> So I hated all the fruit of my labor for which I had labored under the sun, because I must leave it to the man who will come after me. And who knows whether he will be wise or a fool? Yet he will have control over all the fruit of my labor for which I have labored by acting wisely under the sun. This too is futility. Therefore I completely despaired over all the fruit of my labor for which I had labored under the sun. When there is a person who has labored with wisdom, knowledge, and skill, and then gives his legacy to one who has not labored for it; this too is futility and a great evil. (Eccles. 2:18–21).[6]

The head of the household has personal knowledge about the ethical outlook of his children. While they are children, he can instruct them. His main task is to lead by example. This is word-and-deed instruction. Americas have a phrase for what desperate parents tell their children: "Do as I say, not as I do." They suspect that this recommendation will not work in the long run. Their children will see through it. As adults, they are more likely to imitate what the parent did than what he

---

6. Gary North, *Autonomy & Stagnation: An Economic Commentary on Ecclesiastes* (Moulton, Alabama: Axehead Press, [2012] 2030), ch. 4.

ordered. A parent has both a legal and personal connection with minor children under his authority. Family members are bound by love. This is not true of a politician's relationships with those under his authority. He has no personal knowledge about who will inherit what. He votes for bills that affect everyone in his jurisdiction. He is by law blind to the people who will be affected. He is not legally allowed to show favoritism to individuals. This is the principle of the rule of law. "The same law shall apply to the native as to the stranger who resides among you" (Ex. 12:49). He must rely on the threat of negative sanctions to gain compliance. Because of this impersonal aspect of all civil law, the state is incapable of determining which individuals should be the heirs. The heirs of state wealth-redistribution need not show conformity to any ethical system, as long as they do not break state laws. They need not imitate righteous parents in order to collect their inheritances. This reduces the likelihood of imitation of good behavior.

State officials have no such personal knowledge. They are to judge without respect to people's specific character traits. This is what the rule of law mandates for civil government. The state judges specific illegal acts, not the suspect's general ethical character. This is why the state is unfit to redistribute wealth except when enforcing the Bible's legal principle of restitution from the criminal to his victim. The state does not have detailed personal knowledge of citizens. When a state seeks to collect such information, it becomes messianic: redemptive. It should not be trusted.

D. Justice

Point four: sanctions. State central economic planners are in a unique position. They control the allocation of assets that do not belong to them. They act as economic stewards for the population. But because their plans are backed up by monopolistic power, residents cannot stay the magistrates' hands directly. Citizens can at best organize politically, gain a majority, and get the law changed. That takes years. So, state central planners are in a position to do enormous harm. They can use the power of the state to redistribute wealth. They do not own the state's assets personally, but they can determine who gets what out of taxes, and who gets what out of administrative regulation. F. A. Hayek warned in 1944 that the state's power to tax and spend places potentially dictatorial power into the hands of central powers. They can determine where capital flows, what the conditions of the labor market are, and what gets produced. His book, *The Road to Serfdom*, explains this link between power over state economic planning and its power over people.

In today's world, executive bureaucratic agencies have their own courts. These in-house courts adjudicate disputes between residents and the agencies that pay for the courts. They are officially impartial, but this is nonsense. Judges do not bite the hand that feeds them. They are biased in favor of the plaintiffs: agency bureaucrats. This is called administrative law. It is outside the judiciary. Harvard's historian of law, Harold Berman, issued a warning in 1983: administrative law is undermining the Western legal tradition. He issued the warning in the Introduction to his book, *Law and Revolution*.

The biblical state's sanctions are exclusively negative. The state acts in the name of God judicially. If the state uses its monopolistic authority to reward one group at the expense of other groups, it violate the rule of law. Again: "The same law shall apply to the native as to the stranger who resides among you" (Ex. 12:49). The state is a judicial institution. It must not reward one economic group at the expense of others. Again: "You shall not do injustice in judgment; you shall not show partiality to the poor nor give preference to the great, but you are to judge your neighbor fairly" (Lev. 19:15). Again and again and again. Why? Because defenders of secular welfare state theology of the social gospel will not listen and will not respond. God-fearing Christians must reject the social gospel, which is in fact a statist anti-gospel: bad news, not good news.

The fundamental principle of biblical justice is this: *victim's rights*.[7] A civil law-order must impose negative sanctions on a convicted criminal in order to provide economic restitution to the victim. The court transfers wealth from the criminal to his victim (Ex. 21:1, 4).[8]

When politicians use state power extract wealth from successful peo-

7. Gary North, *Victim's Rights: The Biblical View of Civil Justice* (Moulton, Alabama: Axehead Press, [1990] 2029).

8. North, *Authority & Dominion*, vols. 3–4, *Part III: Tools of Dominion*, ch. 43.

ple in order to reward people who have experienced economic losses, this violates the principle of the rule of law. It substitutes wealth-redistribution for restitution. The successful person has not violated the law, yet he suffers economic losses as a result. The graduated income tax is the textbook case of wealth redistribution. People with greater income are taxed at higher rates than people with low income. In the United States, half of the taxpayers pay no federal income tax. They have been granted the right to take deductions from their income, thereby reducing their net income below the taxable limit.

The state rewards economic failure and penalizes economic success. People respond to economic incentives. The number of people who get onto the welfare rolls increases: "free money." The number of investors who are willing to bear greater economic uncertainty with their capital for the sake of profit declines.

In a free market, the economic sanctions are monetary profit and loss. This is not true of the state. That is because there is no open competition, i.e., no product substitution. A state exercises a near monopoly. It shares jurisdictions with other civil governments, but there is an inescapable chain of command: an appellate court system. A supreme court must declare the outcome in disputed court cases: Ex. 18).[9]

E. Capitalization

Point five: succession. The essence of liberty is the freedom to do whatever is not explicitly prohibited by civil law. The model is Adam in the garden. The state is supposed to declare what is prohibited, and then enforce the law predictably over time. There should be judicial continuity. Judicial continuity creates a sense of public trust. People know what to expect from the state. There are known rules of procedure: in elections, in the legislature, in the courts, and in executive bureaucracies. People can then more safely make long-term economic plans, secure in the knowledge that politicians, bureaucrats, and judges will not arbitrarily confiscate their wealth.

When a society lives under predictable law enforcement, entrepre-

9. Ibid., Part I, ch. 19.

neurs can make long-term plans. They can afford to take a less uncertain path to wealth. They have decades to let it compound. The shorter the time horizon, the more that entrepreneurs must rely on more uncertain investment strategies that earn a high rate of return when successful, but which are more subject to uncertain events that can reduce capital substantially. The way to achieve these high rates of return is through debt. If a person buys an investment for $10,000, and it goes to $20,000, he makes 100% on his money. But if he borrows $7,500, and adds $2,500 of his money, he makes $20,000, but it only cost him $2,500 plus some interest on the borrowed money. He made 300% on the borrowed portion, and 100% on the $2,500. But if the investment falls by 50%, it is now worth $5,000. He still owes the lender $7,500, and he also lost his $2,500. He sells his investment and repays the lender $5,000. He still owes the lender $2,500. *Leverage is a two-way street.* Someone looking for a high short-term rate of return will use debt. He has no time to wait for a slow, steady rate of return. He puts himself at risk. Another example: if he owns an investment worth $10,000, and it falls by 50%, it is now worth $5,000. To get his capital back to $10,000 after taxes and inflation, he must make well over 100% on his investment. Conclusion: it is not easy to recover from a bad investment.

This is why uncertainty about the civil government leads to high-risk, short-term investing. The law of large numbers eventually catches up with high-risk investors. The investment strategy will produce a major loss. This delays the appreciation of capital. There is less capital to invest. The compounding process suffers a major setback. The investor leaves less wealth to his heirs.

If the state transfers wealth to economic failures, this de-capitalizes productive individuals, families, and businesses. The rate of economic growth will slow. At the same time, those who receive the confiscated money from the state will spend it on consumption, not capital accumulation. There will be lower economic growth. This is why the policy of state-enforced wealth redistribution reduces dominion by successful people, businesses, and societies.

The dominion covenant is basic for the long-term expansion of capital. The primary goal of increased capital is increased production, not increased consumption.

Conclusion

A high degree of predictability is required for the preservation of liberty. It is also required for economic growth.

The future is uncertain. Men are not omniscient. They see as through a mirror, darkly. They must devote mental energy to estimating what the future will bring. Then they must devise a plan to deal with some of the most probable effects of uncertainty in their lives. The more uncertainty that people expect, the more money they need in reserve. Money is the most marketable commodity. It can be used to deal with a wide variety of unforeseen circumstances.

Most people want the state to provide multiple economic safety nets to protect them against unforeseen negative outcomes. Multiple safety nets require a lot of revenues. They require taxes. They also require forecasters who accurately forecast the future. But state planners have little personal incentive to forecast accurately. They can only rarely be fired, and never for having made inaccurate forecasts. This is not true of investors, who place their own money at risk/uncertainty. They can gain personally or suffer loss personally, unlike state bureaucrats. This is why the idea of a state-guaranteed safety net is inherently suspect. It involves coercion in order to fund it and administer it. It reduces the amount of money in the private sector that could be used to hedge against both uncertainty and risk.

Then there is the issue of predictability of the courts. Do the courts predictably enforce property rights? If so, owners can use their wealth to hedge against uncertainty that is imposed by the physical environment and the social order. If not, owners must allocate wealth to the protection of their property: locks, alarm systems, weapons, and lawyers—especially lawyers. If people can predict the likely outcome of a court, they are less likely to bring a lawsuit that will likely go against them. They will settle the matter out of court.

The value of private property rises when courts protect owners from invasion and fraud. This makes people wealthier. A classic study of this is Hernando De Soto's book, *The Other Path* (1989).[10] It is a study of

10. Hernando De Soto, *The Other Path: The Invisible Revolution of the Third World* (London: Tauris, 1989).

the economy of Peru. He shows that the most effective way to raise the wealth of the poor is to grant property rights to poor people to buy land in squatter settlements. Another way is to make it easier for the poor to start businesses. Politicians and bureaucrats maintain social control by making it difficult for people to start small businesses.

The Mosaic law governing property was short. The legal code had to be read aloud to the assembled people once every seven years at the feast of booths (Deut. 31:9–13). The people could understand the code's legal principles. The code was not tens of thousands of pages. The more complex a legal code, the more arbitrary the interpreters of this code can be. Arbitrariness increases uncertainty. This is a case for limited civil government. The Mosaic law is God's model.

Conclusion to Part V

A. Covenant, Not Contract

The state has no future beyond the final judgment. It does not extend into eternity. The individual does. The church does.

Citizenship is established by an oath, either implicit (citizens by birth) or explicit (naturalized citizens and magistrates). To this oath are attached sanctions: negative only.

A magistrate is a judicial agent: a trustee. He acts judicially as a guardian. He acts in the name of God to citizens, and in the name of citizens to God. A magistrate is also an economic steward. He acts on behalf of God and on behalf of citizens. All of this is hierarchical.

The state is a judicial unit. Responsibility is corporate. Thus, methodological individualism does not apply well to the state. The state is more than the participants. God holds it responsible as a corporate unit. Wealth and poverty apply to the state. All economic approaches that rely on methodological individualism as the sole tool of economic analysis founder on family, church, and state.

The time horizon of a state is multi-generational. The time horizon of elected officials in marginal districts is the next election. There is a serious disconnect here. The state is supposed to consider long-run effects of its policies. But the state is represented by officials. Elected officials have a far shorter time horizon than tenured bureaucrats do. Bureaucracy is inherently anti-democratic. It does not respond to the voters' short-term demands. The voters cannot bring short-term negative sanctions against bureaucrats. Neither can politicians.

Because magistrates must make economic decisions on behalf of citizens, they must make interpersonal comparisons of subjective utility. They must "balance" or "weigh" the goals and aspirations of multiple citizens. They must also make estimates regarding God's assessment of these aspirations. So, in order to make accurate assessments of multiple subjective valuations, they must rely on their ability to assess God's assessments. They act as God's fiduciary agents in his allocation of state capital. But they also act as the state's fiduciary agent with God and with the world outside. There are multiple acts of economic imputation.

This must be done without reference to internally generated money prices. The state is an agency that relies on the division of labor. But this is not marked by a money economy internally. This division of labor is far more personal than impersonal in a non-profit, non-market organization. Money is geared to voluntary exchange, so most services performed in a church, family, or state cannot be out-sourced.

In a covenantal unit, pricing is not based on product substitution. So, the logic of exchange that applies to a free market does not apply in a covenantal unit. There is no product substitution allowed by law. This is why that which Mises called catallactics is highly limited. This is why he never attempted to apply the science of human action outside the market.

B. Edmund Burke's Error

One of the most important mistakes in the history of Western political theory was Edmund Burke's confusion of two categories: covenant and contract. This confusion has undermined the theoretical foundation of Western conservatism ever since. Burke wrote *Reflections on the Revolution in France* (1790). Here is probably the most famous passage in this deservedly famous book. He wrote of society as a contract.

> Society is indeed a contract. Subordinate contracts, for objects of mere occasional interest, may be dissolved at pleasure; but the state ought not to be considered as nothing better than a partnership agreement in a trade of pepper and coffee, callico or tobacco, or some other such low concern, to be taken up for a little temporary interest, and to be dissolved by the fancy of the parties.

This passage is fundamentally incorrect. Why? *Because there is no such thing as a social contract.* The idea of the social contract was one of the most pernicious ideas in the eighteenth century. A contract is a formal agreement between individuals. It is a legal document. It spells out responsibilities for individual performance. Society is not based on any such formal agreement. *Society is a loose system of cooperating individuals and institutions.* Some of these institutions are contract-based. Others are covenant-based.

In contrast to a contract, a covenant is a formal public agreement under God. Participants are bound by a binding oath. This oath explicitly or implicitly calls down God's negative sanctions if the terms of the covenant are broken. God does not authorize signers of contracts to use His name in this way (Matt. 5:33–37). The use of His name to seal a covenant judicially establishes a high degree of responsibility on men's part to obey the terms of the covenant. Breaking the terms of a covenant involves far more personal risk than breaking the terms of a contract.

Burke failed to understand that a civil covenant is not a contract. A covenant is far more authoritative because it is under special sanctions by God. This is why we are to hold the state in higher regard than an economic contract. God's negative sanctions are a greater threat than some earthly court's negative sanctions.

Burke made another mistake. He failed to see the inter-generational aspect of all private ownership, which is based on contracts. The key distinguishing mark of the state is not its future-orientation. The state shares this with all institutions. The key to the state is the binding oath under God and in front of men.

Burke failed to see that the free market is basic to any system of future-oriented responsibility. He also failed to discuss parents' training of children as governed by the requirements of free market competition for resources, including human labor. He used the idea of an inter-generational future-oriented contract to justify the state. But this same future-orientation is far more relevant to economic inheritance than to affairs of state. Why? Because property owners can increase the present value of their property by paying attention to expected future demand for the long-term net output of every asset. It is far easier for someone to assess the future value of a piece of property that he owns, compared to the future net productivity of state officials. A person can do little to affect the performance of state officials. He can do a great deal to add to the value of what he owns.

Burke did not frame his discussion in terms of binding oaths taken by citizens under God, but he did correctly seek to distinguish the authority of the state from the authority of a contract. The state possesses greater authority than a market contract, he wrote. He was correct, but he did not offer a reason that distinguishes a state covenant from a market contract. He spoke of reverence for the state. But why should the state be revered? I have an answer: because it is *not* based on a contract. He called the state a partnership. This muddled judicial categories even more. A partnership is a long-term business relationship. It ceases to be legally binding when either partner dies. But a corporation does not die. Burke did not foresee the rise of corporations over the next 70 years.

He waxed eloquent about the state's long-term authority over all aspects of society. This outlook, wherever believed, adds to the legitimacy of the state in areas that ought to be outside of its lawful jurisdiction.

> It is to be looked on with other reverence; because it is not a partnership in things subservient only to the gross animal existence of a temporary and perishable nature. It is a partnership in all science; a partnership in all art; a partnership in every virtue, and in all perfection. As the ends of such a partnership cannot be obtained in many generations, it becomes a partnership not only between those who are living, but between those who are living, those who are dead, and those who are to be born. Each contract of each particular state is but a clause in the great primaeval contract of eternal society, linking the lower with the higher natures, connecting the visible and invisible world, according to a fixed compact sanctioned by the inviolable oath which holds all physical and all moral natures, each in their appointed place.[1]

This inter-generational aspect of civil government is not unique to the state. It also applies to family government and church government. It is also an inescapable aspect of the individual covenant, because someone will inherit. Because of economic inheritance, there is equally a "great primaeval contract of eternal society" in market affairs, as well

1. Edmund Burke, *Reflections on the Revolution in France* (1790), Book 2, Chapter 1, paragraph 159.

as civil affairs. This is why inheritance is an inescapable concept, both for individual ownership and collective ownership.

Christians should defend the idea of the civil covenant based on its God-given role as the sanctions-bringer against criminals in history. It defends the other covenants from violence, theft, and fraud. Christians should not view the state as different from the other covenants with respect to the categories of past, present, and future. They all are marked by these three categories.

C. The Social Gospel

The moral and legal foundations of capitalism are based on biblical ethical norms. This is why free market societies prosper. If private property is upheld by custom and civil law, then capitalism can and will flourish. If future-orientation becomes widespread—an outlook that is the result of optimism concerning the future—then the rate of investment will increase. If a rejection of envy is widely adopted, then cooperation across economic classes will increase. If taxes remain lower than Samuel's warning figure of 10% (I Sam. 8:14, 17),[2] then high economic growth will be maintained. If wealth gained through entrepreneurship is upheld by the people who influence public opinion, there will be economic growth.

Societies can for a time adopt the fruits of a biblical worldview, but without adopting Christianity. They will prosper. Conversely, Christian societies ever since 1914 have adopted non-Christian attitudes toward time and wealth. Fertility rates have declined. This has reduced the future output of the crucial economic resource: human creativity.[3]

Civil government is supposed to preserve justice, defend the nation's boundaries from invasion, and provide peace. It is not to tax at excessive rates: as much as 10%. It is required by God to defend private property: "You shall not steal" (Ex. 20:15).[4] It is required to create the judicial

2. Gary North, *Disobedience & Defeat: An Economic Commentary on the Historical Books* (Moulton, Alabama: Axehead Press, [2012] 2029), ch. 14.

3. Julian Simon, *The Ultimate Resource* (Princeton, New Jersey: Princeton University Press, 1971).

4. North, *Authority & Dominion*, ch. 8.

conditions for creativity to flourish. Its own creativity is limited to discovering and then enforcing biblical principles of civil law in specific circumstances. This will produce a free market social order. This in turn will lead to economic growth (Lev. 26:1–13,[5] Deut. 28:1–14[6]). The biblical concept of the state is simple to summarize. Small is beautiful. Less is more.

This conclusion has been denied by most American Protestant academics in the social sciences and in seminaries ever since the end of World War II. The advocates of the social gospel denied this by the late 1880s, but they were generally theological liberals. They were ecumenists. They did not get support from fundamentalists. They got opposition. The Federal Council of Churches began in 1908. It was theologically liberal and pro-social gospel. John D. Rockefeller, Sr. put up 5% of the initial funding. Its name was changed to the National Council of Churches in 1950.[7] The outlook of the NCC slowly began to infiltrate into the evangelical academic community. Social gospel-teaching Evangelical seminary professors and college professors faced opposition from donors who were opposed to the welfare state. These donors believed their Bibles. They sensed that the social gospel was not taught in the Bible, even though they could not articulate their ideas in academic jargon. Academic evangelicals had to persuade them that the social gospel is truly biblical. To accomplish this task, they first denied that biblical law is binding. Most church members believed this already. They had been taught this from the pulpit for three centuries. That made them vulnerable.

The old social gospel did not penetrate Protestant evangelical churches outside of the mainline denominations. The social gospel leadership was frustrated. Fundamantalists never accepted it. Conservative evangelicals resisted. Then, in 1977, a new, evangelical-friendly version of the social gospel appeared. Its main wedge was a book by a history professor, Ronald J. Sider: *Rich Christians in an Age of Hunger* (1977). The title was provocative. It was guilt-producing. So was

5. Gary North, *Boundaries & Dominion: An Economic Commentary on Leviticus* (Moulton, Alabama: Axehead Press, [1994, 2012] 2026), chaps. 32, 33.

6. North, *Inheritance & Dominion*, chaps. 69, 70.

7. C. Gregg Singer, *Unholy Alliance: The History of the National Council of Churches* (New Rochelle, New York: Arlington House, 1975).

the text. It was co-published by the evangelical Protestant InterVaristy Press and the liberal Catholic Paulist Press. This ecumenism made it unique. It represented a common theology: the social gospel. I hired David Chilton in 1981 to write a refutation: *Productive Christians*.[8] Sider never responded in print. I debated him in 1981 at Gordon-Conwell Seminary. The other major advocate in that period was a professor of sociology, Tony Campolo.[9]

The high-water mark of the new social gospel came about the time that InterVarsity Press' symposium on wealth and poverty was published: 1984. Three chapters promoted the welfare state. Mine opposed it. That November, voters elected Ronald Reagan to his second term by the largest electoral college victory since James Monroe's second victory in 1820. He was vociferously opposed to the welfare state. Evangelical laymen voted overwhelmingly for him. The new social gospel, always a small movement outside of Christian academia, got even smaller. It is represented today by Jim Wallis, the director of a small organization, Sojourners. I devote a department on my website to Wallis: "Questions for Jim Wallis." I began posting questions in September 2005. He has never publicly acknowledged my existence or publically answered any of my questions. He is a Left-wing political activist who makes $190,000 a year running a tax-exempt charity,[10] an officially nonpartisan organization. (I ran the tax-exempt Institute for Christian Economics from 1975 to 2001, when I shut it down. I never took a salary. I received no book royalties.)

With the bankruptcy of the Soviet Union in the late 1980s, and then its disappearance on Christmas Day, 1991, the appeal of liberation theology faded rapidly in Roman Catholicism. Liberation theology had been a vocal Left-wing movement in Latin America and in some Catholic religious orders. After 1991, it went out of style among intellectuals, both inside and outside the Catholic Church. Pope Francis is a closet liberation theologian. He was trained in Latin America during the heyday of the movement. But there is no strong liberation theology move-

8. David Chilton, *Productive Christians: A Biblical Response to Socialist Economics* (Moulton, Alabama: Axehead Press, [1981, 1985] 2022).

9. Campolo lost much of credibility after President Bill Clinton's scandal with Monica Lewinsky in 1998. Campolo had been one of Clinton's spiritual advisers.

10. See charitynavigator.org/ein/237380554 (accessed October 15, 2022).

ment in the Church today. Baptized Marxism has lost its cachet. It has become out of date, which is fatal among theological liberals.

Nevertheless, the old political slogan is true: "You can't beat something with nothing." There has to be a biblically mandated and positive alternative. There is. That is what this multi-volume book is all about.

Conclusion

There are numerous themes is this book. Here are a few of the more prominent themes. The most prominent theme is this: "What do economists know, and how can they know it?" This is the issue of epistemology. It raises the following issues.

- Autonomy vs. theonomy
- Creator/creature distinction
- The one (unity) and the many (plurality)
- Permanent law (Parmenides) and historical flux (Heraclitus)
- The subjective imputation of economic value
- Subjective value (nominalism) vs. objective value (realism)
- The ordinal ranking of economic value vs. cardinal ranking
- The objective manifestation of prices
- The interpersonal comparison of subjective utilities
- Representative imputation of economic value
- Delegated sovereignty vs. original sovereignty
- Methodology: individual, holistic, and covenantal
- Deductive theory vs. inductive theory
- Value-free economic theory vs. value-derived economic theory
- Product substitution as the foundation of market pricing
- Monetary high bid wins. Should it?
- Praxeology (universal social science) and catallactics (market theory)
- Future-orientation vs. present-orientation
- Man as the image of God
- Man as God's agent in history
- Guardianship, sharecropping, and auctioneering

- Four-way responsibility
- Scarcity as the starting point of economic analysis
- Ownership as the starting point of economic analysis
- Economic growth and the limits of time
- Plan reconciliation in institutional covenants
- Equality vs. liberty
- Ethics and economic growth
- Production vs. consumption as the supreme economic goal
- Personal self-interest and economic growth
- Kingdom competition as zero-sum

I have offered a rival way of approaching economics specifically and social science generally: in terms of the five-point structure of the biblical covenant. I assert, though do not prove here, that humanistic economic science also has its version of this model, but with different content, especially on the key point, sovereignty.

1. Sovereignty: man (either individual or collective)
2. Authority: reason
3. Law: evolutionary
4. Sanctions: profit/loss or bureaucratic
5. Inheritance: economic growth

I argue that the supposed autonomy of economic science is a myth. Economics as a separate discipline does not stand on its own two feet. It is derived. It imports its values from outside the discipline. It imports objective value theory through the back door of statistical aggregates. Economists invoke science to add credibility to their advice, which is the only reason they get paid by the state: widespread faith in the authority of science. But this invocation is a sham. Why? Because it is scientifically impossible to compare interpersonal subjective values, given the premise of modern economics: subjective (imputed) value theory. *Therefore, there is no such thing as scientific economic policy advice.* Yet economists refuse to discuss this issue, which was recognized as early as 1938 in an exchange between Roy Harrod and Lionel Robbins in *The Economic Journal.* Robbins surrendered to Harrod.[1] This debate is

1. Gary North, *Sovereignty & Dominion: An Economic Commentary on Genesis* (Moulton, Alabama: Axehead Press, [1982, 2012] 2022), ch. 5.

long forgotten. Economists continue to provide policy advice, and states continue to pay them.

I have proposed a theology-based solution to this epistemological dilemma, and also numerous other epistemological dilemmas. I do not expect the economics profession to embrace these solutions, or even acknowledge their existence. Since members of this profession rarely discuss epistemology, I have no good reason to assume that they will pay any attention to this book.

A good example of the dualism of modern economic thought are the two standards of truth that economists apply to discussions of the way the world works economically. These two standards are completely opposed to each other. One is the theory of equilibrium. The real world is compared with a hypothetical realm in which there are neither profits nor losses, because all participants possess omniscience regarding the future. In other words, all people possess one of the incommunicable attributes of God. The other is pure randomness, which does not exist either in theory or practice. A theory of how the world works is tested for coherence by means of a tool based on incoherence. Yet both omniscience (equilibrium) and randomness are invoked at different times as a test of a theory's correspondence with the real world. This fundamental dualism (antinomy) is not mentioned in economics textbooks, or even in monographs on methodology.

The two questions treated as one: "What can economists know, and how can they know it?" The economics profession has long had two answers treated as one: "We don't know, and we don't care." They should know. If they do not know, at least they should care.

I knew about some of these problems in 1975, when I wrote this essay: "Economics: From Reason to Intuition." I had already begun my economic commentary on the Bible. In September 1977, the month my son was born, I increased my pace: ten hours a week, 50 weeks a year. I set a deadline: February 11, 2012, when I would turn 70. As it turned out, that was the day my son got married. I finished writing with a couple of weeks to spare. A typesetter completed the 31-volume project.

My goal today is to complete my four-volume treatise on Christian economics. I have finished three volumes: the student's edition, the teacher's edition, and the activist's edition. Ahead is the scholar's edition. The set will cover the five points of the biblical covenant structure in all of the five biblical covenants: dominion, individual, family, church, and state. I may have time to write a book on economic epistemology. The basics of that book are covered in the Appendix, which I wrote in 1975. It was published in 1976. I wrote it on a portable manual typewriter: the bad old days.[2]

Will I complete all this? That depends on James 4:15. Or, if you prefer, *b'ezras hashem.*

---

2. Gary North, "What You Can Learn from My 1974 Desk," *GaryNorth.com,* September 4, 2015, garynorth.com/members/14233.cfm.

Appendix

Economics: From Reason to Intuition*

This, then, is a further sense in which Economics can be truly said to assume rationality in human society. It makes no pretence, as has been alleged so often, that action is necessarily rational in the sense that ends pursued are not mutually inconsistent. There is nothing in its generalisations which necessarily implies reflective deliberation in ultimate valuation. It rests upon no assumption that individuals will always act rationally. But it does depend for its practical raison d'etre upon the assumption that it is desirable that they should do so. It does assume that, within the bounds of necessity, it is desirable to choose ends which can be achieved harmoniously.

Lionel Robbins[1]

A. Epistemology

Epistemology asks this: "What can man know, and how can he know it?" Modern economics as a discipline suffers from the same crucial limitations found in all other post-Kantian fields of scholarship. Ulti-

* This is a slightly revised version of my essay with the same name, which was published in Gary North (ed.), *Foundations of Christian Scholarship: Essays in the Van Til Perspective* (Vallecito, California: Ross House, 1976).

1. Lionel Robbins, *An Essay on the Nature and Significance of Economic Science* (London: Macmillan, 1932), 157.

mately resting on a foundation of pure contingency and chaos, the economics profession affirms rationality as its *raison d'etre.* Yet economists cannot escape the fundamental rational antinomies of Kantian thought: unity vs. plurality, structure vs. change, law vs. freedom, science vs. personality, deduction vs. induction, theory vs. brute factuality, definition vs. application. When pushed to the limits of exposition, every economist finally rests his case on "intuition" or "experience" to bridge the unbridgeable Kantian gap between mind and matter. Reason collapses into mystery at the heart of the economist's task. What is the economist's task? This is a little hard for the economists to say exactly. James Buchanan in 1964 cited two classic definitions from a pair of University of Chicago economists. Jacob Viner: "Economics is what economists do." Frank Knight: "And economists are those who do economics."[2]

The problem, to use Cornelius Van Til's phrase, is that for the most part, economists are not epistemologically self-conscious. In 1952, Fritz Machlup, while acting as chairman of an American Economic Association's workshop in methodology, remarked: "Usually only a small minority of American economists have professed interest in methodology. The large majority used to disclaim any interest in such issues."[3] Things have only become worse since then. The total triumph of mathematical economics has created a new, highly specialized economic technician who is buried in an esoteric universe of his own. Walter Adams remarked: "A methodological addict, he shows singular unconcern with the world as it exists. His standard of success—his pay-off matrix—is to impress the tastemakers of an ever-narrowing professional specialty. He is more and more cut off from specialists in other fields, and finds it increasingly difficult to communicate to the lay world. The result is a sort of apartheid: economists are no longer able to see the real world, and the world no longer can understand what economists are saying."[4] The quality of scholarship is increasingly Alexandrian: endless unreadable articles which have a half-life of six years or less, falling

---

2. James Buchanan, "What Should Economists Do?" *Southern Economic Journal,* XXX (Jan. 1964), 213.

3. Fritz Machlup, "Introductory Remarks," *American Economic Review, Papers and Proceedings,* XLII (May 1952), 34.

4. Walter Adams, "Economic Science, Public Policy, and Public Understanding," *Diogenes* (Fall 1969), 24.

into oblivion with rare exception almost immediately.[5] Yet the basis of personal and departmental advancement is in the publication of such articles in a handful of specialized journals.[6]

New Left economists, whether Marxian, extreme Galbraithian, or whatever, temporarily challenged the establishment economists to re-examine their calling in the late 1960s, but nothing came of this. Still, there was far more interest—critical interest—in epistemology since 1965 than could have been reasonably predicted in 1963. As Bronfenbrenner commented, in 1964 he could not find any indication of radical economics in America. "Only five years later, in late 1969, the end of ideology had itself ended."[7] Walter Weisskopf could fight the good Galbraithian battle against methodological neutrality and sterility with his lively and unread *Alienation and Economics* (1971). But criticisms against irrelevance are, for the profession, annual rituals that have zero effect. The fact of the matter is, as Bronfenbrenner stated it: "The general economist may be travelling the way of the Dodo or Passenger Pigeon Highway to extinction. He survives—as I am a survivor—as dilettante, journalist, or elementary [principles] teacher, or as an exotic variety of multiple-specialist whose several specialisms fall in more than one of our ordinary classification boxes."[8] And it does not help the situation to read Joseph Schumpeter's remark that "Economists in particular, much to the detriment of their field, have attached unreasonable importance to being understood by the general public...."[9] Yet he was eminently readable and a generalist; two decades later he would have found less reason to bother with writing that sentence. But the evil had already been accomplished; he got his wish!

One thing seems certain, however. Since 1965, we have not heard

5. A. W. Coats, "The Role of Scholarly Journals in the History of Economics: An Essay," *Journal of Economic Literature*, IX (1971), 42.

6. John J. Siegfried, "The Publishing of Economic Papers and Its Impact on Graduate Faculty Ratings," ibid., X (1972), 31–49.

7. Martin Bronfenbrenner, "Radical Economics in America: A 1970 Survey," *Journal of Economic Literature*, VIII (1970), 747. Cf. *Wall Street Journal* (Feb. 11, 1972); *Business Week* (March 18, 1972).

8. Bronfenbrenner, "Trends, Cycles, and Fads in Economic Writing," *American Economic Review, Papers & Proceedings*, LVI (May 1966), 539.

9. Joseph A. Schumpeter, *A History of Economic Analysis* (New York: Oxford University Press, 1954), 10.

speeches like the one John Kennedy delivered at Yale University in 1962. It was one of those typical "end of ideology" performances by the consummate pragmatist of the era.

> Today these old sweeping issues have largely disappeared. The central domestic problems of our time are more subtle and less simple. They relate not to basic clashes of philosophy or ideology, but to ways and means of reaching common goals—to research for sophisticated solutions to complex and obstinate ideas.... What is at stake in our economic decisions today is not some grand warfare of rival ideologies which will sweep the country with passion, but the practical management of modern economy. What we need are not labels and cliches but more basic discussion of the sophisticated and technical questions involved in keeping a great economic machinery moving ahead. I am suggesting that the problems of fiscal and monetary policy in the Sixties as opposed to the kinds of problems we faced in the Thirties demand subtle challenges for which technical answers—not political answers—must be provided.[10]

As it turned out, "can do" Liberalism couldn't, and the United States government bogged down in a fruitless war in Vietnam. We saw the nation blow apart. Anyone wishing to read a post-mortem on JFK's faith in technocratic solutions can go through David Halberstam's *The Best and the Brightest.* The naïveté of this kind of worldview is officially dead, if not yet operationally defunct (due to tenure and other forms of guild control) in the economics profession. The established men may believe in technocratic wisdom, but they are at least more humble today.

B. What Is Economics?

There have been a number of influential economists over the years who have outspokenly denied the validity of the question. Vilfredo Pareto, the late-nineteenth-century social scientist, Gunnar Myrdal, and T. W. Hutchison were among these.[11] Schumpeter, whose *History*

10. John F. Kennedy, quoted by Theodore Roszak, *The Making of a Counter Culture* (Garden City, New York: Doubleday Anchor, 1969), 11.

11. Israel Kirzner, *The Economic Point of View* (Princeton: Van Nostrand, 1960), 7.

of Economic Analysis is a classic, was another.[12] Others, most notably Lionel Robbins, vigorously denied this form of skepticism. When open disagreement can exist on so fundamental a point as the definition of what constitutes a science, the extent of the intellectual confusion is indicated. Drawing hermetically sealed definitional boundaries is not possible, given the nature of human thought and the inescapable fact of unity and diversity in all created structures, but men need operational definitions for their work. Buchanan's warning in 1964 is significant: "Economics, as a well-defined subject of scholarship, seems to be disintegrating...and realistic appraisal suggests that this inexorable process will not be stopped."[13]

Israel Kirzner's very fine study of *The Economic Point of View* (1960) surveys several definitions of economics that have been employed by members of the profession since the seventeenth century: the study of trade, of wealth and welfare, of greed, of getting the most from the least, of money and measurement, of economic choice in a scarce world, of human action. But there is one common feature that stands out over three centuries, and William Letwin called attention to it forcefully: "Nevertheless there can be no doubt that economic theory owes its present development to the fact that some men, in thinking of economic phenomena, forcefully suspended all judgments of theology, morality, and justice, were willing to consider the economy as nothing more than an intricate mechanism, refraining for the while from asking whether the mechanism worked for good or evil. That separation was made during the seventeenth century."[14] The autonomy of academic economics from "metaphysics," namely any revelation from God, is the hallmark of all contemporary economic practice. Perhaps the strongest statement on behalf of the total autonomy of economics came from Ludwig von Mises, who equated liberalism and free market economics.

> Liberalism is based upon a purely rational and scientific theory of social cooperation. The policies it recommends are the application of a system of knowledge which does not refer in any way to sentiments, intuitive

12. Schumpeter, *History*, 10.
13. Buchanan, op. cit., 222.
14. William Letwin, *The Origins of Scientific Economics* (Garden City, New York: Doubleday Anchor, [1963] 1965), 158–159.

> creeds for which no logically sufficient proof can be provided, mystical experiences, and the personal awareness of superhuman phenomena. ...They [the policies] are radically opposed to all systems of theocracy. But they are entirely neutral with regard to religious beliefs which do not pretend to interfere with the conduct of social, political, and economic affairs."[15]

The most widely respected work in the area of modern economic epistemology is Lionel Robbins' *An Essay on the Nature and Significance of Economic Science* (1932). "The economist studies the disposal of scarce means," he wrote. "Economics is the science which studies human behaviour as a relationship between ends and scarce means which have alternative uses."[16] Economics is a science of human choice among scarce alternative resources, according to Robbins. Biblically, we would say that he accepts the existence of the effects of Genesis 3:17–19, which separates him from the utopians, Marx, and many of the New Left economists.

So far, so good, but it does not stop here. Everyone who claims to be a modern scientist wants his colleagues to regard him as utterly neutral and objective. Of course, he admits in theory that this is ultimately impossible, citing Heisenberg, Kuhn, and so forth to show he is epistemologically literate, but at least all good scientists are neutral and objective with respect to revelational religion. Robbins was no less a part of this tradition of neutrality. "The economist is not concerned with ends as such. He is concerned with the way in which the attainment of ends is limited. The ends may be noble or they may be base. They may be 'material' or 'immaterial'—if ends can so be described. But if the attainment of one set of ends involves the sacrifice of others, then it has an economic aspect."[17] *Ultimate ends are scientifically irrelevant.* The academic economist is primarily—perhaps entirely—a technician. Robbins believed that, in sealing off economics from questions of ultimate ends, he had accomplished a necessary intellectual task, but in fact he opened up an overwhelming problem for epistemology, one

15. Ludwig von Mises, *Human Action* (New Haven, Connecticut: Yale University Press, 1949), 155.

16. Robbins, *Nature and Significance*, 16.

17. Ibid., 25. Cf. Mises, *Human Action*, 95–96.

which almost no economist has had the courage to face publicly. Frank Knight was an exception.

> The "scientific" view assumes that changes in man can be completely accounted for in terms of external and prior natural conditions. A theory which recognizes ends and allows man real initiative in changing himself or his environment is in contradiction with a scientific conception of human nature and transfers the discussion to a different realm of discourse. In the writer's opinion the contradiction is insurmountable in the present stage of intellectual development. Philosophy and experience have not taught us concepts which enable us to think comfortably in the terms of what experience and common sense force us to recognize as real and valid.[18]

This may be the reason that Armen Alchian, a leading economist and formerly chairman of the department at UCLA, refused to use the word "choice" in front of a colloquium of graduate students and scholars in 1969. I was one of them. He hedged by using "demonstrated preference" or similar terms. The concept of choice implies an unscientific, methodologically unverifiable concept of human freedom, or so he believed.

There is nothing in Robbins' work to indicate that he understood the issue he was raising. He simply went on: "Economics is neutral as between ends. Economics cannot pronounce on the validity of ultimate judgments of value."[19] And on: "Applied economics consists of propositions of the form, 'If you want to do this, then you must do that.'"[20] The economist may only advise men in terms of their stated ends. I suppose the economist in Nazi Germany or the Soviet Union in the 1930s would not have questioned the national ends of liquidation or mass imprisonment; he only would have examined the technical questions concerning the least expensive means of accomplishing these ends. Economics is pure technique, and therefore value-free, you see. Economists promise not to tell moralists what to think in the realm of ends, and by this treaty they gain autonomy for their own technical activities. Moralists

18. Frank H. Knight, *On the History and Method of Economics* (Chicago: University of Chicago Press, 1956), 194n.
19. Robbins, *Nature*, 147.
20. Ibid., 149.

are supposed to agree not to influence the form or content of economics. As Friedman put it: "Positive economics is in principle independent of any particular ethical position or normative judgment."[21] Economics is therefore rational, as contrasted to moralistic or value-laden.

Why this religious quest for neutrality, for a value-free science? George Stigler, Friedman's colleague, who also won the Nobel Prize in economics, offered one straightforward explanation: "The reason for assigning such an austere role to economics is this: it is the fundamental tenet of those who believe in free discussion that matters of fact and of logic can (eventually) be agreed upon by competent men of good will, that matters of taste cannot be reconciled by free discussion. Assuming this to be true, it is apparent that if value judgments were mixed with logic and observation, a science would make but little progress."[22] F. A. Hayek announced a similar faith in human reason. Speaking of those who favor socialistic solutions, he wrote: "Yet if we have not convinced them, the reason must be that our arguments are not yet quite good enough, that we have not yet made explicit some of the foundations on which our conclusions rest."[23] It is more than a little ironic that Hayek and Stigler, the proponents of faith in reason, both supporters of free market ideas, both colleagues at the University of Chicago, although not in the same department, could agree on the whole question of reason in the social sciences. Stigler was an inductionist, while Hayek's *Counter-Revolution of Science* is one of the most eloquent pleas for a deductivist approach. When groups of Chicago School economists and Austrian School economists used to get together in the late 1960s and early 1970s, they had to avoid the whole issue of epistemology if the conference was not to break down entirely. So much for the efficacy of (supposedly) screening out value judgments for the sake of sweet reason and ultimate intellectual accord.

21. Milton Friedman, *Essays in Positive Economics* (Chicago: University of Chicago Press, 1953), 4.

22. George Stigler, *The Theory of Competitive Price* (New York: Macmillan, 1942), 15–16.

23. F. A. Hayek, "The Defense of Our Civilization Against Intellectual Error," in *What's Past Is Prologue* (Irvington-on-Hudson, New York: Foundation for Economic Education, 1968), 41.

C. Reason: Inductive

The vast bulk of economists regard themselves as essentially empirically oriented inductivists. They are men who rely, ultimately, on "the facts." They are not empiricists in the old German Historical School mold, however. That late-nineteenth-century group of Prussian academic socialists, led primarily by Gustav Schmoller, was initially committed to the premise that economic theory is always relative to time and place, and that only by exhaustive monographic studies of cultural history could scholars come to judgments about economic theory.[24] The approach of this school was holistic and organic: all of human life had to be studied, not simply an "isolated segment" known as economic life. This approach was so utterly fruitless in the production of economic theorems that it was generally abandoned by 1900. There were just too many data to handle coherently. The unsophisticated positivism of the German Historical School could not sustain itself against the demands of intellectual specialization. In order to examine human history, the investigator has to have an idea of what he is looking for, which in the area of economic history means that he needs some basic economic theory. "Facts" do not speak for themselves, and "laws" do not leap off of the pages of historical data.

Today's empirical economist is committed to the idea of economic theory. His model is generally that of the natural sciences. Friedman's description of positive economics is standard: "Its task is to provide a system of generalizations that can be used to make correct predictions about the consequences of any change in circumstances. Its performance is to be judged by the precision, scope, and conformity with experience of the predictions it yields."[25] He went on to state that the decisive test "is whether the hypothesis works for the phenomena it purports to explain."[26] The test is therefore factual: "Only factual evidence can show whether it [theory] is 'right' or 'wrong' or, better, tentatively 'accepted' as valid or 'rejected.'"[27] Economics is empirical, inductive, *a posteriori*, fact-oriented. Facts cannot prove a theory, but they may

24. Schumpeter, *History of Economic Analysis*, 807ff.
25. Friedman, *Essays*, 4.
26. Ibid., 30.
27. Ibid., 8.

fail to disprove some theories.[28] The process is: . . . facts . . . theory . . . facts . . . theory—endlessly, always in a refining process.[29] If you can find a better theory (at no extra cost), choose it.

Friedman then confronted a basic post-Kantian antinomy, the problem of defining "theory," "fact," and explaining the interrelationship of each to each and both to the human mind.

> More generally, a hypothesis or theory consists of an assertion that certain forces are, and by implication others are not, important for a particular class of phenomena and a specification of the manner of action of the forces it asserts to be important. We can regard the hypothesis as consisting of two parts: first, a conceptual world or abstract model simpler than the "real world" and containing only the forces that the hypothesis asserts to be important [Weber's "ideal type"—G. N.]; second, a set of rules defining the class of phenomena for which the "model" can be taken to be an adequate representation of the "real world" and specifying the correspondence between the variables or entities in the model and observable phenomena.
>
> These two parts are very different in character. The model is abstract and complete; it is an "algebra" or "logic." Mathematics and formal logic come into their own in checking its consistency and completeness and exploring its implications. There is no place in the model for, and no function to be served by, vagueness, maybe's, or approximations. The air pressure is zero, not "small," for a vacuum; the demand curve for the product of a competitive producer is horizontal (has a slope of zero), not "almost horizontal."
>
> The rules for using the model, on the other hand, cannot possibly be abstract and complete. They must be concrete and in consequence incomplete—completeness is possible only in a conceptual world, not in the "real world," however it may be interpreted. . . . In seeking to make a science as "objective" as possible, our aim should be to formulate the rules explicitly in so far as possible and continually to widen the range of phenomena for which it is possible to do so. But, no matter how successful we may be in this attempt, there inevitably will remain room for judgment in applying the rules. Each occurrence has some features peculiarly its own, not covered by the explicit rules. The capacity to judge that these are or are not to be disregarded, that they should or

28. Ibid., 9.
29. Ibid., 139.

> should not affect what observable phenomena are to be identified with what entities in the model, is something that cannot be taught; it can be learned but only by experience and exposure to the "right" scientific atmosphere, not by rote. It is at this point that the "amateur" is separated from the "professional" in all sciences and that the thin line is drawn which distinguishes the "crackpot" from the scientist.[30]

First, just how coherent is the model? Friedman asserted that it can be consistent and complete. I suspect that he was here giving more credit to a rival discipline—mathematics—than the discipline's best minds ever claim for it. Kurt Gödel's hypothesis denies that a mathematical proposition can be simultaneously consistent and complete, which is precisely what Friedman naïvely asserts as an ideal for the logic of the economic model.

Second, how do the rules for using the model actually connect it with the data? Why is such a contact possible? Eugene Wigner, the Nobel Prize winner in physics, has called attention to this very anomaly: it is an unreasonably effective correspondence which secular scientists simply cannot explain.[31] If the rules are incomplete, how can they be fitted with the "complete" model?

Third, the "real world," which Friedman was careful to put in quotation marks, is really the product of our senses, as interpreted by our minds. In Kantian language, concepts without percepts are empty, while percepts without concepts are blind. So, the data are never raw; there is no operational brute factuality. The data are already interpreted as we receive them. How do we know, for example, when a perceived trade cycle is nothing more than the product of our own ingenuity? The great mathematical economist Ragnar Frisch once demonstrated the existence of a particular economic cycle before a group of professional colleagues—a regularity where none had been perceived before by any of them. Harlan McCracken describes the finale: "When the group was thrilled and almost dumfounded by the results, they were mildly informed that the omega operations had been performed on a relief map of Europe."[32]

30. Ibid., 24–25.

31. Eugene P. Wigner, "The Unreasonable Effectiveness of Mathematics in the Natural Sciences," *Communications on Pure and Applied Mathematics*, XIII (1960), 1–14.

32. McCracken, "Comments," *American Economic Review, Papers & Proceedings*, XLIII (May 1953), 277. Cf. Gunther Stent, *The Coming of the Golden Age: A View of*

Finally, what of Friedman's appeal to "the capacity to judge" and "experience"? Here we have an appeal, ultimately, to some form of intuition as the means of bridging the gap between the model and the perceived historical data (which may or may not be in conformity to the economic world "out there"). There is no strict one-to-one application of the abstract mental model and perceived reality, for then the model would be as complex as reality itself, swallowed up in the immensity of brute factuality. Yet it is believed to be in conformity to the basic outline of the already perceived facts. But how do we know? How can we have such faith in the coherence of our minds, the orderliness of nature, and the intuitive ability of our minds (or whatever it is) to bridge the gap? We must exercise faith—a remarkable quantity of faith. Without it, there could be no economics. So our neutral, rationalistic practitioners simply put this statement of faith in the back of their minds and forget it. Epistemology, at the truly crucial points, is not a popular topic among secularists.

Ultimately, Friedman asserted, "The construction of hypotheses is a creative act of inspiration, intuition, and invention; its essence is the vision of something new in familiar material."[33] He was quite correct, of course, but this does not answer the question. How is man so endowed, for what purpose does he have the gift? How, in fact, are we sure on rational grounds that he does have it? We need a theory to explain the phenomenon, and intuition, being nonrational at bottom, cannot be made to fit any rationalistic theory. We think we perceive men in the activity of linking theories and facts, but can they do this accurately, really, and if so, how? In effect, the secularist replies, "he just can, that's all!" Faith, faith, wonderful faith!

Is there some accepted, fairly stable body of acceptable theory? Probably not, says Friedman. "Observed facts are necessarily finite in number; possible hypotheses, infinite" [I do not understand this—G. N.][34] Furthermore, "Any theory is necessarily provisional and subject to change

the End of Progress (Garden City, New York: Natural History Press, 1969), 115 ff.; Benoit Mandelbrot, "New Methods in Statistical Economics," *Journal of Political Economy*, LXXI (1963), 421ff.

33. Friedman, *Essays*, 13.

34. Ibid., 9.

with the advance of knowledge."[35] In short, all we can say, somehow, in faith, is that "some parts of economic theory clearly deserve more confidence than others."[36] (Try and find one that all economists agree on!) You can check these statements by comparing them with "facts." But which facts? Facts selected by which theorist? Not all facts, since our knowledge can never be exhaustive.[37] Remember, "we cannot perceive 'facts' without a theory."[38] Yet within the shifting sands of knowledge, there is somehow structure enough to establish an academic discipline. Or at least maybe there is.

Van Til put this problem in a starkly penetrating analysis.

> If man is made the final reference point in predication, knowledge cannot get under way, and if it could get under way it could not move forward. That is to say, in all non-Christian forms of epistemology there is first the idea that to be understood a fact must be understood exhaustively. It must be reducible to a part of a system of timeless logic. But man himself and the facts of his experience are subject to change. How is he ever to find within himself an a priori resting point? He himself is on the move.... If we do not with Calvin presuppose the self-contained God back of the self-conscious act of the knowing mind of man, we are doomed to be lost in an endless and bottomless flux.[39]

Is there a coherent world out there, out beyond the powers of our perception? Does it, or some part of it, conform to the logical structure of our minds? Is there some means by which we can discover such order? How do we find the rules that might allow us to make deductions from our theories and predictions about the facts? The facts are like beads for the secularist, said Van Til, and the theories are like string. But on the premises of the secularist, the beads have no holes in them, and the string is infinitely long. Furthermore, there may be more than one string! The only way to string them is unknown, and this the secularist calls "intuition." Friedman was no different from epistemologists in other academic disciplines. Either theory is swallowed up in the facts,

---

35. Ibid., 41.
36. Idem.
37. Ibid., 32.
38. Ibid., 34.
39. Cornelius Van Til, *An Introduction to Systematic Theology* (Phillipsburg, New Jersey: Presbyterian and Reformed, [1961] 1978), 167, vol. V of *In Defense of the Faith.*

or else the facts are swallowed up by the theory, or else theory remains wholly removed from all facts. Van Til's words are inescapable:

> The point we are now concerned to stress is the atomistic character of the non-Christian methodology. The idea of system is for it merely a limiting notion. It is merely ideal. What is more, it must forever remain but an ideal. To become reality this ideal would have to destroy science itself. It would have to demolish the individuality of each fact as it came to know it. But if it did this, it would no longer be knowledge of a fact that is different from any other fact. The method of non-Christian science then requires that to be known facts must be known as part of a system. And since the Christian idea of a system as due to the counsel of God is by definition excluded, it is man himself that must know this system. But to know the system he must know it intuitively. He cannot know it discursively because discursive thought, if it is to be in contact with reality at all, must partake of the piecemeal character of non-rational being. Each individual concept that pretends to be a concept with respect to things that have their existence in the world of time must partake of the *de facto* character of these facts themselves.[40]

Intuitive knowledge is all that is left for man, and intuitive knowledge, not being discursive, participates in the chaos of random factuality, i.e., is not rational knowledge. Friedman, ending as he did with intuition, destroyed the logical character of hypothetically rational inductive economic science. *At the heart of "rational" inductive thought is a bedrock of irrationalism.* Without a doctrine of divine creation, the inductive rationalist builds his foundation on the sand of pure chance, and whirl does not give up his kingdom.

I have not singled out Friedman as a stick man. He was an eloquent defender of modern economic science, and his chapter on methodology has become standard in the profession. Other expositions echo his. Gregor Sebba, a mathematical economist, has raised similar issues. He wrote that "Classical economics made the tremendous discovery that the quantifiable features of a modern economy can be represented by a general mechanistic model capable of mathematization and presumably

40. Cornelius Van Til, *Apologetics* (Syllabus, Westminster Theological Seminary, 1959), 76–77.

prediction."[41] Positive economics, officially neutral with respect to values, can predict the future. But with prediction comes control, Sebba argued. New forms of macroeconomic planning are possible through the use of input-output techniques developed by both Soviet and Western economists. "Here the distinction between 'technical' and 'economic' problems obviously no longer applies."[42] But then a problem appears which had been held back by the hypothetical value neutrality of positive economic theory. "Unlike classical theory, it is not confined to the question what the terminal state of the economic system will be, given its initial state and its laws of operation; normative economics can simultaneously consider the initial and the terminal state and select the minimum path from one to another. The theory of allocations has the markings of a rigorous, predictive, general theory of planning."[43] Hayek demonstrated eloquently in his *Road to Serfdom* (1944) that central planning can never be neutral; it is based on the value preferences of the central planners.

Positive economics, because it involves knowledge, necessarily involves power. And power is never neutrally applied. Sebba saw this clearly, and he drove home his point.

> Control then consists of prediction offered as purely technical, neutral, powerless advice. The sons of Adam Smith fear control of man over man. And rightly so, for such control implies the dehumanization of the human realm. The ethos of classical economics revolts against this consequence. But its epistemology works towards it. So long as the theory is unpredictive, the conflict can remain unresolved and even undetected. But should the theory become predictive, it may yet turn against its origins and become instrumental in subverting economic freedom.[44]

The *nature-freedom antinomy* of all modern thought reasserts itself once again. On the one hand, knowledge of the world is seen as giving men power and therefore freedom from an impersonal, capricious universe. Yet with the advent of power, man falls under the sway of his own creation, like Dr. Frankenstein and his monster. Man, defined as being

41. Gregor Sebba, "The Development of the Concepts of Mechanism and Model in Physical Science and Economic Thought," *American Economic Review, Papers & Proceedings*, XLIII (May 1953), 261.

42. Ibid., 263.

43. Ibid., 264.

44. Ibid., 266.

no more than a natural creature, becomes as subject to his own laws as nature is. *Secular law eats away at the foundations of secular freedom.*[45] Classical economics destroys itself in an orgy of planning. The attempt at being epistemologically neutral to God and all values becomes dust in the mouth; values, never truly banished from science's closed universe, reappear in power.

D. Reason: Deductive

For almost a century, deductive reasoning in the social sciences has been out of favor. Its defenders are limited almost exclusively in economics to the followers of Ludwig von Mises. Inductive reason, supposedly the characteristic of the natural sciences, has been adopted by most modern economists. Now, however, the perception on the part of some social scientists of the implications of Thomas Kuhn's *The Structure of Scientific Revolutions* (1962) has begun to shake their faith in the paradigm of purely inductive research. It has become more and more obvious to the readers of Kuhn's book that there is no scholarship apart from intellectual presuppositions. Academic guilds form around an accepted body of these premises, and they in turn become the foundation of "normal science"—the drudge-like repetitive science of the vast majority of men in any given era or discipline. Thus, research is guild-oriented and essentially *a priori:* the questions asked, the ways in which the questions are to be answered, the form of presentation of the answer are all determined by the prevailing definition of the particular discipline as set forth by the academic guild. Thus, Kuhn's analysis argues, science is never purely inductive, objective, or neutral. It is governed by presuppositions that are thought to be "rational" and "inescapable." From time to time younger members of the guild do escape them, overturning the accepted paradigm; this constitutes a scientific revolution.

The writings of Ludwig von Mises constitute the strongest case for

45. It seems to me to be quite likely that input-output analysis will prove to be premature, and that Mises' argument that without a free market and private ownership, no rational planning is possible, will reassert itself. But to the extent that modern economists believe that they have predictive power due to any economic tool, there is a tendency for that tool to become a means of economic planning and external control.

pure deductive rationalism. He took seriously the second half of Kant's slogan, "precepts without concepts are blind." There is no scientific investigation by the social scientist that is not in terms of fixed intellectual categories. His was the consistent Kantian world of humanism. Man is the starting point. "*Panta rei*, everything is in ceaseless flux, says Heraclitus; there is no permanent being; all is change and becoming. ... For epistemology, the theory of human knowledge, there is certainly something that it cannot help considering as permanent, viz., the logical and praxeological [science of human action] structure of the human mind, on the one hand, and the power of the human senses, on the other hand."[46] Mises brought back the old debate between Parmenides and Heraclitus. Parmenides held, in Van Til's words, "that only that can exist which is fully subject to the laws of human logic. In other words Parmenides assumes that the reach of human logic is the limit of possible existence."[47] But Heraclitus countered that the essence of the world is flux, beyond the static categories of universal human reason. Along with all post-Kantians, Mises held to both positions: logic is static and can understand some things "out there," but there is some aspect of flux and chaos in the universe, and it is here that man finds his freedom from totalitarian humanistic law. In other words, as far as human nature is concerned, "epistemology must look upon it as unchanging."

Man needs an unchanging point of reference, Mises believed, if he is to be able to say anything accurate about anything. *The unchanging point of reference is the human mind.*

> Kant, awakened by Hume from his "dogmatic slumbers," put the rationalistic doctrine upon a new basis. Experience, he taught, provides only the raw material out of which the mind forms what is called knowledge. All knowledge is conditioned by the categories that precede any data of experience both in time and in logic. The categories are a priori; they are the mental equipment of the individual that enables him to think and—we may add—to act. As all reasoning presupposes the a priori categories, it is vain to embark upon attempts to prove or disprove them.[48]

---

46. Lugwig von Mises, *The Ultimate Foundation of Economic Science: An Essay on Method* (Princeton: Van Nostrand, 1962), 1.

47. Cornelius Van Til, A *Christian Theory of Knowledge* (Nutley, New Jersey: Presbyterian and Reformed Publishing Co., 1969), 171.

48. Mises, *Ultimate Foundation*, 12.

What are these categories? They are independent of biological evolution. Evolution is continuous, while the catagories appeared in man discontinuously.[49] They are not innate ideas. "They are the necessary mental tool to arrange sense data in a systematic way, and transform them into facts of experience...."[50] They are *pragmatic*: "Only those groups could survive whose numbers acted in accordance with the right categories, i.e., with those that were in conformity with reality and therefore—to use the concept of pragmatism—worked."[51] Apparently, had the world been a different kind of world, those using the categories would not have survived, and the categories would have disappeared—not, somehow, evolving into something else. Where categories are concerned, life is one huge crap shoot; you either have them, or you don't. Or, paraphrasing one scholar, "When you're hot, you're hot, and when you're not, you're not."[52]

The reason that the categories function is that the universe is orderly, in part. "No thinking and no acting would be possible to man if the universe were chaotic, i.e., if there were no regularity whatever in the succession and concatenation of events. In such a world of unlimited contingency nothing could be perceived but ceaseless kaleidoscopic change. There would be no possibility for man to expect anything."[53] Therefore, he concluded, "Reasoning is necessarily always deductive. ...All human knowledge concerning the universe presupposes and rests upon the cognition of the regularity in the succession and concatenation of observable events. It would be vain to search for a rule if there were no regularity."[54]

This is empiricism's Achilles heel: it rejects the category of regularity in the microscopic sphere, looking instead for statistical laws of probability in aggregate events. Empiricists fail to search for explanations in terms of individual human action.[55] It is a misuse of the methodology of the natural sciences, on the assumption that people are not acting beings. Empiricism postulates pure randomness of individual events.[56]

---

49. Ibid., 8, 14.
50. Ibid., 16.
51. Ibid., 15.
52. Jerry Reed, "When You're Hot, You're Hot" (RCA Records, 1971).
53. Mises, *Ultimate Foundation*, 19.
54. Ibid., 19.
55. Ibid., 23.
56. Ibid., 21–22.

Mises came to the heart of the epistemological problem:

> Following in the wake of Kant's analysis, philosophers raised the question: How can the human mind, by aprioristic thinking, deal with the reality of the external world? As far as praxeology [the science of human action] is concerned, the answer is obvious. Both, a priori thinking and reasoning on the one hand and human action on the other, are manifestations of the human mind. The logical structure of the human mind creates the reality of the action. Reason and action are congeneric and homogeneous, two aspects of the same phenomenon.[57]

Mises was far more epistemologically self-conscious than most contemporary economists. He knew the ground on which all modern secularists must stand if they are to defend the idea of modern science from total chaos, and so he affirmed, as Kant did, the creative ordering power of the human mind. This, as Van Til argued throughout his career, is the heart of modern Kantian thought. Mises acknowledged it and built upon it.

The historical sciences, however, are different from praxeology and its most developed subdivision, economics. History is concerned with the flux of human life, not regularities. "What distinguishes the descriptions of history from those of the natural sciences is that they are not interpreted in the light of the category of regularity."[58] Men must look to history for *meaning*; unlike natural events, men act in terms of final causes. The interpreter searches for meaning in the minds of the participants: what did it mean for them? "The autonomy of history or, as we may say, of the various historical disciplines consists of their dedication to the study of meaning."[59] The goal is radical autonomy: "History is man-centered; it has nothing to do with any point of view of God or some quasi-God. . . ."[60] Man provides the meaning. God's knowledge is not available to man.[61] However, the mind is bounded by the limits of

57. Ibid., 23.

58. Ibid., 27–28. Cf. the exchange on this point between Gary S. Becker, an empiricist of the Chicago School, and Israel Kirzner, a follower of Mises: Becker, "Irrational Action and Economic Theory," *Journal of Political Economy*, LXX (Feb. 1962); Kirzner, "Rational Action and Economic Theory," *JPE*, LXX (Aug. 1962); "Reply" and "Rejoinder," *JPE*, LXXI (Feb. 1963).

59. Ibid., 42.

60. Ibid., 43.

61. Ibid., 37, 64.

understanding: the "meaning of the whole" is beyond us.[62] There are no general laws in history; historical events are entirely unique.[63] The historian must select the "relevant" facts. Yet despite this process of selection, historiography must be neutral. He wrote: "A historian must first of all aim at cognition. He must free himself from any partiality. He must in this sense be neutral with regard to any value judgments."[64] The historian must select, yet be neutral. He did not explain how this is possible. (Neither has any historian.)

The rock-bottom data that resist classification in terms of the categories of the social sciences are those that are historically unique. Here, the historian must use "sympathy" or "understanding" in order to make these data intelligible. However, such understanding must not contradict the teachings of neutral social science. No matter how many historical documents testify to the existence of a devil, "no appeal to understanding could justify a historian's attempt to maintain that the devil really existed otherwise than in the visions of an excited human brain."[65] The same, of course, is true of any relationship between witches and the devil.[66]

How objectivity is to be guaranteed, or even thought to be possible, in the historical sciences is never explained. How does the historian know that his sympathetic understanding of the motives or hopes of past individuals has any relationship with the past? How can he be certain that his understanding links up with theirs? There can never be such assurance. Furthermore, how can the bedrock data of history be related to any system of general understanding? How is it possible to make sense out of the infinite data of history? Mises assumed too much for the historical disciplines. He gave too much credit to the ability of the irrationalist powers of the Kantian noumenal "understanding" to make intelligible judgments and statements about Kant's phenomenal realm.

How do we link the *a priori* categories of the mind with the external reality of the social sciences? On this point, Mises was forthright. We

62. Ludwig von Mises, *Epistemological Problems of Economics* (Princeton: Van Nostrand, 1960), 48.

63. Mises, *Theory and History: An Interpretation of Social and Economic Evolution* (Auburn, Alabama: Mises Institute, [1957] 2007), 212.

64. Mises, *Human Action*, 48.

65. Ibid., 51.

66. Mises, *Epistemological Problems*, 100.

cannot explain this connection. *The scientist needs ultimate presuppositions that cannot be proven.* Life and death are mysteries.

> Science, which is dependent both on discursive reasoning and on experience, does not present us with a unified picture of the world. It reduces phenomena to a number of concepts and propositions that we must accept as ultimate, without being able to establish a connection between them. It proves incapable of closing the gap that exists between the system of the science of human thought and action and the system of the sciences of physical nature. It does not know how to find a bridge between sentience and motion or between consciousness and matter. What life and death are elude its grasp.[67]

There is an inescapable dualism in Mises' Kantian universe, and Mises was perfectly willing to admit its existence.

> But as long as we do not know how external (physical and physiological) facts produce in a human "soul" definite thoughts and volitions resulting in concrete acts, we have to face an insurmountable dualism. In the present state of our knowledge, the fundamental statements of positivism and monism are mere metaphysical postulates devoid of any scientific foundation. Reason and experience show us two separate realms: the external world of physical and physiological events and the internal world of thought, feeling, and purposeful action. No bridge connects—as far as we can see today—these two spheres. Identical external events result sometimes in different human responses, and different external events produce sometimes the same human response. We do not know why.[68]

But if a gap of total ignorance exists between the external event and human will, then the will is totally separated from the external world. This is the most fundamental of all Kantian dualisms. Action, argued Mises, "is the outcome of a man's will. Of course, we do not know what will is. We simply call *will* man's faculty to choose between different states of affairs. . . ."[69] This seems to be the equivalent of Friedman's *intuition*. It is the mysterious bridge between thought and action, between stimulus and response. Secularists can never be sure whether this relationship is

67. Ibid., 44.

68. Ludwig von Mises, "The Treatment of 'Irrationality' in the Social Sciences," *Philosophy and Phenomenological Research*, IV (June 1944), section VI.

69. Ibid., section II.

active—thought leading to action—or passive—response to a stimulus.

How do we know if our *a priori* mental concepts correspond with the facts of the external world? "The question whether or not the real conditions of the external world correspond to these assumptions is to be answered by experience."[70] *Experience:* we are back to Friedman's intuitional, experiential link. We are back to testing once again—testing, on the assumption that there is the mind-matter link. Mises acted in faith that this mystical link exists, although he denied any mysticism in such an affirmation. "Science is sobriety and clarity of conception, not intoxicated vision."[71] But what is experience? How does it relate mind and external matter? Is it the same as will? Is it the same as intuition? How sure are we of the correspondence of the two realms? Not very. "But if the answer is affirmative, all the conclusions drawn by logically correct praxeological reasoning strictly describe what is going on in reality."[72] If the answer is in the affirmative, our *a priori* mental concepts correspond with data—some data, i.e., the relevant data—of the external world. Here is a huge "if clause" in Mises' epistemology. It is, in fact, a statement of faith, incapable of proof, as he admitted, and yet the very intellectual foundation of his *a priori* rationalism.

Our ignorance of the nature of this link between mind and matter is the source of our personal freedom. On the other hand, our faith in its existence is the source of our knowledge and power. Here is the Kantian nature-freedom antinomy in its sharpest form. We need power to escape the chaos of nature—to gain freedom as men in nature—yet this power destroys our freedom, or threatens to. Mises wrote:

> We do not know how out of the encounter of a human individuality, i.e., a man as he has been formed by all he has inherited and by all he has experienced, and a new experience definite ideas result and determine the individual's conduct. We do not even have and surmise how such knowledge could be acquired. More than that, we realize that if such knowledge were attainable for men, and if, consequently, the formation of ideas and thereby the will could be manipulated in the way machines are operated by the engineer, human conditions would be essentially altered. There

70. Mises, *Ultimate Foundation*, 44.
71. Mises, *Epistemological Problems*, 46.
72. Mises, *Ultimate Foundation*, 45.

> would yawn a wide gulf between those who manipulate other people's ideas and will and those whose ideas and will are manipulated by others.[73]

If autonomous man can use his mind to shape nature, why can't an elite of power-seeking men use science to shape society's masses? Here is the heart of the dilemma sketched by C. S. Lewis in his *Abolition of Man* and *That Hideous Strength*. It is an inescapable contradiction in all post-Kantian thought. Secularists must affirm the existence of the mind-matter link, yet they dare not affirm it.

Within the framework of this antinomy, man's ignorance of the nature of this link—indeterminacy—protects him from manipulation by other men. Yet it is the determinacy of the link that allows him to control nature (of which man is said to be a part). Thus, we are said to be able to rationalize only a few segments of reality. "Reason and science deal only with isolated fragments detached from the living whole and thereby killed."[74] Mises then retreated into Kantian mysticism in order to preserve man's freedom and living humanity. "This personal experience of wholeness, unity, and infinity is the loftiest peak of human existence. It is the awakening to a higher humanity. It alone transforms everyday living into true living. It is not vouchsafed to us daily or at all places. The occasions on which we are brought closer to the world spirit must await a propitious hour."[75]

To recapitulate, the foundation of economic reasoning is the existence of universal, timeless categories of human logic.[76] All facts require theories to interpret them; there can be no uninterpreted factuality for men to deal with intellectually. Thus, facts cannot refute accurate theories, since they have existence only in terms of theories. The theories are autonomous. "They are not subject to verification or falsification on the ground of experience and facts."[77] On this issue, Mises was forced to appeal to *experience* in answering the question concerning the existence of the mind-matter link.[78] Thus, he both affirmed and denied experience as a means of checking the validity of his theorems' applicability.

73. Ibid., 58.
74. Mises, *Epistemological Problems*, 44.
75. Ibid., 45.
76. Ibid., 27. See also pages 198, 204.
77. Mises, *Human Action*, 32.
78. Mises, *Ultimate Foundation*, 44.

Experience in some necessarily unstated way links theory to fact, yet it cannot criticize theory. But it can somehow *warn* theory: "If the facts do not confirm the theory, the cause perhaps may lie in the imperfection of the theory. The disagreement between the theory and the facts of experience consequently forces us to think through the problems of the theory again. But so long as re-examination of the theory uncovers no errors in our thinking, we are not entitled to doubt its truth."[79] And experience *can* criticize *bad* theory: "Precisely because the phenomena of historical experience are complex, the inadequacies of an erroneous theory are less effectively revealed when experience contradicts it than when it is assessed in the light of correct theory."[80] But these inadequacies are, apparently, revealed in part, though less effectively than by theory, through the contradictions of experience. It is impossible to give a precise definition of "experience" as found in Mises' writings.

On the one hand, we are asked to believe that science is value-free, since "no standard of value of any kind is contained in the system of economic or sociological theory or in the teachings of liberalism, which constitute the practical application of this theory to action in society."[81] On the other hand, we are not supposed to regard as in any way value-laden the following statement: "Every individual desires life, health, and well-being for himself and his friends and close relations."[82] Conclusion:

> To the man who adopts the scientific method in reflecting upon the problems of human action, liberalism must appear as the only policy that can lead to lasting well-being for himself, his friends, and his loved ones, and, indeed, for all others as well. Only one who does not want to achieve such ends as life, health, and prosperity for himself, his friends, and those he loves, only one who prefers sickness, misery, and suffering may reject the reasoning of liberalism on the ground that it is not neutral with regard to value judgments.[83]

In contrast, the Bible states explicitly, "But one who sins against me injures himself; All those who hate me love death" (Prov. 8:36). Even if

79. Mises, *Epistemological Problems*, 50.
80. Ibid., 29.
81. Ibid., 40.
82. Ibid., 38.
83. Ibid., 39.

all men were to agree about the true nature of health, joy, and the good life, it does not follow that all men truly want these things.

Mises' hypothetical neutrality is uncritically naïve. He held to a value-free science that in turn presupposes agreement among all men concerning "the good life." What he assumed is the universal validity of the goals of Western civilization, which is in itself an overwhelming mental abstraction.[84]

> Of course, the objections the economists advanced to the plans of the socialists and interventionists carry no weight with those who do not approve of the ends which the peoples of Western civilization take for granted. Those who prefer penury and slavery to material well-being and all that can only develop where there is material well-being may deem all these objections irrelevant. But the economists have repeatedly emphasized that they deal with socialism and interventionism from the point of view of the generally accepted values of Western civilization.[85]

While Western civilization may well have been the product of a world-view based on the idea of the sovereignty of the God of the Bible, a possibility that Mises did not mention, today our universe is closed to God, he insisted. "It is not to be denied that the loftiest theme that human thought can set for itself is reflection on absolute questions. Whether such reflection can accomplish anything is doubtful."[86]

> Our own thinking is utterly powerless to discover anything whatever about what such a superhuman or divine being would think. But within the cosmos in which our action is effective and in which our thinking paves the way for action, the findings of our scientific reasoning are so securely established as to render meaningless the statement that, in a broader setting or in a deeper sense, they would have to lose their validity and yield to some other cognition.[87]

God and His revelation are therefore irrelevant for the content of economic science, since "whatever firmly withstands the logical scrutiny of our reason can in no way be refuted by the assertions of meta-

---

84. Robert A. Nisbet, *Social Change and History* (New York: Oxford University Press, 1969), 245–246.

85. Mises, *Theory and History*, 33.

86. Mises, *Epistemological Problems*, 49.

87. Ibid., 50.

physics."[88] In short, "We may leave aside the genuine dogmas such as Creation, Incarnation, the Trinity, as they have no direct bearing on the problems of interhuman relations."[89] We can say nothing about God at all. However, God *is* "wholly other from man."[90] He is incapable of action (being perfect).[91] He is socially irrelevant.[92] The only universals for man are the universal categories of his own mind.[93] Without these, men could not think or act, so these *have* to exist.[94]

Man's dignity stems from his freedom. Yet he lives in a determinate universe in which universal laws rule. Still, "The main fact about human action is that in regard to it there is no such regularity in the conjunction of phenomena. It is not a shortcoming of the sciences of human action that they have not succeeded in discovering determinate stimulus-response patterns. What does not exist cannot be discovered."[95] Yet that such patterns may exist.

> ...in the present state of human science it is impossible to reduce the emergence and the transformation of ideas to physical, chemical, or biological factors. It is this impossibility that constitutes the autonomy of the sciences of human action. Perhaps natural science will one day be in a position to describe the physical, chemical, and biological events in which the body of the man Newton necessarily and inevitably produced the theory of gravitation.... The sciences of human action by no means reject determinism. The objective of history is to bring out in full relief the factors that were operative in producing a definite event. History is entirely guided by the category of cause and event. In retrospect, there is no question of contingency. The notion of contingency as employed in dealing with human action always refers to man's uncertainty about the future and the limitations of the specific historical understanding of future events.[96]

88. Idem.
89. Mises, *Theory and History*, 46.
90. Mises, *Ultimate Foundation*, 37. This is the language of the neo-orthodox Swiss theologian Karl Barth. Barth was a faithful disciple of Kant, as was Mises.
91. Ibid., 3.
92. Mises, *Epistemological Problems*, 24, 57, 150.
93. Ibid., 91, 204.
94. Ibid., 98.
95. Mises, *Theory and History*, 9.
96. Ibid., 93.

In principle, there is no contingency. All is determined, and natural science may fuse with human science to produce the society of total planning. It is only a question of gaining adequate knowledge.

There is a Kantian dualism between determinism and indeterminism. Man needs to preserve both his power and his freedom. "Free will means that man can aim at definite ends because he is familiar with some of the laws determining the flux of world affairs. There is a sphere within which each man *can* choose alternatives. He is not, like other animals, inevitably and irremediably subject to the operation of blind fate. He can, within definite limits, divert events from the course they would take if left alone."[97] *Man is therefore morally responsible.* The question is: To Whom? "Comparing himself with all other beings, man sees his own dignity and superiority in his will."[98] But Mises had already admitted that we do not know what the will is. It fills the gap between external causality and the rational categories of human thought. And man loses his freedom once that bridge is erected; men can control the responses of others once we know how the link is to be made. So, free will therefore means simultaneously that we cannot bridge that gap, that we cannot be controlled. Our so-called free will requires a determinate universe to hold off nature's blind fate, and it needs an indeterminate universe to hold off the controllers. Mises, as all post-Kantians, was impaled on the horns of the nature-freedom dilemma, also known as the personality-science dilemma. In short, it was Kant's dilemma.

Mises had no consistent theory of law, no link between mind and reality, other than "experience" and "will," both left undefined. Yet in his humanistic confidence he said of the natural sciences: "They provide the only mental tool that can be used in the ceaseless struggle for life. They have proved their practical worth. And no other way of knowledge is open to man, no alternative is left to him."[99] No alternatives, by *a priori* dictum—and this cannot be refuted by theology or facts. This is the closed universe of nineteenth-century neo-Kantian rationalism. It is overconfident even in its all-encompassing contradictions.

---

97. Ibid., 179.
98. Idem.
99. Ibid., 305.

E. Living With Dualism

Unlike Mises, Prof. Frank H. Knight (d. 1972) had a sense of the intellectual dualisms of secular thought. He was also a neo-Kantian. He separated the natural sciences from the human sciences in terms of epistemology, something that Paul Samuelson refused to do.[100] Social science must "strive to tell the whole truth, to recognize all the facts" in its quest for exhaustive knowledge.[101] Yet we are involved in an intellectual antinomy: the science ideal vs. the ideal of free human personality. "As far as science is concerned, free will, which is the only real dynamism, is either an illusion or simply a methodological limitation."[102] Free will is of very limited scope in life, he affirmed, in spite of the fact that it is "infinitely important." Here is the basic dilemma of all attempts at explaining social causation:

> There is equal insistence that causality is an active principle, and, on the other hand, upon concrete methods of problem-solving which are "scientific" in the sense of natural science as purely empirical, phenomenalistic, and positivistic. The main criticism of the book [R. M. MacIver's *Social Causation*] is that the author sees both horns of this intellectual dilemma but fails to recognize it and to see that it has no real solution.[103]

How do we link mind and external reality? Again, Knight admitted, there is no secular, rational solution.

> With regard to the relation between deduction and observation, or intelligence and the senses, in our knowledge of nature, there is not much that should need to be said. Surely anyone who has made any progress at all in the study of philosophy, or even in private reflection about its problems, can be assumed to know that any simple antithesis between

---

100. Knight, *History and Method*, 121. Cf. Paul Samuelson, "Economic Theory and Mathematics—An Appraisal," *American Economic Review, Papers & Proceedings*, XLII (May 1952): "There are no separate methodological problems that face the social scientist different in kind from those that face any other scientist" (61). This is the modern, post-Heisenberg viewpoint; Mises and Knight are clinging to Newtonian concepts of natural science.

101. Knight, 131.

102. Ibid., 140–141.

103. Ibid., 137.

> observation and inference is utterly untenable, if not downright foolish. The question as to the primary or immediate data of consciousness is perhaps the main perennial, unsolved and probably unsolvable problem of the theory of knowledge as a whole.[104]

Thus, since it cannot be solved, it is "downright foolish" to bring it up any longer, at least if the proposed antithesis is "simple." We must live with our inescapable intellectual contradictions.

Then how do we know the "facts" of economic scarcity or the idea of a "best" apportionment of scarce resources? We know "by living in the world 'with' other intelligent beings; we neither know them *a priori* nor by one-sided deduction from data and sense observation."[105] We know by "living." What kind of knowledge is economic knowledge? "Methodologically considered, economics is a highly abstract 'concrete deductive' science, similar to geometry or to mathematical mechanics; but in addition its data are intuitive in a far higher or purer sense than is true of mathematics itself."[106] We are back, once again, to *intuition*. Economists always get back to intuition.

Then how relevant are Friedman's categories of prediction? Not very, answered Knight. "A more fundamental weakness of inductive prediction in economics is that empirical (i.e., statistical) data never present anything like an exhaustive analysis of phenomenal sequences down to really elementary components, and the correlation of and extrapolation from composite magnitudes or series never can be very reliable."[107]

Theory or fact: where do we start? How do we string together the infinite number of hole-less beads with our infinitely long string of theory? Schumpeter simply concluded that we have to push very, very hard on the string: "It stands to reason that these two activities are not independent of one another but there must be an incessant give and take between them."[108] In short, "there is not and there cannot be any fundamental opposition between 'theory' and 'fact finding,' let alone between deduction and induction."[109] Then why the endless battles

104. Ibid., 159.
105. Ibid., 164.
106. Ibid., 168.
107. Ibid., 176n.
108. Schumpeter, *History of Economic Analysis*, 45.
109. Idem.

between inductivists and deductivists? And how can you solve the problem of fitting facts with the proper theories if you deny that the problem even exists?

Alfred Marshall, the influential nineteenth-century Cambridge economist, wrote that an economist "needs the three great intellectual faculties, perception, imagination and reason: and most of all he needs imagination."[110] He is echoed by Kenneth Boulding: "Decision making by instinct, gossip, visceral feeling, and political savvy may stand pretty low on the scale of total rationality, but it may have the virtue of being able to take in very large systems in a crude and vague way, whereas the rationalized processes can only take subsystems in their more exact fashion, and being rational about subsystems may be worse than being not very rational about the system as a whole."[111] Finally, we have the testimony of Michael Arbib.

> Any science that supposedly captures reality in two or three equations is inadequate to describe the systems formed by both brain and society—systems with billions of variables. Thus it would seem that, given the incomplete state of our formal theories, we must complement them with our everyday knowledge as members of society. In short, our rational analysis of society must strike a balance between precise description of certain subsystems and, quite frankly, intuition and feeling about other problems.[112]

Modern man has no epistemology. He wants to stand on balanced ground, but where is balance to be found? What are the criteria of true balance? How does one apply these criteria to the data of the external world? How does one go about proving the existence of such criteria of balance? The whole epistemology of modern man collapses into intuition, feeling, and endless measurement of increasingly useless minute data.

---

110. Alfred Marshall, quoted by Vincent W. Bladen, "John Stuart Mill's *Principles:* A Centenary Estimate," *American Economic Review, Papers & Proceedings*, XXXIX (May 1949), 4–5

111. Kenneth Boulding, "The Economics of Knowledge and the Knowledge of Economics," ibid., *Papers & Proceedings*, LVI (May 1966), 11.

112. Michael Arbib, "Complex Systems: The Case for a Marriage of Science and Intuition," *The American Scholar*, XLII (Winter 1972–1973), 53. Arbib was a professor of computer science at the Massachusetts Institute of Technology.

Knight argued that one thing that scientists need is *a sense of corporate honor*. "Without a sense of honor (as well as special competence) among scientists—if, say, they were all charlatans—there could be no science."[113] To support the superstructure of rational science we have to have honesty—indeed, honor, an essentially feudal, military concept. Science rests on ethics. Can ethics be neutral? If not, value-free science rests on value-laden assumptions about man, honesty, and fairness. Economic science is not and cannot be autonomous. It therefore cannot be rational. It is intuitional and ethics-oriented. Its secular neutrality is a sham.

Epistemologically, there is simply no legitimate way open for post-Kantian economists to defend their affirmation of neutrality. Neutrality implies a fixed, straightforward, universally recognized link between the external world and the logic of the human mind. But it is this link that is both affirmed and denied by modern philosophers of the social sciences. By appealing to intuition again and again in order to fill the gap between mind and matter, the modern social scientist must abandon his confidence in neutrality. The noumenal realm of will, feeling, intuition, or experience is nonrational, by definition. Kantians can say nothing about its operations.

What goes on in the noumenal realm is closed to pure reason, that is, the logical and mathematical reasoning of phenomenal science. All is mystery in Kant's noumenal realm, as Richard Kroner has shown so well in his book, *Kant's Weltanschauung* (1914). Logical neutrality implies a fixity of reference, and the noumenal realm is a zone of pure contingency—total chaos, as far as logic can determine. It is the realm of Kant's God, Kant's ethics, and Kant's "things in themselves." Once washed in the chaos of intuition, neutrality emerges as a myth. The determinacy of logic erodes in the acid sea of chance.

There is absolutely no likelihood that the *a priori* approach of Prof. Mises and the *a posteriori* approach of Prof. Friedman will ever be reconciled, in spite of the fact that each approach ultimately appeals to the irrational and the intuitive in the crucial task of uniting the laws of thought and the world beyond. From Parmenides and Heraclitus to Mises and Friedman, the basic opposition has in no meaningful way

113. Knight, 157.

been bridged, despite the stupendous effort of intellectuals to overcome it. Nevertheless, on the most fundamental of all issues, Parmenides and Heraclitus could join hands, just as Mises and Friedman did: the issue of human autonomy. Van Til put it quite well:

> It is not the differences between them but that fact that all of them, whatever their differences, have in common the assumption of human autonomy that is basic to an understanding even of their internal differences. I do not speak of the *autonomy of theoretical thought* but of the *pretended* autonomy of apostate *man*. It is this and, as it appears to me, basically *only* this which all schools of apostate thought have in common. Assuming this autonomy apostate man gives a rebellious covenant-breaking response to the revelational challenge that he meets at every turn. The face of the triune God of Scripture confronts him everywhere and all the time. He spends the entire energy of his whole personality in order to escape seeing this face of God.[114]

Conclusion

The Bible tells us what mankind is apart from grace: blind, rebellious in need of salvation, perverse. Every man requires limits on his thought processes—*balance*, to use Arbib's concept—and this means authoritative revelation. He is unable to find such a balance on his own. He needs biblical law to help him construct social and economic institutions, each with its proper legitimate sphere of authority. Men are not autonomous, and by claiming full autonomy, they hurl themselves into the intellectual void of intuition. The faith of the secular economist in the full autonomy of the discipline is a shaky faith indeed.

This should not give comfort to the pietist or the Barthian who is antinomian to the core anyway. There are far too many of both groups who are unwilling to discover the common grace (or restraining grace)[115] of secular economists like Mises, Friedman, or Knight. Brushing off their scholarship with a brief comment like the following gets us

114. Cornelius Van Til, "Response" to Herman Dooyeweerd, in E. R. Geehan (ed.), *Jerusalem and Athens* (Nutley, New Jersry: Presbyterian & Reformed, 1971), 96–97.

115. Gary North, *Dominion and Common Grace: The Biblical Basis of Progress* (Moulton, Alabama: Axehead Press, [1987] 2024).

nowhere: "They're just secularists, so they have nothing to teach us, so we can adopt guild socialism that is neither intelligent nor revealed in the Bible, but we like it because it sounds radically Christian!"

There is no social hope in an antinomian retreat into the vague socialism of the German Historical School or other anti-theoretical economics systems. Where Mises and Friedman say things that are in conformity to the Bible, we should take their careful expositions seriously. We have the responsibility of recognizing what is and what is not in conformity to the Bible's concrete revelation whenever we read the works of secular economists. Abandoning reason in the name of vague "Christian feelings of charity" is no substitute for prayerful scholarship into the implications of our acts. Christian reconstruction will not be the result of pietistic singing about the joy, joy, joy, joy down in the heart, nor will it be the result of endless affirmations of empty Dooyeweerdian spheres. It will be the result of the concrete application of biblical law in the external spheres of life and the application of sovereign grace in the hearts of men. Antinomianism, whatever its form, leads to cultural impotence. Because the secular economist has no epistemological cloak does not, in and of itself, clothe the Christian in robes of purple. The Christian has to make his own clothing.

In order to make myself perfectly clear, as President Nixon used to say, let me spell out precisely what I mean. The slogan of too many Christians has been "no creed but the Bible, no law but love." Another is the familiar "we're under grace, not law." This is pure antinomianism. It makes Christianity utterly impotent to challenge the scholarship of the secularists. It makes it impossible to construct intellectual or institutional alternatives to the various secular systems. We are not under the curse of law, but we are under its limitations for our external conduct, including social conduct. The *progressive sanctification* of the Christian—fighting the good fight, pressing on to the mark for the prize of God's high calling (Phil. 3:14)—is in terms of law. If a Christian is an economist, then his own progressive sanctification must be in terms of the Bible's revelation concerning both the theory and facts of economic thought. The "mind-matter" link is there, because he is made in the image of God, and God comprehends His own creation. The rebellion of Adam made God's verbal revelation necessary in order to restrain man's apostate thought, including economic thought. Without the Bible and its concrete economic instruction, the "mind-matter" link will inevitably be warped; the theories of economics, as well as the facts selected in terms of these theories, will be in error, sooner or later.

Scripture Index

Boldface entries indicate a passage has been quoted or discussed at length.

Old Testament

New Testament

About Gary North

Gary North (1942–2022) was one of the most influential and prolific Christian writers, thinkers, and strategists of the last generation. He was the author of approximately 80 books on a wide array of subjects from economics, history, and social issues to ethics, theology, and ecclesiology. His 31-volume economic commentary on the Bible and his 4-volume introduction to Christian economics are veritable modern classics. After receiving his PhD in History from the University of California, Riverside, he served on the staffs of the Foundation for Economic Education, the Chalcedon Foundation, and Congressman Ron Paul. He went on to establish, with his wife Sharon, the Institute for Christian Economics, Dominion Press, *Remnant Review*, Free Christian Educational Resources, and GaryNorth.com. Thousands of his essays, articles, and columns have been published in *The Wall Street Journal*, *National Review*, *The American Spectator*, *The Freeman*, and a host of other publications. He was the intellectual mentor to an entire generation of Christians concerned about the cultural disarray of Western Civilization in general and the United States in particular.

Made in United States
Cleveland, OH
05 November 2026

47659988R00278